W9-BOA-551

Date Due

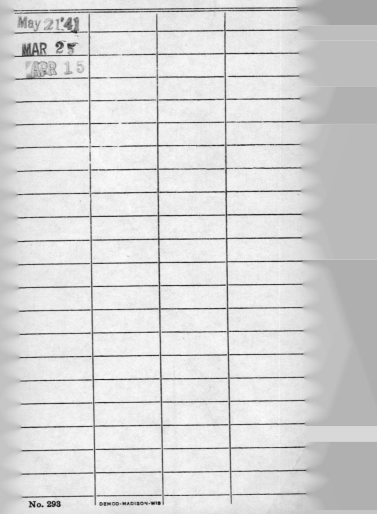

May 21 '41			
MAR 25			
APR 15			

No. 293   DEMCO-MADISON-WIS

THE

FORMATION OF CHRISTENDOM

BY

T. W. ALLIES, K.C.S.G.

VOL. II

THE CHRISTIAN FAITH
AND SOCIETY

LONDON: BURNS & OATES, Limited

NEW YORK, CINCINNATI, CHICAGO: BENZIGER BROTHERS

1903

CONTENTS

LECTURE VII

THE GODS OF THE NATIONS WHEN CHRIST APPEARED

LECTURE VIII

THE FIRST AND THE SECOND MAN

CONTENTS

LECTURE IX

THE SECOND MAN VERIFIED IN HISTORY

LECTURE X

THE FIRST AGE OF THE MARTYR CHURCH

LECTURE XI

THE SECOND AGE OF THE MARTYR CHURCH

LECTURE XII

THE THIRD AGE OF THE MARTYR CHURCH

LECTURE XIII

THE CHRISTIAN CHURCH AND THE GREEK PHILOSOPHY

PART I

LECTURE XIV

THE CHRISTIAN CHURCH AND THE GREEK PHILOSOPHY

PART II

by one man, the representative of the whole people; and the effect of this change, an effect no doubt unforeseen, at least in its extent, by its framer, was gradually to absorb the manifold races inhabiting these vast regions into the majesty of the Roman law, order, and citizenship. The three centuries which follow Augustus are occupied in working out the drama of this unity. During this time the provinces appear to come out more and more as parts of one whole. Some which at its beginning had only just entered the circle of Roman power and thought, as Gaul, become entirely interpenetrated with the law, language, customs, and civilisation of the sovereign city. Spain was nearly as much, and Northern Africa perhaps even more Latinised: in all, local inequalities, and the dissimilarity arising from conflicting races, customs, and languages, are more and more softened down, though never entirely removed; and while throughout this period the great city continues the head, yet the body assumes an ever-increasing importance, until at length its members engage the equal solicitude of that central potentate to whom all equally belong. In the times of so-called Roman liberty, the plunder of lands which received pro-consuls for their annual rulers, served to replenish the fortunes of nobles exhausted by the corruption requisite to gain high office; but if the dominion of one at Rome seemed an evil exchange to a nobility which deemed itself born to enjoy a conquered world, at least it served as a protection to those many millions for whom the equality of law and order, the fair administration of justice, and the undisturbed possession of property constituted the chief goods of life. Cicero and his peers might grieve over the extinction of what they termed liberty, but Gaul, Spain, Africa, and Asia exulted in deliverance from the oppression of a Verres, a Fonteius, a Gabinius, a Piso, or a Clodius, in the communication of citizenship, and in the peace of a common civilisation.

I. With a passing glance at the progress of this unity, which, great and magnificent as it is, is yet external, let us turn to an object filling the whole of this vast empire with its varied manifestations : for this object leads us to the consideration of another unity, wholly internal, without which that of government, law, and order must be apparent rather than real, or at best, however seemingly imposing, be deprived of the greater part of its efficacy.

1. It has been said that the empire contained in it many lands and many races, but these likewise worshipped their own distinct gods, which were acknowledged and sanctioned as national divinities for the several countries wherein they were locally established. Had Augustus ordered an enrolment not only of the numbers, the landed property, and the wealth of his subjects, but of their gods, his public register, or Breviarium, would have included at least ten distinct systems of idolatrous worship. First of all, there would be the proper gods of Rome, then those of the Hellenic race ; and these, though the most similar to each other, yet refused a complete amalgamation. But besides these there were on the west the Etrurian, the Iberian, the Gallic, and the Germanic gods ; on the east, the Carian and Phrygian, the Syrian, the Assyrian, the Arabian ; on the south, the Phœnician, Libyan, and Egyptian. All these different races, inasmuch as they were subjects of the empire, enjoyed undisturbed the right of worshipping their ancestral gods,[1] who, so long as they did not overstep their local

[1] Tertull. *Apolog.* xxiv. "Ideo et Ægyptiis permissa est tam

boundaries, were recognised; they possessed priests, rites, temples, estates, and self-government; they held the soil, and their worship was legal. It was a matter of Roman policy not to interfere with them. Nay, their several worshippers could carry their rites along with them in their various sojourns and settlements, and even in Rome build altars, and adore Egyptian, Asiatic, African, or Gallic gods. These various systems agreed all in one point, that they were systems of polytheistic idolatry : they all divided the attributes of the godhead, assigning them to more or fewer objects, and worshipping all these by visible symbols which the power worshipped was deemed to inhabit ;[1] but they did not make the same division with a mere difference of name ; on the contrary, they ran into and across each other with the most bewildering multiplicity, variation, and contradiction. Even in the same system, if we may give this name to any of the various mythologies, the several divinities were perpetually interfering with each other's province. When the Roman made vows for the removal of his ailments, in his uncertainty to which god the ailment belonged, or who was most proper to remove it, he addressed his vow to several together; or in public supplications, being often uncertain to whom exactly the prayer or offering should be made, he cautiously expressed himself, " whether it be a god or a goddess." And the various Hellenic, Asiatic, or Egyptian cities often possessed local gods, whose worship was supreme there,

vanæ superstitionis potestas, avibus et bestiis consecrandis, et capite damnandis qui aliquem hujusmodi Deum occiderint. Unicuique etiam provinciæ et civitati suus Deus est, ut Syriæ Astartes, ut Arabiæ Disares, ut Noricis Belenus, ut Africæ Cælestis, ut Mauritaniæ Reguli sui," &c.; and Minucius Felix, Octavius vi., in like manner.

[1] See Aug. *de Civ. Dei*, l. viii. 24.

while they exercised far less influence, or were even scarcely known elsewhere.[1]

Now, merely as a specimen of what this worship was all over the Roman empire, let us take the brilliant Athens, Greece's eye, the world's university. First of all ruled in her the worship of Pallas-Athené: she was the lady of the land, who had won it for her own after a hard contest with Poseidon. Her chief sanctuaries were the temple of Athené, guardian of the city, with its old statue fallen down from heaven on the Acropolis. On the Acropolis likewise the Parthenon, built expressly for the gorgeous Panathenaic festival; and in the lower city the Palladium with the statue of the goddess supposed to have been brought from Troy. Yet the worship of the "high goddesses," Demeter and Persephoné, was also richly endowed with shrines and festivals, and affected scarcely less the feelings of the Athenians. Then Jupiter, as "supreme," was honoured with unbloody offering before the Erechtheium, dedicated to Athené; whilst as "Olympian" he had the colossal temple begun by Peisistratus and finished after many hundred years by Hadrian, and as "guardian of the city" distinct festivals. Yet more manifold was the invocation of Apollo, as the Pythian, the Delphic, the Lycian, as the ancestral god of the Ionians. The multiform Artemis had her temples and worshippers as the Tauric, by the name Brauronia; as the port-goddess, by the name Munychia; as the goddess of the hunt, by the name Agrotera, who had the credit of the victory won at Marathon; as presiding over birth, she was called Chitone, while Themistocles had built a temple to her as the Counsellor. Heré had only a

[1] Döllinger, *Heidenthum und Judenthum*, pp. 528, 529.

doorless and roofless temple on the road to Phalerum ;
but the god of fire was worshipped in Athens abundantly.   Hermes had his peculiar statues in every
street, irreverence to which might be fatal even to an
Alcibiades, the city's darling ; while Aphrodité had a
crowd of temples and shrines, whose unchaste worship
found but too many frequenters.   Poseidon had to
content himself with a single altar in his rival's city,
and with games in its harbour ; but Dionysos had
three temples, with brilliant festivals ; Mars was not
without one ; Hestia was throned in the Prytaneum ;
the Earth, Kronos, and Rhea had their temples and
festivals, as also the Erinnyes, who were worshipped
only in two other places in Greece.   Here alone in
Greece was a sanctuary and a rite to Prometheus ;
while the Asiatic mother of the gods had a splendid
temple where the archives of the state were kept.
Besides, there was the worship of the Hours and the
Graces, of Eileithyia, goddess of victory and of birth,
of Æsculapius and Themis, of the Kabirian Anakes,
the Arcadian Pan, the Thracian Cotytto and Bendis,
the Egyptian Serapis.   Mercy and Shame, Fame and
Endeavour had their altars ; and the hero-worship
numbered Theseus, Codrus, Academus, Solon, the
tyrant-slayers Harmodius and Aristogeiton ; and Hercules, originally a hero, but here and elsewhere widely
honoured as a god.[1]

Athens, if the most superstitious as well as the
most intellectual of cities, may be taken as the type
of a thousand others of Hellenic race scattered over
the Roman Empire from Marseilles to Antioch.   Say
that she had twice as many deities and festivals as
her sister cities, enough will remain for them where-

[1] From *Heidenthum und Judenthum*, pp. 101-2.

claimed a certain superiority over all these gods, would scarcely have yielded to any Grecian city, even were it Athens, in the number or variety of her deities, the frequency and solemnity of her festivals; while in the costliness of victims offered to her gods, and in the strictness of her ceremonies, she probably far surpassed that and all other cities. Her sterner worship of originally shapeless gods, presiding over the labours of a simple agricultural life, had long yielded to the seductions of her dangerous Grecian captive. The rude block Terminus, and Jupiter the Stone, ceased to satisfy those who had beheld the majesty of the father of gods and men embodied by the genius of a Phidias; and she had ended by going further in breaking up the conception of one god, and in the personification of particular powers, operations, physical functions, and qualities than any nation of antiquity.[1] But though the beautiful forms of the Hellenic gods, as expressed by the skill of unrivalled sculptors, had carried her away, yet the nature of her worship was in strong contrast with that of Greece. Her religion had rested originally on two ideas, the might of the gods friendly to Rome, and the force of ceremonial over these gods;[2] and still when she accepted the gods of conquered nations for her own, it was to secure the possession of their might, and to have them for friends instead of foes; while her own worship was a matter of routine and habit jealously guarded by unchanging ceremonies, and prosecuted not out of affection, but for the material security of daily life, which, according to the deeply-rooted feeling of the people, could not go on without it.

[1] *Heidenthum und Judenthum*, p. 469.
[2] *Ibid.* pp. 468, 480.

The individualised and humanised Latin and Hellenic gods, if they had much in common, still could not be thoroughly amalgamated; but Rome, as the mistress of Western Asia and Egypt, came upon Oriental religions of a very different stamp. Instead of this wide Pantheon of gods, each of whom had his occupation, these Asiatics generally regarded the deity in a sexual relationship, as one male and one female god, representing the active and passive forms of nature,[1] and worshipped with a mixture of fear and voluptuousness. Such were Bel and Mylitta, Moloch and Astarte, and by whatever different names the same idea was presented. The worship of the great mother Cybele, so widely spread through Asia Minor, approached in many respects in character to that of this female goddess. But it is needless to go further into the specific differences of these various idolatries; only bear in mind that they in their several countries occupied the domain of public and private life, as the worship of which I have given the details did at Athens. So it was before the influence of external conquerors reached them. After this a certain change ensues. The Roman Empire was accomplishing in the west as well as in the east what the progress of Grecian rule and thought had commenced three hundred years before[2] under Alexander and his successors, the bringing together and in some sort fusing the multiform and often contradictory worship of the nations surrounding the Mediterranean Sea. Not merely in Rome, but in all the chief cities of the Empire, the Asiatic, the Egyptian, the Libyan deities, and many others of subject nations under the Roman sway, were worshipped side

---

[1] *Heidenthum und Judenthum*, p. 344.
Ibid. p. 312.

by side.   Accordingly, in the time of Augustus, and
at the year of Rome 750, where we are taking our
stand, there prevailed all over the hundred millions of
men ruled by him a polytheistic idolatry bewildering
by its multiplicity, internal contradictions, fluctuations,
and mixtures, yet imposing by its universal extent
and prevalence.   The only exception seems to have
been the Jewish worship of one God, whether in its
chief seat, the small province of Judæa, or as it was
seen in the lives of Jewish settlers scattered throughout
the empire.   It must be remarked that this Jewish
worship of the true God was sanctioned as that of a
national god belonging to the Jews, and sacrifice was
perpetually offered for Augustus in the temple at Jerusalem.   But the Jews did not, as a rule, make efforts
to convert the Gentiles to their religion, nor seek to
exhibit it as antagonistic to the prevailing idolatry,
and as claiming to subdue and cast it out.   They
were content to keep their own worship to themselves,
and with the toleration which the Roman law thus
allowed them.   Yet even so in every place where they
dwelt in any numbers some of the better heathens
were found to be attracted to their worship by the
intrinsic beauty of their belief in one God.

2. But such an exception as this hardly made a
perceptible break in that continuous mass of evil and
falsehood which then surrounded young and old,
learned and ignorant, rich and poor in its grasp.
The sea stands in Holy Writ as the well-known
image of the world's disobedience to the divine
promptings, of its impetuosity and lawlessness.   What
image is there in nature so striking and awful as the
long waves of the Atlantic bearing down in storm
upon a helpless ship, and sweeping it upon an iron-

bound coast! So broke that wild sea of human error
over the individual mind of man. The observer looked
round upon all the nations, and it was everywhere the
same—a multiplicity of gods filling up the whole circle
of human life, many-named, many-natured, but all
without truth, purity, and justice; full of violent and
sensual deeds, and still viler imaginations. What stay
was there for the spirit of man against that universal
flood? Its vastness was everywhere. Who was strong
enough, who wise enough, to resist what all his fellows
accepted? And the struggle of a single soul against
it might seem like that of "some strong swimmer in
his agony" alone at night amid the waste of waters.

3. For this polytheism was no dormant, otiose power
withdrawn into the background and crouching apart
from the actions and feelings of daily life. Its presence was indicated in every home by the little images
of the Lares; homage was done to it at every table
by libations; every house had its consecrated emblems;
every street its statues of Hermes and serpents; in
the forum there were feasts in honour of the gods;
the shops, taverns, and manufactories had little altars
on which wine and incense were offered to them;
there were idolatrous emblems on the foreheads of the
dead, on their funeral pyre, on their tombs. The
places of amusement were specially dedicated to the
gods; the theatres had representations in honour of
them; the circus had their images, chairs, carriages,
robes borne in procession; the amphitheatre was consecrated to them, and as being so Tertullian called it
"the temple of all demons." So much for private
and social life. But not only so. All political acts
were bound up with a crowd of religious formalities
and outward signs of divine concurrence, and were

carried on with a ceremonial, every part of which was prescribed as having an exact inward meaning. Then there were continually recurring vows to the gods made for the great, made for private individuals, made for the emperor and his family. Three special ceremonies were used to obtain favours from them or to deprecate calamities, feasts, the solemnly bearing their images on cushions, processions with naked feet.[1] To this we must add the priestly colleges, pontifices, flamines, augurs, and magistrates, whether distinct or co-ordinated. Then, besides, consider the magical character of the prayers, and the strict use of formularies without mistake, omission, or addition, which were supposed to ensure success apart from the intention of those offering them. Thus the whole life of the Romans was filled with invocations, propitiations, purifications, and even in any small matter a whole string of gods had prayer and service offered to them, and no one of their names might be omitted. Consider again the great frequency of the offerings, whether propitiative or consultatory; and, further, how particular beasts belonged to particular gods. The mere expense of victims was felt as a great burden. It was reckoned that on the accession of Caligula 160,000 animals, chiefly oxen and calves, were sacrificed in the Roman Empire in token of the general joy; and Augustus and Marcus Aurelius devoted such a multitude of beasts to their sacrifices that what had been said of the former was repeated as to the latter, how the white oxen had written to him, saying, "If you conquer, we are lost." Indications of the will of the gods were to be taken on all occasions; nothing was to be done in public or private without consulting

---

[1] "Epulæ, lectisternia, nudipedalia."

the auspices.   Then there was the institution of the
Haruspices, in its two branches of examining the
entrails of the victims, and divining the meaning of
all prodigies.   One is still amazed at the ever-untiring
solicitude which the senate showed to have all these
things carefully watched—eclipses, rainbows of unusual
colours, shooting-stars, misbirths, human or bestial;
showers of earth, stones, chalk, or ashes; mice gnaw-
ing the golden vessels of a temple; bees swarming
on a public place, but especially a shrine touched by
lightning.   Such things struck senate and people with
consternation; special supplications were ordered to
appease the causers of them.[1]

These are the external manifestations of polytheism
which struck every eye, and affected the mind by
their constant recurrence.   But if we go beneath the
surface and examine the root, we shall find an universal sense in the minds of all men in that day of unseen
power over and above the material operations of nature.
It was too strong as well as too general and invariable
to be called an opinion, and it so acted on the nerves
and feelings of men that I term it not so much a
logical conviction as a sense of the close contact
between man and nature, or rather an unseen power
behind the veil of nature and working through it.
Various as the forms of idolatry were—Egyptian,
Asiatic, Libyan, Greek, or Roman; or again, Iberian,
Gallic, German—all teemed with this sense.   To the
adherents of these religions, one and all, the world
was very far from being a mere system of nature
governed by general laws,[2] it may rather be said that

[1] These incidents are taken from various places in *Heidenthum und
Judenthum*, pp. 531, 549, 550, &c.
[2] Champagny, *Les Antonins*, liv. v. c. 3.

this was precisely what it was not. They looked upon nature in all its forms as an expression of the divine will, and therefore the unusual productions of nature became to them intimations respecting that will. And having lost the guidance of a fixed moral and religious teaching, they were ruled by an ever-watchful anxiety to gain acquaintance with that will. On this sense rested the universal belief that it was in man's power to hold intercourse by means of charms, spells, adjurations, with spirits of greater might and knowledge than his own—that is, magic or witchcraft. Hence the evocation of the spirits of the dead to reveal secrets of their prison-house, or necromancy. Hence the recurrence to oracles, running through all pagan history, of which there were many scattered through the Roman world, and which, after a temporary discredit, rose again into name in the time of Hadrian. Not less general was the belief that men and women might be possessed by spirits who ruled their words and actions according to an overmastering will. Then divination existed in endlessly various forms; and of its force we can gather a notion by Cicero's remark that it lay like an oppressive burden on the minds of men, so that even sleep, which should be the refuge from anxieties, became through the meaning attached to dreams the cause of a multitude of cares.[1] To this must be added the use of sortileges, amulets, and talismans in countless number and variety; and the belief that the actions and fortune of men were swayed by the course of the stars—that is, astrology. It was not the vulgar and ignorant merely whose minds were filled with these things. Scarcely a philosopher, scarcely a statesman, scarcely a ruler can be found

---

[1] *De Divinat.* ii. 72.

whose mind, even if proof against a genuine devotion
to a divine providence, was not open to one or more
manifestations of the dark mysterious power pressing
upon the confines of human life, and every now and
then breaking through the veil of visible things with
evidences of malignant might.   A more determined
and unscrupulous conqueror than Sylla, a more genuine
philosopher than Marcus Aurelius, a more sagacious
user of religion than Augustus, we shall not easily
find ; yet each of these, like their ordinary countrymen, had this sense of the supernatural and intangible
above, beneath, and around them.   Sylla, on the eve
of any battle, would, in the sight of his soldiers,
embrace a small statue of Apollo, which he had taken
from Delphi, and entreat it to give an early fulfilment
of its promises.[1]   Marcus Aurelius, in his war with
the Marcomanni, collected priests from all quarters to
Rome, and was so long occupied in offering rites to
their various foreign gods that he kept his army waiting for him.   And Augustus watched carefully the
most trivial signs, and was distressed if in the morning
his left shoe was given to him for his right.   Even
that Julius before whose genius all men quailed, and
whose disbelief of a future state stands recorded at
a notable point of Roman history, never mounted a
chariot without uttering certain words for good luck
and preservation against calamity.[2]   We shall therefore judge most inadequately of the force which the
innumerable rites, temples, festivals, pomps, ceremonies,
prayers, invocations, priesthoods, sodalities, initiations,
and mysteries of polytheism exercised upon the minds
of men, unless we take into full account that remark-

[1] Valerius Max. i. c. 2, 3.
[2] Merivale's *History of the Romans*, ii. 447.

able sense of contact and sympathy between the external world and man——of invisible power betraying itself through palpable agents, whether in reasoning or unreasoning productions, whether in the animal or vegetable world——which served as its basis. The line between religion and superstition in paganism no eye can trace ; but at least the foundation of true worship plunged deep out of sight into the secret recesses of abject fear.

4. But what was the moral influence of this multiform, universal, all-embracing, and all-penetrating worship ?

Varro, whom Cicero calls the most acute and learned of writers, and whose great work in forty-one books he praises as containing the names, classes, offices, and causes of all divine and human things, divided theology into the fabulous, the natural, and the civil. In the first, he said, are many fictions unworthy of the nature and dignity of immortal beings : such as that one god sprung from the head, another from the thigh, another from drops of blood ; such, again, as that gods were thieves or adulterers, or became slaves to men. In fact, this fabulous theology attributed everything to them which might happen not merely to a man, but to the most contemptible of men.[1]   Let us leave what he calls natural theology, which is the discussion of philosophers concerning the physical nature of the gods, and proceed to the third, which he calls civil, and which is that which the citizens, and especially the priests of human communities, are bound to know and administer. This treats of what gods are to be worshipped, and with what rites and sacrifices. The first theology, he says, belongs to the theatre, the

_____

[1] See Varro, quoted by St. Aug. *de Civ. Dei*, lib. vi. 5.

second to the universe, the third to the city. St. Augustine, commenting at length upon his division, proves that the first and the third, the fabulous and the civil, are, in fact, identical, since the universe is a divine work, but the theatre and the city works of men. The theatre is indeed made for the city, and the very same gods are ridiculed on the stage who are adored in the temple; the same have games exhibited in their honour and victims sacrificed to them. The images, features, ages, sexes, bearing of the gods in the one and in the other are the same. Thus this fabulous, theatrical, and scenic theology, full of everything vile and criminal, is actually a part of the civil, cohering with it as limb with limb in the same body.[1]

Conceive, then, every revolting detail of adultery, prostitution, incest, or of dishonesty, or of violence, which the perverted invention of modern writers has ever dressed up for the theatres of great cities in this and other countries. They will perhaps yield in turpitude to that which the theatres of the Roman Empire exhibited. But what these theatres represented in mimic action was the exact image, as reflected in a mirror, of what was transacted at the solemn service of the gods in unnumbered temples.[2] The exact image, so far as it went, yet stopping short in some respects, for our eye-witness above cited declares that gratitude was due to the actors, inasmuch as they spared the eyes of men, and did not lay bare upon the theatre all that was hidden within the walls of temples. It was not enough, then, that all the many

[1] De Civ. Dei, l. vi. 5, 6, 7.
[2] "Illam theatricam et fabulosam theologiam ab ista civili pendere noverunt, et ei de carminibus poetarum tanquam de speculo resultare: et ideo ista exposita, quam damnare non audent, illam ejus imaginem liberius arguunt." De Civ. Dei, vi. 9; id. vi. 7.

games and spectacles in which such things were represented were dedicated to the gods, acted under their
especial sanction, even enjoined by them as means of
gaining their favour or averting their wrath, which
alone would have made them answerable for the
immorality so portrayed; not enough, even, that
actions of this quality were in the theatres ascribed
to the gods who presided over them; but these acts
of immorality were not the fictions of poets or the
acting of players, but the very substance of the
theology itself in which the worship of all these
nations was embodied. Priapus appeared to make a
laugh on the stage exactly in the costume in which
he was worshipped in the temples, or in which he
entered into the rites of marriage; a costume of inde-
scribable turpitude, the shame of our human nature.
The players on the stage and the statues in the
temples equally exhibited Jove bearded and Mercury
beardless, Saturn in decrepitude and Apollo in youth-
ful beauty. In the rites of Juno, of Ceres, of Venus,
of the mother of the gods, words were uttered and
scenes acted such as no decent person would suffer to
be spoken or acted before his own mother; or rather
they contained, as a portion of themselves, the worst
crimes which the theatres represented; nay, crimes
which they stopped short of acting, and persons so
infamous that they were not tolerated even on the
stage, where yet to take part was a civil dishonour.
What, then, was the nature of those rites wherein
those were chosen to take part whom the utmost
license of the stage banished from its boards?[1] Let
us conceive—if such a conception can be adequately

[1] "Quæ sunt ergo illa sacra quibus agendis tales elegit sanctita
quales nec thymelica in se admittit obscœnitas." *De Civ. Dei*, vi. 7.

represented to the mind——that the vilest drama ever acted upon a modern theatre was being daily carried on in all the churches of Christendom by troops of priests and priestesses, with all the paraphernalia of costliest worship, with prayers, invocation, and sacrifices, as a service acceptable to the Ruler of man's lot, and as an account of what that Ruler had Himself done, and of what He loved to be imitated by others. That would be a picture of heathen worship in the time of Augustus; that would be the moral food on which was nurtured that crowd of nations which acknowledged Cæsar's sway; that the conception of divine things wrought into the minds of the hundred millions of men who formed the Roman empire.

Was it surprising that all worshippers of the gods should look for their example rather in Jupiter's actions than in Plato's teaching or the moral judgments of Cato ?[1] A nature subject in itself to the sway of passion was stimulated by an authority supposed to be divine to the commission of every criminal excess ; and herein lay a strong proof of the malignant and impure character of these gods.

On the other hand, the same eye-witness challenges the defenders of the pagan gods to produce a single instance wherein moral precepts of living were delivered to their worshippers upon divine authority. True, indeed, there were here and there whispers of secret rites in which a pure and chaste life was recommended, but where were the buildings dedicated to the public preaching of such truths ? Places there were in abundance consecrated to the celebration of

[1] "Omnes cultores talium deorum—magis intuentur quid Jupiter fecerit, quam quid docuerit Plato vel censuerit Cato." *De Civ. Dei*, ii. 7.

infamous games, rightly termed "Fugalia," since they put modesty and decency to flight, but none where the people might listen to divine commands repressing avarice, ambition, or unchaste desire. Thus with the positive inculcation of all evil, under cover of their own example, was united the negative absence of all moral teaching.[1]

For even the prayers which accompanied these sacrifices and this ceremonial, and this lavish exhibition of every human wickedness under divine names, were not addressed for moral goods, but for wealth, bodily strength, temporal prosperity. Horace but expresses the general mind when he says :

"Sed satis est orare Jovem quæ donat et aufert ;
    Det vitam, det opes, æquum mi animum ipse parabo."
                                —*Epist.* i. 18, 111.

They were moreover viewed as carrying with them a sort of physical force, not as prevailing through purity of intention in those who offered them. In fact, the gods to whom they were addressed were powers of nature, or malignant and impure powers, but in neither case beings who looked for a moral service from rational creatures.

One other turpitude the Asiatic idolatry added to the Greek and Roman forms. By consecrating the sexual relations themselves in one male and one female god, they effected this crowning connection of idolatry with immorality, that unchaste acts became themselves acts of sacrifice, and so of worship.[2] This is the strange perversion borne witness to by Herodo-

---

[1] *De Civ. Dei*, ii. 6. "Demonstrentur vel commemorentur loca— ubi populi audirent quid dii præciperent de cohibenda avaritia, ambitione frangenda, luxuria refrænanda." See also sec. 28.

[2] See *Heidenthum und Judenthum*, p. 398. Herodotus, i. 199. Baruch, vi. 42–3.

tus, and corroborated by the prophet Jeremiah. A great seat of this worship was the city of Hierapolis, in Syria, where was one of the most magnificent temples of the ancient world, dedicated to Derketo, and rich with the offerings of Arabians, Babylonians, Assyrians, Phœnicians, Cilicians, Cappadocians, and all nations of the Semitic tongue. Nor was this worship confined to the East, for hence, as from a centre, the adherents of the Syrian goddess spread themselves in begging troops over the provinces of the empire. And the worship of Venus at Eryx, and other places in the West, with the thousands of female priestesses dedicated to it, reproduced the same abomination.

As the great result of all that we have said, we find the notion of sanctifying the human will absent from the religious rites of the polytheistic idolatry in all its forms. To this corresponded the absence of the notion of holiness in the gods. And this leads us finally to the remarkable character which defines it as a whole. This worship was throughout a corruption,[1] the spoiling, that is, of something good ; a turning away from the better to the worse. The worship itself had been originally good. The corruption lay in the alteration of the quality and the object of the worship. Worship had been implanted in man, and prescribed to him. It was at once the need of his nature and the command of Him who gave that nature. It had for it, first, positive institution, and then tradition and custom, and throughout, the conscience, the reason, and the heart of man. The reason of man ever bore powerful witness to the unity of the Godhead ; the breaking

[1] See S. Athan. *con. Gentes*, 5–9. In like manner S. Theophilus, lib. i. ad Autolyc. c. 2.

up of that unity, as exhibited by this idolatrous polytheism, in contradiction to the original prompting and
continued witness of the reason, is a very strong proof
of that moral corruption in the will which first generated it, which continued its existence, and which,
while multiplying, degraded its forms from age to age.
But man was free to decline from the good in which
he had been placed.   The corruption which was left
in his power he exerted; he changed the quality of
the service, and the person served.   The productive
cause of idolatry on the part of man was the soul of
man turning away from the notion of a good and holy
Creator, the contemplation of whom was its present
support and future reward, to visible things.   Of these
things the chief were bodily pleasures.   Thus this
corruption of the soul, in process of time, and continually becoming worse, produced this whole pantheon
of gods, originally the creation of its own lusts, and
subsisting as a perpetual food and support of those
lusts.   For this cause it had broken up the one perfect idea of God the Creator and Ruler of all persons
and things into a multitude of gods, whose functions
became more and more divided, until the ether, the
air, the earth, and the water swarmed with these supposed beings, which took possession even of wood and
stone, dwelling in the statues erected to them; and
every desire which the soul in its corruption could
entertain had its corresponding patron, helper, and
exemplar.   In this descending course cause and effect
were perpetually reacting on each other, and as the
corruption of the human soul had generated these
gods, so their multiplication and degradation intensified
its corruption from age to age.[1]

[1] In order to form a notion how far this division of gods could

Derketo and Mylitta, of Anubis and Serapis, of Thor and Woden, and so many more, receive man's adoration, and rejoice above all things in possessing his heart. These it is who have seduced him by exhibitions of visible beauty, have lain in wait for him by fountain, forest, and field, and filled the groves and high places with the charms which best pleased him under the name of worship; or have promised to disclose future things to him; or, again, have harrowed his soul with phantasms and terrors of the unseen world. These incoherent systems; these deities, whose functions ran into and athwart each other; these investings of human passions, and even unnatural and monstrous vices, with immortality and terrible power; these rivals ever quarrelling with each other, and jealous for the possession of man's homage, all serve the purpose of those behind the scenes, are puppets under their command, and have a common end and result in the captivity of their victim. More even than this; while they seem disunited and contradictory, they are really one, marshalled by the power, directed by the mind, held in the hand of him who is called "the ruler of this world," "the power of darkness," "the might of the enemy," who "holds the power of death," "the ancient serpent, who leads into error the whole world," "that malignant one in whom the whole world is lying," "the prince of the power of the air, the spirit who now works in the children of disobedience," who musters "the principalities, the powers, the world-rulers of this life's darkness, the spirits of wickedness in ethereal places," to serve him in his conflict with man's flesh and blood; in short, for St. Paul's language goes one point even beyond that of his Master, and terms him not merely the ruler, but "the god of this world;"[1] that is to say, this manifold idolatry is the establishment of his kingdom, the enthronement of his godhead over men, the mark of their captivity and prostration before him.

The statements of our Lord and His apostles being so express and definite as to the existence of this diabolic kingdom, and as to the personal sway of a sovereign over it, let us look once more at this idolatry itself by the light thus shed upon it.

And first, whether we regard men as made to be members of a well-ordered society, enjoying temporal prosperity in this life, or as further intended for happiness in a future life, resulting from their present actions,[2] the condition in which the heathen nations are actually found at our Lord's coming is quite unintelligible unless we suppose the reality of a diabolic power exercised upon them. The polytheism which we have witnessed holding all human life in its grasp, while it did not teach and uphold the great laws of morality, did, on the other hand, actively inculcate the violation of those laws by continually representing to the minds and eyes of men such a violation in the acts of the deities worshipped. It was a perpetual incitement of men to crimes, as well against social order as against all the sanctities of private life; it fostered the savageness of slavery, and the utmost cruelty in carrying on war, because its deities, being diverse for every nation, and belonging exclusively to the nation, had obliterated the idea that all men were of one blood, and thus delivered over the captive and

[1] See John xii. 31 ; xiv. 30; xvi. 11 ; Luke xxii. 53; x. 19 ; Apoc. xii. 9 ; Heb. ii. 14; 1 John v. 18; Ephes. vi. 12; ii. 2 ; 2 Cor. iv. 3.

[2] These two subjects occupy respectively the first five and the second five books of St. Augustine's *City of God*, where the argument is carried out in great detail.

the slave to the pitiless hatred or equally pitiless luxury of their fellow-men. So much for its action on human society as terminating with this life, while for a life to come it had no doctrine and made no preparation, but had suffered the earlier teaching of a future retribution to be considered as a fable fit for children and old women. Looking at such a condition of human society from the moral point of view, we may conclude with certainty that man would never, if left to himself, have devised it.

Secondly, regarding this polytheism as an object presented to the human intellect, nothing more unreasonable and monstrous than this crowd of deities can even be conceived. The human reason demands imperatively the unity of the Godhead, since infinite power at least enters into the conception of the Godhead, and to divide or limit infinity is an unreason. All the great works and order of the world bore witness likewise to this unity of the Godhead, and were sufficient to prove it; [1] and even in the worst times of paganism we find this proof exhibited with a force and lucidity to which even now little can be added. And in the worst times, again, we find the natural witness of the human soul breaking out in moments of sudden trial or great anguish, and calling upon the one God for help. [2] Yet in spite of this we see whole nations renowned for their intellectual productions, and men among them in whom the force of reason has rarely or never been surpassed, bowing their necks to this yoke of polytheism, and accepting this tissue of monstrous error, paying homage to it in their life, and dying with

[1] Rom. i. 20.   See the Stoical argument for the unity of the deity in Cic. de Nat. Deor. 2.
[2] Tertullian de Testimonio Animæ, 2.

it on their lips ; as Socrates offering the cock to Æsculapius, and Seneca the libation to Jove the liberator.
We know not how to account for this, were man's
reason left alone.   We can see an adequate ground
for it only in "men having been made unreasonable,
and in the demoniacal error overshadowing the earth,
and concealing the knowledge of the true God.[1]

Let us take a third view of it, neither the moral
nor the logical, but the view of it as an existing fact,
as something which for many hundred years occupied
the earth, ruled nations, moulded the institutions and
characters of men.   Here we do not speak merely of
the multitude of temples, of priests or priestesses
serving in them, of sacrifices offered by these, of
prayers, vows, festivals in honour of the gods——because
all these enter into the notion of a service rendered
by man to the power superior to him, and in their
utmost perversion there is nothing which may not be
accounted for by a simply human corruption stealing
into and spoiling an originally good institution ; but
all these in the actual condition of paganism were
mixed up with and penetrated by other elements, and
accompanied by effects not to be so accounted for.
Let us take the universal persuasion that the statues
of the gods were inhabited by the deities which they
represented, as bodies by souls.[2]   Here was the notion
of a spiritual power taking possession of material
forms.   But how was this notion introduced, propagated,
and maintained in men's minds ?   By certain visible

---

[1] Οὕτω τοίνυν ἀλογωθέντων τῶν ἀνθρώπων, καὶ οὕτω τῆς δαιμονικῆς
πλάνης ἐπισκιαζούσης τὰ πανταχοῦ, καὶ κρυπτούσης τὴν περὶ τοῦ ἀληθινοῦ
Θεοῦ γνῶσιν.   S. Athan. de Incar. 13.

[2] See S. August. de Civ. Dei, viii. 24.   "Immundi spiritus, eisdem
simulacris arte illa nefaria colligati, cultorum suorum animas in suam
societatem redigendo miserabiliter captivaverant,"

and palpable effects,[1] of which those who were eye-witnesses give us many details. Take again the oracles which existed throughout the heathen world, and, as dealing with the same subject-matter, divination in all its forms. However much of deceit there might be here, was there not also, in many instances, an exhibition of power and knowledge beyond that of man, which no mere deceit could produce? Take again magic, the invocation, adjuration, and compacting with spirits, which ran through heathen society in numberless shapes; and take lastly the fact of spirits seizing upon and possessing the bodies of men, speaking by their voice, and controlling their minds. The four classes which we have just given, comprehend in themselves an innumerable multitude of facts which are apparent in pagan history, in all which the corruption of the human soul is an agent or patient, but for which that corruption by itself supplies no adequate cause. A spiritual power is behind, laying hold of and acting upon this corruption, and by fault of the human will making an inroad into the visible world, and partially mastering it, bending it to an evil purpose, and making it serve as an agent to man's captivity. Let us briefly cite as to the reality of this spiritual power the witness of its victims and the witness of its opponents.

First, as to its victims. Scarcely a writer, whether poet, historian, philosopher, or biographer, can be found among the heathens of Greece and Rome who does not attest facts belonging to one or more of these four

---

[1] Called by S. Athan. ἡ τῶν δαιμόνων ἀπάτη—μανία—φαντασίαι. Thus, *De Inc.* 47. πάλαι μὲν δαίμονες ἐφαντασιασκόπουν τοὺς ἀνθρώπους, προκαταλαμβάνοντες πηγὰς ἢ ποταμούς, ἢ ξύλα, ἢ λίθους, καὶ οὕτω ταῖς μαγγανείαις ἐξέπληττον τοὺς ἄφρονας. Νῦν δὲ τῆς θείας ἐπιφανείας τοῦ Λόγου γεγενημένης, πέπαυται τούτων ἡ φαντασία

classes which surpass human power, and suggest an invisible spiritual agency. The poet who writes expressly to deny such an agency speaks of the whole world as bowed beneath the fear of it; another poet,[1] referring tacitly to this very passage, felicitates the man not who has a pure conscience, but who through knowledge of natural things has trampled these fears under his feet. Nor is such a belief confined to the vulgar; but scarcely a man of eminence, a soldier, or a statesman can be cited who does not in his life and actions acknowledge it, shrink from it, or cower beneath it. It is too powerful for Alexander or even Julius to escape; and the philosophers who affect to deny it in their systems exhibit it in their conduct. They have all the conviction of an evil power beyond and above nature, but taking hold of natural forms, and ever lying in wait to burst forth from them upon human life. The Greek name for superstition is fear of the demons; and what S. Paul said of the Athenians, that he found them in all things too fearful of the demons, might be applied to the whole circle of nations surrounding the midland sea.

Secondly, as to the opponents of this power. Now they offer a triple witness to its existence. The first of these is in the facts mentioned in the New Testament. The strongest, most terrible, and most inexplicable instance of this power lies in those diabolical possessions with which so many of our Lord's miracles are concerned. Again, as to the reality of divining

---

[1] "Humana ante oculos fœde quam vita jaceret
In terris, oppressa, gravi sub religione," &c.   Lucret. i. 63.

"Felix qui potuit rerum cognoscere causas,
Atque metus omnes et inexorabile fatum
Subjecit pedibus, strepitumque Acherontis avari."
—Virg. *Geo.* ii. 491.

powers arising from the presence of a demon in a human form, we have the evil spirit in the girl at Philippi acknowledging in St. Paul a servant of the most high God, and, when cast out by the Apostle in the name of Christ, leaving his victim destitute of those powers which had brought gain to her masters, who forthwith try to avenge themselves for their loss by exciting a persecution against the Apostle.[1]

A second witness is found in the rites and offices of the very power set up to dethrone and abolish this other power. The Church called upon every one who was received into her bosom to begin by renouncing the usurpation of this great enemy, which was thus declared to be universal. She provided forms for exorcising him. One of her Apostles warned those to whom he wrote that men could not partake at once of the Christian sacrifice and the heathen; for as truly as one was the chalice of the Lord, the other was the chalice of devils; as one was the table of the Lord, the other was the table of devils.[2]

A third witness is found in the unanimous testimony of all Christian writers as to the reality of the demoniacal powers with which they were waging war; as to their perpetual interference with human life; as to the open and palpable effects which they produced; as to their unwilling retirement in the face of that Stronger One who was come upon them. It was not merely the fervid Tertullian who offered to rest the truth of Christianity and the life of any ordinary Christian upon his power publicly to expel a demon. Athanasius, who weighs every word he utters, says also, "Let him who will, try the truth of what we have said, and in the very presence of the spectral

---

[1] Acts xvi. 16.   [2] 1 Cor. x. 21.

ruption, to all which a consummating force is added by the indwelling of diabolic power, it remains to give a glance at certain conditions and circumstances under which it was acting on the minds of men. We have here taken it and examined it by itself, abstracting it from those circumstances, but it never so appeared to those who lived under it. The wonderful error which so enfolded these widespread nations never exhibited itself to them bare and naked. On the contrary, it came to them interwoven with the dearest claims of the family, the city, the country, with the force of habit and tradition, with the dread of change, with the past history and future hopes of their fatherland, coloured moreover with the radiant dress of a rich and ever-advancing civilisation.

To judge of its power, vitality, and chance of permanence, we must look at it under these conditions. And if, when we regard this idolatrous polytheism in itself, one is lost in wonder at its ever having arisen, at its existence, at its continuance, so, when one regards it as throned in the customs, feelings, convictions, and interests of society, one wonders how any moral force could ever overthrow it. At the present time not only are their religions outside of Christianity, but there are also sects within it, so irrational, so devoid of the witness given by internal truth and harmony, so unable to render any account of themselves and their claims which will satisfy a mind looking for consistency, that, regarding them merely as facts, one cannot account for them, yet notwithstanding they may have existed for several hundred years, and had a large share in forming national habits of thought, or even national character; nay, perhaps their secret strength lies in some fold of this character itself. And because they are never seen by themselves, their intrinsic absurdity does not come before their adherents, and the last thing which these think of examining is the foundation of their sect, inasmuch as in fact it has never approached them otherwise than as a condition of their daily life. So we shall understand paganism better by considering it as interwoven with civilisation, polity, and national feelings. We will treat of it briefly under these three heads.

1. First, the whole eastern part of the Roman Empire was made up of many various nations having a long and sometimes renowned history, kingdoms and polities much anterior to Rome herself, of which the Romans had taken violent possession, but wherein remained still the fruits of a rich and undisturbed civilisation. And this word comprehends all the natural life of man, all the discoveries gained by his invention or experience, and accumulated by wealth descending from age to age, all the manifold ties of social intercourse, all the pleasures of the intellect, united, moreover, in their case with an art even now unrivalled in portraying the beauty of the human figure, and in the elegance with which it adapted material forms to the conveniences of life. So rich and varied an inheritance unfolded itself in a thousand Hellenic cities studding the shores of the Mediterranean. The culture itself since the time of Alexander might be termed Hellenic, but it embraced Egypt, and Syria, and all Western Asia. And so completely was idolatrous polytheism interwoven with culture, so inextricably was it blended with the bulk, so gradually had it grown with the growth, and wound its fibres about the tree and the branches, that

the worship might be absolutely identified with the
civilisation.   The gods of Greece were the heads of
the most illustrious Grecian families; their hero-
worship consecrated every city, every grove, every
field.   The gods of Egypt were blended with the long
renown of the Nile-land, with every Egyptian custom,
with the beginning and the end of life.   Not less had
the gods of Syria and Western Asia occupied their
respective lands.   These deities struck their root into
the home of man, into the union of the sexes, into the
loves of parent and child, of brother and sister.   They
had their mementos in every street of busy traffic;
they watched over the Acropolis; not a fountain but
laid claim to their patronage, nor a field which was
fruitful but by their supposed influence.   These countries had lost their political independence, but the
material ease of life under the majesty of the Roman
name they retained.   There was a passionate love for
this world's goods, comforts, and enjoyments in the
Greek, Syrian, Asiatic, Egyptian, and Libyan races,
all of them more or less worn, and effete, and deeply
sensualised; but their glory was this great Hellenic
civilisation, with which polytheism might be termed
one and the same thing.

   2. When we turn to the West, the seat of the
sovereign city and of the empire itself, we find that
from the very beginning and through many centuries
the political constitution of the city had been indis-
solubly blended with the worship of the Roman gods.
The religion of Rome was much more than national;
her polity seemed only another name for her worship.
Her temples were as much a part of her political life
as her forum.   So far at least she had embodied in
her whole structure the legend of her Etruscan teacher,

wherein the dwarf Tages sprung from the soil to communicate the worship claimed by the gods.[1]   Her soil
and her worship were indivisible.   And even after
seven centuries, when the city was embracing the
world in its arms, this union practically existed.
Rome indeed admitted, as we have said, the gods of
the conquered nations into her pantheon, but it was
on the same tenure as the nations themselves shared
her civic rights.   Jupiter Capitolinus was a sort of
suzerain not only to the gods of the Grecian Olympus,
but to the dark forms of the Nile deities, to the
Syrian, the Libyan, the Gallic, the Germanic, the
Sarmatian Valhalla.   When the greatest of her poets
would express unending duration, he joins together
the race of Æneas enthroned on the Capitol with the
god who dwelt there :

> "Nulla dies unquam memori vos eximet ævo,
>   Dum domus Æneæ Capitoli immobile saxum
>   Accolet, imperiumque Pater Romanus habebit."

The Roman father is the Capitoline Jupiter.   "I am
not a king ; the only king of the Romans is Jupiter,"
said the most royal of the race, and the founder of
her empire, when, seeing all prostrate at his feet, he
put away reluctantly the diadem offered by his creature.   Thus even he who had seized the reality of
power, who would have omens when he pleased, and
whose will was his law, left the crown on the head of
Jupiter.   In Rome, all through her history "piety
and patriotism were the same feeling." [2]   When her
empire became world-wide, this sort of devotion did
not cease.   Rome had long been deified ; and the

[1] Merivale, iii. 496.
[2] Beugnot, *Destruction du Paganisme*, i. 8.

double import of her name [1] expressed strength against
the foe without, and nourishment to the child within.
She was at once a warrior-goddess clothed in mail to
meet the enemy, and a mother offering her bosom to
her citizens clustered around her.   And so in her new
constitution, adapted for the world, her emperor too
was deified, as the first of her children, her living
representative, the embodiment of her force and love,
the visible wielder of her unseen power.   All that is
sacred in home and country to us the Roman signified
when he swore by the genius of the emperor.   Nothing could be more tolerant than this polytheism, if
the innovation extended only to the borrowing or
creating a new divinity, to reforming a rite or a cere-
mony,[2] or to such like modifications of worship which
admitted that on which it rested ; but nothing more
intolerant than the same polytheism when the worship
itself was attacked.   A movement against the Capitoline Jupiter would be not only sacrilege but high
treason, and the refusal to call to witness the emperor's
genius was in fact to deny his imperial authority.
The worship of the gods was as much identified with
the Empire of Rome in the West as with the civilisation of Greece throughout the East.

   3. But as if these two powers were not ties sufficiently strong to hold polytheism together, there was
another feeling distinct from both, which formed its
last bulwark.   The iron hand which held in its grasp
these vast countries, many of them so large that by
themselves they might have been empires, was strong
enough to prevent or crush insurrection, but provided
only the majesty of the Roman peace was accepted,

----

[1] ῥώμη, strength ; ruma, a mother's breast.
[2] Beugnot, i. 17.

did not seek to disturb a large remnant of local feeling and interest still representing the former life and polity of the several provinces.   Now whatever of national, tribe, or race feeling existed, was grouped everywhere about the worship of the native gods.[1] The Nile-land had ceased to be a royal seat, and was governed by a simple Roman knight as prefect of the emperor; but not for this had the Nile gods abdicated their dark sway over their votaries.   In them the Egyptians still felt that they had something which was their own.   Thus, whatever force of patriotism still lurked in the several parts of the empire was nurtured by its own form of polytheism, which it in turn invested with the memories dearest and most ineradicable in man, of past independence or renown. Not only the Egyptians, but the various Asiatic and Libyan races, the Gauls and Germans under Roman sway, were thus attached to their native gods with a feeling no doubt akin to that of the English towards "Old England," or the Russians towards "Holy Russia."

Two more conditions of society throughout the whole empire we have yet to consider in their bearing on the maintenance of polytheism : first, the concentration of the vast power of the state—in itself an acknowledged omnipotence, without the restriction or reservation of individual rights—in one hand, the hand of the emperor, the sole representative of the people.   By this it would seem that all the upper classes of society, the classes at ease as to their maintenance, the classes who have leisure to think and will to act in political matters, were deprived of so much of their freedom, and such deprivation would tend to

---

[1] Οἱ ἐγχώριοι θεοί.

support an existing institution. Secondly, the despotism above was met by a corresponding despotism below. The rights of the slaveholder over the human labourer left as little margin of freedom to daily toil as the right of the imperial autocrat to the freedom of conscience in the rich. The servants throughout the world of Rome being slaves, were as much in the hand of their masters as those masters were in the hand of the prince.

We can now take a prospect of human society in reference to the polytheism of the empire from the standing-point of Augustus in the last twenty years of his reign. The worship of her gods was so intertwined with the political constitution of Rome from her birth through seven centuries and a half, that it might be said to be one thing with it. Almost as close was the identification of the several religious systems of the East with the enjoyments of civilised life which they prized so highly, and which the Empire of Rome secured to them. Further in the background the national gods of the many races included in the empire were the last inheritance of their former independent life. Again, not only was the emperor as Pontifex Maximus the official head of this polytheism, but as representing the whole power of the state he was its guardian, and whatever assailed it was an insult to the majesty which he embodied; while the slavery in which the masses were lying seemed to represent in human society the chances of war, which had all ended in the dominion of Rome and the subjection of the whole pantheon of incongruous gods to the sovereignty of the Capitoline Jupiter. These were general conditions to that multifarious whole of nations and races. Then if Augustus sought to examine more narrowly the society of Roman citizens spread through his empire, he would find it divided very unequally as to numbers into two classes. The vast majority were those who take things as they find them, and who belonged with more or less fidelity and heartiness to the idolatrous polytheism. The worship which came to them as part and parcel of the empire, of civilised and of national life, they accepted without thought. To all these an indefinite number of immoral gods was throned in possession of Olympus; to all these the result of such worship was, as we have seen described by St. Augustine, the utter perversion of morality, the consecration of fables equalling in turpitude the utmost license of the theatres. But everywhere among the educated classes were to be found a small number of sceptical minds : philosophers they termed themselves : it was fashionable to follow some philosophic system or sect, and these fell mainly into two. Now the Epicureans and the Stoics, while they left the existing polytheism in practical possession, as a matter of custom and state religion, and so delivered themselves from any unpleasant consequences of denying the prevailing worship, concurred entirely in this, that the one by the way of atheism, the other by that of pantheism, destroyed all religion of the heart and inner conduct; because they equally removed the notion of a personal God, and its corresponding notion of a personal being in man outliving the body and the world of sense, and meeting with a personal retribution. Whether the power they acknowledge be nature, as in Lucretius, or a hidden physical force running through all nature, which might be called Jupiter, Juno, Hercules, or the name of any other god, as in Marcus Aurelius, the notion of a personal Creator, provident and rewarding, was equally

destroyed.   Nor before the preaching of the Gospel
does there appear a single individual who drew out
of the existing polytheism such a conclusion.   On the
contrary, in Augustus and his successors the imperial
idea of unity in religion was to make out that all these
systems of polytheism, running into and athwart each
other, came practically to the same thing, differing in
name only.   Their obedience to Jupiter of the Capitol
was the only bond of unity, and pledge of the empire's
duration, conceived by the Roman rulers.

II. Thus in the time of Augustus no human eye,
whether we look at the mass of mankind or the thinking few, could see any sign either that the dominant
polytheism was about to fall, or that the lost doctrine
of the divine Unity and Personality could be extri-
cated from the bewildering mass of error and superstition which had grown over, disguised, and distorted it.
Darker still, if possible, became the prospect under
his successor, Tiberius, whose reign had reached the
climax of moral debasement, when Sejanus was all-
powerful at Rome.   Hope for the human race there
appeared none, when such an emperor devolved his
omnipotence on such a prime minister.   Then in the
judgment-hall of a procurator in a small and distant
eastern province, there passed the following dialogue
between an accused criminal and his judge:—"Pilate
went into the prætorium again, and called Jesus, and
said to Him, 'Art thou the king of the Jews?'
Jesus answered him, 'Sayest thou this thing of thyself,
or have others told it thee of me?'   Pilate answered,
'Am I a Jew?   Thine own nation and the chief
priests have delivered thee up to me: what hast
thou done?'   Jesus answered, 'My kingdom is not
of this world.   If my kingdom were of this world,

my servants would strive that I should not be delivered to the Jews; but now my kingdom is not from hence.' Pilate therefore said to Him, 'Art thou a king, then?' Jesus answered, 'Thou sayest that I am a king. For this was I born, and for this came I into the world, that I should bear witness to the truth. Every one that is of the truth heareth my voice.' Pilate saith to Him, 'What is truth?'" He who thus declared Himself to be a king, the cause of whose birth and advent into the world, the function of whose royalty, was to bear witness to the truth, received from the power which then ruled the world the punishment allotted to the slave who was worthy of death. For many ages a false worship had overshadowed the earth, hiding the true God from men, and setting up instead a multitude of demons for gods. And during this time the thinkers of Greek and Roman society had been asking, What is truth? And now the officer who asked that question of the Truth Himself, replied to it by crucifying Him. And when the body of that Crucified One was the same day taken down from the cross and laid in its sepulchre, the power which reigned in polytheism and spoke by the mouth of the judge, seemed to have given the final answer of triumphant force to its question, What is truth? and falsehood might be thought to reign supreme and victorious in the world.

It was with the resurrection of that Body, in which Truth was enshrined, that the resurrection of truth among men began. He had said to His disciples a few hours before, not "I show the truth," but "I am the Truth." His birth and His advent took place that His witness might be given to it, the witness to it being that very birth and advent, His appearance among men, and the reception He would meet with. The crucifixion itself—the reply of triumphant force to its own unanswered question—was the witness which, first in Him, and then in His followers, should make itself heard over the earth, now held in captivity by falsehood. And since Truth is His proper Name and His personal Being from eternity, and by being the Truth He who spoke is the second Person in the Godhead, the perfect Image of all Truth, let us consider the import of His Name as the summing-up of the great antagonism which He then planted on the earth.

For He named Himself the Truth because He is the Son and the Word of the Father. "Thus the Father, as it were uttering Himself, begot His Word, equal to Himself in all things. For He would not fully and perfectly have uttered Himself, if there were anything less or anything more in His Word than in Himself. . . . And therefore this Word is truly the Truth; inasmuch as whatever is in that knowledge of which He is begotten, is also in Himself; and whatsoever is not in it, is not in Himself. . . . The Father and the Son know each other, the one by generating, the other by being generated." [1]   Thus it is that He is the perfect Word, the absolute Image of God; and being the Image of God He created man in the beginning a copy of that Image, and according to its resemblance, in that He created him in the indivisible unity of a soul intelligent and willing—a created copy of the Trinity in Unity. But though by the original constitution of the soul this copy could not be destroyed, being the very essence of the soul, yet the resemblance might be marred, and the harmony which reigned in

[1] St. Aug. *de Trin.* l. xv. c. 14, tom. viii. 984.

the original man between the soul, its intellect, and will, through the indwelling of God's Spirit, was broken by the act of sin; whereupon that Spirit withdrew from him, and left the copy of the divine Image defaced and disordered. All the heathenism we have been considering is the sequence of that disorder, part of which is the grievous obscuration of truth, that is, of the whole relation between God and man, of which idolatrous polytheism is the perversion. It was the exact representation of the soul's own disorder, being the distortion but not the extinction of worship; the fear of many demons, instead of the fear of one God; slavish instead of filial fear.

But as the Truth of the Father is beheld and expressed in generating His Son, His Word, His perfect Image, so truth to man is the resemblance of created things to the archetypal idea of them in God; the resemblance of the works of the divine art to the Artificer's intention. In this long act of heathenism we see the work of the divine Artificer marred and obscured, and the marring and obscuration seem to have gone as far as was possible without touching the essence of the soul. Who, then, should restore, but He who had first created? Who should give back to the copy the lost harmony, and reimprint the defaced resemblance, save the perfect Image of God? Thus, when the corruption had run its course, and the original disobedience had reproduced itself all over the earth in a harvest of evil and disorder, the time for the work of reparation was come, and the Divine Word, the Image of the Father, took flesh.

Magnificent as had been the dower of the First Man, and wonderful the grace which held his soul in harmony with itself, and his bodily affections in obedience to his soul, incomparably more magnificent was the dower of human nature in its reparation, inconceivably grander the grace which ruled the Soul and Body of the Restorer. For whereas the first man's person had been simply human, the Person of the Second Man was the Divine Word Himself, the perfect Image of the Father; and whereas the grace of the first man was such that he was able not to sin, the grace which had assumed the nature of the Second Man was a Person who could not sin, the fountain of grace itself, measureless, absolute, and personal. The Image of God Himself came to restore the copy of that Image in Man; his appearance as man among men was the reconveying of the Truth to them, because He was the Truth Himself. The Truth in all its extent; the Truth in the whole moral order and every relation which belongs to it; the Truth by which all the rational creation of God corresponds to the Idea of its Creator, was the gift which He brought to man in His Incarnation.

But this truth is not merely external to man. In order to be received and appropriated by him, he must become capable of it. The Restorer works his restoration by an inward act upon the soul, its intellect and will. The image of God sets up His seat within His work, the copy. Man is sealed by the Holy Spirit with the likeness and resemblance of the Father's Face, the Son; and having the Son within him, and giving a home within the soul to the divine character, and making this his treasure, man is formed after God.[1] The supreme likeness, which is beyond all others, is impressed on human souls by the Spirit of the Father and the Son. As the defacing of the

[1] St. Cyril. Alex. tom. v. 1, pp. 544, 557 a.

likeness, the result of the original fall, caused the obscuring of the Truth, so its restoration was itself the recovery of the Truth.

And this restoration is itself the witness to the Truth of which He spoke before Pilate as the object of His birth and advent. But to make the witness operative and fruitful, the greatest wonder in this list of wonders is required, the suffering of the Truth Himself. He said of the corn of wheat, which was to bear fruit in unnumbered hearts, that it would remain alone unless it fell into the ground and died. And so His crucifixion in the nature which He had assumed was the act from which the renewal of truth went forth ; and not only in His Person, but likewise in His chosen witnesses this special mode of vivifying the truth, and making it fruitful, should be repeated. Not only must the absolute Truth of God appear in our nature itself in order to be accepted, but the nature in which it appeared should offer the sacrifice of itself ; and this particular mode of propagating the truth should be observed in that chosen band whom He termed specially His witnesses. Their witness should be their suffering ; in them too the Truth should be crucified, and so become fruitful.

And as man in his original creation had been a copy, however faint, of the eternal relations of the Godhead in itself, so his restoration springs from those same eternal relations. In it the Father, the Son, and the Holy Spirit are seen working.[1] It springs from the Father, in that He is the Father of the only-begotten Son, the Original of the Image, and so the Father of all those who are the copies of that Image. It springs from the Son, in that He is the perfect

[1] St. Cyril. Alex. *in Joh.* x. p. 858 b.

Image of the Father, and by dwelling in a created nature has raised it to the dignity of His Person, from which the grace of Sonship comes. It springs from the Holy Spirit, whose work as the Spirit of the Father and the Son is to imprint the copy of the Son on man. He performs in every one of the redeemed by communicating to them a participation of the divine nature, by dwelling in them, by contact and coherence with them, a work infinitely less in degree, but yet of the same order with that work of His whereby all the fulness of the Godhead dwelt by personal unity in our Lord's Manhood.[1]

But we left our Lord before Pilate, bearing witness to the truth. It remains to see how that truth became impressed on the world.

[1] Petav. *de Trin.* lib. viii. c. 7.

LECTURE VIII

THE FIRST AND THE SECOND MAN

"Totus Christus caput et corpus est. Caput unigenitus Dei Filius, et corpus ejus Ecclesia, Sponsus et Sponsa, duo in carne una." St. Aug. *De Unitate Ecc.* tom. ix. 341.

"Totus Christus, id est, caput et membra." St. Thomas, Prolog. ad 1 Sentent. art. 4.

LET us look back on the space which we have traversed, and gather up in a few words the sight which it presents to us. We have man before us as far as history will carry us back, as far as reasoning, planting itself on the scanty traces of history, will penetrate into the cloudland of prehistoric times : and the result stands before us exhibited in the manifold records still remaining of the most renowned ancient civilisation. Here, then, we see nations whose genius, whether in history, poetry, and literature, or in works of art, or in civil government, we still admire, comprising men in many of whom the powers of reason reached their utmost limit ; nations inhabiting the most varied climates and countries, and amongst them the fairest in the world, nations formed under the most different circumstances and pursuing the most distinct employments, some agricultural, some commercial, some inland, some nautical, but alike in this, that they were enthralled by systems of a false worship, of which it is hard to say whether it was the more revolting to the reason by its absurdity, or to the conscience of man by its foulness. And this false worship does not lie distinct and apart from the concerns of daily civil and domestic life, but is intertwined with all the public and private actions of men, forming their habits and ruling their affections. Moreover, the polytheistic idolatry described above as existing at the time of Augustus in every province of his empire except one, in almost [1] every country which touched upon it, or was known to it, is the result, the summing-up, the embodiment of man's whole history up to that time, so far as we know it: it is that into which this history had run out, its palpable, it almost seemed its irresistible, form. And it amounts to a complete corruption, first of the relation between man and his Creator, secondly of the relation between man and his fellow, thirdly of the relations of man in civil government, that is, of states and political communities, to each other.

Now, looking at this polytheistic idolatry simply as a fact, without for the moment any attempt to give a solution of it from authority, looking at it just as modern science would regard the facts of geology or astronomy, there is one thing, we may suppose, which it proves with a superabundance of evidence not found to belong to any other fact of history; and that is, the intrinsic corruption of man as a moral being. That which in theological language is called the Fall of man is, apart from all revealed doctrine on the subject, brought in upon the mind with irresistible force by the mere enumeration of the gods which heathendom worshipped, and of the worship paid by it to them; a force which is indefinitely increased by every inquiry into the moral and religious state of man as he lived under this worship.

[1] An exception must be made in favour of Persia, where the original monotheism was preserved with more or less corruption.

Now, then, let us consider what solution the Christian faith does give of this fact, which exists, be it remembered, independently of this solution, and would exist with all its force undiminished, if this were rejected.

I. The Christian faith, as a solution of this wonderful maze of polytheistic idolatry, with all its accompaniments and consequences, carries us back to the first father of the race, whose development we have been following in it.   This, it says, is nothing else [1] but the body of Adam carried out through thousands of years, the body of Adam fallen under a terrible captivity.   Not only does the Christian faith set before us man as one race descended from one, but because he is this one race, descended from one, it represents him as having come into such a state.   To understand this we must contemplate the original creation, the fall of man, and its consequences, in their several bearings on each other, which will then lead us on to the nature and mode of the restoration.

In speaking of the creation of man we may first consider the union of the soul and body simply by themselves; that is, in order to obtain a clear view of our subject, we may form to ourselves a purely ideal state of simple nature.   Such a state would include two things; one positive, the other negative. [2]   Positively, human nature in this condition would have all natural faculties in their essential perfection, and the assistance and providence of God naturally due to it: negatively, it would have nothing superadded to nature, nothing not due to it, whether evil or good, that is,

---

[1] "Das Heidenthum ist nichts anderes als der gefallene und nicht wiedergeborne Mensch im Grossen."   Möhler, *Kirchengeschichte*, i. 169.

[2] Suarez, *de Gratia*, Proleg. 4, cap. i. sec. 3.

neither sin on the one hand, and what follows sin, the guilt which entails punishment, nor on the other hand any gifts of grace, or perfections not due to nature.

Human nature, if created in such a state, would have no supernatural end; its end would be to love God with a natural love, as the Author and Ruler of the world.

Of such a state it is requisite for our present purpose to say only two things further. The first, that it is not contrary to any attribute of God to have created human nature in such a state. The gift of eternal beatitude, arising from the vision of God, which such a creature would not have had for its end, is simply and absolutely a gratuitous gift of the divine bounty, which God is not bound to bestow on any creature as such. Secondly, God did not in fact so create man.

Going on from this state of simple nature, we may consider another state in man, in which, beyond all his natural faculties,[1] he would have a certain special perfection, consisting in the absence of immoderate concupiscence, or in the perfect subjection of the sensitive to the rational appetite, so that the inferior appetite should not be allowed to set itself in motion against the superior, or to anticipate reason. For human nature, regarded in itself as the union of a spirit and a body, is as it were divided in its natural affections, which tend in diverse directions, and thus totters, so to say, in its gait; when, therefore, it receives an inward peace in its own proper faculties, it is said to be supplemented, or to receive its integrity.

Now it is much to be noted that this special gift of

---

[1] Suarez, *de Gratia*, Proleg. cap. ii. sec. 3.

integrity would not be connatural to man, that is, not
given to him by force of his nature itself. It is true
indeed that as such a gift perfects nature in regard to
all natural acts, and supplies a sort of natural de-
ficiency arising out of the combination of a spiritual
with a material substance, wherein a conflict is engendered, in such a sense it may be called natural : but
strictly speaking it is a gift superadded to nature.

It must further be noted that this state of nature
in its integrity, however high and beautiful, is not
only entirely distinct from but of an inferior order to
the state of human nature raised to the gift of Divine
Sonship. Between human nature in this condition
and human nature raised to the gift of sonship, there
would be more than the difference [1] that with us
exists between the kindly-treated servant and the
adopted son : for human nature in this integrity
would still not by virtue of it possess sanctifying
grace, or, in consequence, have God and His vision
for its supernatural end.

But, thirdly, it was not merely in this state that
God created man, but in a state which not only included this, but had grace for its basis,[2] that is to say,
every perfection which it had sprang out of this, that
it was united to God by grace. This is a state of far
superior order, absolutely gratuitous, and beyond anything which is due to nature. The first man, Adam,
then, was not only a union of soul and body, not only
did he possess this nature in its integrity, but he was
created in grace, so that there was a union of the
Holy Spirit with him, whereby he was exalted to the
condition of a supernatural end and adopted sonship,

---

[1] Kleutgen, *die Theologie der Vorzeit*, ii. p. 559.
[2] Suarez, *de Grat.* Proleg. 4, cap. v. sec. 3.

and in this union was rooted the integrity of his nature, and the supernatural power of so ruling all the lower faculties of his soul that the higher could mount undisturbedly to God : and certain other gifts over and above, such as immunity from error or deception, so long as he did not sin, immunity from even venial fault, immunity from death, and from all pain or sorrow.   Such was the original condition which grace bestowed on human nature, wherein man had not only a supernatural end, but the power to attain it easily.[1]

Now it is evident that man, by being created in grace, was raised to an astonishing height of dignity, to which not only his nature, but any created nature whatsoever had no claim.   All that the justice and goodness of God required him to do in creating such a being as man of two substances, soul and body, was to bestow on the compound being so united such perfections as made the several substances complete in their own order.   Such would be the ideal state of simple nature as delineated above.   It was a gift beyond nature, such as nature in its first beginning could not claim, to bestow on it the integrity which in the second place we considered.   But how far beyond this, passing it by an unmeasured chasm, was that dower of sonship rooted in sanctifying grace which God actually bestowed on His favoured child ?   It is obvious at first sight that the divine gift here intended, being in Adam's actual creation the root of all which was over and above the natural faculties of body and soul in their union, was bestowed absolutely by the pure goodness of God, and therefore could be bestowed with such conditions attached to it as pleased

[1] Kleutgen, *die Theologie der Vorzeit*, vol. ii. 650.

the Giver.   In all that is beyond the mere faculties and
needs of nature—in forming which God's own being is
a sort of rule to Him—He is absolutely free to give as
pleases Himself, to what degree He pleases, on what
terms He pleases.   What, then, were the conditions
on which He invested Adam with the gift of sonship,
and created him in grace as its foundation ?   He
created him, not only as the individual Adam, but as
the Head of his race, so that his race was summed up
in him, and a unity was founded in him attaching his
whole race as members to his body, in such manner
that the supernatural gift of sonship bestowed on him
was to descend from him by virtue of natural propagation to every member of that body, which thus
became a supernatural race from a supernatural father.
So absolute was this unity that the order maintained in
the case of every other creature put under the dominion
of the man so formed was not followed in his case.   For
whereas they were created with the difference of sex,
each a male and a female, he was created alone, as the
Head, and then she, by whose co-operation the race was
to be continued, was formed out of him.   It was not
a second man who was so formed from the first, but
one made with reference to him, in dependence on
him, to be a help meet for him, not for herself, with
an independent being, but for him.   This formation
of Eve from Adam, which has a meaning of unfathomable depth in the development of the race, is
an essential part of the original design.   " Therefore," says Adam, speaking in an ecstasy sent upon
him by God, the words of God, "this is now bone of
my bone and flesh of my flesh : she shall be called
woman, because she was taken out of man.   Therefore shall a man leave his father and his mother, and

shall cleave unto his wife, and they shall be one flesh."
First, the Eve so formed from him is one flesh with
him; secondly, the race springing from both is one
flesh likewise with him. The consequence intended
by that one flesh was the transmission of that magnificent inheritance in which Adam was standing
when he so spoke. In this he was Father and
Head, for this created alone, then Eve built up
from him, from whom afterwards was to issue their
joint race. On the further condition of his personal obedience to God and fidelity to His grace, he
held the whole supernatural gift of grace conferring
sonship, both for himself and for his race: on these
terms it was bestowed by the charter of God, the
original Giver. Thus, the greatness of his Headship
was visible in two things, the power of transmitting
his quality of divine sonship to his race by propagation, and the dependence of that quality, in them
as well as in himself, on his personal fidelity to God.

But the First Man, the Father and Head of the
race, did not stand in his inheritance. He broke
the divine command, and lost the gift of sonship,
and with it all the prerogatives attendant on that
gift, which were above nature and rooted in grace,
and which the eminent goodness of God had bestowed upon him: and by the terms of the original
charter lost the gift, not only for himself, but for
his race. But he did not, therefore, destroy that
relation between the Head and the Race, which was
part of the original foundation of God. This continued; but whereas it had been intended to communicate the blessing of adoption, it now served to
communicate the demerit of adoption lost, the guilt,
and with it the punishment incurred by that loss.

This is the original sin, the sin of the nature, not of the person, inherited by the members of Adam's body; and as there can be no sin without free-will, the sin of the whole nature included in Adam as its Root and Head, which sinned by Adam's abuse of his free-will.

Let us try to determine as accurately as we can the position into which Adam and his race fell.

Did, then, Adam simply lose with the forfeiture of sanctifying grace the gift of sonship, the super-natural inheritance, all which God had bestowed on him beyond that ideal state of pure nature which we described in the first instance? God, we said, might have created man originally in this condition, and man so created, that is, in virtue of this creation, would not have been under any sin, nor exposed to the anger of God. Did man, by Adam's sin, fall back into it? Not so. His state after his fall differed from such a state of pure nature in that he had upon him the guilt of lost adoption, of adoption lost by the first Adam's fault, and in proportion to the greatness of the loss, and the gratuitousness of the gift originally bestowed, was the anger with which, on the donor's part, the loss was regarded. How would a king, a man like ourselves, regard one whom he had raised out of the dust to be his adopted child, and who had been unfaithful to the parent who had so chosen him with more than natural affection? Such an anger we can indeed understand when felt against the person sinning; but we fail to enter into it as resting on the race, because the secret tie which binds the head and the race into one is not discerned by us; because too the greatness of the divine majesty, the awfulness of His sovereignty, and

the wrath of that majesty slighted, are feebly appreciated by us.   But this image may at least give us
some notion of the nature of that divine anger which
pressed upon Adam and his race after the fall.   Not
only, therefore, was the gift of sonship and the prerogatives attending it withdrawn, but this withdrawal
was a punishment, which their absence in the pre-
sumed case of an original state of simple nature
would not have been.   Thus death was a punishment
to Adam and his race; the body's weakness and
disease, the soul's sorrows and pains, the disobedience of the inferior appetites to the reason, the resistance of the reason to the law of God, were all
punishments, and a remarkable point of the punishment is to be seen in this.   Adam, as the head of
his race, was in virtue of natural propagation to have
bestowed on the children of his flesh, the members
of his body, his own supernatural inheritance.   Thus
a singular honour was conferred on the fathership
of Adam.   But now when, in virtue of this natural
propagation, he, continuing to be the head of his race,
transmitted to it the guilt of adoption lost instead
of the blessing of adoption conferred, a peculiar
shame was set by God upon this fathership of Adam,
and upon all the circumstances attending it: so that
henceforth in the disinherited race the bride veiled
her head, and the act of being a father became an
act of shame.

The condition, therefore, of Adam and his posterity after his fall differed from the condition which
would have been that of simple nature by the whole
extent of the guilt incurred by the nature in its fall
from sonship.

And herein lies one peculiarity, and one strangely

distressing condition of his state, in that while he lost by the fall the grace in which, as an indwelling gift, his whole supernatural state had been rooted, he yet did not lose that condition of being formed and intended for a supernatural end which grace alone could enable him to attain. For the supernatural vision and love of God he had been created, and in his fall he did not sink to be merely a natural man; but his original end was still held out before him as that which he might reach supported by that grace the aids of which were in a different measure promised to him in order to lead a life of penance, and as the earnest of a future restoration.

This, however, is far from being a complete statement of his case, and we must go back to the circumstances of his fall in order to add that further still more peculiar and remarkable condition which, added to the one just described, made up the whole of his fall.

Adam had not disobeyed the divine command, and so broken the covenant of his sonship, by the simple promptings of his own will. Another had intervened; had suggested to the woman doubts against her Maker and Father. She had yielded to these doubts, and disobeyed; and then Adam had suffered himself to be drawn with her in her disobedience. Who was this other? He was the prince and leader of spirits created good, but fallen into enmity with God. Thus, the favourite son of God had listened to the persuasion of God's chief enemy, and his fall from sonship had been, by the judgment of the offended Parent, not a simple fall from his supernatural estate, but a fall likewise into servitude to that enemy. This servitude also, with the guilt of the nature in which he had sinned,

Adam transmitted to the members of his body in and by their nature. Adam with his race was the captive taken in war by the enemy of God, and the life which he was allowed to live had the condition of this servitude impressed on it, with this alleviation only, that the assistance of the divine grace offered to him by the mercy of God in his state of penance could protect those who accepted it from the effects of this servitude, and ultimately deliver them.

Here, then, is the condition of Adam's posterity in consequence of his fall; members of a Head who had broken his allegiance to his Creator and Father, and so inheriting with their nature the disinherited state into which he had cast himself; captives, moreover, of that powerful spirit, God's antagonist, who had tempted Adam, seduced him, and led him to his fall.

Now the heathenism which we have been contemplating is the carrying out in time and space of this body of Adam in those who, by their personal fault, fell away from the aids of grace which were accorded to man after his fall—aids given first to Adam for the whole race, and then renewed to Noah for the whole race; and the false worship, so blent and mingled with heathenism, which seemed as if it were the soul of its body, is the sign and stamp of that captivity to the evil spirit which the first man's sin inaugurated.

How powerful was the bond between Adam and his race, how great and influential the headship which the Divine choice had vested in him, we see in that mysterious transmission of guilt which passed from him to his children. And it must be expressly noted that it was not a transmission of punishment alone. Rather, the divine justice cannot punish where there is no guilt; and as in this case Adam's fall, and that of his posterity with him, was not merely a loss but a punishment, so it had the special nature of guilt, not only in him but in his posterity, and was a sin both of the person and of the nature in him, of the nature only in them. We see the force and range of the divine endowment of Adam here, though it be in the tenacity of the calamity which ensued to his race; but it must be remembered that such in this respect as the punishment was, the blessing would have been. Adam was created both an individual and a race. In him were two things—the single man and the head; but of these two things the headship was peculiar to himself, while such as the individual Adam was, his race was to be. He had it in his power to break the covenant of his sonship with God, but not the tie between himself and his race.

And this sheds a light upon the darkest part of that terrible picture which collected heathenism presents to us. Man, as a social animal, is incessant in his action on his fellow-man; the parent and the family form the child; the companion and the neighbourhood lead forth the child into manhood. This work is perpetually going on in all its parts, and society is the joint result. When, therefore, we see this society once fallen into the possession of a false worship, which perverts the very foundations of morality, and instils deadly error into the child with the mother's milk, no thoughtful mind can gaze without horror upon beings involved in such a maze,[1] yet intended for an eternal duration. Man's nature, as a race, seems turned against him; and in addition to the guilt under which each individual of the race is born,

---

[1] This is called by St. Peter, 1. i. 18, ἡ ματαία ἀναστροφὴ πατροπαράδοτος.

and the nature which each inherits, wherein the internal harmony of peace is broken, and neither the appetites obey the reason nor the reason is obedient to God, comes the force of habit, of education, of culture, of companionship, of man's business and leisure, his play and his earnest, the force of his language, the expression of his thoughts upon himself and others, the whole force, in fact, of man's social being when it is put under possession of an evil power, man's adversary. But this social nature was to have been to him the means of the greatest good. As by his natural descent from Adam unfallen would have come the grace of sonship, so the whole brotherhood of those who shared that gift would have helped and supported each in the maintenance of it. The human family would have had a beauty and a unity of its own as such; an order and a lustre would have rested on the whole body, confirming each member in the possession of his own particular gift. The concatenation of evil in the corrupt society is the most striking contrast to the fellowship of good in the upright; and while it is distinct from that guilt which descends to man as the sin of his nature, yet springs like it from the original constitution of that nature as a race. It is the invasion of evil upon good carried to its utmost point, wherein we discern most plainly "the prince of this world" wielding that "power of darkness" by which the Apostle described the whole state of the world, out of which these nations, which made the empire of Augustus, were a part.

We have thus contemplated four distinct pictures. The first of these was human nature bare and naked by itself, a merely ideal view of man, as a being compounded of soul and body, each possessing only the

faculties which belong to them as spiritual and corporeal natures, the result of which is a substantial
union, because the spiritual substance becomes the
form of the corporeal, not by making the body, when
already animated by another principle, to participate
of spiritual life, but by becoming itself the principle
first animating it.   And we set forth this condition
of human nature in order to throw light upon our
second picture—the first man as he was actually
created, possessing, as a gift superadded by the purest
divine bounty to this his natural constitution, a divine
sonship founded in grace ; which transcendent union
of the Holy Spirit with his soul kept the soul with all
its faculties in a loving obedience to God, and the
body in obedience to the soul ; and added even to
this state the further gratuitous prerogatives of immunity from error, fault, pain, distress, and death.   Our
third picture was man in this same state, but constituted besides by the divine will, whose good pleasure
was the sole source of all this state of sonship, to be
father of a race like to himself, receiving from him,
with its natural generation, the transmitted gift of
sonship ; that is, from our view of him as an individual person we went on to consider him as the head
of a body—the root of a tree.   Fourthly, we have
looked on the same man stripped by a fault, personal
to himself but natural to his race, of this divine
sonship—reduced to a state like that which the first
would have been, but altered from it by two grave
conditions, one of guilt lying on himself and his race
on account of this gratuitous gift of sonship lost,
another of captivity to that enemy of his Creator and
Father who had seduced him to fall.   And this
picture included in it the double effect of guilt trans-

Body, which corresponds to Adam's original Headship, but as far transcends it as the grace of the Incarnate Word transcends the grace bestowed on the first man. As Adam, had he stood in his original state of son, would have transmitted the gift of a like sonship to his whole race—as, falling, he did actually transmit to that race the guilt of adoption lost, so the Second Adam, out of His own uncreated Sonship, but through the nature which He had assumed, bestowed the dower of adopted sons and the gift of justice on His race. From the one there was punishment generating through the flesh,[1] from the other, grace regenerating through the Spirit. From the one, nature stripped and wounded, yet still bound to its head by an indissoluble tie; by the other, the Spirit of the Head, the Spirit of Truth, Charity, Unity, and Sanctity, ruling His Body and animating it, as the natural soul animates the natural body. Precisely where the mystery was darkest and the misery greatest, the divine grace is most conspicuous, and the divine power most triumphant. The very point which brings out Adam's connection with his race has an exact counterpart in Christ's Headship of His people, and an inscrutable judgment serves to illustrate an unspeakable gift. In exact accordance with the doctrine that the sin of Adam is man's sin, and the guilt of Adam man's guilt, is that boundless and unimaginable grace that the Incarnate Word did not merely assume an individual human nature, but espoused in that assumption the whole nature; that on the cross He paid the debt of the whole nature, whether for original or actual sin; that

[1] "Adam unus est, in quo omnes peccaverunt, quia non solum ejus imitatio peccatores facit, sed per carnem generans pœna: Christus unus est, in quo omnes justificentur, quia non solum ejus imitatio justos facit, sed per spiritum regenerans gratia." St. Aug. tom. x. p. 12 c.

His resurrection is our collective justification; that the gift of sonship is bestowed on men not as individual persons, but as members of His Body, before they have personally merited anything, just as the guilt came on them, as members of Adam, before they demerited anything personally. Exactly where the obscurity of the fall was the deepest, the light of the restoration is brightest; and where the sentence was most severe, the grace most wonderful. But to deny the first Adam would entail the loss of the Second; and he who declines the inheritance of the father stripped and wounded cannot enter into the Body of the Word made flesh.

But thirdly, as in that terrible corruption of heathenism, wherein immorality was based on false worship, we saw the body of Adam run out through time and space into the most afflicting form which evil can assume in the individual and social life of man, so in that Body which is ruled by the Divine Headship we see the counterpart, the triumph of grace, individual man taken out of that state of fallen nature, and invested with a membership answering to the dignity of the Head. The one great Christian people, the Kingdom of Christ, stands over against that kingdom of violence, disorder, impurity, and false worship. As there is a unity of the fallen Adam, a force of evil which impact only gives, so much more is there a unity of the Second Adam, which is not a collection of individuals, but a Body with its Head. The first unity consists in the reasonable soul, informing the flesh which was moulded once for all from the clay and descended to the whole race; and the race so descending was polluted by a common guilt, on which, as an ever-fertile root, grew the whole trunk of man's personal sins, of falsehood, enmity, corruption of morals, division, having the common quality of egotism. The second unity consists in the Holy Spirit of the Head communicated to the soul and body of the faithful people, both being restored by that grace of which truth and charity, unity and sanctity, are the tokens, the full virtue being planted in the cross of the Head, and from the cross diffusing itself to His Body.

II. And so we are brought again to Him who stood before Pilate to make the good confession, and who declared that the cause of His coming into the world was to bear witness to the truth. In what form was that witness to be made, and how was it to be efficacious? This is that point which we have now to illustrate. Adam's disobedience was a single act, the power of which, springing out of his headship, extended through the whole line of his race; through the consequences of this act the truth was obscured to them, and human life involved in manifold error. What was that action on the part of Christ, the purpose, as He declares, of His Incarnation, which had an equally enduring effect? If the guilt communicated was not transitory, then should the corresponding grace be perpetual. And how was it so? The Son of God, as the Head of His race, does not stand at disadvantage with Adam, but rather, we are told His grace is superabundant in its results over the other's sin: and He Himself declared that He had completely finished the work given Him to do.[1] But here He describes this work to be the bearing witness to the truth. For, indeed, it was worthy of the eternal wisdom to clothe Himself in flesh [2] in order that truth,

[1] John xvii. 4.
[2] St. Thomas, *Summa contra Gentiles*, l. i. c. i.

the good of the intellect, and the end of the whole universe, might stand forth revealed to His rational creatures : and He who made all things in truth would Himself restore truth, when it had been obscured by the traducer.

1. Let us take the character which He acknowledged and claimed before Pilate : His character of King, and the kingdom in which it is exercised.

The Person of Christ, as that of the eternal Word, is the Truth itself. But He has assumed a body, and in that body He declares that He is a king, and that the exercise of His royalty is the bearing witness to the truth.[1] His words therefore indicate no less than the creation of a kingdom to which the truth should be the principle of subsistence. But what in the material or temporal kingdom is that by force of which it subsists ? Plainly power. A kingdom may be larger or smaller in population, wealth, extent, stronger or weaker in the quality of its people ; but as long as it retains in itself that in which power culminates, sovereignty, it will be a kingdom. If this power departs from it, if it falls into subjection to a foreign authority, or if its own subjects successfully rebel against its power, it ceases to be. In the kingdom, therefore, of which Christ speaks, the maintenance of truth corresponds to what the maintenance of power is in a material kingdom.

But power in the material kingdom moves men to the natural end of society ; it preserves order, administers justice, allows and assists all natural forces to develop themselves, and it must be in its supreme

---

[1] John xviii. 37. "Thou sayest that I am a king. To this end was I born, and for this cause came I into the world, to bear witness unto the truth."

exercise one and indisputable : that is, it culminates in sovereignty. So in the spiritual kingdom truth, the corresponding power, moves men to the supernatural end, and truth culminates in infallibility. But where is this power seated, and how does the King wield it ?

The same who here calls Himself King and declares it to be the function of His royalty to bear witness to the truth, in describing elsewhere the very creation of His kingdom says to His apostles, "You shall receive power by the Holy Ghost coming upon you," bidding them also to remain in Jerusalem " until they were endued with power from on high." [1]   But a few hours before that scene in the hall of Pilate He had told them also that He would send them the Spirit of Truth, who should abide with them for ever, and should lead them into all truth.   He creates therefore the kingdom of the truth by sending down the Spirit of the Truth to dwell for ever with those to whom He is sent ; and this Spirit of the Truth is His own Spirit, whom He Himself will send as the token of His ascension and session ; the Spirit who dwelt in the Body which He had assumed, and in which He spoke before Pilate, should be sent by Him when that Body had taken its place at the right hand of God, should invest with His own power those to whom He was sent, and should never cease to be with them in His character of the Spirit of Truth.   Here, then, is that power in the kingdom of the Truth which enables it to bear a true and a perpetual witness.   It is the power of the King, for it is His Spirit : it is the power of the kingdom, for it remains in it, is throned in it, and makes it to be what it is.

[1] Acts i. 8 ; Luke xxiv. 49.

But to create a kingdom of the truth, and to bear perpetual witness in that kingdom to the truth, is not only to state what is true. These expressions mark out an organisation in and by means of which truth is perpetuated. And further, the spirit in man is both reason and will; and that man may act, the intellect which has truth for its object must work on the will which has good for its object. And so the witness which our Lord speaks of is that action of the truth upon the will which produces a life in accordance with it : it is truth not left to itself, but supported by grace. This power of the Spirit of Truth is therefore double, as intended to work on the two powers of the soul, the reason and the will : it is the double gift of Truth and Grace; as He is the Spirit of Grace no less than the Spirit of Truth, and all grace is His immediate gift.

Thus the Word made flesh, being full of Truth and Grace from His own Person, communicated that Truth and Grace as the power which should form His kingdom for ever, abide in it, and constitute its being a kingdom ; the gift of truth and grace being the very presence of His own Spirit, who took possession of His kingdom on the day of Pentecost and holds it for ever.

This whole possession of Truth and Grace dwelling in a visible body is the work of the eternal Word, who assumed a body for that purpose. It is the counter-creation to the kingdom of falsehood which began with the sin of the first man believing a falsehood against his Maker, and which spread itself with his lineage into all lands.[1] And as in the natural creation He not only created but maintained—for He did not make His creatures and then depart from them, but

[1] See St. Aug. tom. iv. 1039 e. "Ipse ergo Adam," &c.

from that time they exist in Him—so in the supernatural the act of maintaining is equivalent to the act
of creating, it is a continued creation. As the guilt
had a force which was fruitful, which continued and
propagated itself, and produced a widespread reign of
falsehood, how much more should that mighty and
astonishing grace of a Divine Person assuming a
created nature be fruitful, continue, and propagate
itself in the maintenance of a visible kingdom, whose
distinctive character and its very life should be the
possession and communication of the truth ! Should
the Creator of man in His greatest work be less
powerful than His seduced creature in his fall ? And
if the fall, pregnant with falsehood, bore fruit through
ages in a whole race, should not the recovery likewise
have its visible dominion, and stand over against the
ruin as the kingdom of truth ?

It is as King ruling in the kingdom of truth that
the Divine Word incarnate redeems man from captivity,
which began in a revolt from the truth, and in becoming
subject to falsehood. All who are outside His kingdom
lie in this captivity ;[1] the life which He gave voluntarily is the price paid for their liberation ; and as age
after age, so long as the natural body of Adam lasts,
the captivity endures, so age after age the liberation
takes effect by entering into His kingdom. And this
is the most general name, the name of predilection,

---

[1] Οἴδαμεν ὅτι ἐκ τοῦ Θεοῦ ἐσμεν, καὶ ὁ κόσμος ὅλος ἐν τῷ πονηρῷ
κεῖται· οἴδαμεν δὲ ὅτι ὁ υἱὸς τοῦ Θεοῦ ἥκει, καὶ δέδωκεν ἡμῖν διάνοιαν ἵνα
γινώσκωμεν τὸν ἀληθινόν· καὶ ἐσμὲν ἐν τῷ ἀληθινῷ, ἐν τῷ υἱῷ αὐτοῦ
Ἰησοῦ Χριστῷ.   1 John v. 19.   Two persons are here opposed to each
other, ὁ πονηρός and ὁ ἀληθινός. Compare the Lord's Prayer, ῥῦσαι ἡμᾶς
ἀπὸ τοῦ πονηροῦ.   Matt. vi. 13, and John xvii. 14, 15. ἐγὼ δέδωκα
αὐτοῖς τὸν λόγον σου, καὶ ὁ κόσμος ἐμίσησεν αὐτούς, ὅτι οὐκ εἰσὶν ἐκ τοῦ
κόσμου, καθὼς ἐγὼ οὐκ εἰμὶ ἐκ τοῦ κόσμου. οὐκ ἐρωτῶ ἵνα ἄρῃς αὐτοὺς ἐκ
τοῦ κόσμου, ἀλλ᾽ ἵνα τηρήσῃς αὐτοὺς ἐκ τοῦ πονηροῦ.

which both in prophecy marked the time of Messiah the King, and was announced by His precursor, and taken by our Lord to indicate His having come. The eternal duration of this kingdom may be said to be the substance of all prophecy, and it was precisely in the interpretation of a vision describing under the image of a great statue the four world-kingdoms, that is, the whole structure, course, and issue of the heathenism which we have been contemplating, that Daniel contrasts these kingdoms with another. "In the days of these kings shall the God of heaven set up a kingdom which shall never be destroyed; and the kingdom shall not be delivered to another people, but it shall break in pieces and consume all these kingdoms, and shall stand itself for ever." As King in this kingdom through all the generations of men from the moment that He stood in Pilate's hall until He comes to judge the world, our Lord bears witness to the truth, His witness and His royalty being contemporaneous and conterminous to each other.

2. This perpetual possession and announcement of the truth is indicated by another image which is of constant recurrence,[1] wherein Christ is the Inhabitant, His people the Inhabited, while both are the House or Temple, for that in which God dwells is at once His House and Temple. Thus Moses is said to have been "faithful in all his house as a servant, but Christ as a Son over His own house, whose house are we." Here the King who bears witness to the truth is the God who sanctifies the faithful people by dwelling in them and building them in the truth.

[1] Heb. iii. 1–6; Ephes. ii. 19–22; 1 Cor. iii. 9, 10–15; 2 Cor. vi. 16; 1 Pet. ii. 4, 5.

It is not merely the individual believer, but the whole mass of the faithful which grows up to be a holy temple; and the ever-abiding Spirit of truth, whose presence is the guarantee of truth, is the equally abiding Spirit of sanctity, whose presence imparts holiness. The Son dwells in His own house by His Spirit for ever: as He ceases not to be incarnate, He ceases not to dwell in His house, and could falsehood be worshipped in His temple, it would cease to be His. That was the work of heathenism, when a false spirit had caused error to be worshipped for truth; the specific victory of the Word incarnate was to set up a temple in which the truth should be worshipped for ever, "the inhabitation of God in the Spirit." But living stones make up this temple, that is, individual spirits, endued with their own reason and will, yet no less fitted in and cemented together by His grace, and so forming a structure which has an organic unity of its own, being the House and Temple of One. It is in virtue of this inhabitation that the Church is termed the House of God, the pillar and ground of the truth, inasmuch as it contains, as between walls,[1] the faith and its announcement and proclamation, that is, the law of the King of Truth declared by His heralds. "We speculate," says St. Augustine, "that we may attain to vision; yet even the most studious speculation would fall into error unless the Lord inhabited the Church herself that now is."[2] And again: "In earthly possessions a benefit is given to the proprietor when he is given possession; not so is the posses-

---

[1] Τοῦτο γὰρ ἐστὶ τὸ συνέχον τὴν πίστιν καὶ τὸ κήρυγμα. St. Chrys. in loc. Compare St. Irenæus, lib. i. c. 10. Τοῦτο τὸ κήρυγμα παρειληφυῖα, καὶ ταύτην τὴν πίστιν, ὡς προέφαμεν, ἡ Ἐκκλησία, καίπερ ἐν ὅλῳ τῷ κόσμῳ διεσπαρμένη, ἐπιμελῶς φυλάσσει, ὡς ἕνα οἶκον οἰκοῦσα.

[2] St. Aug. in Ps. ix. tom. iv. 51.

the whole body, and yet so strong that a wound may transfix the whole structure, leaving the life untouched. And, in addition to this physical marvel, the incorporeal mind, which has its seat in this material structure, and whose presence is itself its life, rules like an absolute monarch with undisputed sway over his whole dominion, so that the least movement of volition carries with it a willing obedience in the whole frame, and for it instantaneously the eye gazes, the ear listens, the tongue speaks, the feet walk, the hands work, and the brain feels with an incomparable unity. The marvel of the body is that things so many and various by the rule of the artificer impressed upon them are yet one, concur to one end, and produce one whole, from which no part can be taken, and to which none can be added without injury, the least and the greatest replete with one life, which so entirely belongs to the whole body that what is severed from the body at once dies. " Now, as the body is one, and has many members, but all the members of this one body, being many, are one body, so also," says St. Paul, "is Christ," giving the name of the Head to the whole Body. What the human head is to its own body, that our Lord is to His Church. Perhaps no other image in the whole realm of nature would convey with such force the three relations[1] which constitute spiritual headship, an inseparable union, by which the head and the body form one whole, an unceasing government, including every sort of provision and care, and a perpetual influx of grace. This is on the part of the head, while as to the body perhaps no other image but this could equally convey the conjunction of many different members with various functions, whose union makes

[1] Petavius on the Headship of Christ.

the structure, and whose unity is something entirely distinct from that which all the parts in their several state, or even in their collocation and arrangement, make up, for it is the life which makes them one. Thus it is an unfathomed depth of doctrine, which is conveyed in the words, "God gave Him to be Head over all things to the Church, who is His Body, the fulness of Him who fills all things in all." For though no language could exhaust or duly exhibit the meaning of the kingdom or the temple in which the abiding work of our Lord is indicated, we have in this title yet more strikingly portrayed the intimate union and common life of His people with Christ, and His tender affection for them, since the King of Truth who redeems and the God of Truth who sanctifies, is at the same time the Head who by His own Spirit of the truth rules and vivifies His own Body. If it be possible to dissociate the idea of the King from His kingdom, or that of God from the temple of living souls in whom He is worshipped, and whose worship of Him makes them one, yet in the human frame to dissever the head from the body is to destroy the propriety of both terms, and it is as a whole human body that the apostle represents Christ and His people to us.

4. Yet, as if this were not enough, St. Paul goes on to delineate Him as the Bridegroom, whose love after redeeming sanctifies one who shall be His bride for ever, one who obeys Him with the fidelity of conjugal love, one whose preservation of His faith unstained is not the dry fulfilment of a command, but the prompting of wedded affection. The image seems chosen to convey intensity of love, first on the part of the Bridegroom as originating it, and then on the part of the Bride as responding to it. But no less does

the unity of person in the Bride, given by St. John as well as by St. Paul, indicate in the Church something quite distinct from the individuals who compose her. For she is the pattern of the faithful wife in that she is subject to Christ; and in these words a fact is stated,[1] a fact without limit of place or time, which therefore marks that she who is so described can never at any time be separated from the fidelity and love due from her to her Head and Husband. And this is not true of the individual souls belonging to her, for they, having been once faithful members of the body, may fall away and be finally lost. The Bride alone is subject to Christ with a never-failing subjection. And He on His part loves her as His own flesh, a union of the two loves of the Head for the Body, and of the Bridegroom for the Bride, which is true with regard to Him of the Church alone, since individuals within her He may cast off, but her alone He cherishes and fosters for ever. It is indefectible union and unbroken charity with Him which her quality of Bride conveys.

5. And out of this wedded union by that great sacrament concerning Christ and the Church, of which in the same passage St. Paul speaks, that they two shall be one flesh, springs the whole race, in the generation of whom is most completely verified his title of the Second Adam. From the womb of the Church, become from a Bride the Mother of all living, the Father of the age to come bears that chosen race, and royal priesthood, and holy nation, and purchased people. And here we see expressed with great force the truth that all who belong to the Father's supernatural race must come by the Mother. Her office of

[1] Passaglia, *de Ecclesia*.

for images whose union might express a work so un-
exampled and unique.   Rather, it is truer to say that
these natural affections themselves, the gift of that
most bountiful giver, were created by Him originally
to be types, foreshadowings, and partial copies of
that more excellent supernatural love which He had
decreed to show to man, since first of all things in
the order of the divine design must the Incarnation
have been.   The whole structure of the family, and
the affections which it contains, must spring out of
this root, for nature was anticipated by grace in man's
creation, and must ever have been subordinate to it.
And now, when the full time of grace is come, these
titles of things which by His mercy have lasted through
the fall, serve to illustrate the greatness of the restoration.   For this, which has many names, all precious
and dear, is but one creation, having the manifold
qualities of redemption and sanctification, of organic
unity in one body, wherein many members conspire
to a corporate life, which life itself is charity, and in
which is the production of the holy race.   As we gaze
on the Kingdom, Temple, Body, Spouse, and Family,
one seems to melt and change into the other.   The
Kingdom is deepened and enlarged by the thought
that the King is the eternal Truth who is worshipped
therein ; and the worship passes on into the love of
the Incarnate God for the members of His own Body,
whom He first saves, then fosters and cherishes as His
own flesh : and here again is blended that tenderest
love of the Bridegroom for the bride, which further
issues into the crowning love of the Father for His
race.   The mode of the salvation seems to spring
from the nature of God Himself, since all paternity
in heaven and earth springs from that whereby He is

Father of the only-begotten Son, who, descending from heaven with the love of the Bridegroom for the bride, binds together in sonship derived from his own the members of His body, the bride of His heart, the subjects of His kingdom, who are built up as living stones into that unimaginable temple raised in the unity of worshipping hearts to the ever-blessed Trinity. To this grows out, as the fulness of Him who fills all in all, that body of the Second Adam, of which in the body of the first Adam He had Himself deposited the germ.

When the angel described to the Blessed Virgin herself that miracle of miracles which was to take place in her, the assumption of human flesh by the Son of God, he used these terms: "The Holy Ghost shall come upon thee, and the power of the Most High shall overshadow thee." When the Son of God, at the moment of His Ascension, declared to His Apostles the creation of His mystical body, by using similar words, He referred them back to His own conception: "You shall receive power, the Holy Ghost coming upon you:" having already on the day of His Resurrection told them, "I send the promise of My Father upon you; but wait you in the city until you be endued with power from on high." [1] Our Lord Himself thus suggests to us the remarkable parallel between the formation of His natural and His mystical body. He who framed the one and the other is the same, the Holy Ghost: the Head precedes, the Body follows; because of the first descent, that Holy Thing which was to be born should be called the Son of God; because of the

---

[1] Luke i. 35. Πνεῦμα ἅγιον ἐπελεύσεται ἐπὶ σε, καὶ δύναμις ὑψίστου ἐπισκιάσει σοι. Acts i. 8. λήψεσθε δύναμιν, ἐπελθόντος τοῦ ἁγίου Πνεύματος ἐφ᾽ ὑμᾶς. Luke xxiv. 49. ἕως οὗ ἐνδύσησθε δύναμιν ἐξ ὕψους.

second, "you shall be my witnesses in Jerusalem, and
in all Judea, and Samaria, and to the farthest part of
the earth;" and this is said in answer to their question whether He would then restore the kingdom to
Israel: that is, the second descent of the Holy Ghost
forms the kingdom whose witness to Christ is perpetual; forms the body with which and in which He
will be for ever by this power of His Spirit dwelling
in it to the end of the world. We have therefore
here all the various functions and qualities which,
under the five great titles of Kingdom, Temple, Body,
Spouse, and Mother, delineate His Church, gathered
up into that unity which comprehends them all, and
from which, as a source, they all flow, "The Power of
the Holy Ghost coming upon men."[1] This creation
is as absolutely His, and His alone, as the forming of
our Lord's own Body in the Virginal Womb; it is the
sequel of it; the fulfilment among men of those divine
purposes for which God became Incarnate; in one
word, the Body of the Head perpetually quickened by
His Spirit. And here we may remark those striking
resemblances between the natural and mystical Body
which this "power of the Holy Ghost," the former of
them both, indicates. For in the first the manhood[2]
cannot be severed from the Person of the Word, nor
in the second can the body of the Church be severed
from Christ the Head and His Spirit. Secondly, in
the first the Person of the Word and His manhood
make one Christ, and in the second Christ the Head
and the Church the Body made one complete Body.
Thirdly, in the first the manhood has its own will, but

[1] The Church is so called by St. Augustine.
[2] These five are taken from Passaglia, *de Ecclesia*, lib. i. cap. 3,
p. 34, 5.

in this divine Body, which makes the whole Christ, it is the presence of the Holy Ghost, as of the soul, which gives it unity and life. The conclusion was drawn by a great Saint, and no less great a genius, fourteen hundred years ago, and I prefer St. Augustine's words to any which I can use myself: " Our spirit by which the whole race of man lives is called the soul; our spirit, too, by which each man in particular lives is called the soul; and you see what the soul does in the body. It quickens all the limbs: through the eyes it sees, through the ears it hears, through the nostrils smells, through the tongue speaks, through the hands works, through the feet walks; it is present at once in all the limbs that they may live; life it gives to all, their functions to each. The eye does not hear, nor the ear nor the tongue see, nor the ear nor the eye speak, but both live; the functions are diverse, the life common. So is the Church of God. In some saints it works miracles; in others gives voice to the truth; in others, again, maintains the virginal life; in others keeps conjugal fidelity; in these one thing, in those another; each have their proper work, but all alike live. Now, what the soul is to the human body, that is the Holy Spirit to the body of Christ, which is the Church: what the soul does in all the limbs of an individual body, that does the Holy Spirit in the whole Church. But see what you have to avoid, what to observe, and what to fear. It happens that, in the human body, or in any other body, some member may be cut off, hand, finger, or foot. Does the soul follow it when cut off? As long as it was in the body it lived: when cut off, it loses life. So too the Christian man is a Catholic while he lives in the body; when cut off, he becomes a heretic; the Spirit does not follow the amputated limb."[1]

But what is this "power of the Holy Ghost coming upon men"? It is the whole treasure of truth and grace, which dwelt first in the natural body of Christ, which He came to bestow on men, which He withdrew not when He ascended, but of which He promised the continuance in the Person of the Holy Ghost, and fulfils by that Person indwelling in the Church. It was the imparting the whole treasure of truth and grace by such an indwelling which made it expedient for Him to go. This made His bodily departure not a loss, but a gain. It was "the promise" of which He spoke on that last night. It was expressly declared to be a perpetual presence, leading, as it were, by the hand[2] into all truth—an all-powerful, all-completing, all-compensating presence, such as that alone is or can be which maintains the intellect of man in truth, because it maintains his will in grace. Thus, instead of the two wild horses of which the great heathen[3] spoke, this presence guides the soul in her course and bears her aloft on those twin divine yoke-fellows,[4] faith and charity.

Correlative, therefore, to the Person of Him who is at once King, and God, and Head, and Bridegroom, and Father, is that singular creation of His Spirit, by which, in the Kingdom, Temple, Body, Spouse, and Mother, He deposited the treasure of the truth and

---

[1] St. Aug. serm. 267, tom. v. p. 1090 e.

[2] Luke xxiv. 49 and John xvi. 13. ἐκεῖνος, τὸ πνεῦμα τῆς ἀληθείας, ὁδηγήσει ὑμᾶς εἰς πᾶσαν τὴν ἀλήθειαν· and 14, 15. ἐγὼ ἐρωτήσω τὸν Πατέρα, καὶ ἄλλον παράκλητον δώσει ὑμῖν, ἵνα μένῃ μεθ᾿ ὑμῶν εἰς τὸν αἰῶνα, τὸ πνεῦμα τῆς ἀληθείας.

[3] Plato.

[4] πανταχοῦ συνάπτει καὶ συγκολλᾷ τὴν πίστιν καὶ τὴν ἀγάπην, θαυμαστήν τινα ξυνωρίδα. St. Chrys. 3rd Hom. on Ephes. tom. xi. p. 16.

grace which He became man to communicate. It was not as individual men, living a life apart, but as common children of one race, joint members of one body, that the guilt of the first father fell upon them; it is only on them as children of a higher race and members of a far greater body, that the grace of the Deliverer is bestowed. The distinctions of race and the divisions of condition drop away as they are baptized into one body, and made to drink of one spirit. The new and supernatural life cannot be communicated save by this act of engrafting into a new body. As Eve from the side of Adam sleeping, so the Church from the side of Christ suffering; as Eve bears still to Adam the children of men, so the Church to Christ the children of Christ. These are not two mysteries, but one, unfathomable in both its parts, of justice and of mercy; but the whole history of the human race bears witness to the first, and the whole history of the Christian people to the second. It would be amply sufficient to prove what we have been saying, that the first communication of the supernatural life is conferred by being baptized into one body and made to drink into one spirit. But this is not all. There is a yet dearer and more precious gift, which maintains and increases the life so given. Our Lord stands in the midst of His Church visibly forming from day to day and from age to age that Body of His which reaches through the ages; He takes from Himself and gives to us. He incorporates Himself in His children. He grows up in us, and by visible streams from His heart maintains the life first given. Here, above all, is the one Christ, the Head and the Body. This is but an elemental truth of Christian faith, though it is the highest joy of the Christian heart. It was in an instruction to catechumens that St. Augustine said, "Would you understand the Body of Christ? Hear the Apostle saying to the faithful, 'But you are the Body and the members of Christ.' If, then, you are Christ's Body and His members, it is your own mystery which is placed on the Lord's table; it is your own mystery which you receive. It is to what you are that you reply amen, and by replying subscribe. For you are told, 'the Body of Christ,' and you reply, amen. Be a member of the Body of Christ, and let your amen be true. Why, then, in bread? Let us bring here nothing of our own, but listen to the Apostle himself again and again, for in speaking of that sacrament he says, 'We that are many are one bread, one body.' Understand and rejoice. Here is unity, verity, piety, charity. One bread. Who is that one bread? We being many are one bread. Remember that the bread is not made of one, but of many grains. When you were exorcised, it was as if you were ground; when baptized, as if you were kneaded together with water; when you received the fire of the Holy Ghost, it was your baking. Be what you see, and receive what you are. This the Apostle said of the bread. Of the chalice what we should understand is clear enough even unsaid. For as to make the visible species of bread many grains are kneaded with water into one, as if that were taking place which Holy Scripture records of the faithful, 'they had one mind and one heart in God,' so also in the case of the wine. Many grapes hang on the bunch, but their juice is poured together into one. So too Christ the Lord signified us; willed us to belong to Himself; consecrated on His own table the mystery of our peace and unity. He who receives the

mystery of unity and holds not the bond of peace receives not a mystery for himself, but a witness against
himself." [1]

Thus the coherence of the natural and mystical
Body of Christ was at once exhibited and effected in
the great central act of Christian worship, and the
whole fruit of the Incarnation was seen springing from
the Person of Christ, and bestowed on men as His
members in the unity of one Body. Thus were they
taken out of the isolation, distraction, and enmity
—that state of mutual strife and disorder which
heathendom expresses—and made into the one divine
commonwealth; and thus the Body of Christ grows
to its full stature and perfect form through all the
ages of Christendom.

And if there be one conviction which, together with
the belief in the Incarnation itself of the Word, is
common to all the Fathers, Doctors, Saints, and
Martyrs of the Church—which together with that
belief and as part of it is the ground of their confidence in trouble, of their perseverance in enduring,
of their undoubting faith in times of persecution, of
their assurance of final victory, it is the sense which
encompassed their whole life, that they were members
of one Body, which, in virtue of an organic unity in
itself and with its Head, was to last for ever. The
notion that this Body, as such, could fail, that it could
cease to be the treasure-house of the divine truth and
grace, would have struck them with as much horror as
the notion that Christ had not become incarnate, and
was not their Redeemer. The Body which the Holy
Ghost animated on the day of Pentecost never ceased
to be conscious of its existence—conscious that the

[1] St. Aug. serm. 272, tom. v. p. 1104 c.

power of its Head, the Eternal Truth, was in it, and
would be in it for ever.   Confidence in himself as an
individual member of the Body, the Christian had not,
for he knew that through his personal sinfulness grace
might be withdrawn from him, and that he might fall
away ; confidence he did not place either in his own
learning, knowledge, and sanctity, or in these gifts as
belonging to any individual Christian ; his confidence
lay in the King who reigned in an everlasting Kingdom, in the Head who animated an incorruptible Body.
To sever these two would have been to decapitate
Christ.[1]   The thought that the Bride of Christ could
herself become an adulteress, and teach her children
the very falsehoods of that idol-worship which she was
created to overthrow, would have appeared to him the
denial of all Christian belief.   And such a denial
indeed it is to any mind which, receiving the Christian
truth as a divine gift, looks for it also to have a logical
cohesion with itself, to be consistent and complete, to
be a body of truth, not a bundle of opinions.   Let us
take once more St. Augustine as expressing, not a private feeling, but the universal Christian sense, when
he thus reprehended the Donatist pretension, that
truth had deserted the Body of the Church to dwell
in the province of Africa.   " But, they say, that
Church which was the Church of all nations exists no
longer.   She has perished.   This they say who are
not in her.   O shameless word !   The Church is not,
because thou art not in her.   See, lest therefore thou
be not, for though thou be not, she will be.   This

---

[1] "Quid tibi fecit Ecclesia, ut eam velis quodammodo decollare ?
Tollere vis Ecclesiæ caput et capiti credere, corpus relinquere, quasi
exanime corpus.   Sine caussa capiti quasi famulus devotus blandiris.
Qui decollare vult, et caput et corpus conatur occidere." St. Aug.
tom. v. p. 636.

word, abominable, detestable, full of presumption and falsehood, supported by no truth, illuminated by no wisdom, seasoned with no sense, vain, rash, precipitate, and pernicious—this it was which the Spirit of God foresaw, and as against these very men, when He foretold unity in that saying, 'To announce the name of the Lord in Zion, and His worship in Jerusalem, when the peoples and kingdoms join together in one that they may serve the Lord.'" [1]

Now, to suppose that anything which is false has been, or is, or can be taught by the Church of God, is to overthrow the one idea which runs through the titles of the Kingdom, Temple, Body, and Spouse of Christ ; it is to make the Mother of His children an adulteress, to deny that power of the Holy Ghost coming down on the day of Pentecost, and abiding for ever, with His special function of leading into all truth, that presence of the Comforter in virtue of which the Apostles said for themselves and for the Church through all time, "It has seemed good to the Holy Ghost and to us." With all men who reason, such a supposition is equivalent to the statement that Christ has failed in what He came on earth to do, for "the Word was made flesh, that He might become the Head of the Church." [2]   Next, therefore, in atrocity to that blasphemy which assaults the blessed Trinity in Unity upon His throne is the miserable and heartless blasphemy which, by imputing corruption of the truth to the very Kingdom and Temple, the very Body and Spouse of the Truth Himself, the Incarnate God, would declare the frus-

---

[1] St. Aug. in Ps. ci. tom. iv. p. 1105 d.

[2] St. Augustine, tom. iv. p. 1677. "Elegit hic sibi thalamum castum, ubi conjungeretur Sponsus Sponsæ. Verbum caro factum est, ut fieret caput Ecclesiæ."

tration of that purpose which He became man to execute, the falsifying of that witness of which He spoke in the hall of Pilate, and would so annihilate that glory to God in the highest, and on earth peace to men of good-will, which was the angelic song on the morning of His birth, and is daily [1] in the mouth of His Bride. The truth can as little cease out of the House and Temple of God as the Father and Son can cease sending the Spirit to dwell in it: the truth can as little cease to be proclaimed and taught in its own kingdom as the King can cease to reign in it. The conjugal faith of the Bride of Christ cannot fail, because He remains her Bridegroom. The power of the Head, the double power of truth and grace, cannot cease to rule and vivify His Body, because He is its Head for ever. The Mother cannot deceive her children, because she is of one flesh with the Son of Man, in the union of an unbroken wedlock.

It has been said above that the power of that bond which from the origin of man united the race to its head was shown not only in the guilt which the act of that head was able to inflict on the body, not only in the exact transmission of the same nature, thus stained, from age to age, but likewise in that social character of the race in virtue of which such a thing as a man entirely independent of his fellow-men, neither acting upon them, nor acted upon by them, never has existed nor can exist. It was in that connected mass which this social nature creates, that corporate unity of human society, that heathenism appeared most terrible, because corruption seemed to propagate itself, and evil by this force of cohesion to become almost impregnable. But it was especially

---

[1] By the "Gloria in excelsis," &c., in the Mass.

in creating a corporate unity which should show the force of our social nature for good, as the corruption had shown it for evil, that the power of the Restorer shines forth. The true Head of our race came to redeem and sanctify not so many individuals, but His Body. Surely there is no distinction more important to bear in mind.[1] "No single member by itself can make a body; each of them fails in this; co-operation is required, for when many become one, there is one body. The being or not being a body depends on being united or not united into one." And, again, beautiful as the individual member, the hand or the eye, may be in itself, far higher is the beauty which belongs to the body as the whole in which these members coalesce and are one. Each member too has a double energy, its own proper work, and that which it contributes to the body's unity, for this is a higher work which the co-operation of all produces; each a double beauty, its beauty as a part, and that which it adds to the whole : and these two, which seem to be separate, have the closest connection, for a maimed limb impairs the whole body's force, and as to its beauty, as it is incomparably finer than the beauty of any part, so is it marred by a slight defect in one part, as the fairest face would be spoilt by the absence of eyebrows, the fairest eyes lose their lustre, and the countenance its light, by the want of eyelashes. It is, then, in the beauty of the Body of Christ that the

---

[1] Οὐδὲν γὰρ αὐτῶν καθ' ἑαυτὸ σῶμα δύναται ποιεῖν, ἀλλ' ὁμοίως ἕκαστον λείπεται εἰς τὸ ποιεῖν σῶμα, καὶ δεῖ τῆς συνόδου· ὅταν γὰρ τὰ πολλὰ ἓν γίνηται, τότε ἐστὶν ἓν σῶμα . . . . τὸ γὰρ εἶναι ἢ μὴ εἶναι σῶμα ἐκ τοῦ ἡνῶσθαι ἢ μὴ ἡνῶσθαι γίνεται. . . . τῶν γὰρ μελῶν ἡμῶν ἕκαστον καὶ ἰδίαν ἐνέργειαν ἔχει καὶ κοινήν· καὶ κάλλος ὁμοίως καὶ ἴδιον καὶ κοινόν ἐστιν ἐν ἡμῖν, καὶ δοκεῖ μὲν διῃρῆσθαι ταῦτα, συμπέπλεκται δὲ ἀκριβῶς, καὶ θατέρου διαφθαρέντος καὶ τὸ ἕτερον συναπόλλυται. St. Chrys. on 1 Cor. xii. tom. x. pp. 269, 271, 273.

Christian mind would exult, not merely in the several graces of those who are its members, but in that corporate unity which they present. We see in the course of the world that great image of the prophet, lofty in stature and terrible to behold, whose head is of gold, whose breast and arms of silver, the thighs of brass, the legs of iron, the toes mixed of iron and clay. This is the form of the first Adam, seen in his race; and over against it likewise is the one man Christ, forming through the ages, gathering His members in a mightier unity. This is the Word made flesh, the Second Adam, " so that the whole human race is, as it were, two men, the First and the Second." [1]

So much, then, is the creation of the Church superior to the creation of a single Christian as the creation of a body is superior to that of a single bone or muscle. This superiority belongs to the nature of a body as such. It is another thought, which we only suggest here, *whose* body it is. And here it appears in two very different conditions, the one as it is seen by us now, the other as it will be seen hereafter. There is, I conceive, no subject in all human history comparable in interest to that which the divine commonwealth as such, when traced through the eighteen centuries which it has hitherto run, presents. What nation can be compared to this nation? what people to this people? what labours to its labours? what sufferings to its sufferings? what conflicts to those which it has endured? what triumphs to those which it has gained? what duration to that portion only of its years which is as yet run out? what promise to its future? what performance to its past? What is

[1] St. Aug. *Op. imp. contr. Julian.* lib. ii. tom. x. p. 1018 d.

the courage and self-denial, what is the patience and
generosity, what the genius, the learning, the sustained
devotion to any work, shown by any human race, compared to those which are to be found in this race of
the Divine Mother?   How do those who are enamoured
of nationalities fail to see the glories of this nation,
before which all others pale their ineffectual fires?
How do those with whom industry is a chief virtue,
and stubborn perseverance the crowning praise, not
acknowledge her whose work is undying and whose
endurance never fails?   These men admire greatness
and worship success.   Let them look back fourteen
hundred years, when that great world-statue seemed
to be breaking up into the iron and clay which ran
through its feet.   Then this kingdom was already
great and glorious, and crowned with victory, and
filled the earth.   The toes of that statue have mean-
while run out into ten kingdoms, and the islands
which were forest and swamp when this kingdom
began have become the head of a dominion which
can be mentioned beside that of old Rome.   Still
in undiminished grandeur the great divine republic
stands over against all these kingdoms, penetrates
through them, stretches beyond them, and while
they grow, mature, and decay, and power passes from
one to the other, her power ceases not, declines not,
changes not, but shows the beauty of youth upon the
brow of age, and amid the confusion of Babel her
pentecostal unity.   If success be worshipful, worship
it here; if power be venerable, bow before its holiest
shrine.

But if this be the Body of Christ here in its state
of humiliation, during which it repeats the passion of
its Head, if these be the grains of wheat now scattered

among the chaff,[1] what is that one mass to be which these shall make when the threshing-floor is winnowed out? We see the Body in its preliminary state of suffering, where it has a grandeur, a duration, and a beauty like nothing else on earth. What it shall be in its future state St. John saw when he called it the great City invested with the glory of God, the Bride adorned for her husband; and St. Paul hints, when he speaks of the perfect man compacted and fitly framed together by what every joint supplies, and grown up to full stature in the Head. There is in the redeemed, not only the exceeding greatness of the quality of their salvation, that is, the gift of divine sonship; nor, again, that this gift is heightened by its being the purchase of the Son of God, so that He is not ashamed to call those brethren whom He has first washed in His own blood: but over and above all this, one thing more, that the whole mass of the redeemed and adopted are not so many souls, but the Body of Christ. Faint shadows, indeed, to our earthly senses are House and Temple, Kingdom and City paved with precious stones of that mighty unity of all rational natures, powers, and virtues, each with the perfection of his individual being, each with the superadded lustre of membership in a marvellous whole, under the Head-ship of Christ. The exceeding glory of this creation, which will be the wonder of all creation through eternity, is that God the Word made flesh, the Head and His Body, make one thing, not an inorganic, but an organised unity, the glorified Body of a glorified Head.

---

[1] "Grana illa quæ modo gemunt inter paleas, quæ massam unam factura sunt, quando area in fine fuerit ventilata." St. Aug. in Ps. cxxvi. tom. iv. p. 1429.

Once more let us note the consistency and unbroken evolution of the divine plan.

In the first creation of the human race the Body of Christ is not only foretold but prefigured, not only prefigured but expressed in the very words uttered by Adam in his ecstasy, the words of God delineating that act of God, the greatest of all His acts of power, wisdom, and goodness, whereby becoming man, and leaving His Father and His Mother,[1] He would cleave to the wife He so took, the human nature which in redeeming He espoused. This, and no other, was the reason why Eve was formed out of Adam. It is the beginning of the divine plan, which is coherent throughout. Designed in the state of innocency, it remains intended through the state of guilt. Unfolded in the state of grace, it is completed in the state of glory. Then the final issue will be seen: what that forming of Eve from the side of Adam, and of the Church from the side of her Lord, signified: what that growth through thousands of years, through multitudinous conflicts, through unspeakable sorrows, through immeasurable triumphs. This will be the entrancing vision bestowed on His beloved by the Second Adam.

---

[1] See Origen on Matt. xiv. 17. καὶ ὁ κτίσας γε ἀπ' ἀρχῆς τὸν κατ' εἰκόνα ὃς ἐν μορφῇ Θεοῦ ὑπάρχων ἄρρεν αὐτὸν ἐποίησε, καὶ θῆλυ τὴν ἐκκλησίαν, ἐν τὸ κατ' εἰκόνα ἀμφοτέροις χαρισάμενος· καὶ καταλέλοιπέ γε διὰ τὴν ἐκκλησίαν κύριος ὁ ἀνὴρ πατέρα ὃν ἑώρα, ὅτε ἐν μορφῇ Θεοῦ ὑπῆρχε, καταλέλοιπε δὲ καὶ τὴν μητέρα καὶ αὐτὸς υἱὸς ὢν τῆς ἄνω Ἱερουσαλήμ, καὶ ἐκολλήθη τῇ ἐνταῦθα καταπεσούσῃ γυναικὶ αὐτοῦ, καὶ γεγόνασιν ἐνθάδε οἱ δύο εἰς σάρκα μίαν. διὰ γὰρ αὐτὴν γέγονε καὶ αὐτὸς σάρξ, ὅτε ὁ λόγος σὰρξ ἐγένετο καὶ ἐσκήνωσεν ἐν ἡμῖν, καὶ οὐκέτι γέ εἰσι δύο, ἀλλὰ νῦν μία γέ ἐστι σάρξ, ἔπει τῇ γυναικὶ λέγεται τὸ, ὑμεῖς δέ ἐστε σῶμα Χριστοῦ καὶ μέλη ἐκ μέρους, οὐ γάρ ἐστί τι ἰδίᾳ Χριστοῦ σῶμα ἕτερον παρὰ τὴν ἐκκλησίαν οὖσαν σῶμα αὐτοῦ, καὶ μέλη ἐκ μέρους. καὶ ὁ Θεός γε τούτους τοὺς μὴ δύο ἀλλὰ γεγομένους σάρκα μίαν συνέζευξεν, ἐντελλόμενος ἵνα ἄνθρωπος μὴ χωρίζῃ τὴν ἐκκλησίαν ἀπὸ τοῦ κυρίου.

LECTURE IX

THE SECOND MAN VERIFIED IN HISTORY

Magnum principium, et regni ejus non erit finis. Deus fortis, domi-
nator, princeps pacis."

In order to complete the view taken in the preceding
lecture of the work of Christ as the second Adam
over against the work of the first Adam, it is necessary
to dwell at greater length upon a point of which only
cursory mention was made therein.   It was our object
there to bring out the relation of Christ to the Church,
but this cannot be done without fully exhibiting the
relation to the same Church of the Holy Spirit.   To
the Incarnation the Fathers in general give the title
of the Dispensation of the Son, and as the equivalent,
the result, the complement and crown of this Dispensation, they put the Giving of the Spirit.[1]   This Giving
of the Spirit occupies the whole region of grace, and
is co-extensive with the whole action of the Incarnate
God upon men whom He has taken to be His brethren.
The Holy Spirit in this Giving is He who represents
the Redeemer, and executes His will, not as an instru-

[1] As St. Irenæus, v. 20. "Omnibus unum et eundem Deum Patrem
præcipientibus, et eamdem dispositionem incarnationis Filii Dei creden-
tibus, et eamdem donationem Spiritus scientibus ; " and St. Aug. tom.
v. app. p. 307 f. "Ecce iterum humanis divina miscentur, id est,
vicarius Redemtoris : ut beneficia quæ Salvator Dominus inchoavit
peculiari Spiritus Sancti virtute consummet, et quod ille redemit, iste
sanctificet, quod ille acquisivit, iste custodiat." This striking sermon
is quoted by Petavius as genuine, but placed by the Benedictines in the
appendix.

ment, not as one subordinate, but as the very mind of Christ between whom and Christ there can far less enter any notion of division or separation than between a man and his own spirit. He is that other Paraclete, abiding for ever, who replaces to the disciples the visible absence of the first Paraclete, the Redeemer Himself: He is the Power constituting the Kingdom of Christ; the Godhead inhabiting His Temple; the Soul animating His mystical Body; the Charity, kindling into a living flame the heart of His Bride; the Creator and Father of His Race.

This connection between the Dispensation of the Son and the Giving of the Spirit was delineated by our Lord Himself when He first appeared to His assembled disciples after His resurrection. As they were gazing in wonder and trembling joy on that Body which had undergone His awful passion, as He showed them the wounds in His hands and His feet, He told them how His sufferings were the fulfilment of all that in the Law, the Prophets, and the Psalms had been written concerning Him. And thereupon it is said, He opened their mind to the understanding of these Scriptures. It was thus that the Christ was to suffer, it was thus that He was to rise again on the third day. Hitherto He has dwelt upon His own dispensation, as the ful- filment of all prophecy, now He proceeds to its fruit; that in the name of this Christ repentance and remis- sion of sins should be proclaimed to all nations, begin- ning at Jerusalem. "And you," He says, "are the witnesses of these things. And, behold, I send the promise of my Father upon you: but stay you in the city of Jerusalem until you be endued with power from on high." Again, at another occasion of equal solemnity, when He was with His assembled disciples in visible form for the last time, at the moment preceding His ascension, He uses the same emphatic words, charging them not to depart from the city, but to await there that promise of the Father, the baptism in the Holy Ghost, which they were to receive in common together. That baptism was to be the power in virtue of which they should be His witnesses for all time unto the ends of the earth : the power which instead of restoring a local kingdom to Israel, as was in their thoughts when they questioned Him, was to create an universal kingdom to Him in the hearts of men. It is then as the result of His passion, and the token of His resurrection, that the Son sends down upon His disciples the promise of the Father, that is, the perpetual presence of the Spirit of the Father and the Son, the Spirit of Truth and Grace, that permanent and immanent power from on high, who, dwelling for ever in the disciples, makes the Church.

But these words, so singular and so forcible, which He uses on these two occasions, at His Resurrection and His Ascension, are themselves a reference to the long discourse which He had held with His Apostles on the night of His passion. It is in this discourse, from the moment that Judas left them to the conclusion of the divine prayer——and if we can make any distinction in His words, surely these are the most solemn which were ever put together in human language, since they are the prayer not of a creature to the Creator, but the prayer of One divine Person to Another——it is in this discourse that He describes the power from on high with which, as the promise of the Father, He, the Son, would invest His disciples. It is here He says that He would ask the Father, who should give them another Paraclete, the Spirit of truth, to abide with them for ever : whom the world would not receive, nor see, nor know, but whom they should know, because He should abide with them and be in them.   This other Paraclete, co-equal therefore with Himself, whom the Father should send in His name, and whom He should send from the Father, the Spirit of holiness as well as the Spirit of truth, should teach them all things, and remind them of all His teaching. And His coming, though invisible, should profit them more than His own visible presence.   For while He declared Himself to be the Way, the Truth, and the Life,[1] He revealed to them here that it was by that very way that the Spirit of truth should lead them by the hand into all truth.   It was in this Truth, that is, in Himself, that they should be sanctified, and that they should be one, the glory of the Incarnation, which had been given to Him, passing on to them as the members of His Body, by the joint possession of the spirit of truth and holiness, whose presence was the gage that the Father loved them, as He loved Christ, the Body being identified with the Head.   In all this He was describing to them the work of that other Paraclete, His own Spirit, " who was to sanctify what He had redeemed, and to guard and maintain posses-sion of what He had acquired."[2]   This is but a small portion of that abundant revelation, which our Lord then communicated to His Apostles, concerning the Power from on high with which they were to be invested.

---

[1] There is in the original words here something which is lost both in the Vulgate and in the English translation.   First, c. xiv. 6.   ἐγώ εἰμι ἡ ὁδὸς, καὶ ἡ ἀλήθεια, καὶ ἡ ζωή· then c. xvi. 13.   ὅταν δὲ ἔλθῃ ἐκεῖνος τὸ Πνεῦμα τῆς ἀληθείας, ὁδηγήσει ὑμᾶς εἰς πᾶσαν τὴν ἀλήθειαν.   As Christ is the ὁδὸς, so His Spirit is the ὁδηγῶν.   " Ego sum via et veritas ; ille vos docebit omnem veritatem," does not render this : and as little, " I am *the way*, the truth, and the life ; He shall *lead* you into all truth."
[2] St. Aug., quoted above in note.

The words of our Lord to His Apostles at the three great points of His Passion, His Resurrection, and His Ascension, stand out beyond the rest in their appeal to our affections. The last words of a friend are the dearest, and these are the last words of the Bridegroom, and they are concerning His Bride. When He was Himself quitting His disciples He dwells upon the Power which was to create and maintain His Church, upon the gift of His Spirit, His other self, in which gift lay the formation of His kingdom. It is thus He expresses to us the point with which we started, that the Giving of His Spirit is the fulfilment of all that Dispensation wherein the Eternal Word took human flesh.

It is not only then the unanimous voice of the Fathers which sets the Giving of the Spirit over against the Incarnation of the Son. They are but carrying on that which our Lord so markedly taught; their tradition was but the echo of His voice, as their life was the fulfilment of it.

But it was a double malady in man which God the Word became man to cure. It was the whole nature which was affected with a taint, and the soul through the whole race touched in both its powers of the intellect [1] and the will. That false worship which we have seen spreading through the earth, and that deep corruption of manners which was interlaced with it, were the symptoms of this malady. The perversion of the truth concerning the being of God, and all the duties of man which grow out of this being, was inextricably blended with the disregard of these duties in the actual conduct of man. It was in vain to set the

---

[1] This word is used as the equivalent of λόγος, *ratio*, *Vernunft*, in man.

truth before man's intellect without a corresponding power to act upon his will. Therefore the apostle described the glory of the only-begotten Son, when He dwelt as man among us, by the double expression that He was "full of grace and truth." Viewed as the Head of human nature, its Father and new beginning, He is the perpetual fountain to it of these two, which no law, not even one divinely given, could bestow. For the law could make nothing perfect, because it could not touch the will; and the law gave the shadow, but not the very truth of things. But when that unspeakable union of the divine nature with the human had taken effect in the unity of one Person, Truth and Grace had an everlasting human fountain in the created nature of the Incarnate Word. Now was the fountain to pour forth a perpetual stream upon the race assumed. And this it does by the descent of the Spirit. In this descent upon the assembled Church the Grace and Truth of the divine Head, with which His Flesh, carried by the Godhead, overstreams, find themselves a human dwelling in the race. Such an operation belongs only to the Divine Spirit, for God alone can so act upon the intellect and will of creatures as to penetrate them with His gifts of Truth and Grace, while He leaves them their free-will, their full individuality, as creatures. This, then, was the range of that power with which our Lord foretold to His apostles that they should be invested, and for which He bade them wait. The whole field of truth as it respects the relation of God to His creatures as moral beings, and the whole extent of grace, as it touches the human will, for the performance of every act which a reasonable creature can execute, made up the extent of that divine indwelling in men which the Spirit of Christ assumed upon the day of Pentecost. This was the power of the Holy Ghost which then came down upon men. Through the whole divine discourse which preceded His passion, our Lord dwells upon this double power, referring to Himself as the Truth, to His Spirit as the Spirit of the Truth, to Himself as the Vine, and so that root of grace which should communicate its sap to the branches, and to His Spirit, who should take of His and give it to them; uniting both ideas of Truth and Grace in that one word, " Sanctify them in Thy Truth," that is by incorporation with Me, who am the Truth, in My Spirit, who is the Truth. And so the eternal Word, having assumed a human Body, when He withdraws His corporal presence, proceeds to form that other human Body, the dwelling-place of His Spirit, in which His Truth and Grace are to become visible.

Thus the transfusion of Truth and Grace from the Incarnate Word to His mystical Body is the generic character of the Giving of the Spirit.

Two differential marks distinguish this giving from any which preceded the coming of our Lord.

First, the Spirit should come upon them, but should never depart from them. " He shall give you another Comforter, to abide with you for ever, the Spirit of Truth." This giving was not an intermittent operation, whether extraordinary, such as had shown itself in Moses and the Prophets, for their inspiration in writing, or their guidance in particular trials, nor that ordinary one whereby from the beginning He had enabled all the good and just to lead a life acceptable to Him. It was a far higher gift,[1] wherein, as

---

[1] See Petavius *de Trin.* vii. 7, where he states it to be the general belief of the ancient writers that a new and *substantial* presence of the Holy Ghost began at the day of Pentecost.

St. Augustine says, by the very presence of His majesty no longer the mere odour of the balsam, but the substance itself of the sacred unguent was poured into those vessels, making them His temple, and conveying that adoption in virtue of which they should not be left orphans, but have their Father invisibly with them for ever. No intermittent operation, and no presence less than that of His substance, would reach the force of the words used by our Lord, " I will ask the Father, and He shall send you another Paraclete, the Spirit of Truth, to abide with you for ever ; " for that word " other " conveys a comparison with Himself, from whom they had never been separated since He had called them, in whose continuance with them alone was their strength, their unity, their joint existence and mission, without whom they could do nothing. All this to them that " other " Paraclete was to be, in order that the departure of the Former Paraclete should be expedient for them. For in this continuity of His presence was involved the further gift that the Paraclete was to come to them as a Body, and because of this manner of coming He replaced the Former. Had He come to them only as individuals, they would have suffered a grievous loss, the loss of the Head who had made them one. But He came to them as the Body of Christ, and by coming made them that Body, being the Spirit of the Head. That rushing mighty wind filled the whole house in which they were sitting, and they all were filled together with the presence ; and as a sign that the old confusion and separation of mankind were in them to be done away, speaking in one tongue the one truth which was evermore to dwell with them, they were heard in all the various languages of the nations present at the feast.   "The society by which men are made the one Body of the only Son of God belongs to the Spirit,"[1] and He came upon all together in one House to indicate, as He made, that one Body.   "The mode of giving," says St. Augustine, "was such as never before appeared.   Nowhere do we read before that men congregated together had by receiving the Holy Ghost spoken with the tongues of all nations."[2] "Therefore He came upon Pentecost as upon His birthday."[3]

It is His presence alone which confers four gifts upon the body which He vivifies.

It was the will, says St. Augustine,[4] of the Father and the Son that we should have communion with each other and with Them by means of that which is common to Them, and by that gift to collect us into one, which, being one, They both have ; that is to say, by the Holy Ghost, who is God, and the gift of God.   For, says St. Thomas,[5] the unity of the Holy Spirit makes unity in the Church.   It is not by similarity, or by juxtaposition, or by agreement, how much less by concessions and compromises, that unity exists in the body of Christ, but because the Spirit is one, because all gifts, however various, all functions, however distinct, are distributed by this One.

For the same reason truth dwells in this Body, because He is the Spirit of Truth.   Our Lord Himself has defined His great function in this particular, to lead His disciples by the hand[6] into all truth, to teach all things, and remind of all things which made

[1] St. Aug. tom. v. 398 g.   [2] St. Aug. tom. iii. pp. 2, 527.
[3] Ib. tom. v. 47.   [4] Ib. tom. v. 392 e.
[5] St. Thomas in Joh. i. lec. 10 : "Nam unitas Spiritus Sancti facit in Ecclesia unitatem."   [6] ὁδηγεῖν.

up His own teaching. This function began on the day of Pentecost, and lasts to the day of judgment, and belongs to the Body of Christ, and to it alone, and belongs to it because it is animated by the Spirit of Truth. And this animation is like the Head, the same yesterday, to-day, and for ever. It is not of any past time more or less than of the present or the future. It is the illumination which belongs to that whole last day, through which the Body of Christ grows, teaches, labours, and suffers, until the mortal day break into the light of eternity.

His third gift to the Body is that of charity, and for the same reason, because He is this Himself. He who is the mutual Love of the Father and the Son, the Gift and Spirit of divine redeeming Love, creates in this human dwelling-place that one charity, which bears His name, and is of His nature. It is this charity in the one body which joins the wills of men together as His Truth joins their intellects. If the Body of Christ has one prevailing charity, which reaches to all its members, and encompasses the least as well as the greatest, it is because the heart is divine.

The fourth gift which He bestows upon the Body is sanctification, and it may be said to be the result of the other three. This, again, is His own name and nature, and many have thought and said, His personal attribute, to make holy; and that, as Father-ship indicates the First Person, and Sonship the Second, so the making holy names the Third, the bond of the most blessed Trinity. But this, at least, may be said to be the final cause of the body which He animates, the imparting of holiness. In virtue of this gift, all the means and aids and rules of holiness are stored up in the Body.   And this does not mean that there is not a continual falling away from the rule and practice of holiness in particular members, but it means that while these, in spite of the Body's nurture and solicitude, fall away from it and perish, the Body lasts for ever, the rules and aids and means of holiness lasting for ever within it, because it is the Body of the Spirit of holiness.

Now these four gifts, Unity, Verity, Charity, and Sanctity, can none of them exist in the Body without the other, and all of them exist together there, because they have one divine root, that indwelling of the Holy Spirit which is the fruit of the Incarnation, and whereby the mystical Body of Christ corresponds to His natural Body.   Of this Body the beginning is Unity, the substance Truth, the bond Charity, the end Sanctity.   Countless heresies and schisms have sought to break up the co-inherence of these gifts, but in vain. The only success which the indwelling Spirit allows them is to detach from the Body those who are unworthy to remain in it, and to prolong for a time their maimed existence by some portion of some of His gifts.   Truth, for instance, has such a vitality that many a heresy will live for ages on that fragment which it has detached from the mass ; unity and charity have such force that even their shadow, that is, the joint possession of a fragmentary truth, and the good-will thence proceeding, will prolong for a time a sort of corporate existence.   Holiness has so attractive a power, that zeal and self-denial, which present the seeming of it, will make the fortune of a sect for a time.   But in the union and the completeness of these four gifts, the great Body of Christ stands out through all the ages inimitable and un-approachable. Alone it dares to claim them thus united and complete, for alone it can present their realisation.

These four gifts, then, dwell in the Body in a higher degree than that in which they adorn the members of the Body, as in it, by force of the Spirit's indwelling, they ever exist together. Let us now see the qualities which the Spirit imparts to the members of the Body, by virtue of their incorporation into it.

First of all is the forgiveness of sins. The Spirit takes them out of that state of alienation in which they are born, and unites them to His Body; and in so doing He effaces both the birth-sin and every actual sin which they may have committed. This is that plenary forgiveness of sins, the pure gift of God un-preceded by any merit on man's part, which greets the new-comer out of Adam's body of sin into the Body of Christ. It is imparted by and from the Body, and to its members alone.

The second quality is that illumination of the mind, irradiated by the truth, the whole compass of which exists in the Body. This illumination is the root of the virtue of faith, by means of which the individual mind appropriates the divine truth presented to it. The force of the virtue differs in the individual as the keenness of sight in the natural man, but the visual power is the same in quality in all. By it the mind of the believer lays hold in ever-varying degree, one more and one less, of that great harmony of truth which is held in its completeness, its manifold appli-cations, and all but infinite relations, only by the Body. For the truth with which we deal is not unlocalised and scattered, the prey, as it were, of the individual mind, which can hunt it down and take it as a spoil, but it is a divine gift, orbed in the sphere which was created for it, the Body of that Word who is the Truth. Hence the first question to the applicant for baptism : What askest thou of the Church of God ? and the answer is, Faith.

The third quality is the adoption of Sonship, which flows directly from incorporation into the Body of Christ, and to which man has no sort of title in himself or from his own nature, but which comes to him only by kindred with Him who, on the morning of His Resurrection, greeted that great penitent who bore the figure of the Church with that paschal salutation of the Second Adam, " Go to My brethren, and say, I ascend to My Father and to your Father, to My God and to your God." And the divine virtue of hope well corresponds to this quality, the effects of which in a state of trial and conflict are to so great a degree future and unseen. It seems, moreover, to be as a special link and tie between the virtue which purifies the intellect, and that which corrects the will and makes it obedient. Thus through it we pass on to the fourth quality of Sanctification, which is the completion of the other three and their end, the harmony of each individual will with the divine will, the work of charity. That divine virtue is the special fruit of the passion of Christ, which was to gather up into one what sin had disunited and torn away, first from its Author, and then from the order by Him created, which was to heal the animosities thus introduced, and to change the world from a conflict wherein each sought to better himself at the expense of his neighbour, into a community cemented together with mutual affection. It was with reason, therefore, that St. Augustine would not allow the possession of charity, save in the unity of that one Body which Christ had created,[1] and without charity there is no sanctification.

The four qualities thus slightly sketched, forgiveness of sins, illumination of faith, adoption to sonship, and sanctification by charity, which come to the individual by and with incorporation into the Body, are not given to him irrevocably, but are conditional upon his perseverance. They are portions and derivations of that vast treasure of Truth and Grace which the Body holds in their entireness and for ever, because of the perpetual indwelling of the Spirit who makes its life, but which He dispenses as it pleases Him to the members, and which He may withdraw from them in default of their co-operation. Vast are the losses thereby incurred, not to the treasure-house, which remains inexhaustible, but to those who fall out of it back into the world, or rather that body of Adam from which they were taken. But these losses touch not the beauty and the glory of that Body of Christ, which goes on through the ages, and takes up its own, fulfils its appointed work, and reaches its intended end.

Thus on the day of Pentecost a new Power, the Spirit of the Incarnate God, descended not upon single men, but upon an assembly of men, binding it in a unity, conveying to it a truth, kindling in it a charity,

[1] Epist. 185, tom. ii. p. 663. "Proinde Ecclesia Catholica sola corpus est Christi, cujus ille caput est, Salvator corporis sui. Extra hoc corpus neminem vivificat Spiritus Sanctus, quia sicut ipse dicit Apostolus: Caritas Dei diffusa est in cordibus nostris per Spiritum Sanctum, qui datus est nobis. Non est autem particeps divinæ caritatis, qui hostis est unitatis. Non habent itaque Spiritum Sanctum qui sunt extra Ecclesiam."

and working through these a sanctification never before known; which Power, thenceforth dwelling in that Body, was to collect and draw into itself out of all nations and ranks of men those who should form the Church, that is, the Kingdom and Temple, and House, and Body, and Family of Christ. The virtue of Him, who had assumed our flesh, not transiently but for ever, was to work in it, and to go out hence-forward from it. In the Body, through the life of His Spirit, Christ should teach and bear witness to that truth of which He spoke in the hall of Pilate. He had said concerning it that "this gospel of the kingdom should be proclaimed through the whole world, for a witness to all nations, and then that the end should come."[1] To the continuance, the indis-solubility, the purity of this power He has pledged His word in such a way that they who deny it must in doing so deny Him. He has even made the unity of this Body the special mark to men of the truth of His mission, beseeching His Father in that last prayer, "Neither pray I for these alone, but for those also who through their word shall believe in Me, that they all may be one, as Thou, Father, art in Me, and I in Thee, that they also may be one in Us, that the world may believe that Thou hast sent Me."

There are three analogies[2] which illustrate this creation of our Lord—a creation in itself as singular as His assumption of man's nature.

---

[1] Matt. xxiv. 14.

[2] See Möhler, *Die Einheit in der Kirche*, p. 176. "Der Körper des Menschen ist eine Offenbarung des Geistes, der in ihm sein Dasein bekundet, und sich entwickelt. Der Staat ist eine nothwendige Erscheinung, eine Bildung und Gestaltung des von Gott gegebenen Κοινωνίαν."

First, that of the relation between the soul and body. The soul is the life of the body; the body, as it were, the mansion and home of the soul, its bearer. Through the body the qualities of the soul become visible and known; its powers exercise themselves, and personal unity so binds the two together that we love or hate, admire or despise, the one for the sake of the other; the grief of the soul acts upon the body, the sickness of the body depresses the soul. Through the acts of the body we learn the very existence of the soul, and in these acts it portrays itself. Human nature has been so made by its Creator that the qualities of soul and body, of spirit and matter, are imputed in the individual man to each other. Now to the Body we have been considering the Spirit of Christ is, as it were, the soul. It is nothing strange, then, if it was His will to create such a Body, if it be the result of His Incarnation, that the like effects which exist in the case of every human soul and body should take place here. To this Body also the power and virtue of its soul are communicated; and, since Christ by His Spirit animates it, in honouring it He is honoured; in despising it, He is despised. There is an imparting to it of the qualities which He has; and thus it is that unity and sanctity, truth and charity dwell in it as the operation of His mind. Thus every man contains in himself, in the union of soul and body, an image of that tie, by which Christ and His Church are one.

Secondly, because God has created man for society, He has implanted in him an irrepressible instinct of communion with his brother men. This instinct it is which, under circumstances of every possible variety, results in one end, the State. The human commonwealth, whatever external shape it wear, whatever division of its powers it make, springs from this.   In virtue of this original formation of man, that he is made to live together, and gregariously, not separately, the supreme power of government, the power of life and death, dwells in the community, and obedience to it has a divine sanction.   Thus, the commonwealth has a variety of powers which the individual has not.   Moreover, it has powers which do not arise from the mere aggregation of individuals, rather which belong to it as a community, as a whole, for instance, sovereignty in all the details of its exercise. But now the very object for which Christ became Incarnate was to constitute a divine commonwealth. He is the King : it is the tenderness of a God Incarnate that He calls and makes His Kingdom His Body. The powers, then, which belong to the earthly commonwealth belong, with the changes which the change of subject carries, to the Divine.   They who have so great a reverence for human government, who respect in the nation an ultimate irresponsible power, ought, if they were consistent, when they acknowledge Christ as having come in the flesh, to acknowledge His government in the kingdom which He has set up.   All that his country is to the patriot, the Church is to the Christian, but in so much higher a degree, as the object for which Christ came is above the needs and cares of this present life.   Has the City of God, then, less claim upon Christians than the City of Romulus had upon Romans ?   Thus, in the natural duty of the citizen, as well as in the compound nature of man, is contained a reminder of the Christian's relation to the Church, and a picture and ensample of the Church's authority.

Thirdly, there is the analogy presented by the trans-

gift of the Incarnate God.[1]   Thus the descent of the
Spirit at Pentecost is a true and real counterpart of
the creation of man in Eden; but they who share it
are become kindred of God through His flesh, and by
so sharing it together, they form that society which
failed through Adam's sin.   In the first creation,
the Omnipotent Creator, in His bounty towards His
favourite child, as foreseeing the assumption of that
nature by Himself, attached to the gift of natural life
the Spirit of sanctification; in the second, having
assumed that nature, He gave through His own Body,
first taken out of us, then crucified, now risen and
exalted, the gift of the Spirit, Who, with all the
endowments springing from Him, as the Inspirer of
truth and charity, of unity and holiness, dwells in
that Body for ever.

Thus in the union of the soul and body, in the constitution and authority of the human commonwealth,
and in the race's natural unity, God holds before us
three analogies, which each in some respect, and altogether very largely, illustrate His finished work.   All
natural productions of His providence are subordinate
to this work of His predilection, of His unbounded
love and sovereign magnificence, that creation which
is at once the Body, the Kingdom, and the Family
of the Incarnate Word.

From all that has gone before we gather this conclusion, that to become a Christian was to enter into
a spiritual and physical [2] unity with Christ by incor-

---

[1] For instance, two passages on the Incarnation in St. Cyril of
Alexandria, tom. iv. pp. 819-824 and 918-920, set forth the whole
sequence of the Fall and the Restoration, and how wonderfully the gift
of the Spirit replaces what was lost in Adam.

[2] See St. Cyril. Alex. *in Joän.* p. 997 e.   ἐν δὲ τούτοις ἤδη πως καὶ
φυσικὴν τὴν ἑνότητα δεικνύναι σπουδάζομεν, καθ᾽ ἣν ἡμεῖς τε ἀλλήλοις καὶ

poration into that Body which He had created as the result of his becoming man. This it was for the individual to become a Christian. But Christianity itself was neither a mere system of belief, nor an outward order representing that belief, but "the great and glorious Body of Christ,"[1] possessing and exhibiting the whole truth of doctrine, possessing and distributing all the means of grace, and presenting together to God those whom it had reconciled with Him, and made one, as the members of the Son by the indwelling of the Spirit.

Let us now trace the exact correspondence of the historical fact with the dogmatic statement just given.

The Acts of the Apostles exhibit to us the creation of the divine society by the descent of the Holy Ghost on the day of Pentecost. When they were all together, the sound as of a rushing mighty wind was heard, filling the whole house wherein they were sitting. Tongues as of fire were seen, the tongues apportioned severally, the fire one.[2] Resting upon each, this fire was to kindle in all that eternal flame of charity which was to draw into one the hearts of men. Our Lord had spoken of this fire as being that which He was come to light upon the earth. Fire, whose inward nature it is at once to illuminate and

οἱ πάντες Θεῷ συνδούμεθα· κ.τ.λ.; and p. 998. τίς γὰρ ἂν καὶ διέλοι καὶ τῆς εἰς ἀλλήλους φυσικῆς ἐνώσεως ἐξοικέοι τοὺς δι' ἑνὸς τοῦ ἁγίου σώματος πρὸς ἑνότητα τὴν εἰς Χριστὸν ἀναδεσμουμένους ;

[1] St. Iren. iv. c. 33, 7. ἀνακρινεῖ τοὺς τὰ σχίσματα ἐργαζομένους, κένους ὄντας τῆς τοῦ Θεοῦ ἀγάπης, καὶ τὸ ἴδιον λυσιτελὲς σκοποῦντας, ἀλλὰ μὴ τὴν ἔνωσιν τῆς ἐκκλησίας· καὶ διὰ μικρὰς καὶ τὰς ὑψούσας αἰτίας τὸ μέγα καὶ ἔνδοξον σῶμα τοῦ Χριστοῦ τέμνοντας καὶ διαιροῦντας, καὶ ὅσον τὸ ἐπ' αὐτοῖς ἀναιροῦντας, τοὺς εἰρήνην λαλοῦντας καὶ πόλεμον ἐργαζομένους, ἀληθῶς διυλίζοντας τὸν κώνωπα, καὶ τὸν κάμηλον καταπίνοντας.

[2] Acts ii. 3. ὤφθησαν αὐτοῖς διαμεριζόμεναι γλῶσσαι ὡσεὶ πυρός, ἐκάθισέ τε ἐφ' ἕνα ἕκαστον αὐτῶν, καὶ ἐπλήσθησαν ἅπαντες Πνεύματος ἁγίου.

warm, to purify and unite, was thus appropriately selected as the outward sign, both expressing and conveying the fourfold office of the Comforter, who came to be "no longer an occasional visitant, but a perpetual Consoler and eternal Inhabitant [1] of this His chosen Home.   As each in that assembly spoke in the one tongue of the country, he was heard by those present in the several tongues of all the nations of the earth represented at that great feast by the Jews who dwelt in them.   And this was the mark, says St. Augustine,[2] of the Church which was to be through all nations, that no one should receive the Holy Spirit, save he who should be jointed into the framework of its unity.   This mark signified that the confusion of Babel, dividing the race into nationalities jealous of each other and perpetual enemies, was to be reversed and overcome by the one Power whose force to unite should be greater than the force of sin to sever.   Thus, the City of God should be gathered out of all nations, fed by the exulting and abounding river of His Spirit, the fountain proper and peculiar to the Church of Christ.   The one truth [3] again, should

---

[1] Non jam visitator subitus, sed perpetuus consolator et habitator æternus."   St. Aug. tom. v. d. app. p. 307.

[2] *Contra Cresconium*, tom. ix. p. 418.   "Hic Spiritus sanctus veniens in eos tale signum primitus dedit, ut qui eum acciperent linguis omnium gentium loquerentur, quia portendebat Ecclesiam per omnes gentes futuram, nec quemquam accepturum Spiritum sanctum nisi qui ejus unitati copularetur.   Hujus fontis largo atque invisibili flumine lætificat Deuscivitatem suam, de qua Propheta dixit : Fluminis impetus lætificat civitatem Dei.   Ad hunc enim fontem nullus extraneus, quia nullus nisi vita æterna dignus accedit."

[3] Ἡ ἀλήθεια : there seems to be no one word in the New Testament of more pregnant signification than this, which in a great number of instances bears the sense of *the whole body of the divine revelation*.   The root of this meaning would seem to lie in Christ Himself, who as the Divine Word is the αὐτοαλήθεια, the εἰκὼν of the Father ; on which title St. Athanasius and St. Cyril of Alexandria specially dwell, while St. Hilary expresses the Blessed Trinity by " Æternitas in Patre, Species in Imagine, Usus in Munere," on which see St. Augustine's magnificent

be characterised by the utterance of the one voice, conveying in harmony the whole revelation of God ; speaking to all nations, not in the broken languages of their division, but in the Unity of His Person, carried by His Body.   We have then in the one Fire the one inward power ; in the one language its outward expression, in the assembly its receptacle, the House of God. This Body appears at once as formed and complete. In it sits and prays in her silent tenderness and unapproachable grandeur, as the Mother of the risen Lord

comment, *de Trin,* l. vi. 10, p. 850 ; and as our Lord is from eternity the Truth, so in and by His Incarnation He becomes in a special sense the Truth to man : ἐγώ εἰμι ἡ ὁδὸς, καὶ ἡ ἀλήθεια, καὶ ἡ ζωή : and so the Spirit who proceeds from the Father and the Son, "ille ineffabilis quidam complexus Patris et Imaginis" (St. Aug.), is τὸ Πνεῦμα τῆς ἀληθείας, who ὁδηγήσει ὑμᾶς εἰς πᾶσαν τὴν ἀλήθειαν : and again, 1 John v. 6, τὸ Πνεῦμά ἐστι τὸ μαρτυροῦν, ὅτι τό Πνεῦμά ἐστιν ἡ ἀλήθεια.   This is the first meaning.   Secondly, as derived from it, the Truth is the whole body of the divine revelation.   In this sense it is used in a great many places of St. John's Gospel and the Apostolic Epistles, *e.g.,* John i. 14, 17 ; viii. 31 ; xvi. 13 ; xvii. 17 ; xviii. 37 ; 1 John ii. 21 ; iii. 19 ; 2 John i. 1–3 ; 3 John 3, 4, 8, 12 ; 1 Tim. iii. 15, where, because this whole body of truth dwells in the Church of Christ and there alone, it is emphatically called the "House of God, which is the Church of the living God, the pillar and ground of the Truth ;" 1 Tim. ii. 3 ; Rom. xv. 8 ; 2 Cor. iv. 2 ; xiii. 8 ; Gal. iii. 1 ; v. 7 ; Ephes. i. 13 ; iv. 21–24 (in which passage the Apostle contrasts heathen man with Christian, the one, τὸν φθειρόμενον κατὰ τὰς ἐπιθυμίας τῆς ἀπάτης ; the other, τὸν κατὰ Θεὸν κτισθέντα ἐν δικαιοσύνῃ καὶ ὁσιότητι τῆς ἀληθείας, and again, the mass of the Gentiles, as τὰ ἔθνη περιπατεῖ ἐν ματαιότητι τοῦ νοός αὐτῶν, ἐσκοτισμένοι τῇ διανοίᾳ, while Christians ἐν αὐτῷ ἐδιδάχθητε, καθώς ἐστιν ἀλήθεια ἐν τῷ Ἰησοῦ) ; 2 Thess. ii. 8–13 ; 1 Tim. iv. 3 ; vi. 5 ; 2 Tim. ii. 15, 25 ; iii. 7, 8 ; iv. 4 ; Titus i. 1 and 14 ; Heb. x. 26 ; Jac. v. 19 ; 1 Pet. i. 22 ; 2 Pet. ii. 2.   In this second sense, as signifying the whole body of the divine revelation, the expression has been searched for, but without success, in the Gospels of St. Matthew, St. Mark, and St. Luke, and in the Acts.

Thirdly, as the effect of this revelation to man, the Truth signifies uprightness, as equivalent to justice or sanctity, in the individual.

Fourthly, it means sincerity, absence of hypocrisy : and

Fifthly, correspondence to fact.

In the Apocalypse our Lord is designated "the holy, the true," "the Amen, the Witness faithful and true," the rider of the white horse, "called faithful and true," "whose name is the Word of God," iii. 7, 14 ; xix. 11.

and Head, and the Mother too of His race, the most beloved, the most lovable, and the most loving of creatures,[1] whose great function in the Church for ever is to pray for the members of her Son, and to solicit the graces of His Spirit, which as the Mother of the sacred race she gains and distributes to all and each that belong to it, a Second Eve who corresponds to the Second Adam, as the First Eve in the divine plan corresponded to the First Adam. In it the Apostles, so long before chosen and designated by their Lord, and having already received from Him portions of their supernatural power on the day of His Resurrection and during the forty days of His secret instruction, teach and govern. In it Peter at their head exercises that primacy, which is exhibited with so much grandeur, and, imaged out by a new name imposed at his first calling, promised at his great confession, and confirmed and conveyed on the sea-shore of the lake of Galilee. He stood with the eleven and lifted up his voice, in virtue of his primacy to describe to the men of Judea and the inhabitants of Jerusalem the nature of the event which they were witnessing, and the fulfilment of all the promises made through their prophets concerning that presence of God in the pouring out of His Spirit among men in the last days. That first discourse of his at the head of his brethren is the summary as it were of his perpetual office of teaching and promulgating the dispensation of the Christ in the midst of the Church. Its immediate effect was the aggregation of three thousand persons to the Body, who were told that this was the way in which they should receive remission of

[1] "La creatura, la più amabile, la più amata, e la più amante di Dio." St. Alfonso, *Gran Mezzo della Preghiera*, p. 280.

sins and the gift of the Holy Ghost.[1]   The subsequent
teaching of Peter and the Apostles, accompanied with
miraculous cures, produced further aggregations among
all ranks of the people.   And the mode of salvation
for all time is pointedly marked out by the words,
" the Lord was adding to the Church day by day such
as should be saved."

We have only to repeat the process which is thus
described as having taken place at Jerusalem in the
first months after the day of Pentecost, by carrying
it through the various cities of the Roman empire,
Damascus, Antioch, Rome, Alexandria, and between
these all round the shores of the Mediterranean, to
have a just picture of the mode in which the Divine
Society grew and gathered into itself more and more
of those who listened to the truth which it announced.
What is important to dwell upon is that men uni-
formly became Christians in one way, by being received into the Divine Body, through which reception
forgiveness of sins and the gift of the Holy Ghost were
conveyed to them.   From the whole account contained
in the sacred Scriptures, and from all that remains to
us of history, the great fact is established for us that
Christianity came into the world at its first beginning
a society created by the Holy Ghost, and held together
and informed by Him as its soul, who is sent down
upon it as the Promise of the Father from the Incarnate Son.

Further, it was in and by their reception into this
society that men received all the fruits of the Incarnation ; it was in it that all the gifts of the Holy
Ghost dwelt, and through it that they were dispensed.
By hearing the truth announced by its ministry peni-

[1] Acts ii. 38.

tence was engendered in the listeners, itself a prevent-
ing grace of the Holy Ghost, which gave inward effect
to the outward word. As a working of this penitence
they came, according to the instruction of the teachers,
to be baptized. By and in the act of baptism they were
received into the divine society, and made partakers of
the full operation of the Spirit who dwelt in it. They
had the supernatural virtues of faith, hope, and charity
infused into them, each according to the measure of
the grace accorded to him, and to help the exercise of
these virtues, that they might be borne as it were with
the wings of a Spirit, the sevenfold gifts of wisdom,
understanding, counsel, fortitude, knowledge, piety, and
fear, were added to the soul. None of these virtues
and gifts were possessed by believers as individuals;
all of them came to men as members of her who was
dowered with the blood of Christ,[1] and whose bridal
qualities imparted to her children all which that blood
had purchased. In her was stored up that great, inexhaustible source of abiding life, the Body and
Blood of her Lord: in her the redeeming Word
gave direct from His heart the vivifying stream.. In
her was the gift of teaching which illumined the understanding, and not only drew from without, as we have
seen, those who should be saved from the ignorance
of the pagan or the carnalism of the Jew, but which
erected in the world the Chair of Truth,[2] that is, the

---

[1] " Non te fefellit sponsus tuus : non te fefellit qui suo sanguine te
dotavit." St. Aug. tom. v. 1090 b.
[2] "Quod tunc faciebat unus homo accepto Spiritu sancto, ut unus
homo linguis omnium loqueretur, hoc modo ipsa unitas facit, linguis
omnibus loquitur. Et modo unus homo in omnibus gentibus linguis
omnibus loquitur, unus homo, caput et corpus, unus homo, Christus et
Ecclesia, vir perfectus, ille sponsus, illa sponsa. Sed erunt, inquit, duo
in carne una ; judicia Dei vera, justificata in idipsum : propter unitatem." St. Aug. in Ps. xviii. 2, tom. iv. 85 f.

rule and standard of right belief, which was the continuance of the pentecostal gift, the illuminating and kindling fire, and the speaking tongue of unity, which the Body of Christ possesses for ever. It was by enjoying these endowments together in her bosom, by the actions of a life pervaded with these principles, by the joint possession and exercise of these supernatural powers which at once opened to the intellect a new field of knowledge and strengthened the will to acts above its inborn force, that men were Christians. And those who remembered what they had been as Jews, and what they had been as heathens, had no difficulty in recognising such a life as the effect of a divine grace, and no temptation to refer it to anything which belonged to them as individuals, since its beginning coincided with their entrance into a divine society, its growth depended on their membership in that Body. Their union with Christ in this Body was something direct and palpable; to them the several degrees of that one ministry constituted by Christ were the joints and articulations of the structure; the teaching thence proceeding as it were the current of life; by their being parts of the structure they were saved from the confusion of errors which swept freely round them without through the craft of men and the seduction of deceit.[1] "Possessing the truth in charity," or "sanctified in the truth," was the expression of that divine life in common whereby they were to grow up into one, and be called by the name of their Lord,[2] because inseparably united to Him by the nerves and ligaments of one Body.

And this makes manifest to us how Christians,

---

[1] Ephes. iv. 11–16. ἀληθεύοντες ἐν ἀγάπῃ. Joh. xvii. 19. ἡγιασμένοι ἐν ἀληθείᾳ.
[2] 1 Cor. xii. 12. οὕτω καὶ ὁ Χριστός.

while scattered through every city of the great Roman
Empire, formed one Body. It was by virtue of the
unity of spiritual jurisdiction which directed the whole
ministry of that Body. The command of our Lord
was, "Go, and make disciples all nations," "proclaim
the gospel to every creature;" the Body assembled
and empowered at Pentecost was to carry out this
command. How did it do so? The teaching and
ruling power was distributed through a ministry
wherein those of a particular order were equal as
holding that order: bishops as bishops were equal,
priests as priests. But not the less by the distribution of the places where the ministry was to be fulfilled, subordination was maintained through the whole
Body. Had it been otherwise, as each bishop had
the completeness of the priesthood in himself, his
sphere of action, that is, his diocese, would have constituted a distinct body. But no such thing was ever
imagined in the Church of those first centuries. The
bishops were, on the contrary, joint possessors of one
power, only to be exercised in unity.[1] The unity was
provided for in the Apostolic body by the creation of
the Primacy, without which the Body never acted, the
Primate being designated before the Body was made;
the Primate invested with his functions on the sea-
shore of the lake of Galilee before the Ascension, the
Body on which he was to exercise them animated on
the day of Pentecost. Spiritual jurisdiction being
nothing else but the grant to exercise all spiritual
powers, two jurisdictions would make two bodies; a
thousand would make a thousand; so that the more

---

[1] So says the great maintainer of episcopal power, St. Cyprian, in his
famous aphorism : "Episcopatus unus est, cujus a singulis in solidum
pars tenetur."

the Church grew, the more it would be divided, were it not that the root of all its powers in their exercise is one. A spiritual kingdom is absolutely impossible without this unity of jurisdiction ; and in virtue of it the whole Church, from north to south and from east to west, was and is one Body in its teaching and its rule ; that is, in the administration of all those gifts which were bestowed at the day of Pentecost, and which have never ceased to be exercised from that day to this, and which shall never cease to the end of the world. Thus as it is through the Body that men are made and kept Christians, so the Primacy is that principle of cohesion and subordination without which the Body cannot exist.

Let us carry on the history of the divine Body to another point. How was the Truth transmitted in it ?

Peter and his brethren having received through the great forty days from our Lord the complement of His teaching concerning His Kingdom, were empowered by the descent of the Holy Ghost to begin its propagation. And for this work they use the same instrument which their Lord had used—the living spoken word. They labour together for some time ; after several years they divide the world between them ; but in both these periods they found communities and supply them with everything needful for complete organisation and future increase and progress by their spoken teaching, which therefore contained the whole deposit of the truth. The gospel of which St. Paul so repeatedly speaks was that which he communicated by word of mouth, and St. Peter and all the rest did the same. Communities were planted by Apostolic zeal over a great part of the Roman

Empire before as yet anything was written by their founders. The whole administration of the sacraments, and the order and matter of the divine service, were arranged by this personal teaching of the living word. All that concerned the Person of our Lord, all that He had taught, done, and suffered, was so communicated. One reason of this is plain. It was not the bare gospel, but the "gospel of the kingdom," [1] which was to be proclaimed to all nations. It was not a naked intellectual truth of which they were the bearers, but a kingdom which they were to build. They were not disseminating a sect of philosophy, but founding an empire. They were a King's heralds, and every king has a realm. Thus the Kingdom of the Word was proclaimed by the word spoken through many voices, but as the outpouring of one Spirit given on the day of Pentecost. This whole body of their teaching, therefore, was one Tradition; that is, a delivery over of the truth to them by inspiration of the Spirit, as the Truth who had become incarnate taught it, and a delivery of this truth from them to the communities which they set up. The first communication of the Christian faith to the individual was never made by writing. How, said the Apostle, should they invoke one whom they did not believe, but how believe in one of whom they had not heard, and how hear without a preacher, and how preach except they were sent? [2] It did not occur to him to ask, how should they believe in one of whom they had not read? On the contrary, he gives in these few words the whole order of the truth's transmission. He conceived not heralds without a commission, any more than faith without trust in the

<hr>

[1] Matt. xxiv. 14.   [2] Rom. x. 15.

word of the heralds. But here is the great sending, at and from the day of Pentecost, the root of perpetual mission from which the heralds derive their commission ; they are sent, they proclaim, they are heard, they are believed, and this faith opens the door for the admission of subjects into the kingdom, according to the law which they proclaim. Thus are described to us at some length the acts of that wise masterbuilder whose words we have just cited ; but though he laboured more abundantly than all, all acted after the same manner. The Church was founded by personal teaching, of which the living word was the instrument, and the whole truth which was thus communicated was termed the Tradition [1] or Delivery.

We now come to the second step. Before the Apostles were taken to their reward, the same Spirit, who had instructed them that they were to found the spiritual kingdom by means of the living word, inspired them to commit to writing a portion of that great tradition which they had already taught by mouth.[2] But they never delivered these writings to men not already Christians. One evangelist expressly says that he drew up a narrative in order that his disciple might know the certainty of what he had already been instructed in catechetically, which was, that great system of oral teaching by question and

---

[1] ἡ παράδοσις. It will be shown hereafter that the four great writers, Irenæus, Tertullian, Clement of Alexandria, and Origen, unanimously refer to Tradition in this sense.

[2] See St. Irenæus, ii. 1, expressly stating this of St. Mark's and St. Luke's Gospel, and of the Apostles generally : " quod (Evangelium) quidem tunc præconaverunt, postea vero per Dei voluntatem in Scripturis nobis tradiderunt ;" which is repeated by Euseb. *Hist.* ii. 15, who declares that the Roman Christians, not content τῇ ἀγράφῳ τοῦ θείου κηρύγματος διδασκαλία, besought Mark with many prayers ὡς ἂν καὶ διὰ γραφῆς ὑπόμνημα τῆς διὰ λόγου παραδοθείσης αὐτοῖς καταλείψοι διδασκαλίας, which St. Peter afterwards approved.

answer, that grounding of the truth in the memory,
intellect, and will, which Christianity had inaugurated.
He wrote after the pattern of those who had delivered over the word to us, having been its original
eye-witnesses and servants.[1]   A second evangelist declares that what he was putting into writing was a
very small portion indeed of what his Lord had done.[2]
Another very remarkable thing is that the Apostles
are not recorded to have put together what they had
written themselves, or others by their direction, so as
to make it one whole; far less that they ever declared
what was so written to contain the complete tradition
of what they had received.   But what they did was
to leave these writings in the hands of particular
churches, having in every case addressed them to
those who were already instructed as Christians, and
not having left among them any document whatever intended to impart the Christian faith to those
who were ignorant of it.   These writings were in
the strictest sense Scriptures of the Church, which
sometimes stated, and always in their form and construction showed that they were adapted to those
who had been taught the Christian faith by word of
mouth.   Moreover, it was left to the Church to gather
them together, and make them into one book, which
thenceforward should be *the Book;* it was left to the
Church to determine which were to be received as
inspired writings, and in accordance with the teaching
already diffused in her, and which were not.   And
this collection of the several writings from the particular Churches to which they were addressed into
one mass would seem not to have taken place until at
least three or four generations after the whole order

[1] Luke i. 2-4.   [2] John xx. 30.

and institutions of the Church had been established by oral teaching, which filled as with a flood the whole Christian people. Then, finally, the authority of the Church alone established the canon of Scripture, and separated it off from all other writings.

Now as the planting of the Church by oral teaching was a direction of the Holy Spirit, from whom the whole work of mission proceeded, so all these particulars concerning the degree in which writing was to be employed, and the manner in which that writing was to be attested, and the persons to whom it was to be addressed, were a direction of the same Spirit. That a spiritual kingdom could not have been established save by oral teaching Christians may infer with certainty, because, in fact, that method was pursued. That a portion of the great Tradition should be committed to writing they may for the same reason infer to have been necessary for the maintenance of the truth, because it was so done. That these writings were the property of the Church—her Scriptures— may be inferred with no less truth, because they were addressed only to her children, and presupposed a system of instruction already received by those who were to read them. And, finally, that they were to be understood in their right sense only by the aid of the Spirit who dictated them, is, their being given in this manner once admitted, an inference of just reasoning. It is plain, when once these things are stated, that these writings were not intended to stand alone, as ordinary books, and to be understood by themselves. Not only were they part of a great body of teaching, but a portion of a great institution, to which they incessantly alluded and bore witness. They would speak very differently to those without and to those within the kingdom of which they were documents. They would remind the instructed at every turn of doctrines which they had been taught, corroborating these and themselves explained by them. Some of them indeed were letters, and we all know how different is the meaning of letters to those who know the writer and his allusions, and to those who do not. A word of reference in these documents to a great practice of Christian life would kindle into a flame the affection of those who possessed that practice, while it would pass as a dead letter to those who had it not.[1] Such word, therefore, would be absolute proof of the practice to the former, while it would seem vague and indeterminate and no proof at all to the latter.

From what has been said we may determine the relation of the Church to the Scriptures. The Church planted everywhere by the personal oral teaching of the Apostles and their disciples, with her worship and sacraments, accepted these writings, which they left, as conformable to that teaching they had delivered by word of mouth. Moreover, she esteemed those writings as sacred because proceeding from the dictation of the one Spirit. Finally, she put them together and gave them a place apart from all other books, as forming, in conjunction with the unwritten word, her own canon or rule of faith. Thenceforth they were to be for all ages a necessary portion

---

[1] As one instance out of many take the words of St. Paul, 2 Cor. i. 22 : "He that *confirms* us with you is Christ, and that has *anointed* us is God ; who has also *sealed* us, and given the pledge of the Spirit in our hearts." How differently would this passage appear to one who had received the confirming chrism, with the words conveying it, "*Signo* te signo crucis, et *confirmo* te *chrismate* salutis ;" and to one who had lost the possession of this Sacrament. Those who have deserted the ecclesiastical tradition and practice read the Scriptures with a negative mind, and so fail to draw out the truth which is in them.

of the divine Tradition which was her inheritance from the Incarnate Word, distributed by His Spirit. They were to be in her and of her. To her belonged, first, the understanding of them ; secondly, the interpreting them to her children, out of the fund of that whole Tradition lodged in her, and by virtue of that indwelling Spirit, who, as He had created, maintained her ; as part and parcel, moreover, of that whole kingdom, of that body of worship and sacraments, which she is.

And this brings us to a further point of the utmost importance. For the Truth, which is the subject matter of all this divine Tradition or Delivery from the Incarnate Word, in order to be efficacious and permanent, approached men in the shape of a society invested with grace.[1] It was not proposed as a theory which is presented simply to the reason, and accepted or rejected by it. True, it was addressed to the reason, but only when illuminated by faith could the reason accept it. Here, again, it showed itself manifestly as " the gospel *of the kingdom*." It was the good tidings proclaimed, not simply and nakedly to man's intellect, but as the gift and at the same time the law of that kingdom which accompanied its publication by the bestowal of power to accept it, and to make it the rule of conduct. There were many whom the word, though proclaimed to them as to others, did not help, because it was not mixed with faith in those who heard it. St. Paul preached to many when the heart of one Lydia was opened to receive what he announced.[2] Thus with the first hearing of the message coincided the beginning of grace to accept it.

[1] Eine Gnadenanstalt : our language does not supply the expression.
[2] Heb. iv. 2 ; Acts xvi. 14.

But so likewise the Church supplied a storehouse of grace for the continuance of the truth in those who had once received it. Truth and grace, as they come together in her, so they remain together inseparable. Wisdom, understanding, counsel, and knowledge, which perfect the intellect, are linked in her with fortitude, piety, and fear, which perfect the will. And this which is true of the individual is true of the mass. In the Body, as well as in each single member of it, and the more because the Body is an incomparably grander creation, it is the sanctified intellect which must receive, harmonise, and develop the truth. If the sevenfold fountain of the Spirit's gifts is one in the individual, much more is it one in that Body out of whose plenitude the individual receives. Thus wherever the Apostles preached the word, if faith made it fruitful, they bestowed the sacraments.

We shall see, if we observe it closely, that it is a triple cord through which the Holy Spirit conveys His life perpetually to the Body; and in His life is the Truth.

First, there is the succession of men. As the Word Incarnate taught, so men bear on His teaching. Personal labours, intercourse from mouth to mouth, the action of men on men, the suffering of men for men, this was from the beginning, this is to be for ever, the mode of spreading His kingdom. It is not a paper kingdom, it cannot be printed off and disseminated by the post. But from His own Person it passed to Peter and the Apostles, and from them to a perpetual succession of men, whose special work it is to continue on this line by a chain never to be broken. These are the messengers, or heralds, or stewards, or ministers, or teachers, or shepherds. They are all and each of these according to the manifoldness of the gift which they carry. Through the unbrokenness of this line the continuity of the gift is secured. Through it the Redeemer, King, and Head touches, as it were, each point of time and space, and with a personal ministry lays hold of each individual through the vast extent of His Kingdom in time and space. And the gift is as living and as near to Him now as it was when St. Paul spoke of it as communicated by the imposition of his hands to his disciple; nay, as it was when He Himself breathed on His Apostles together assembled, and said, " Receive the Holy Ghost;" and will be equally living and direct from Him to the last who shall receive it to the end of time. And all this because these men who are taken up into this succession are the nerves of His mystical Body, through which runs the supply to all the members. This is the indestructible framework which He has wrought for carrying on to men His own teaching, until the whole mass grow up to that fulness of the perfect stature which He has foreseen and determined.

The second succession is that of the Truth itself committed to these men. For that plenitude of teaching which the Apostles delivered orally to the Church has never ceased to rest in her, and out of it she dispenses to all the ages her divine message. But part of this teaching by the further ordering of the Spirit of Truth has been incorporated in writing. And no one can doubt that this incorporation has given a firmness and stability to the teaching which we do not see how it could otherwise have possessed. Thus the great Tradition of the Truth poured out upon the Church has been partly written and partly unwritten; not as if there were two teachings separable from each other, but one and the same which runs in a perpetual blending. Through the written teaching we receive the very words consecrated by our Lord's use: we have the priceless privilege of knowing how He spoke; of catching the accents of His voice, and the look of His eyes, and the gestures of His body, portrayed in that narrative. The words of Him who spake as never man spake live and sound for ever in our ears; and we recognise in the structure of His sentences, which convey in a clause principles of endless application, forces on which a universe can be built, the Father's Word, and the world's Creator, and the Church's Head. Parable and apophthegm and answer, metaphor and plain speech, when used by Him, are all impregnated with this power. And now that we possess this peculiar language of the Word Incarnate, embodied and fixed for ever to our senses as well as our affections, it seems as if we could not have done without it. Then the mode in which His own Apostles apply and illustrate His doctrines, and exhibit to us the formation of the society which He came to institute, possesses a value only subordinate to His own words. The written word, it has been said,[1] gives to the whole Church through all times a sense of the truth and consistency of her teaching like that which the sense of personal identity gives to the individual respecting his own being. And again, what memory is to the single man, such is the whole tradition of the Truth in the bosom of the Church. But it is through the unwritten teaching deposited in her by the Apostles that she possesses the key to the true understanding of that which is written. The one in her practice has never been severed from the other. So dear has

[1] By Möhler.

the written word been to her that almost the blackest epithet in language, "traitor," is derived from the name which she gave to those who, under fear of persecution, surrendered to the heathen her sacred books. With these in her hand, or rather in her heart, she has directed and carried out that great system of instruction which the Apostles laid down and established by their acts. For to her what they did was as sacred as what they said, or what they wrote; and numberless acts of theirs constituted her teaching originally, and have prolonged and continued it on since.

For, besides the succession of men and the succession of doctrine, there is in her likewise the succession of institutions. As chief of these, but involving a number of subordinate rites, the Apostles with their first oral teaching delivered likewise to the Church sacraments, instituted, not by them, but by their Lord Himself, which at once embodied the truth taught by them, and conveyed the grace by which that truth was to find a home in men's heart and mind. No sooner was the first teaching of Peter at the head of the Apostles uttered, and the gift of forgiveness of sins and of adoption disclosed, than three thousand persons received the double gift by the baptism which followed. Thus they established in the Church seven great rites, encompassing the whole of human life. The regenerating power which was the beginning of the whole change that they sought to work in man was stored up in one; the confirming and developing it in a second; the feeding and increasing it in a third; the removal of obstacles to it in a fourth; the supporting and restoring the human nature so elevated, when under pressure of sickness and in fear of death, in a fifth; the blessing and consecrating the union of the species in a sixth; and, finally, the conferring that distinctive power which transmitted through all ages her Lord's gift to the Church in a seventh. This is that great and marvellous sacramental system by which the Church, dowered, as we have said, in her quality of Bride with her Lord's blood, applies that blood to His members, according to their needs. This is the perpetual consecration of matter to a supernatural end, of which the highest example is found in the Body of the Head Himself, and so it is an enfolding of human nature with the Incarnation, and a transforming it into the image of its Head. But such, likewise, is the summary of the whole written and unwritten teaching of the Church; such also, in few and brief words, the perpetual work of the succession of men whom we have described.

Thus the three successions, of men, of doctrines, and of institutions, are woven by the Holy Spirit together as three strands of a rope which cannot be broken: in the union of these three His perpetual presence dwells; and this is the spinal cord whereby He joins the Body with the Head.

Let us take instances wherein the force of this union is seen.

The first gift He bestowed upon men when the gospel of the kingdom approached them was the forgiveness of sins. This is a power belonging to God alone, as sin is an offence against His majesty. The conferring of this power upon the Apostles by our Lord Himself is explicitly recorded. But then two sacraments exhibit the application of this power, first, that of baptism, where it is given plenarily; secondly, that of penance, where it is given under restriction.

And further, an order of men is instituted for this perpetual application. Here, then, we see the force of the triple cord carrying on through all ages this great truth of the forgiveness of sins in and by the Church of God. The very definite mention of the grant of this power in the written tradition is not left exposed by itself to the action of unbelieving reason. It has a double bulwark in the two institutions which assert its perpetual exercise as a matter of history, and in the order of men established to carry it out.

Take again the doctrine of the Real Presence, upon which infidelity falls as being a proof charge of human credulity,[1] on which faith and love rest as the sovereign gift of God. The recorded words of our Lord Himself express it distinctly and emphatically; further words of His in the sixth chapter of St. John allude to it with equal force, and St. Paul repeatedly refers to it. But this is not enough for the solicitude with which the Holy Spirit has guarded it against all attack. As the great central rite of Christian worship it is presented day after day, in myriads of churches, from age to age, to the eyes and hearts of men. The act in which Christians assemble, in which they offer up at once their repentance and their requests, their thanksgivings and their praises, to Him who has formed them into one Body, lives upon this truth. And further, the order of men which is the backbone of the Church, the great Christian priesthood, made by our Lord in instituting the rite and conferring the gift, exists for its continuance. Against such a truth, defended with such bulwarks, both infidelity and heresy dash themselves with impotent rage in vain.

Thirdly, we have in the epistles of St. Paul a men-

[1] See Macaulay's Essays.

tion of the bishop's office and the duties belonging to
it. The mention is incidental, and the words not so
determinate as in the former instances given. Those
who are outside the Body, in their attack upon the
necessity of episcopacy, thought that they could cut
through these words so as to make it doubtful whether
the office of bishop, as distinguished from that of priest,
was of original institution. But then history disclosed
the fact that when the last apostle was taken from the
earth not a church existed which was not under episcopal jurisdiction, and through the whole world, by
the institution of bishops, was fulfilled the prediction,
" Instead of thy fathers thou shalt have children,
whom thou mayest make princes in all lands." Thus,
while the written record was interpreted, the unwritten teaching of the Church found a plain and
unanswerable proof in her invariable practice. All
through her long history she is seen to be governed
by bishops ; and the words of St. Paul, flanked by the
institution and the practice, are more than sufficient
to maintain the truth.

Once more let us take the primacy of St. Peter's
see in the Church. This, as is well known, rests in
the written word mainly on three great passages of
St. Matthew, St. Luke, and St. John. These, indeed,
are so specific and definite that they convey the dignity intended as clearly as the passages above referred
to convey the forgiveness of sins or the Real Presence.
But over and above these, what an overwhelming proof
in the unbroken succession of those who exercised the
primacy from the beginning, and are referred to from
age to age by the doctors, fathers, and historians of
the Church ! Beside the charter of institution stands
the long record of the work wrought in virtue of it,

the witness of the Church to it in councils, the obedience to it in fact. As the priesthood exists in
attestation of the Real Presence, so the primacy stands
beside our Lord's words, first promising and then conferring it, like the comment of eighteen hundred years,
uniform and consistent.

What we have here applied in the case of the forgiveness of sins, the Real Presence, episcopacy, and
the primacy of the Church, might be carried out in
the case of many more doctrines forming a part of the
great deposit. But it may be well to cite one instance of a truth not contained in the written word
at all, which through the unwritten teaching of the
Church has passed into universal practice. This is
not the abolition only of the Jewish Sabbath, constituted as it was by the most express divine command,
for to that abolition there is a passing reference in an
epistle of St. Paul, but the further substitution of the
day of the Resurrection, the first day of the week for
the seventh, with a modified observance. This rests
solely upon the deposit of the Church's unwritten
teaching, corroborated by universal practice from the
apostolic times.

Viewing, then, the transmission of the Truth as a
whole, and the creation of the mystical Body of Christ
as its home, and the Holy Spirit as the perpetual
Indweller who fills that treasure-house of Truth and
Grace, we may consider its maintenance as secured
by the triple succession or tradition of men, of doctrine, and of institutions which are inseparably joined
together in that its home. But there are some words
of our Lord so distinctly and translucently expressing
all this statement respecting the mode in which His
Truth was first and is ever to be transmitted, and the

the Body of Christ, *the* Teacher: so that this function of magisterial teaching is the great distinctive office of His Church, coming from above, and invested with the authority of the God-man, by which it draws to it disciples, whose consent is not the ground but the result of its authority.   Fourthly, there is the creation of the sacraments, as containing the grace which is needed for the reception of this Truth, and they are summed up in the first, which is the beginning of the new life, illumination, and perfection, and which is given in the covenant name of God, as the Christian God, and is the mark of the triune Creator, Redeemer, and Sanctifier, impressed on his own people of acquisition.   Thus Grace is for ever associated with Truth as the means whereby alone on earth Truth shall prevail and be received, and that only as the teaching of that Body whose Head is full of Grace and Truth. Fifthly, there is marked the manner of the teaching, the nature of the magisterial office created as that of a living body of men: "teaching them to observe all things whatsoever I have commanded you." The fund from which this teaching is drawn is that whole communication of truth from the Incarnate Word Himself, given to them by word of mouth, of which we have spoken above as the great Tradition or Delivery; and out of which a part is incorporated in the written word, while the whole dwells ever in the Body created to receive it, from which it is to be imparted by perpetual oral teaching.   The teaching, therefore, rests upon the perpetual presence of the Body representing Christ, and as in the days of His flesh He teaches through it, and has fixed part of His tradition in it by writing, not to the exclusion of the rest, but as the charter of a sovereign, the title-deeds of an empire, to be perpetually applied, interpreted, and developed in that whole system of institutions, by that whole race of teachers, in the life of that one Body, which He was creating. And lastly, to this perpetual living line of teachers, to this perpetual living doctrine, to this perpetual living framework of grace, He has promised His own presence without fail to the end. In this triple succession He is seen, lives, and rules, and this is His Kingdom, His Temple, His Body, His Bride, His Family, to whom He says, " Behold, I am with you all days, even to the end of the world."

From these words of our Lord, as from the whole previous argument, we gather that while the Truth which Christ imparted to His Apostles was one and complete, its development in its various relations was designedly left as the proper work of such a Body as He created. He Himself spoke as God in human flesh, uttering, that is, creative words, which gathered up in a sentence a germ of truth capable of a long series of applications, and requiring them in order to be understood. And the aptitude to make these applications, so that the truth proclaimed by Him and committed to His Apostles should penetrate through and leaven the whole human society, He gave to His mystical Body. Let us take an instance of this. The Pharisees approached Him one day to entangle Him by their words, and proposed to Him a dilemma from which they thought that He could not escape save by ruining His influence with one great party, or by encountering the danger of being charged with seditious teaching by another. They put to Him the question whether it was lawful to give tribute to Cæsar or not. Whereupon He asked them to show Him the tribute-money, and pointing to the image of the emperor upon it, uttered those famous words, " Render therefore to Cæsar the things which are Cæsar's, and to God the things which are God's." Now these words were laid up in the treasury of His Church, and by them she has had to determine the relation between the civil and the spiritual powers in the society created by Him who spake them.   Here is a vast development from a small seed : but it is a seed cast by the world's Creator and the Body's Head. And His teaching is full of such seeds, as the history of His Church is one great process of developing and harmonising and conveying to man the truth thus cast into the fallows of her soil.   It is not new truth, for He gave the germ, and no power in man could have developed it without the germ, any more than it could produce the oak without the acorn.   It is the same truth, as He taught it, but with that process passed upon it which He intended when He gave it in such a form, and when He made a living Body, to be called by His name, to propagate His teaching, to collect His members into one, and to fill the earth with the knowledge which He brought.

Such a work, therefore, the root and authorisation of which we have been attempting to delineate in this lecture, stretches over the whole field which Truth and Grace occupy, and over all the relations of men which are summed up in what they are to believe and what they are to do.   These ramifications are all but endless.   But to all these extends that giving of the Holy Ghost in his fourfold character of the Spirit of Unity, Verity, Charity, and Sanctity, which is the result of the Incarnation, and which makes the Church.   What we have said here has a special relation to Truth, and to Christian morals as resting upon

Christian dogma.* But it is impossible to separate
Truth from Grace, in their actual operation as powers :
faith and charity in the Christian are linked together,
as the intellect and the will are one soul. What we
have said is but an introduction to a sketch of the
great evolution of dogmatic truth through eighteen
centuries : but in recording its rise, the secret of its
growth, and the source of its strength, it was impossible not to bring out the great fact that Christianity
was nothing less than a divine life produced in the
world over against the existing heathenism, and laying
hold of the whole soul of man, in which, as we have
just said, intellect and will are inseparable. It did
not consist in anything which individuals believed,
however true ; but in a society of which Truth and
Grace were the joint spring, and it was produced in
the midst of a world which had to a great extent
forfeited both Truth and Grace, while both returned
to it as the gift of Christ assuming man's nature.
This error and distraction of heathenism, and this
great unity of Christian life grounded in faith and
charity which rose up against it, were profoundly felt
by all the Fathers, being eye-witnesses of the old
world and the new. Their writings express it again
and again, with the vividness which only eye-witnesses,
who are likewise actors and sufferers, feel. In nothing,
perhaps, do they so differ from modern writers as in
the energy with which they appreciate the supernatural
character of the Christian, and the wonderful being
and endowment of that Christian Body which impressed this character on its members. One cause,
we may suppose, of this was the sight of heathenism
before them with all its impurities and its impotence
to produce good. So they were not even tempted to

that naturalism which is the besetting sin of our age and these countries. It would have seemed to them not only an ingratitude but an absurdity to refer to the inborn force of humanity a change equally of the intellect and of the will which they saw to belong only to the power of Christ revealed in His Church. We will cite one such passage as a conclusion to this discussion, and because it represents the whole train of thought which we have been drawing out.[1]

" Before He came, Who was sent, at once a mystery, a sacrifice, priest, and God, all sacred and mystical communications made by angels to our forefathers, or their own deeds, were foreshadowings of Him, in order that every creature should proclaim that One was to come for the salvation of all. For as the sin of impiety had torn us from the One true Almighty God, and rent our whole being, it was meet that He in His mercy should command many things to utter a cry for the One to come, that thus called upon, the One should come, and that things should bear witness to His having come. Thus it behoved us to come to the One free from our burdens, and being dead in our souls, and mortal on account of our sins, that we should love the Sinless One, Who died for us in the flesh. Made one believing in Him Risen, and rising with Him in spirit, it was meet that we should be justified in the One Just. Nor were we, His members, to despair of rising again in our flesh, seeing that our Head has gone before us. Cleansed now by our faith, and hereafter by vision reconciled to God by our Mediator, we should adhere to the One, enjoy the One, remain one."

[1] St. Aug. *de Trin.* c. vii. 11, tom. viii. 817.

LECTURE X

THE FIRST AGE OF THE MARTYR CHURCH

"Magnum hæreditatis mysterium! Templum Dei factus est uterus nescientis virum. Non est pollutus ex ea carnem assumens. Omnes gentes venient dicentes, Gloria tibi, Domine."

Antiphon on Vespers of Circumcision.

THE world which Augustus and Tiberius ruled was not conscious of the fact that there was an order of truth, and of morality based upon that truth, the maintenance of which was to be purchased, and cheaply purchased, with the loss of life, or of all that made life valuable. This world was indeed familiar with the thought and with the practice of sacrificing life for one object—an object which collected all the natural affections and interests of a man together, and presented them to him in the most attractive form, his country. Greek and Roman history, and indeed the history of all nations up to that time, had been full of instances in which privations and sufferings were endured, and, if necessary, life itself given up for wife and children, for the dear affections of house and home, for friends, for freedom, for fatherland. Man, civilised and uncivilised, was alike capable of this, and capable of it in profusion. Rome had many a Regulus and Sparta many a Leonidas in the humblest ranks of their citizens: Gaul had thousands as noble as Vercingetorix, and Spain not one but many Numantias. Human nature had never

been wanting in the courage to die for the visible
goods of human life. But to labour, to combat, to
endure pain, sorrow, privations, to suffer in every form
for the invisible goods of a future life, to recognise,
that is, an inviolable order of religion and morality, so
far superior to all that a man can grasp and hold in
his possession, to wife, children, goods, friends, freedom,
and fatherland, and to life adorned and crowned with
these, that any or all of these, and life itself, are to be
sacrificed for its preservation; this may be said to be
a thought of which the whole heathen world ruled by
Augustus and Tiberius was unconscious.[1]   For other
reasons also it was familiar enough with the sacrifice of
life, since the continual practice of war and the permanent institution of slavery had made human life the
cheapest of all things in its eyes.   And further, to die
rather than to live dishonoured was still the rule of
the nobler among the millions who yielded to the sway
of Augustus.   But to die for the maintenance of moral
truth, that is, for faith,—this was known indeed to
the Jews, who had already their "cloud of witnesses"
to it; but it was unknown to heathendom, which has
in all its ranks and times but one man [2] to offer
whose death approaches to such a sacrifice, and
therefore shines with incomparable lustre among
all deeds of purely human heroism.   But the death
of Socrates found in this no imitators, he created
here no line of followers; and he stands alone in

---

[1] Tertullian, *Apol.* 50.   "O gloriam licitam, quia humanam, cui nec
præsumptio perdita nec persuasio desperata deputatur in contemptu
mortis et atrocitatis omnimodæ, cui tantum pro patria, pro imperio, pro
amicitia pati permissum est, quantum pro Deo non licet."   See again
the instances he collects *ad Martyres*, 4 ; and Eusebius, *Hist.* 5, prooem.,
draws the same contrast.

[2] Celsus only alleges the suffering of Socrates as a parallel to that of
the martyrs.   Origen *c. Cels.* i. 3.

this greatness, an exception to an otherwise invariable
rule.

However, in our two preceding lectures we have
been describing something much more than the exhibition of this order of truth; that is, we have set
forth the union of it with a Person, who both exhibits
it in Himself, and is the source of it to others. And
the difference between these two things is very great.
Many at different times have said, "I teach the truth."
One only has said, "I am the Truth:" and to say
it is the most emphatic indirect assumption of Godhead which can be conceived. And with it that One
also joined a similar expression, containing the same
assumption of Godhead, and which equally was never
approached by any other teacher. "I am the Life."
The union of the Truth at once and of the Life with
His Person, which is thus become the root of both to
human nature, was the subject of the last two lectures. Now, as we have said, that there was an order
of truth sacred and inviolable above all things, was
borne witness to by the Hebrew martyrs, and therefore was not new to the chosen race of Israel, though
it was new to heathendom, at the time at which our
Lord appeared. But the union of the Truth and of
the Life with the Person of One appearing visibly in
the world as man, was as new to the Hebrews as to
the heathen, was an absolute novelty to human nature.
And so the Christian Faith also, as a system of belief
and action, that is, as embracing the mind and the will
of man, as giving both Truth and Life, is entirely new
in this respect; that in this double action it is in its
origin and in its whole course and maintenance bound
up with a Person. Thus all which it teaches is not
naked truth, unlocalised as it were, and impersonal,

but is the development of relations in which the disciples of Christ stand to Him; for instance, as King,
as God, as Head, as Bridegroom, as Father.   As these,
He is at once the Truth and the Life.   Thus it is
that the Christian Faith flows out of the Person of
Christ the God-man; and, as its Truth is centred
in that Person, so also its continuous Life depends
on Him.

And further, as the connection of doctrine, or
truth, and of life, that is, action, with a Person is
the point from which all this movement springs,
and thus is absolutely new, so the term to which
it reaches is the creation of something in both
these things correlative to that Person, the creation
of a Kingdom, a Temple, a Body, a Mother, a Race.
In this respect also the term is as new as that from
which it springs.   That He is the Truth and the Life
is shown in this creation, which has a distinctive character, as He has, an unique existence, and an organic
unity with Him.

The subject now before us is to describe as an
historic fact how the duty of maintaining, propagating, and dying for the truth and conduct thus
identified with the Person of Christ, was carried
out through many generations and under difficulties
which seemed to preclude the possibility of its
success; and to show how this great creation, starting from the day of Pentecost, made a home and
established itself in the Roman Empire, by which,
after a conflict of nearly three hundred years, it was
finally recognised.

The worship of the one true God had been fixed in
the children of Abraham, Isaac, and Jacob, as the faith
which made them a nation, that is, as the dogma on

tians had no such justification in Roman eyes for their exclusive worship. They were not a nation nor a province of the Empire; they had not, therefore, that title for their worship which constituted their charter of toleration to all besides, including the Jew, who worshipped the same God. For the Christians worshipped Him, not as their ancestral God, but as the Father of that Son who had taken human flesh, and become the Saviour of men. Their worship of the one true God was not only exclusive, but in and through the fact of the Incarnation claimed the homage of all men to it. It knew of no bond of brotherhood but in Him who had deigned to call men His brethren. Thus its special character and pre-eminent glory were the cause of its persecution, and from the moment that it came before the notice of the Roman governor not as a Jewish sect but as a distinct belief, it was considered as not a lawful religion. Thus too it was that the selfsame point which kindled Jewish hatred entailed Roman persecution. The Christian faith was a mortal offence to the Jew because it extended what had been his special privileges to all the Gentiles. He abhorred the substitution of the Person of the God-man for the race of Abraham after the flesh; as the Roman at once despised and hated a worship which not only adhered to one God, but dethroned from his political supremacy the Capitoline Jupiter, and whose title rested not on tradition and national inheritance, but on a fact touching the whole race of man, and therefore claiming the allegiance of the whole race—the assumption of human nature by a Divine Person. Thus the doctrine in which lay the whole creative force, the truth and the life of Christianity, was that which from the first caused the dislike of the Jew and the persecution of the Gentile—the kingship of Christ, involving the headship of a universal religion, and a power which was not that of Cæsar.

We have, then, now to treat of a period of 280 years, homogeneous in its character from the beginning to the end, for it is the carrying out by a people ever increasing in number and strength of that good confession made before Pontius Pilate—that witness at its proper time of which St. Paul[1] in its first stage said that he was the herald and apostle. The course and life of Christians during these ten generations is to be the prolongation of this testimony, the embodiment of this confession. It is as soldiers, imitators, followers of one Chief, that all appear on the scene in their respective order.[2] It is by a direct virtue drawn from the cross of that Chief that they move onward to their own passion. They endure and they conquer simply as under His command, and because He endured and conquered before them. Their oath of military fidelity is the bond of their discipline ; they prevail because they are His, and because they are one in Him :

> "And they stand in glittering ring
> Round their warrior God and King—
> Who before and for them bled—
> With their robes of ruby red,
> And their swords of cherub flame."

The whole process and cause of Christians during this

---

[1] 1 Tim. vi. 13 ; ii. 6.
[2] " Æmulos nos ergo Sibi esse voluit, ac primus virtute cœlesti injustorum justus obtemperavit arbitrio ; dans scilicet secuturis viam, ut pius Dominus exemplum famulis Se præbendo, ne onerosus præceptor a quodam putaretur. Pertulit ante illa quæ aliis perferenda mandavit." *Epist. Ecc. Smyr.* i. Ruinart, p. 31.

long period, the ground of their accusation, the conduct and principles of the judges, and their judgment, are summed up as in a parable in that scene which passed before Pilate, while the subsequent day of Pentecost is in the same manner an image of the final result won in these three hundred years. For as the crucifixion of the Truth in the Person of Christ is followed by the descent of the Holy Ghost forming the Church, so the persecution and crucifixion of the truth in ten generations of His people is followed by the Empire's public recognition of His eternal kingdom—of that Body of Christ seen visibly in a council of its prelates assembling freely from all lands.

Take first the seventy years which form the Apostolic age. What do we find as the result when St. John, the last Apostle, is taken away? In a large number of cities throughout the Roman Empire a community has been planted after the pattern of that which we have described as arising at Jerusalem, and by the same means, the power of oral teaching. Every such community has at its head its bishop, or angel, who sums up and represents in his own person the people over which he presides. This is exactly the picture presented to us at the close of this period by St. John in the Apocalypse, when he is directed by our Lord personally appearing to him to write seven letters to as many bishops of cities on the seaboard of the province of Asia. Each, with his people, is addressed as a unit. One, " I know thy works, and thy labour, and thy endurance, and how thou canst not bear those which are evil : " a second, " Fear not what thou art about to suffer ; behold, the devil shall cast some of you into prison : " a third, " I have against thee some few things, that thou hast there some who hold the

doctrine of Balaam." [1]   Each has around him his
council of priests, his ministering deacons, his faithful
people.   The last Apostle is still living; but in all
these communities many exist, both of teachers and
taught, who have learned Christian doctrine, either
from the mouth of an Apostle or the comrade of an
Apostle—a Mark, a Luke, a Silvanus, a Clemens.
Thus they live mainly upon oral teaching : the voice
which went forth from the day of Pentecost is sounding freshly in their ears.   Doctrine is in the stage of
simple tradition and authority.   The writings of the
New Testament are completed, but being addressed to
various parts of the Church, are best known to those
for whom they were written.   They are not yet collected and made the common patrimony of the whole
Church.   St. John leaves the earth without performing
any such function; without setting the seal of his
apostolical authority upon the New Testament as a
whole ; nay, the authorship of some of his own writings, as we now receive them, will be partially con-
tested after his death before their final reception.   Of
the absolute number of these Christian communities,
and of the multitude they severally embrace, we have
no account; we can form no estimate, save to infer
that the whole number of the faithful, at the end of
this period, was very small in comparison with the
mass out of which they had been drawn.   Still it was
a germ with a living force of expansion, planted in
every considerable spot of the empire ; and wherever
it was planted, a Christian people, in the full sense of
the word, existed, having a complete spiritual life of
its own, possessing the sacraments which insured the
beginning and the continuance of that life, an order of

[1] Apoc. ii. 2, 10, 14.

worship based on the great central fact which made them a people, and a ministry charged with the power to teach and to convey on to their successors the doctrines delivered to them.

But in the meantime how had the Empire treated it? In these seventy years it has traversed the last seven years of the Emperor Tiberius, and the whole principates of Caligula, Claudius, and Nero; the revolutionary crisis in which Galba, Otho, and Vitellius reigned for an instant, and then the settled time of Vespasian, Titus, Domitian, and Nerva. Now, during this period its treatment by the Empire has been a singular reproduction of what passed in the hall of Pilate. For the Jewish religion was one allowed by Roman law. The profession of it entailed no penalty. Now the first heralds of the Gospel, as Jews, preached their message boldly and publicly, and in doing so it does not seem that Roman law would have interfered with them.[1] At this stage it looked upon Christians as a sect of Jews. As no authority of the Empire had interfered with the public ministry of our Lord, so it would seem to have left the ministry of His disciples in the first instance free. It is from another quarter that opposition arises. The Jew in his jealous anger at the promulgation of a Messiah and a spiritual kingdom which is not after Jewish taste, both because it is a kingdom not of this world, and because it raises the Gentile to co-inheritance with the race of Abraham, drags the Christian missionary before the tribunal of the Roman magistrate and imputes to him "sedition." Then many a Gallio, many

---

[1] This is what Tertullian calls "sub umbraculo insignissimæ religionis, certe licitæ," *Apolog.* 21 ; and *ad Nationes*, i. 11, "Nos quoque ut Judaicæ religionis propinquos."

a Felix, many a Festus have as it were unwillingly
to enter into and decide these questions of the Jewish
law. It would seem that converts to the Christian
faith in these its earliest days might long have escaped
the notice of the magistrate, as belonging to a Jewish
sect, but for this enmity of the Jews themselves. But
as the teachers of the new faith everywhere addressed
themselves first to their countrymen, so everywhere
they found these countrymen alive to their progress
and bitterly set against it.[1]   This state of things is
pretty well expressed by that answer of the Roman
Jews to St. Paul when he excuses himself before them
for having been compelled to appeal to the Emperor
Nero : " as concerning this sect, we know that it is
spoken against everywhere." [2]   This, however, was
Jewish, not Roman, contradiction.   So far as everywhere Jewish hatred and jealousy could malign and
counterwork the progress of the Christian Faith, and
bring suffering on its teachers, it had been done.
But nevertheless with this exception it would seem
that for thirty-five years after the day of Pentecost
that faith had been freely and publicly taught throughout the Empire.   It was through the malignity of his
own countrymen, stirring up a dangerous conspiracy
against him, that St. Paul felt himself compelled to
appeal to the emperor, and the result of his appeal
was that he was set free.   But in the year 64 another
state of things had arisen.   The ruin of a large part
of Rome by fire had brought a great odium upon
Nero.   Now his wife Poppæa is said to have been a
Jewish proselyte, he himself to have been surrounded

---

[1] See Justin Martyr, *Dial. c. Tryph.* 17, who speaks of the Jews as
sending everywhere deputies in order to defame Christians.

[2] Acts xxviii. 22.

by Jewish influences, and nothing is more probable than that Jewish hatred, which had tracked the Christians everywhere, pursued them especially here, and suggested them to him both as authors of the conflagration, and as convenient scapegoats whereon to divert the odium against himself which had arisen from it.   Thus he took the opportunity of exposing to shame and torment, as victims of the popular dislike, and in popular opinion guilty of " hatred of the human race," or of being hated by them, " a vast multitude " [1] of Christians, who, says the heathen historian, were put to the most exquisite suffering, being wrapt in the skins of wild beasts, and torn to pieces by dogs, or crucified, or clothed in garments of pitch and set on fire to illuminate the night.   Thus it is, as decorations of Nero's games, in his gardens of the Vatican, where the obelisk from Heliopolis, once the ornament of his circus, now bears witness to the victory of Christ, that Christians first come before us in the pages of Roman historians, just at the middle of the period we are now describing, thirty-five years after the Ascension.

It may be considered part of this first persecution that the two great Apostles—Peter, who had founded the Roman Church, and Paul, who after its first foundation had helped to build it up—were condemned in the last year of Nero, and by his deputies [2] during his absence, to suffer as Christians, the one the death of a Roman citizen by the sword, and the other that of a slave by crucifixion.   Thus the two great brethren by enduring together the martyr's death, the highest mark of Christian charity, sealed their joint founda-

---

[1] Tacitus, *Ann.* xv. 44.

[2] Ὁ Παῦλος, μαρτυρήσας ἐπὶ τῶν ἡγουμένων, οὕτως ἀπηλλάγη τοῦ κόσμου.   St. Clem. Rom. *ad Cor.* 5.

tion of Christian Rome, that like as the Rome which
had gained the conquest of the world by the strong
hand of violence, had been planted in the blood of one
brother shed by another, so the Rome which was to
be the centre of Christ's kingdom, and in the words
of St. Ignatius "preside over charity," should have
for her founders brethren in supernatural love, pouring
forth their blood together for the seat of that Christian unity which binds the earth in one.

But this persecution by Nero is not transitory in
its consequences.   The emperor had judged that
Christians as such professed a religion not allowed
by the Roman laws, and were guilty therein of a
capital crime.   This crime, if technically expressed,
would amount to sacrilege and treason; [1] for they
could not acknowledge the Roman gods as gods, nor
the emperor as Pontifex Maximus; nor could they
swear by his genius, which was the oath expressing
fidelity to the Roman constitution in its civil and religious aspect.   This was that "hatred of the human
race," that is, in other words, of the Roman Empire, of
which in the eyes of Tacitus and Pliny, of Nero now
and of Trajan afterwards, they were guilty as Christians.   But the singular thing is this, that the Jew,
who was the first to drag them before the Roman
tribunal, who was their omnipresent, ever-ready antagonist and traducer, though he worshipped one only
God, though he abhorred the whole Roman polytheism,
though he swore not by the genius of the emperor,
was exempt from punishment : his religion was recognised by Roman law and the senate its interpreter,

---

[1] Tertull. *Apol.* 10. "Sacrilegii et majestatis rei convenimur : summa
hæc causa, immo tota est."   Lassaulx says, "die beiden Hauptank-
lagen, die Religion-verachtung, die Majestäts-beleidigung."   *Fall des
Hellenismus*, p. 11.

because it was the national and time-honoured religion of a constituent part of the Empire. On the same ground the vilest Egyptian, Asiatic, African idol was allowed the worship of those who claimed it as their ancestral god. The Christian Faith was the sole exception to this universal tolerance, because it was not the religion of a subject nation, because it was new, because, in short, it rested on principles which, if carried out, would sweep away the whole fabric of polytheism on which the Roman State rested. And the act of Nero had its great importance in that it formally distinguished the Christian from the Jewish religion, and took away from it by a legal decision of the State's highest authority the claim to be considered "licit."

Nero then bestows the crown of martyrdom on St. Peter and St. Paul, and on what Tacitus calls, even within Rome alone, a vast multitude. But he does more than this. On the first appearance of Christians before the supreme authority he so applies an existing law to their case as to establish their liability under it to capital punishment, and this liability rests upon them henceforth down to the time of Constantine. It is by no means always carried out; it is often suspended, sometimes for many years together, according to the character of the ruling prince, or the maxims of his government, or the state itself of the Empire. But it is henceforth the legal position of Christians. It is a danger which besets their condition, and may be called into action at any moment, in any city of the Empire, from any motive of private enmity, cupidity, or passion. It is the legal Roman equivalent and interpretation of their Master's words, "You shall be hated of all men for My name's sake."[1]

[1] Matt. x. 22; xxiv. 9.

How often, and in how many instances, it was
carried out in this period of seventy years we have no
means of telling ; but another emperor is named as a
persecutor.   Domitian not only put to death as Christian his cousin, the Consul Flavius Clemens, but, as it
would seem, a great many others at Rome, in the
latter years of his principate.[1]   Domitian and Nero
are mentioned as persecutors by Melito when addressing Marcus Aurelius, and by Tertullian,[2] in the time
of Severus, though it was the object of both to make
the emperors appear to have been not unfavourable
to Christians.   But, independent of any general act
which would constitute an emperor a persecutor,[3] this
liability to punishment,[4] in virtue of which the con-
fessor or martyr was brought before the local magistrates, was that under which individual Christians, in
most peaceful times, and in the reign of emperors
generally just and moderate, endured their sufferings.
The Emperor Tiberius is said by Tertullian to have
brought before the senate a proposition to allow the
Christian Faith as a lawful religion.   Had this been
done, the whole course of Christian history in these

[1] St. Clemens Rom., writing just after Domitian's time, associates
as sufferers with St. Peter and St. Paul in his own time πολὺ πλῆθος
ἐκλεκτῶν, οἵτινες πολλὰς αἰκίας καὶ βασάνους διὰ ζῆλον παθόντες ὑποδεῖγμα
κάλλιστον ἐγένοντο ἐν ἡμῖν.   Ad. Cor. 6.

[2] Euseb. *Hist.* iv. 25 ; Tertull. *Apol.* 5.

[3] In Tertullian's words, " debellator Christianorum," *Apol.* 5.

[4] Thus a late Protestant writer, Schmidt (*Geschichte der Denk- und
Glaubensfreiheit*, p. 165), remarks of the condition of Christians, "Voll-
kommen gewiss ist, dass unter Domitian eine neue Drangperiode für
die Christen begann, die sich in Verfolgungen, in Hinrichtungen, und
Verbannungen äusserte. (*Dio.* 67, 14, und die Ausleger.)   Damals
soll auch der Apostel Johannes nach Pathmos verwiesen worden sein.
Erst Nerva lüftete wiederum diesen Druck, indem er den Verhafteten
die Freiheit gab, und die Verbannten zurückberief. (*Dio.* 68, 1.)   *Es
war dies aber doch nur als eine Amnestie, als ein Gnadenact anzusehen,
nicht als eine Anerkennung der Unsträflichkeit, wie das schwankende
Verhalten des nicht minder hochherzigen und freisinnigen Trajan zur
Genüge darthut.*"

three centuries would have been changed. As it was, every one, in becoming a Christian, accepted the chance that he might thereby be called upon to forfeit the possession of wife, children, goods, every civil right, and life itself.

The end of the reign of the first Antonine, in the year 161, furnishes us with a second fitting epoch at which we may estimate the growth and position in the Empire of the Christian Faith.

During the sixty years which elapse from the death of St. John to the accession of Marcus, the Roman Empire is ruled by three sovereigns, who have each left a fair name and a considerable renown behind them, and who, compared with most of those who preceded or who followed them, may almost be termed great. Trajan by his military successes raised to the highest point the credit of the Roman arms, by his moderation in civil government effaced the remembrance of Domitian's cruelties, and gave the Romans perhaps as much liberty as they could bear. His successor Hadrian, joining great energy, administrative ability, and moderation of his own to the fear and respect for the Roman name, which the powerful arm of Trajan had spread around, was able at once to exercise his army with unwearied discipline, and to maintain the empire at its full tide of power in honourable peace, while Antoninus crowned the forty years of equable and generally just government— bestowed on the Roman world by Trajan and Hadrian —with a further happy period of more than half that length, wherein the glory of the empire may be said to have culminated. Imperial Rome never saw again such a day of power, or such a prospect of security, as when Antoninus celebrated the secular games at the completion of nine hundred years ; and for ages afterwards his name carried respect, and men looked back on his reign as on an ideal period of happiness for those whom he ruled.

One of the most competent observers of our time has marked the last ten years of the reign of Pius as the period at which the independent development of Graeco-Roman heathenism terminated, when it had exhausted all the forms of its own inward life, since the Neoplatonic philosophy which is the only striking product of intelligence that arises afterwards, is manifestly due to the antagonism with Christianity, and is no pure offspring of the heathen spirit.[1] From this time forth Christian influences become unmistakable in their action upon heathen thought and society. This, then, affords another reason why we should endeavour to trace the progress and extension which the Church had reached at this point.

Now a contemporary of Antoninus declares that in his time, that is, about the year 150, there was no race of men, either barbarians or Greeks, none even of Scythian nomads roaming in waggons, or of pastoral tribes dwelling in tents, among whom prayers and thanksgivings were not offered to the Father and Creator of the universe in the name of the crucified Jesus.[2] Thus, in a hundred and twenty years the Church had outstripped the limits of the empire. The germ which in the time of St. John was rooted in the chief cities, had spread out thence and increased, taking more and more possession of the soil in all directions.   Still we must consider the Chris-

[1] Döllinger, *Heidenthum und Judenthum*, Vorwort, iv.
[2] Justin, *Dialog. with Tryphon*, 117.   Tertullian, fifty years later, *adv. Judæos*, 7, goes beyond this.

tian Church in each place of its occupation as a small
minority of the people: nor is there any reason to
doubt the statement made by Celsus, that at the
period when he wrote, the middle of the second
century, the Christian faith counted few of the educated, distinguished, and rich among its adherents;[1]
for Origen, in replying· to him, alleges no specific
example to the contrary. Yet, here too we must
consider the justice of Origen's remark,[2] that these
classes are everywhere few in proportion to the poor
and ignorant, and that Christianity being the day-
star arising on every soul, took of all classes alike.
So much, then, as to the Church's material extension :
now as to its internal growth.

As this period opens, comrades of the Apostles
still abound in the churches. We know of several
instances wherein such persons hold eminent rank.
At Rome, St. Clement is the third successor of St.
Peter ; and St. Irenæus,[3] recording him as such eighty
years afterwards, specially notes that he had seen and
lived with Apostles, and had their preaching still
sounding in his ears, and their tradition before his
eyes ; at Antioch, St. Ignatius, second after the same
St. Peter ; in the See of Jerusalem, St. Simeon, the
brother of James, still survives ; at Smyrna, St. John's
disciple Polycarp is bishop. Many more such St.
Irenæus declares that there were. This would pre-
pare us for the strength with which the principle of
authority and tradition was held, and show how

---

[1] Kellner, *Hellenismus und Christenthum*, p. 85.
[2] Origen *cont. Cels.* i. 27.
[3] Lib. iii. 3. Ἔτι ἔναυλον τὸ κήρυγμα τῶν ἀποστόλων καὶ τὴν παράδοσιν
πρὸ ὀφθαλμῶν ἔχων, οὐ μόνος, ἔτι γὰρ πολλοὶ ἐπελείποντο τότε ἀπὸ τῶν
ἀποστόλων δεδιδαγμένοι: where τὸ κήρυγμα and ἡ παράδοσις τῶν ἀποστόλων indicate the whole body of truth which they communicated to
the Church, whether written or unwritten.

Ephesians.   After saying that he had "received their whole multitude in the person of Onesimus, their bishop," he continues: "It is, then, fitting that you should by all means glorify Jesus Christ who has glorified you; that by a uniform obedience you may be perfectly joined together in the same mind and in the same judgment, and may all speak alike concerning everything, and that being subject to the bishop and the presbytery, you may be altogether sanctified. I am not giving you commands, as if I were any one; for, though I am in bonds for His name, I am not yet perfected in Jesus Christ.   For now I begin to learn, and I speak to you as my fellow-disciples, for I had need to be encouraged by you in faith, exhortation, endurance, long-suffering.   But since charity suffers me not to be silent to you, I have taken on me to exhort you to run together all with the mind of God.   For Jesus Christ, your inseparable life, is the mind of the Father, as also the bishops, placed in their several limits, are the mind of Jesus Christ. Therefore you should run together with the bishop's mind, as indeed you do.   So then in your concord and harmonious charity Jesus Christ is sung.   And each several one of you makes up the chorus; so that all being harmonious in concord, you take up the melody in unity, and sing with one voice through Jesus Christ to the Father, that He may hear you, and perceive by your good works that you are members of His Son.   It is good for you then to be in blameless unity, that you may always have fellowship with God."   And then he adds : "For if I in a short time have had such familiarity with your bishop, and that not human, but spiritual, how much more should I think you happy, who are so fused with him as

the Church with Jesus Christ, and as Jesus Christ
with the Father, that all things may be accordant in
unity." [1]

This is an incidental passage out of a very short
letter, in which the speaker is addressing practical
exhortations to the people of a great church, founded
by St. Paul about sixty years before, dwelt in by St.
John up to about fifteen years of the time at which
he was speaking. We should not in such a writing
expect St. Ignatius to speak with the scientific correct-
ness of a theologian, nor is he completely exhibiting
his subject in a treatise ; yet here, as it were at the
first moment after the Apostles have left the earth, we
have a picture of the Church as a world-wide institution, held together by a divine unity, which has its
seat in the Person of Christ as the mind of the Father.
It is a composite unity which is contemplated in the
image of a harp with its strings pouring forth one
song—the song of Christ—to the Father. It is a
unity wide as the earth ; for the bishops, placed in
their several limits, constitute the mind of Christ, who
is Himself the Father's mind. It is the unity of the
diocese, for it is summed up in the bishop : but it is
the unity likewise of the whole Church, for the bishops
are linked together in One whose mind they collec-
tively represent, and that One is He from whose
Person their authority radiates ; in whom, as he says
in this same letter, "the old kingdom was being destroyed, God appearing in the form of a man, unto
the newness of eternal life." [2]   Again, it is not merely
an outward unity of government, but an inward unity
of the truth held in common, and also held as given
by authority : not truth, as a result of the curiosity of

[1] St. Ignat. *ad Ephes.* i.–iv.   [2] *Ad Ephes.* xix.

the human intellect, rather truth, as a participation in the mind of Christ. Thus the Catholic unity of government is at the same time a unity of belief, which two unities are not, in fact, separable, for their principle is one in the Person of Christ, in respect of whom submission to the Ruler is one and the same thing with belief in the truth revealed by Him, who is King no less than Word, Word no less than King.

We have, then, here the principle of authority and tradition as seated in the hierarchy, and at the same time the whole order and unity of the Church as girdling the world by its chain of the Episcopate, and as possessing the truth and exhibiting it in its quality of an institution. It is before us and at work in its succession of men, in its sacraments which they administer,[1] in its truth which is imparted by the one and delivered by the other. It is no vague congeries of opinions held by individuals with the diversity of individuals, but a body strongly organised, and possessing an imperishable life, the life of its Author. And we have all this mentioned as fulfilled at the distance of one life from our Lord's Ascension, while indeed his kinsman and elder in age, St. Simeon, is still bishop of Jerusalem, and mentioned by one of whom a beautiful though insufficiently-grounded legend says that he was that child whom our Lord had called and placed before His disciples as the model of those who should enter into His kingdom. He was at least so near in time to Christ that this could be said of him. He is

---

[1] Another point on which St. Ignatius dwells repeatedly is the receiving the flesh of Christ in the Eucharist : thus he says of the heterodox, *ad Smyrn.* 6 : " They abstain from the Eucharist and prayer, because they do not confess that the Eucharist is that flesh of our Saviour Jesus Christ which suffered for our sins, which in His goodness the Father raised."

the bishop of Antioch ; he is on his way to be thrown
to the beasts in the Colosseum at Rome ; [1] he is wel-
comed on his way by church after church, and he sees
and describes the bishops, in their several boundaries
through the earth, as each maintaining the mind of
Christ in the unity of His Body.

Such is the Church merely stated as a fact towards
the beginning of the second century.

And the trial which in these sixty years the Church
was going through was well calculated to test her
constitution. It is against the spread of false doctrine that St. Ignatius in these epistles so constantly
appeals to the unity of the faithful among each other.[2]
He warns them to use only Christian nourishment,
and to abstain from strange food, which is heresy.[3]
The Church was then continually receiving into her
bosom converts at all ages of life, some from the Jews,
many more from the Gentiles ; among these, therefore,
minds brought up in Jewish prejudices, and others
which had run havoc in eastern superstitions and
systems of philosophy. In the course of these sixty
years she probably multiplied many times over in
number ; and the multiplication was rather by the
accession of adults than by the education of children
born of Christian parents. The Church was composed
of a small minority of the general population scattered
at wide intervals over an immense empire ; and, so far
from being assisted by the civil power, was under con-

---

[1] He says, *ad Rom.* ii. : Ὅτι τὸν ἐπίσκοπον Συρίας ὁ Θεὸς κατηξίωσεν
εὑρεθῆναι εἰς δύσιν ἀπὸ ἀνατολῆς μεταπεμψάμενος. Merivale, *Hist.* c. lxv.
p. 150, note 1, says, "We are at a loss to account for the bishop being
sent to suffer martyrdom at Rome." This passage in the epistle confirms
the acts of martyrdom. It was the wish of Trajan to make a great
example, and the Bishop of Rome, St. Alexander, was at this time in
prison, and shortly afterwards martyred.

[2] See *Epist. ad Magnes.* 13.   [3] *Ad Trall.* 6.

stant persecution from it. Whatever force her spiritual government possessed could be exercised only by the voluntary submission of her members. Let us weigh the fact that, under these circumstances, a number of heresies arose. Some were of Jewish, some of Gentile parentage. But we are not here concerned either with their cause or with their matter; we dwell at present only on the fact of their existence. In number they were many; in character most diverse; they arose and flourished in different places. Hardly anywhere was the Church free from them. Let us ask only one question here: By what power were they resisted? The human mind had then the fullest liberty of action in Christians. It was by a free choice—a choice accompanied with danger, and persisted in through suffering—that men became Christians. The liberty which men exercised in becoming Christians they could use further against Christian doctrine, by innovating; by mixing it up with other doctrines, with which, perhaps, their minds had been familiar before their conversion; by developing it after their own fashion. The desire of fame, the self-will of genius, the mere luxury of thought, would offer a continual temptation to such a course. Many, from one motive or another, fell into it. The question which we repeat is, What power prevented the one Church from breaking up under this process of free thought into fragments? These heresies began even while the Apostles were teaching. St. Peter, St. Paul, and St. John speak strongly against them. They swarm in the two generations succeeding the death of St. John. How is it that, at the accession of Marcus Aurelius, Christians having passed the limits of the empire, and being found so far as the

wandering tribes of the north, there is still one Church,
surrounded, indeed, by a multitude of sects, differing
from her and from each other, but herself distinguished and unmistakable among them all? We
think the epistles of St. Ignatius furnish us with a
reply to this question. As we have seen above, he
views the Church in each place as a community closely
bound together under a spiritual government which is
summed up in the bishop, while the bishops in their
several dioceses are as closely linked to each other, and
all form one society, wherein is Jesus Christ. And
these two truths are not separated from each other,
but the unity of the part is deduced from the unity
of the whole, and is subordinate to it. See, first,
with what force he states the unity of the diocese.[1]
"Avoid divisions, as the beginning of evils. Follow
all of you the bishop as Jesus Christ the Father, and
the presbytery as the Apostles, and reverence the
deacons as God's command. Let no one without the
bishop do aught of what appertains to the Church.
Let that be deemed a sure Eucharist which is under
the bishop, or under him who has the bishop's authority for it. Wherever the bishop appears, there let
the multitude (of the faithful) be." But this strict
unity of the diocese is derived from that of the whole
Church; for he adds as the reason of the foregoing,
"just as wherever Jesus Christ is, there is the Catholic
Church."[2] This is the first time when the word
"catholic" is known to be used, and it is applied to

---

[1] *Ad Smyrn.* viii.

[2] Compare with this expression of St. Ignatius that of the Church of
Polycarp, fifty years later, describing how after his martyrdom, σὺν τοῖς
Ἀποστόλοις καὶ πᾶσι δικαίοις ἀγαλλιώμενος, δοξάζει τὸν Θεὸν καὶ Πατέρα,
καὶ εὐλογεῖ τὸν Κύριον ἡμῶν καὶ κυβερνήτην τῶν [ψυχῶν τε καὶ] σωμάτων
ἡμῶν, καὶ ποιμένα τῆς κατὰ τὴν οἰκουμένην καθολικῆς ἐκκλησίας. *Acta
Polycarpi*, xix. ; Ruinart, p. 45.

the Church as its distinctive character, to convey the
two attributes of unity and universality, in connection
with the Person of Christ, exactly as it has been used,
an unique term for an unique object, from that day to
this. St. Ignatius further views the Church in each
place as having one faith; and not only so, but the
same faith in every place; one faith at Antioch, one
at Rome, one at every city between them, beyond
them, around them. Here, then, is a double unity,
inward and outward. As the double unity of body
and spirit makes the man, so the double unity of
government and of faith makes the Church. As
neither mind nor body alone makes the man, so neither
faith nor government alone makes the Church, but the
coherence of both. The Incarnation is the joining a
human soul and body with the Person of the Divine
Word; after which pattern the Church, which is His
special creation, is the joining of one faith and one
government in a moral unity. It is by this force, by
the same hierarchy everywhere guarding the same
faith, by the principle of authority and tradition
planted in this one living organisation throughout
the earth, that the attacks of heresy are everywhere
resisted. What St. Paul[1] lays down in dogma, history exhibits in fact. A hundred years after his words
are written, the Church has stretched her limits beyond the empire, has multiplied incessantly, has been
attacked by a crowd of heresies striving to adulterate
her doctrine, and has cast them out of her by this
double unity of her faith and her government, and so
is one Body and one Spirit. Her victory lies not in
being without heresies, but in standing among them
as a contrast and a condemnation.

[1] Ephes. iv. 4–16.

The solidity of internal organisation, and the definiteness of the One Faith which animated it, kept pace with the material increase of numbers. At the expiration of this period it is probable that among all the contemporaries and immediate disciples of the Apostles one only of high rank remained, that Polycarp, joint-hearer with Ignatius of St. John, and to whom in his passage the martyr addressed a letter as well as to his Church; whose own letter written at the time of the martyr's combat, and commemorating the wonderful patience therein shown forth, is yet extant. But in the meantime in every Church the transmission of authoritative teaching passed to those who had grown up themselves in the bishop's council—his presbytery, which Ignatius loved to represent as being to each bishop what the Council of Apostles was to their Lord. And as the death of Apostles themselves had caused no break in this living chain, so the gradual departure of their immediate disciples was made up by the careful handing-on of the same deposit, lodged securely in its receptacle, the succession of men, which carried on the teaching office of the Church.[1]

In the meantime, what was the attitude of the empire to the Christian Faith under Trajan, Hadrian, and Antoninus Pius? Domitian's reign had ended in active persecution, to which Nerva had put a stop on his accession.[2] But though Domitian's edicts had been

---

[1] See Eusebius, *Hist.* iii. 37, who speaks exactly in this sense; and an important passage in Döllinger, *Kallistus und Hippolytus*, 338–343, on the force of the word πρεσβύτερος, as Ecclesiæ Doctor, one particularly charged with the magisterium veritatis. See also Hagemann, *die Römische Kirche*, pp. 607, 608.

[2] Tillemont, *Ecc. Hist.* ii. 132.

reversed, like those of Nero, one of the most ancient laws of the Roman Empire forbade the worship of any god not approved by the Senate.[1]   This, as we have said above, was the sword perpetually suspended over the heads of Christians, without any fresh action on the part of the emperors.   By virtue of this, even when it was forbidden to accuse them, yet if they were brought before justice it was forbidden to absolve them.[2]   And even senators,[3] if accused, were not exempt from this severity.   We find Trajan acting upon this law in the year 111, when Pliny, being governor of Bithynia, brings expressly the case of the Christians before him.   And the terms in which he does this show at once the temper of the Roman magistrate in such cases and the state of the law.

"I have never been present," he says, "at the trials of Christians, and therefore do not know either the nature of their crime, or the degree of the punishment, or how far examination should go.   And I have been in great hesitation whether age made any difference, or the tender should not be distinguished from the strong ; whether they should be pardoned upon repentance, or, when once a man had been a Christian, ceasing to be so should not profit him ; or whether the mere profession without any crime, or whether the crimes involved in the profession should be punished.   In the meantime, with regard to those brought before me as Christians, my practice has been this :

---

[1] Tertull., *Apol.* 5, and Euseb., *Hist.* v. 21, assert the existence of this law.   [2] Tillemont, *E. H.* ii. 182, 183.

[3] See the singular instance given by Euseb. v. 21, in the reign of Commodus.   An informer accuses Apollonius of being a Christian, at a time when the imperial laws made such an accusation a capital offence.   The accuser is put to death ; but Apollonius, who is supposed to have been a senator, having made a brilliant defence before the Senate, suffers martyrdom.

I asked them if they were Christians. If they admitted it, I put the question a second and a third
time, threatening them with death. If they perse-
vered, I ordered them to be led away to execution.[1]
For whatever it was which they were confessing, I
had no doubt that stubbornness and inflexible obsti-
nacy deserved punishment. There were others of a
like infatuation, but as being Roman citizens I directed
them to be sent to the city. Presently the crime
spreading, from being under prosecution, as is usual,
several incidents happened. An anonymous delation
was sent in to me, containing the names of many who
say that they are not Christians, nor ever were. As
at my instance they invoked the gods, and made supplication with frankincense and wine to your image,
which I had ordered for that purpose to be brought,
together with the statues of the gods, and as moreover
they reviled Christ, none of which things, it is said,
real Christians can be induced to do, I thought they
might be let go. Others, being accused by a witness,
admitted that they were Christians, and presently said
that they had been, some three years before, some
many years, and some even twenty, but were no
longer. All venerated your image and the statues of
the gods, and reviled Christ. But they alleged that

---

[1] Duci jussi (confer Acts xii. 19, ἐκέλευσεν ἀπαχθῆναι). The extreme
brevity with which the most urbane, kind-hearted, and accomplished of
Roman gentlemen, as Mr. Merivale conceives him, describes himself
as having ordered a number of men and women to be put to death for
the profession of Christianity, is remarkable and significant. Compare
it with the bearing of his friend Trajan to St. Ignatius below. As
soon as the saint's confession of "bearing the Crucified in his heart"
is specific, Trajan without a word of remark orders his execution.
The "duci jussi" of Pliny and Trajan's manner in sentencing perfectly correspond and bear witness to each other's authenticity. So
later the like tone used by Junius Rusticus, prefect of the city under
Marcus Aurelius, to Justin Martyr, as will be seen further on.

the utmost of their fault or error was this : They were accustomed to meet before dawn on a stated day, and addressed themselves in a certain form to Christ as to a god, binding themselves by oath not to any crime, but not to commit theft, robbery, adultery, the breaking of their word, or the refusal to restore a deposit. After this they were wont to separate, and then reassemble to take a common and harmless meal. This, however, they had ceased to do from the publication of my edict forbidding, according to your command, private assemblies. I therefore thought it the more necessary to examine into the truth by putting to the torture two female slaves, who were said to be deaconesses among them. I found, however, nothing but a perverse and immoderate superstition, and so, adjourning the inquiry, I took refuge in consulting you. For the matter seemed to me worthy of consultation, specially on account of the number of those involved in danger. For many of every age, every rank, both sexes, have been already, and will be endangered, since the contagion of this superstition has spread not only through cities but through villages and country. And it seems capable of being arrested and corrected. At all events there is proof that the almost deserted temples have begun to be frequented, and the long intermitted rites renewed, and victims for sacrifice are found ready, whereof hitherto there were very few purchasers. Hence it is easy to form an opinion what a number of persons may be reclaimed if pardon be allowed." [1]

To which the emperor replies : " You have pursued the right course, my dear Secundus, in examining the causes of those delated to you as Christians. For no

[1] Pliny, *Ep.* x. 97, chiefly Melmoth's translation.

universal rule can be laid down in a certain formula.
They are not to be searched after; but if brought
before you and convicted, they must be punished.
Yet with this condition, that whoever denies himself
to be a Christian, and makes it plain in fact, that is,
by supplicating our gods, though he has been in past
time suspected, shall obtain pardon for his repentance.
But anonymous delations must not be admitted for
any accusation.   This is at once the very worst pre-
cedent, and unworthy of our time."

A great difficulty in tracing the progress of the
Christian Faith in these three centuries is that we
possess nothing like a consecutive secular or religious
history of them.   We only catch glimpses of what
passes at intervals.   Incidents are recorded which,
like a flash of lightning, suddenly reveal the landscape
and the actors.   Such an incident is this letter of
Pliny to Trajan, and his reply.   We have here the
governor of a province before whom Christians are
brought as criminals.   We find that if they acknowledge their faith and persist in professing it, he
sentences them to death.   But embarrassed by their
numbers, and perplexed also by the fact, that, save
the profession of their faith, there appeared nothing
criminal in their conduct, he refers the matter to the
emperor.   The emperor, no Nero or Domitian, but
one renowned for his justice and moderation, praises
what the governor has done; pronounces that Christians as such are guilty of a capital crime, and that
Pliny was right in so interpreting the existing law;
that, however, it is not desirable to seek them out;
that even when brought before justice they are to
be released if they deny their faith, but that if they
persist in it, they are to be punished with death.

Here, then, is the law—an original law of Rome before the Christian Faith began—under which the martyrs suffered at different times, throughout every province and city, without anything which could be called a general persecution on the part of the emperor directed to the destruction of the whole religion. This perpetual liability to punishment might be called into action anywhere in the empire for various causes. The first in time, and one of the most constant, was the enmity of the Jews; then the dislike of the heathens to Christians and their ways, which was further sharpened by local calamities or distress irritating the mind of the population, or by the jealousy of the heathen priests and worshippers at the desertion of their temples.   Then, again, there was the ascription to Christian godlessness, as it was called, that is their refusal to acknowledge the Roman gods, of famines, pestilences, and whatever troubled the popular mind. To these we must add a copious harvest of private grudges, and a host of calumnies, which seem now almost grotesque, but then found wide belief.   But it was the existence of such a law as this, acted on by Pliny before he referred to the emperor, and confirmed by Trajan, that gave force and effect to all these causes of persecution.   And it would appear that when Christians were brought before the magistrates, as guilty of the Christian Faith, it was not in the magistrates' power to decline hearing the case, any more than any other accusation of sacrilege or treason, for it had been determined that Christians were not a mere Jewish sect, and therefore could not in security worship one God, as the Jews did.   It was a ruled point that their worship was unauthorised.

The practice of Trajan himself was in accordance with his answer to Pliny.

The very ancient and genuine Acts of the Martyrdom of St. Ignatius state that having struggled with difficulty through the persecution of Domitian, he had carefully governed his church of Antioch, grieving only that he had not yet reached the rank of a perfect disciple by the sacrifice of his life, for he considered that the confession which is made by martyrdom brings into closer union with the Lord. Trajan then having come to the East, full of exultation at the victories which he had gained, and considering that the subjugation of the Christians was all that was wanting to the perfect obedience of his empire, began to threaten them with the alternative of sacrifice or death. Then Ignatius fearing for his church caused himself to be brought before the emperor, and being in the presence was thus addressed by him: " Who are you, evil spirit, who are zealous to transgress our commands, besides persuading others to come to an evil end?" Ignatius replied, " No one calls the bearer of God an evil spirit, for the demons fly away from the servants of God. But if you mean that I am a trouble to these, and so call me evil to them, I admit it, for having Christ my Heavenly King, I continually dissolve their plots." Trajan said, " Who is a bearer of God?" Ignatius replied, " He who has Christ in his breast." Trajan said, " We then appear to you not to have gods in our minds, whom we use to help us against our enemies." Ignatius answered, " You in your error call gods the demons of the nations, for there is one God who made the heaven, the earth, and the sea, and all that is in them ; and one Christ Jesus, the only-begotten Son of God, of whose friendship may I partake." Trajan said, "You mean Him who was crucified under Pontius Pilate?" Ignatius answered, "Him who crucifies my sin, with its inventor, and condemns all the error and the malice of the demons under the feet of those who carry Him in their heart." Trajan said, "You then carry the Crucified in your heart?" Ignatius replied, "Yes; for it is written, I will dwell in them, and walk in them." Trajan gave sentence: "It is our command that Ignatius, who says that he carries the Crucified One about in him, be taken in chains by soldiers to the great Rome to become the food of wild beasts, for the pleasure of the people." The holy martyr, when he heard this sentence, cried out with joy, "I thank thee, O Lord, who hast thought me worthy to be honoured with perfect charity towards Thee, and to be bound in iron chains together with Thy Apostle Paul." [1]

So, with great eagerness and joy, through desire of his passion, having commended his church to God, he set out on that long journey, "fighting, as he says, with wild beasts all the way from Syria to Rome, over land and sea, by day and by night," a captive under sentence of death, in the hands of soldiers, but receiving at each city a deputation from the bishop and people, who came forth to honour him as their champion. And he has but one anxiety, expressed again and again in that fervent letter to the Roman Christians, that they should not by their prayers intercept his martyrdom. "I entreat you not to be untimely kind to me. Suffer me to be the food of the beasts, since by them I may enjoy God. I am God's grain: let me be ground by their teeth, that I may be found the pure bread of Christ:" [2] and then, presently, "I do not command

---

[1] *Acts of St. Ignatius*, Ruinart, pp. 8, 9.   [2] *Ad Rom.* iv.

you, as Peter and Paul;" thus giving an incidental but most powerful witness of the special relation which those Apostles bore to the Roman Church.

And it may be remarked that while he has words of honour, praise, and affection for the other five churches which he addresses, yet in speaking of Rome his heart overflows with emotion. Upon this church he pours out epithet upon epithet, as "the beloved and enlightened in the will of Him who has willed all things which are according to the charity of Jesus Christ our God," whose people are "united to every command of His in flesh and spirit, filled undividedly with the grace of God, and thoroughly cleansed from every spot of foreign doctrine." She is not only the Church "which presides in the fortress of Roman power," but likewise "worthy of God, and of all honour and blessing and praise, worthy to receive that which she wishes, chaste, bearing the name of Christ and the name of the Father, and presiding over charity." What is the meaning of this last phrase? As she presides in the fortress of Roman power, so she presides over charity. May we thus interpret the mind of the martyr? God in his Triune Being is Charity; the Holy Spirit, the ineffable embrace of the Father and His Image, their Love, or Delight, or Joy, or Blessedness, or whatever human name we may dare to give to what is most divine, is charity: by charity God became man; charity is the individual Christian's state; charity makes men one in the Body of the God-man; charity is the condition of angels and men in the great kingdom to come, the God-formed kingdom. Thus charity is the distinctive mark of the Christian religion, that from which it springs, that which it is, that which it points to, and in which it will be consum-

mated. When, then, St. Ignatius said of the Roman
Church, using the same word in one sentence,[1] that as
she presided over the country of the Romans, so she
presided over charity, does he not with equal delicacy
and emphasis indicate her primacy ? She presides over
that in which the Unity of the Church consists, in
which its truth, its grace, and its holiness coinhere.

The desire of the martyr was accomplished : he
reached Rome on the last day of the great games,
and was thrown in the Colosseum before the beasts,
which, according to his repeated prayers, so entirely
devoured him that only the greater bones remained.
These, says the contemporary account, " a priceless
treasure," were carried back to Antioch.   Somewhat
less than three hundred years afterwards St. Chrysostom, preaching on his day in his city, thus speaks of
him : " It was a divine benefaction to bring him back
again to us, and to distribute the martyr to the cities.
—Rome received his dripping blood, but you are
honoured with his relics.—From that time he enriches
your city, and like a perpetual treasure, drawn upon
every day and never failing, gives his bounty to all.
So this happy Ignatius, blessing all that come to him,
sends them home full of confidence, bold resolution,
and fortitude.   Not, then, to-day only, but every day
go to him, reaping spiritual fruits from him.   For,
indeed, he who comes hither with faith may reap great
goods.   Not the bodies only, but the very coffins of
the saints are full of spiritual grace.   For if in the
case of Eliseus this happened, and the dead man who
touched his bier broke through the bonds of death,
how much more now, when grace is more abundant,

[1] Ἐκκλησία—ἥτις καὶ προκάθηται ἐν τόπῳ χωρίου Ῥωμαίων—προκα-
θημένη τῆς ἀγάπης.

and the energy of the Spirit fuller?——So, I beseech you, if any one be in despondency, in sickness, in the depth of sin, in any circumstance of life, to come here with faith, and he will put off all these." [1]

Before St. Ignatius reached that completion of his faith to which he aspired, he was cheered with the account that his sacrifice had produced its effect, and peace had been restored to his church, with the completeness of its body.[2]

Now in all this—in Pliny's conduct as governor, in his reference to Trajan, in the emperor's reply, in his treatment of St. Ignatius, and in the restoration of peace afterwards——there is, we conceive, a very exact sample of what the position of Christians was in Trajan's time. His answer ruled the question of Roman law for the following two hundred years. It declared the profession of Christianity to be illicit and a capital offence ; but to call this law into action, or to leave it suspended as a threat over the heads of Christians, was a matter of expedience. When the latter took place, the churches were said to be at peace ; when the former, a persecution was said to rage ; but at any time and place an individual might suffer ; while on the other hand a persecution directed to root out the whole Christian name was not yet thought of.

And this state of things seems to continue through Hadrian's principate. In his first year, Alexander,

---

[1] St. Chrysostom, *Hom. on St. Ignatius*, tom. ii. 600.

[2] St. Ignatius in the 11th sec. of his epistle to the Smyrnæans requests them to send a messenger to congratulate the church of Antioch, ὅτι εἰρηνεύουσιν, καὶ ἀπέλαβον τὸ ἴδιον μέγαθος, ἀποκατεστάθη αὐτοῖς τὸ ἴδιον σωματεῖον. The word σωματεῖον, or corpusculum, indicates the completeness of a diocesan church with its bishop, the whole Church being σῶμα Χριστοῦ, as St. Ignatius had said in sec. 1 of the same epistle, ἐν ἑνὶ σώματι τῆς ἐκκλησίας αὐτοῦ.

fifth successor of St. Peter at Rome, having been
imprisoned under Trajan, suffers martyrdom. It
would seem as if the same hand had struck down
about the same time the heads of the two great
churches of Rome and Antioch, the first and the third
in rank, and perhaps ordered the execution of the
bishop of Antioch at Rome, with that of the Roman
bishop, in order to give greater force to the example.[1]
Many other martyrs at Rome and in the north of
Italy are found at this time. It is not at all necessary to suppose the personal action of Hadrian in
these. After this he was engaged during fifteen
years in those splendid progresses, in which he
examined personally every part of his vast empire,
from its northern frontier between Carlisle and New-
castle to the Euphrates. While he was so engaged,
the governors of the various provinces would apply
the existing law in the cases brought before them.
He would have had to interfere, and that with the
whole weight of the imperial arm, if he wished to
check the course of the law. We have, however,
recorded the most interesting fact, that when he was
at Athens in the year 126, Christians for the first
time approached a Roman emperor with a public
defence of their doctrines, and a persecution is said
to have been stopped by the apologies which Quad-
ratus and Aristides presented to him. Perhaps the
rescript to Minucius Fundanus, proconsul of the province of Asia, which Justin has preserved, was a
result of this. It runs thus : " I have received the
letter written to me by your predecessor, the noble

---

[1] There is some doubt about the time of St. Ignatius's martyrdom.
We suppose it to be at the end of Trajan's reign. St. Alexander I. is
reckoned a martyr, and placed in the canon of the Mass next after St.
Ignatius, which seems to indicate a connection between their deaths.

Serenius Granianus.   And indeed it seems to me that
that affair should not be passed by without a diligent
examination, in order that Christians may not be disturbed, nor an occasion of false accusation be opened
to informers.   If, then, the provincials can present
themselves openly with their petitions against Christians, so as to answer before the tribunal, let them do
that, and not betake themselves to mere requests and
outcries.   It would be much more just that you should
take cognisance of the matter, if any one be willing to
accuse.   If, then, any one denounce them, and prove
that they are doing anything illegal, sentence them
according to the gravity of the crime.   But, by Hercules, if it be a mere false accusation, punish the
informer according to its importance."

Here would seem to be a considerable modification
of Trajan's rescript.   The profession of Christianity is
not taken by itself as a capital offence.   Proof must
be given that something illegal has been committed.
So far it approaches to an act of toleration.   It plainly
discourages anonymous and malicious attacks.   But
on the other hand it was not difficult to show that
Christians did commit something illegal.   Any real
accuser bringing them before the tribunal could prove
by their own testimony that they declared the gods
worshipped by the Romans to be demons, while they
refused to swear by the emperor's genius.   Thus,
favourable as this decree was to them, it fell far short
of declaring their religion to be allowable.

And the same emperor who could thus write, whose
curiosity made him acquainted with all the religious
sects of his empire, whose temper, as an exceedingly
accomplished man, having the widest experience of
men and things, and ruling an empire of the most

diverse races with the most various religions, led him
to an eclectic indifference, and so far toleration of all,
yet showed by his personal conduct at a later period
of his life how he would treat the profession of the
Christian Faith if it thwarted a ruling desire.   When,
after fifteen years of incessant travel, study, and
observation, he returned to Rome, and had enclosed
at Tivoli a space of eight miles in circumference,
adorned with copies of the most beautiful temples in
his wide dominion, he offered sacrifices and consulted
the gods as to the duration of his work; but he
received for answer that the gods who inhabited their
images were tormented by the prayers which the
widow Symphorosa and her seven sons offered daily
to their God.[1]   If she and her children would sacrifice, they promised to grant all his demands.   Upon
this Hadrian ordered Symphorosa and her seven sons
to be brought before him, and endeavoured by kind
words to bring them to sacrifice.   She replied, " It
was for not consenting to what you ask that my
husband Gætulius and his brother Amantius, both
tribunes in your army, suffered various tortures, and,
like generous champions, overcame your demons by a
glorious death.   If their death was shameful before
men, it was honourable in the sight of the angels, and
now they are crowned with immortal light.   They
live in heaven, and follow everywhere the King who
reigns there, covered with glory by the trophies they

[1] So the persecution of Diocletian is said to have arisen from Apollo
declaring that the just who were upon the earth prevented him from
uttering true oracles ; and a like answer was received by Julian the
Apostate at Antioch, where the relics of St. Babylas had been translated by Gallus to Daphne, near a celebrated temple of Apollo.   Here
Julian, offering in vain a great number of sacrifices to the demon,
was at length informed that the body of the saint condemned him to
silence, and ordered the Christians to remove it.   St. Chrys. tom. ii,
560.

gained in dying for Him." Hadrian, stung by this reply, could not contain himself, but said: " Either sacrifice this instant to the immortal gods, or I will myself sacrifice you with your children to these gods whom you despise." " And how should I be so happy," said Symphorosa, " as to be worthy with my children to be sacrificed to my God?" " I tell you," said Hadrian, "I will have you sacrifice to my gods." " Your gods," replied she, " cannot receive me in sacrifice. I am not a victim for them; but if you order me to be burnt for the name of Christ my God, know that the fire which consumes me will only increase their punishment." " Choose, I tell you," said the emperor; " sacrifice or die." " You think, doubtless, to frighten me," rejoined Symphorosa; " but I desire to be at rest with my husband, whom you put to death for the name of Christ." Then the emperor ordered her to be taken before the temple of Hercules, to be struck in the face, and hung up by her hair. But finding that these torments only served to strengthen her in the faith, he had her thrown into the Anio. Her brother Eugenius, being one of the chief men at Tibur, drew her body from the water, and buried her in the suburbs of the town.

The next day Hadrian ordered the seven sons of Symphorosa to be brought before him. And, seeing that neither his threats nor his promises, nor the exhibition of the most fearful punishments, could shake their constancy, nor induce them to sacrifice to idols, he caused seven poles to be planted round the temple of Hercules, on which they were raised by pulleys. Then Crescentius, the eldest, had his throat cut; Julian, the second, was run through the breast; Nemesius was struck in the heart; Primitivus in the stomach; Justin in the back; Stactæus in the side; while the youngest, Eugenius, was cleft to the middle.

The day following the death of these brethren Hadrian came to the temple and ordered their bodies to be removed, and to be cast into a deep hole. The priests and sacrificers of the temple called this spot the place of the Seven Executed. Their blood stopped the persecution, which was only rekindled eighteen months afterwards.[1]

As the rescript to Minucius Fundanus did not prevent the emperor from thus acting, neither was it an obstacle to such an incident as this occurring in any part of the empire.

That it was so likewise in the principate of his successor, of all down to this period the most tranquil and the least persecuting, we have strong and clear evidence in the earliest of the extant apologies, that of Justin Martyr, presented to the emperor Antoninus Pius about the year 150. He who would breathe the atmosphere in which the early Christians lived will find it in this work of a distinguished convert from heathen philosophy, which is the more interesting as being composed at a moment when the empire seems to have reached its highest point, and the ruler of it was its most moderate spirit. We may cite a few passages bearing on the condition of Christians.

" To the Emperor Titus Ælius Adrianus Antoninus Pius Augustus Cæsar, and to his son Verissimus the Philosopher, and to Lucius the Philosopher, son of Cæsar by birth, and of Pius by adoption, the lover of learning, and to the sacred Senate, and to all the Roman people, in behalf of those out of every race of men who are unjustly hated and persecuted, I, that

---

[1] *Acts of St. Symphorosa*, from Dom Ruinart, pp. 23, 24.

am one of such myself, Justin, son of Priscus, and grandson of Baccheius, natives of Flavia Neapolis, of Palestine, in Syria, offer this address and supplication.

"Reason dictates that those who are really pious and philosophers should love and honour truth alone, declining to follow the opinions of the ancients if they be corrupt. For right reason not only forbids us to assent to those who are unjust either in practice or in principle, but commands the lover of truth to choose that which is just in word and deed in every way, even before his own life, and with death threatening him. Now you hear yourselves called on all sides Pious, Philosophers, Guardians of Justice, and Lovers of Learning; but, whether you be such in truth, the event will show. For we have come before you, not to flatter you in this address, nor to gain your favour, but to demand of you to pass judgment according to strict and well-weighed reason, not influenced by prejudice, nor by the desire of pleasing superstitious men, nor by inconsiderate passion, nor by the long prevalence of an evil report, in giving a sentence which would turn against yourselves. For, as to us, we are fully persuaded that we can suffer no injury from any one, unless we be found guilty of some wickedness, or proved to be bad men; and, as to you, kill us you may, but hurt us you cannot.[1]

"We ask, then, that the actions of those who are accused before you may be examined, that he who is convicted may be punished as an evil-doer, but not as a Christian. And, if any one appears to be innocent, that he may be dismissed as a Christian who has done no evil. For we do not require you to punish our accusers: they are sufficiently recompensed by their

[1] Justin, 1 *Apol.* 1, 2.

own malice, and their ignorance of what is good. Moreover, bear in mind that it is for your sakes that we thus speak, since it is in our power to deny when we are questioned. But we choose not to live by falsehood.[1]

"And you, when you hear that we are expecting a kingdom, rashly conceive that we mean a human one, whereas we speak of that with God, as is evident even from those who are under examination by you confessing that they are Christians, whilst they know that death is the penalty of the confession. For if we expected a human kingdom, we should deny in order to obtain our expectations; but, since our hopes are not of the present, we do not regard those who kill us, knowing that death is an inevitable debt to all.[2]

"We adore God only, but in all other matters joyfully serve you, confessing that you are kings and rulers, and praying that you may be found to possess, together with your royal power, a sound and discerning mind. If, however, notwithstanding that we thus pray and openly lay everything before you, you treat us with contempt, we shall receive no injury; believing, or rather, being convinced, that every one, if his deeds shall so deserve, shall receive the punishment of eternal fire, and that an account will be required of him in proportion to the powers which he has received from God, as Christ has declared in those words, 'To whomsoever God has given much, of him shall be much required.'[3]

"Though death be the penalty to those who teach or even who confess the name of Christ, we everywhere accept it, and teach it. And if you as enemies meet these words, you can do no more, as we have already

[1] Sec. 7.   [2] Sec. 11.   [3] Sec. 17.

said, than kill us, which brings no hurt to us, but to you, and to all who hate unjustly, and do not repent, the chastisement of eternal fire." [1]

And his concluding words are : " If now what we have said appears to be reasonable and true, honour it accordingly ; but if folly, despise it as foolish ; yet pass not sentence of death against those as enemies, who have done no evil. For we tell you beforehand that you will not escape the future judgment of God, if you continue in injustice, and we shall cry, Let the will of God be done." [2]

Such then is the testimony of a Christian as to the way in which the confessors of his religion were treated ; and it is corroborated by that of the heathen philosopher Celsus, who writes his books against Christianity about this time, and imputes the secrecy practised by Christians in their teaching and their actions to their attempts to escape the punishment of death hanging over their heads. [3] And again having put into the mouth of Christians the remark, that if they blaspheme or strike a statue of Jupiter or Apollo, these gods cannot defend themselves, he subjoins : " Do you not, then, see that your own demon is not merely blasphemed but expelled from every land and sea, while you, his consecrated image, [4] are chained, and led away to prison, and crucified ; and the demon, or as you call him, the Son of God, gives you no protection." And in another place, comparing Christians with Jews, to whom God had made so many promises :

---

[1] Sec. 45.

[2] Sec. 68. Chevallier's translation, sometimes altered.

[3] Origen c. Cels, i. 3. Περὶ τοῦ κρύφα Χριστιανοὺς τὰ ἀρέσκοντα αὐτοῖς ποιεῖν καὶ διδάσκειν εἰπὼν, καὶ ὅτι οὐ μάτην τοῦτο ποιοῦσιν, ἅτε διωθούμενοι τὴν ἐπηρτημένην αὐτοῖς δίκην τοῦ θανάτου.

[4] Σὲ τὸν καθωσιωμένον ὥσπερ ἄγαλμα αὐτῷ δήσας ἀπάγει καὶ ἀνασκολοπίζει. viii. 38, 39.

" See," he says, " what good has He done to them and to you ?   To them, instead of being lords of all the earth, not a clod of soil or a hearth remains ;[1] while of you, if any one still wanders about in hiding, yet justice pursues him with the doom of death."

However, we know that at this time at least the bold words of Justin drew down no punishment from Antoninus, and a rescript of this emperor, dated about two years after the presentation of this first apology, has been preserved, which is more favourable to Christians than that of Hadrian.   It is addressed to that province of Asia which contained so many flourishing Christian churches, and which accordingly was so bitter against them.   They had written to complain of the Christians, and to accuse them as the cause of the earthquakes which had happened.   The emperor replies : " It was my belief that the gods would take care that such men as you describe should not escape. For much rather would they, if they could, punish such as will not worship them.   Now these men you are annoying, and accusing their opinion as atheistical, and charging them with sundry other things which we cannot prove.   Yet it would be serviceable to them to seem to meet their death for such an accusation ; and they surpass you in giving up their lives rather than comply with what you call upon them to do.   But as to the earthquakes which have happened or are happening now, it is not reasonable that you should mention them, you who lose heart when they take place, comparing your conduct with theirs, who have more confidence than you towards God.   And you indeed in such a time seem to have no knowledge of

[1] viii. 69.   By this we should judge that the work of Celsus appeared not long after the punishment of the Jews by Hadrian.

the gods, and neglect the temples, and know nothing of worshipping God ; whence it is that you are jealous of those who do worship him, and that you persecute them to death.   Respecting such men various other rulers of provinces wrote to my divine father, and his reply was, not to trouble such men, except they appear to be contriving something against the Roman Empire. Many too have referred to me about such, and my reply was in agreement to my father's decision.   Now if any one has an accusation to bring against such a one as such, let the accused be released from the charge, even though he appear to be such, and let the accuser be punished." [1]

Here we reach the highest point of toleration which Christians received in the first 130 years.   Instead of Trajan's somewhat reluctant order to punish Christians as Christians, when once convicted, instead of Hadrian's decision that something contrary to Roman law must be proved against them, Antoninus, while quoting the latter, goes far beyond it, and lays down that as Christians they were blameless, and were only to be punished in case some hostility to the Roman Empire could be proved in their conduct.   Moreover, their accuser was to be punished.   And this rescript being repeated to several places, amounted to an assurance that Christians should be left in tranquillity during the principate of Pius.

Putting ourselves into the position of a Roman emperor at this middle of the second century, let us endeavour to form a notion of what Christianity would appear to him.   In the first place, he who had all the threads of Roman organisation gathered in his hand, would certainly recognise it as a sect spread through-

[1] Attached to Justin's first Apology.

out the empire, the Jewish origin of which was known to him, and the author as one crucified by order of a Roman governor under Tiberius.[1] Yet he would hardly distinguish accurately the Church from the different heresies which everywhere sprang up around it, holding more or less of its doctrines and mixing them up with corruptions and abuses.[2] And it would scarcely appear to him as a power in the State, either from its numbers or the influence of the people belonging to it; yet on the other hand it would appear as something not inconsiderable in either of these respects. Moreover, we may suppose it would come before him as a *belief*, and not as an *institution*. It had as yet no public churches.[3] A heathen would say of Christians at this time that they had no temples, altars, or statues;[4] no ceremonial worship, for he could not, as a heathen, get admittance to Christian rites, which moreover were carried on in private houses, and carefully concealed. The emperor would be well aware that Christians had rulers of their own;[5] it was as such that Trajan had fixed upon the bishop third in rank among Christian communities for punishment the most severe and degrading, to be thrown as food for wild beasts, for the pleasure of the people. But nevertheless, the internal constitution of the Church would lie hidden from him: the link which bound together the bishops of the various local communities,

---

[1] See Trajan's remark to St. Ignatius : " You mean Him that was crucified under Pontius Pilate."

[2] See the curious letter of Hadrian about the Alexandrians, in which the Christians spoken of are probably heretics.

[3] They are first mentioned at Rome in the reign of Alexander Severus.

[4] See Origen *c. Cels.* vii. 62.

[5] See Trajan's question, " Who art thou who art zealous to transgress our commands, besides persuading others to come to an evil end?"

were intended to obviate the persecutions arising from the causes above described, to show the purity of Christian morality, the reasonableness of Christian belief, the fidelity of Christian sentiment to the imperial rule as established by a Divine Providence. They were not in the least intended to lay before him the Christian Church as a whole. Thus Justin, replying to the accusation that they were expecting a kingdom, says, " You rashly conceive that we mean a human one, whereas we speak of that with God." We may then, it seems, conclude with certainty that Antoninus was only partially aware of what Christianity was. That discipline of the secret, which was itself the result of persecution—of the Christian Faith having to make itself a place in a world utterly opposed to it,— became at once its protection, and the cause of further persecution ; of persecution, in so far as it put Christians under general suspicion, but of protection, inasmuch as it covered with a veil that complete moral revolution to which the Christian Faith was tending from the first, and towards which it was continually advancing. Could Trajan have foreseen what was apparent under Constantine, his treatment of Christians would have had no forbearance or hesitation in it, his blows no intermission or doubtfulness. As it is, up to the time we are now considering, there are no traces of a general persecution against the Christian name organised by the emperor as head of the State. There are numberless local and individual persecutions starting up in this city and in that, and arising from the fundamental contrariety of Christian belief to the existing heathen worship and the ordinary heathen life. Such we have and no more. And so a great host of martyrs in single combat won their crown.

But the emperor did not set himself to destroy a unity which he did not see.

Now as to the character in Christians which their condition in these hundred and thirty years tended to produce, we can form a clear conclusion. Of the relative proportion of actual martyrs to the whole mass of believers, we can indeed have no accurate notion ; but it is plain that all were liable to suffering as Christians in every various degree up to that ultimate point of witnessing by death. Thus the acceptance of the Christian Faith itself involved at least the spirit of confession, if not that of martyrdom. A man lived for years, perhaps a whole generation, with the prospect of suffering, which it may be never came, or came as the crown of a long period in which heroic virtues had been called forth. Thus St. Ignatius had been more than forty years bishop of Antioch, and had carried his church hardly through the bad times of Domitian, when he gained at last what he deemed perfect union with his Lord, by being ground under the teeth of lions, as "the pure bread of God." What is here expressed with so sublime a confidence by one actual martyr, must have made the tissue of Christian life in general. Those early disciples of the cross put in the cross their victory. The habitual danger which hung about their life must have scared away the timid, the insincere, the half-hearted. Yet alternations of peace rapidly succeeded times of suffering. Throughout these hundred and thirty years there is no long-continued even local persecution. Breathing-times of comparative tranquillity come, wherein Christians can grow, propagate, and mature for the conflict which may at any time arise. Thus while the opposition made to the infant faith is quite sufficient to have destroyed an untrue religion, born of earth or human device, to have scattered and eradicated its professors, it was precisely what would favour the real advance of a faith rooted upon a suffering God, and in which suffering with Him was made the means of union with Him.

And here we halt at the accession of Marcus Aurelius, as a middle point between the day of Pentecost and the time of Constantine.

LECTURE XI

THE SECOND AGE OF THE MARTYR CHURCH

" Magnus ab integro sæculorum nascitur ordo.
Jam nova progenies cœlo demittitur alto.
Ingredere, O magnos, aderit jam tempus, honores,
Cara Dei soboles, magnum Jovis incrementum."

I. THERE is a moment in the history of the Roman
Empire when it comes before us with the most imposing grandeur. The imperial rule has been definitively
accepted by that proud old aristocracy under which
the city of the seven hills was built up from a robber
fortress to be the centre of a world-wide confederation ;
while on their side the nations all round the Mediterranean bow with an almost voluntary homage before
the sceptre of their queen. If the north be still un-
tameable, it has learnt to dread the talons of the
Roman eagle, and cowers murmuring in its forests
and morasses; if the Parthian still shoot as he flies
from the western Cæsar's hosts, he has at least expiated
in the ruin of Ctesiphon the capture of Crassus and
the dishonour of Mark Antony. But far more than
this. On the Cæsar in his undisputed greatness has
dawned the real sublimity of the task which Providence had assigned to him ; to mould, that is, under
one rule of equal beneficence the many tongues and
many nations which a course of conquest, often the
most unjust, had brought to own his sway. And this
point of time is when after the great warrior Trajan

comes Hadrian the man of culture; in whom seems
implanted the most restless curiosity, carrying him
with the speed of a soldier and the power of a prince
over every climate from Carlisle to Alexandria, from
Morocco to Armenia, in order that he may see in each
the good of which so many varying races of men are
capable, and use them all for his grand design. To
him Rome is still the head; but he has learnt to
esteem at their due value the members of her great
body. The first fifteen years of his reign are almost
entirely spent away from Rome, in those truly imperial
progresses wherein the master of this mighty realm,
when he would relieve himself of his helmet, walks
like the simple legionary,[1] bareheaded in front of his
soldiers, under the suns of the south, examining, wherever he comes, the whole civil and military organisation, promoting the capable and censuring the unworthy,
scattering benefits with unsparing hand. York has
known him as a protecting genius; Athens blends
his name with that of her own Theseus as a second
founder; wayward Alexandria exalts him, at least for
the time, as a granter of privileges; the extreme
north and utmost south acknowledge alike the unsparing zeal and majestic presence of their ruler. At that
moment Rome is still Roman. While the Augustan
discipline still animates her legions, the sense of the
subordination of the military power to the civil spirit
of a free State is not wholly lost; her proconsuls and
præfects have passed out of those plundering mag-
nates, who replenished in the tyranny of a year or
two from a drained province the treasures they had
squandered in a life of corruption at Rome, into the

---

[1] The Roman legionary, if he wished to lay aside his helmet, was
only allowed to go bareheaded.

orderly and yet dignified magistrates accountable to the Republic's life-president [1] for their high delegated power. Perhaps the world had never yet seen anything at once so great and so beneficent as the government of Hadrian. But one thing was wanting to the many-tongued and many-tempered peoples ruled by him, that they should of their own will accept the worship of one God, and so the matchless empire receive the only true principle of coherence and permanence in the common possession of one religion. And the thoughtful student of history can hardly restrain himself from indulging his fancy as to what might then have been the result, and into how great a structure provinces worthy of being kingdoms might then have grown by the process of an unbroken civilisation instinct with the principles of the pure Christian Faith. Then the northern flood of barbarism and the eastern tempest of a false religion, which together were to break up the fabric of a thousand years, might have been beaten back from its boundaries. From thence the messengers of light might have so penetrated the world in all directions that the advance of the truth should not have been impeded by any great civil destruction. The nations of Europe might thus have developed themselves from their Roman cradle by a continuous growth, in which there had been no ages of conquest, violence, and confusion, no relapse into chaos, no struggle back into an intricate and yet imperfect order, but the serene advance from dawn to day.

So, however, it was not to be. The time of proba-

---

[1] Champagny remarks, that the emperors were never in the mind of the Romans *sovereigns* in the modern acceptation of the word, but *life-presidents* with absolute power.

tion in the reigns of Hadrian and Antoninus Pius,
wherein a sort of toleration had seemed to be allowed
to Christians, passed away, and the beginning of a far
different destiny broke upon the empire. With the
accession of Marcus Aurelius the great old enemies,
the North and the East, awoke from their trance in
fresh vigour. A Parthian war of four years, a German war of twelve, with pestilence, earthquakes, and
famines through a large part of the empire, try to the
utmost the vigour and temper of one of the most
upright sovereigns known to heathenism. Marcus
Aurelius meets both enemies with equal courage and
ability, but he dies prematurely, and leaves the
rule, carried so temperately by four great sovereigns
successively adopted to empire at mature age, in the
untried hands of the heir of his blood, a youth of
nineteen, born in the purple. In this at least the
great Roman was wanting both to Stoic greatness and
to Roman duty. And it was a fatal error. During
thirteen years this son of the most virtuous heathen
shows himself the most vicious of tyrants. At a
single bound Rome passes from a ruler more just than
Trajan to a ruler more abandoned than Nero; and in
the palace of Marcus Aurelius endures an emperor
who has a double harem of three hundred victims;[1]
who spares the blood of no senator, and respects the
worth of no officer.

When a revolution, similar to that which swept
away Domitian, has removed Commodus, the Roman
world is not so fortunate as to find a second Trajan to
take his place. Three great officers who command in
Syria, Illyricum, and Britain, contend for the prize,
and when victory has determined in favour of Septi-

[1] Champagny, *Les Antonins*, iii. 311.

mius Severus, he rules for eighteen years with a force and capacity which may indeed be compared with Trajan's, but with a deceit and remorseless severity all his own. At one time forty senators are slaughtered for the crime of having looked with favour upon that pretender to the empire who did not succeed. Nor is this a passing cruelty, but the fixed spirit of his reign. The sway of the sword is openly proclaimed. That the army is everything is not only acted on, but laid down as a guiding principle of state to his children. The unbroken discipline of her legionaries had hitherto indeed proved the salvation of the State; but this Septimius fatally tampers with, and in so doing sows the seeds of future anarchy and dissolution.

His death in 211 places the empire in the hands of a youth of twenty-three, all but born in the purple, like Commodus, and his rival in tyranny and dissoluteness of every kind. Caracalla is endured for six years, and being killed by a plot in the camp, is succeeded by his murderer Macrinus. He again, after a year, gives place to a Syrian boy of fourteen, who took at his accession the honoured name of Marcus Aurelius Antoninus, but is known to posterity as Heliogabalus. Once more during a space of four years the crimes of Commodus and Caracalla are repeated, or even exceeded. Indeed in these years from 218 to 222 the story of shame and degradation reaches its lowest point. But the soldiers of the prætorian camp themselves rise against Heliogabalus, massacre him with his mother, and place on the throne his cousin Alexander Severus, at the age of fourteen. Now Alexander has for his mother Mammæa, if not a Christian, at least a hearer of Origen, who gives her son from his earliest youth a virtuous

education, who surrounds him on the perilous height
of the Roman throne with the arms of her affection
and her practical wisdom.   Alexander rules for thirteen
years, a period equal to that of Commodus, and little
less than that of Nero.   Younger than both at his
accession and his death, his reign offers the most
striking contrast to theirs.   Of all heathen rulers he
stands forth as the most blameless.   It is a reign
which, after the obscene domination of Commodus,
Caracalla, and Heliogabalus, with the savagery between
them of Septimius Severus immediately preceding it,
seems like a romance of goodness.   Simple and admirable in his private life, he rivals Marcus Aurelius in
his zeal for the administration of justice, for the choice
of good governors, for devotion to the public service;
and, happier than Marcus Aurelius, on his name rests
no stain of persecution.   " He suffered the Christians
to be," [1] are the emphatic words of his biographer;
concerning which it has been well remarked that little
as this seems to say, it had been said of no one of his
predecessors, though several had not persecuted the
Church.[2]   And therefore this expression must mean
that he left them in an entire liberty as to religion.
It is indeed the exact contradiction of what, thirty
years before, Tertullian had stated respecting the law
in the time of Septimius Severus; for one of his com-
plaints in pleading for Christians was, " your harsh
sentence ' that we are not allowed to exist,' is an open
appeal to brute force." [3]

[1] " Christianos esse passus est."   Lampridius.
[2] Tillemont, *Hist. Ecc.* iii. 250.
[3] *Apolog.* iv. "Jampridem, cum dure definitis dicendo, non licet esse
vos, et hoc sine ullo retractatu humaniore describitis, vim profitemini
et iniquam ex arce dominationem, si ideo negatis licere quia vultis, non
quia debuit non licere."

Alexander Severus, the darling of his people, perished by the hands of some treacherous soldiers suborned by his successor Maximin; and with him ends this period of seventy-four years, which we will consider together, in order to estimate the progress of the Christian Faith. A time of more remarkable contrasts in rulers cannot be found. It begins with Marcus Aurelius, and it ends with Alexander Severus, the two most virtuous of heathen princes. Between them it contains Commodus, Caracalla, and Heliogabalus, the three generally reputed the most vicious; while the definitive course which the history of the empire took is given to it by another, Septimius Severus. Of great abilities and mixed character, he gained the empire as a successful soldier, and was true to his origin in that he established the ultimate victory of pure force over every restriction of a civil constitution. An African unsparing of blood, he sat on the throne of Augustus, and worked out the problem of government which the founder of the empire had started by preparing the result of Diocletian.

The rule of Commodus and his successors fully revealed the fatal truth, that the five princes who from the accession of Nerva had governed as if they were really responsible to the senate, had only been a fortunate chance; that this time of prosperity rested upon no legal limitation of rights between those things wont to exist only in severance,[1] the sovereign's power and the subject's freedom; that it was no result of a constitution which had grown up under a mutual sense of benefit arising from authority exercised conscien-

[1] "Res olim dissociabiles, principatum et libertatem." Tacit. *Agric.* 3.

tiously, and obedience cordially rendered. The age which Tacitus [1] at its commencement had called "most blessed" was indeed over, and as soon as the second Antonine left the scene, a state of things ensued in which tyranny and cruelty were as unchecked as under Nero or Domitian at their worst. It became evident that all had depended on the sovereign's personal character. From Marcus to Commodus the leap was instantaneous; and so, again, afterwards the short-lived serenity and order of Alexander's rule passed at his death into a confusion lasting for more than forty years, which threatened to break up the very existence of the empire.

But in Rome from the accession of Commodus in 180 to the death of Heliogabalus in 222 we find a profound corruption of morals, an excess of cruelty, and a disregard of civil rights, which could scarcely be exceeded. Tacitus, at the beginning of Trajan's reign, burst forth into indignation at the thought that it had cost Rusticus and Senecio their lives, in Domitian's time, to have praised Thrasea and Helvidius Priscus, and that their very writings had been publicly burned, as if that fire could extinguish the voice of the Roman people, the liberty of the senate, and the conscience of mankind. "Truly great," he cried, "was the specimen of patient endurance which we exhibited." [2] What words, then, would he have found to express the degradation of servile spirit in that self-same city a hundred years later, when Plautianus, the favourite minister of Septimius Severus, at the marriage of his daughter with Caracalla, caused a hundred persons of good family, some of them already fathers,

[1] "Primo statim beatissimi sæculi ortu." *Ibid.*
[2] *Agricola*, 2.

secretly to be made eunuchs, in order that they might serve as chamberlains to the imperial bride.[1]   Or to take another example; as Quintillus, one of the chiefs of the senate, both by birth and by the employments which he had held, a man of advanced years and living retired in the country, was seized in order to be put to death, he declared that his only surprise was that he had been suffered to live so long, and that he had made every preparation for his burial.   A third incident will show both the sort of crimes for which men were punished, the protection given by the law to the individual, and the spirit and temper of the senate. It had condemned Apronianus, proconsul of Asia, without giving him a hearing, because his nurse had dreamt that he was one day to reign, concerning which he was reported to have consulted a magician.   Now, in reading the informations laid against him, it was found that a witness deposed that during the consultation some senator who was bald had stretched out his head to listen.   Upon this all the bald senators, even those who had never gone to the house of Apronianus, began to tremble, while the rest put their hands to their heads to make sure that they had still their hair.   However, a certain Marcellinus fell under special suspicion, whereupon he demanded that the witness should be brought in, who could not fail to recognise him if guilty.   The witness looked round upon them all for a long time without saying a word, until upon a sign that a certain senator made him, he declared it was Marcellinus, who forthwith was hurried out of the senate to be beheaded, before Severus was even informed of it.   As he went to execution he

<hr>

[1] See Döllinger, *Hippolytus und Kallistus*, p. 187, who quotes from Dio Cassius, l. 75, p. 1267, Reimar.   This was A.D. 203.

met four of his children, to whom he said that his
greatest grief was to leave them living after him in so
miserable a time.[1]   It was not without reason that
Tertullian at this very moment encouraged the martyrs
to be constant, with the reflection that there was no
one who might not, for the cause of man, be made to
suffer whatever nature would most shrink from suffering in the cause of God. " The times we live in are
proofs," he cried, " of this. How many and how great
are the instances we have seen, in which no height of
birth, no degree of rank, no personal dignity, no time
of life, have saved men from coming to the most unex-
pected end, for some man's cause, either at his own
hands, if they stood against him, or if for him, by the
hands of his adversaries." [2]

It was a time at which the extremes of reckless
cruelty, of profuse luxury, of shameless dissoluteness,
met together ; in which women were forbidden by an
express law to expose themselves on the arena as
gladiators ; in which, when the Emperor Severus would
legislate against adultery, a memorial was handed to
him with the names of three thousand persons whom
his law would touch.[3]   Such was the character of the
time which followed at once on the empire's golden
age ; the time in which the Church of God was length-
ening her cords and strengthening her stakes, and
building up her divine polity amid the worthlessness
of the world's greatest empire, and the instability of
all earthly things.

II. In the last review which we took of her material progress we said that to the eye of Pius Antoninus

---

[1] Tillemont, *Life of Severus*, iii. 75, from Dio : A.D. 206.
[2] Tertullian, *ad Martyres*, 4 : about A.D. 196.
[3] Dio, quoted by Döllinger, *ut supra*.

she would not yet appear from her multitude as a
power in the State.   But before the end of the
seventy-four years which we are here considering as
one period, it was otherwise.   Already in the reign of
Commodus, Eusebius states that the word of salvation
was bringing to the worship of the one God men out
of every race, so that in Rome itself many distinguished for wealth and rank embraced it with their
whole families.[1]   A few years later, when Tertullian
writes his apology, he makes the heathen complain
"that the State is overrun with us, that Christians
are found in the country, in forts, in islands; that
every sex and age and condition and rank come over
to them."[2]   And again, "We are of yesterday, and
have already filled every place you have, your cities,
islands, forts, boroughs, councils, your very camps,
tribes, corporations, the palace, senate, and forum.
Your temples only we leave you.   For what war
should we not be equal, we who are so ready to be
slaughtered, if our religion did not command us rather
to suffer death than to inflict it?"   Elsewhere he
speaks of Christians as "so great a multitude of men
as to be almost the majority in every city."   Now
make whatsoever allowance we will for Tertullian's
vehemence, such statements, laid before adversaries, if
they had not a great amount of truth in them, would
bring ridicule on his cause rather than strengthen it.
Tertullian besides wrote at the time of the general
persecution set on foot by Septimius Severus against
the Christian Faith, which itself was a proof of what
importance it had assumed.   We may perhaps put
the first twenty years of the third century as the

---

[1] Euseb. *Hist.* v. 21.
[2] Tertullian, *Apol.* i. 37; *ad Scap.* 2.

point at which, having passed through the period when it was embraced by individuals with a several choice, it was become the faith of families, and one step only remained, that it should become the faith of nations.[1]

Let us consider a moment the mode of its increase. It was twofold. The plant of which a root was fixed by the Apostles and their successors in each of the cities of the empire grew, gathering to itself in every place the better minds of heathenism, and exercising from the beginning a marked attraction upon the more religious sex and upon the most down-trodden portion of society; women were ever won to it by the purity which its doctrines inculcated, slaves by its tender charity: it gave a moral emancipation to both. If we possessed a continuous and detailed history of the Christian Faith in any one city, say Rome, or Alexandria, or Antioch, or Ephesus, or Carthage, or Corinth, for the first three centuries, what a wonderful exhibition of spiritual power and material weakness it would offer! By fixing the mind on Christianity as merely one object, as an abstraction, we lose in large part the sense of the moral force to which its propagation bears witness. It was in each city a community,[2] which had its centre and representative in its bishop, which had its worship, discipline, and rule of life presided over by him; its presbytery, diaconate, and deaconesses; its sisterhoods and works of charity, spiritual and temporal: a complete government and a complete society held together by purely spiritual

[1] De Rossi, *Archeol. Christiana*, 1866, p. 33, makes this estimate.
[2] From a passage in the account of the Martyrs of Lyons, A.D. 177 (Euseb. *Hist.* v. 1, p. 201, l. 3), it appears that the word "Church" was only given to a mother or cathedral church by writers of that time.

bonds, which the State sometimes ignored, not unfre-
quently persecuted, but never favoured. Such was
the grain of mustard-seed, from north to south, from
east to west, in presence of the political Roman, the
sensitive and lettered Greek, the sensuous African,
the volatile and disputatious Alexandrian, the corrupt
Antiochene. It had one sort of population to deal
with at Rome, quite another in the capital of Egypt,
a third at Ephesus, which belonged to the great
goddess Diana, and the statue which had fallen down
from heaven, a fourth at Carthage, where the hot
Numidian blood came in contact with the civilisation
of Rome, a fifth at Corinth, the mistress of all art
and luxury. And so on. Now in each and all of
these cities and a hundred others the divine plant
met with various soils and temperatures; but in
them all it grew. It had its distinct experiences,
encountering many a withering heat and many a
stormy blast, and watered full oft with blood, but in
them all the seed, dropped so imperceptibly that the
mightiest and most jealous of empires was unconscious of what was cast into its bosom, became a tree.
It was an organic growth of vital power. Christianity,
during the ten ages of persecution, is the upspringing
of several hundred such communities, distinct as we
see here, and as described above by St. Ignatius, but at
the same time co-inherent, as we saw in the beginning,
and as we shall find presently. As, then, all the cities
of the Roman Empire had a secular political and
social life, and a municipal government of their own,
so had the Christian Faith in each of them a corresponding life of spiritual government and inward
thought; and if we had the materials to construct
the history of this Faith in any one, it would give

East and the whole Greek name, St. Peter set up the
chair of his disciple Mark. There the Evangelist taught
and there in due time suffered. Dragged by an in-
furiated populace through the streets he thus gave up
his soul. But the plant which he so watered with his
blood was of extraordinary vigour. It not only grew
amid the intensest intellectual rivalry of Greek and
Jew in the capital, but likewise in course of time
occupied the whole civil government which obeyed the
præfect of Egypt. From Alexandria, Egypt and the
Pentapolis of Cyrene derived their Christian faith and
government; and so powerful was this bond that the
bishop of the capital exercised control over all the
bishops of the civil diocese, as it was then termed.
He was in power a patriarch long before he had that
name, or even the name of archbishop. How great
and strict this rule was we may judge from an incident
preserved by Photius,[1] which occurred in the very last
year of the period we are considering, in 235. Heraclas, bishop of Alexandria, a former pupil of Origen,
had inflicted upon that great writer a second expulsion
from the Church for his erroneous teaching. Origen
on his way to Syria came to the city of Thmuis, where
Bishop Ammonius allowed him, in spite of the above-
mentioned censure of Heraclas, to preach. When
Heraclas heard this, he came to Thmuis and deposed
Ammonius, and appointed in his stead Philippus as
bishop. Afterwards, on the earnest request of the
people of the city, he restored Ammonius to the office
of bishop, and ordained that he and Philippus should
be bishops together. The latter, however, voluntarily
gave way to Ammonius, and succeeded him at his

[1] Photius, συναγωγαὶ καὶ ἀποδείξεις, quoted by Döllinger, *Hippolytus
und Kallistus*, pp. 264, 265.

death. Such, ninety years before the Nicene Council, which recognised and approved these powers of the bishop of Alexandria, as being after the model of those exercised by the bishop of Rome,[1] was his authority by the natural force of the hierarchic principle which built up the Church. And so little were these Christian communities, which we have seen so complete in their own organic growth, independent of the bond which held the whole Church together, and of which the authority of the Egyptian primate was itself a derivation.

These, then, were the two modes in which the Christian Faith pursued and attained its orderly increase ; as a seed it grew to a plant in each city, and as a plant it ramified, or as Tertullian says, carried " the vine-layer of the faith "[2] from city to city, from province to province. In the meantime the last disciples of the Apostles, those who, from the especial veneration with which they were regarded as teachers of the Faith and " second links in the chain of tradition," were termed Presbyters,[3] had died out. St. Polycarp, at the time of his martyrdom in 167, was probably the sole remaining one, though his pupil St. Irenæus had known others. When the latter, upon

---

[1] Can. 6, Concil. Nic. τὰ ἀρχαῖα ἔθη κρατείτω, τὰ ἐν Αἰγύπτῳ καὶ Λιβύῃ καὶ Πενταπόλει, ὥστε Ἀλεξανδρείας ἐπίσκοπον πάντων τούτων ἔχειν τὴν ἐξουσίαν, ἐπειδὴ καὶ τῷ ἐν Ῥώμῃ ἐπισκόπῳ τοῦτο σύνηθές ἐστιν. See Hagemann, *die Römische Kirche*, 596-8.

[2] "Traducem fidei et semina doctrinæ." *De Præscrip.* 20.

[3] See Döllinger, *Hipp. u. Kall*, pp. 338-343, for the meaning of this word in the time of St. Irenæus, as carrying with it a special magisterium fidei. "Presbyteros " was added as a title of honour to the name of Bishop. In St. Irenæus the same persons have as Bishops the succession of the Apostles, as Presbyteri "the charisma of the truth." Papias marks the Asiatic Presbyteri as those who had heard of St. John ; and Clement of Alex. speaks of Presbyteri who, occupied with the office of teaching, and deeming it diverse from that of composition, did not write. *Eclogæ* xxvii. p. 996.

the martyrdom of St. Pothinus in 177, is raised to the government of the See of Lyons, we may consider that no one survived in possession of that great personal authority which belonged to those who had themselves been taught by Apostles ; and so at the third generation from the last of these the Church throughout the world stood without any such support, simply upon that basis of the tradition and teaching of the truth, and of the succession of rulers, on which the Apostles had placed it, to last for ever.   Now in this position it had already, throughout the whole course of the second century, been violently assaulted by a family of heresies, which growing upon one root—a natural philosophy confusing the being of God with the world —burst forth into an astonishing variety of outward forms.   Gnosticism completely altered and defaced Christian doctrine under each of the four great heads, the Being of God, the Person of Christ, the nature of man, the office and function of the Church.   Into the Godhead it introduced a dualism, recognising with the absolute good an absolute evil represented by matter : it denied the reality of the Incarnation ; it made the body a principle of evil in man's nature : but we will here limit ourselves to the characteristic and formal principle of the system from which it derived its name, to Gnosis as the means of acquiring divine truth.   Now the Christian religion taught that revealed truth was to be attained by the individual through receiving, upon the ground of the divine veracity, those mysterious doctrines superior but not contrary to reason which it unfolded ; and that the communication of such doctrines might continue unimpaired and unchanging, it taught that our Lord had established a never-failing authority charged with the execution of this office, and assisted by the perpetual presence of His Spirit with it to the end.   But the Gnostics admitted only in the case of the imperfect or natural man that faith was the means for acquiring religious truth ; to the spiritual, the proper Gnostic, gnosis should take the place of faith : for to many a heathen, accustomed to unlimited philosophical speculation, the absolute subjection of the intellect to divine authority, required by the principle of faith, was repugnant.   Now this gnosis was in their mind not knowledge grounded upon faith, but either philosophic science, or a supposed intuition of truth, which was not only to replace faith, but the whole moral life, inasmuch as the completion and sanctification of man were to be wrought by it.   And thus instead of an external authority the individual reason was set up as the highest standard of religious truth, the issue of which could only be rationalism in belief and sectarianism in practice.

This formal principle of Gnosticism when duly carried out would deny the idea of the Church, its divine institution, its properties and prerogatives.   For the Gnostic mode of attaining divine truth, as above stated, contains in it such a denial.   Besides this, the Gnostic doctrine that matter was the seat of evil, destroyed the belief that Christ had assumed a body : the Gnostic doctrine that the supreme God could enter into no communion with man made their Æon Christ no member of human society, but a phantom which had enlightened the man Jesus, and then returned back to the " Light-realm."   Not being really the Son of God, he could have no Church which was his body : not really redeeming, for sin to the Gnostic had only a physical, not a moral cause, he was but a teacher, and therefore had created no institution to convey

As such it is not without significance that he encountered the first of the Apostles in Samaria, endeavouring to purchase from him the gifts of grace and miraculous power, and that he likewise afterwards encountered him at Rome. To this the first manifestation of Gnosticism succeed heretical doctrines concerning the Person of our Lord, which sprung out of Judaism ; but no sooner are these overcome than Gnosticism in its later forms spreads from Syria and Alexandria over the whole empire, everywhere confronting the Church, seducing her members, and tempting especially speculative minds within her.   A mixture itself of Platonic, Philonic, Pythagorean, and Parsic philosophy, affecting to gather the best out of all philosophies and religions, in which it exactly represented the eclectic spirit of its age, arraying itself in the most fantastic garb of imagination, but at the bottom no dubious product of the old heathen pantheism, it set itself to the work, while it assumed Christian names, of confusing and distracting Christian truth.   From the beginning of the second century it was the great enemy which beset the Church. It may, then, well represent to us the principle of heresy itself, and as such let us consider on what principles it was met by the Church's teachers.

Now to form a correct notion of the danger to which the Christian people at this time was exposed, we must have before us that it was contained in several hundred communities, each of them forming a complete spiritual society and government.   These had arisen under the pressure of such hostility on the part of the empire that it is only in the time of the last emperor during this period, Alexander Severus, that churches are known to have publicly existed at

Rome.[1] For a very long time all meetings of Christians and all celebration of their worship were secret. It is obvious what an absolute freedom of choice on the part of all those who became Christians this fact involved.   Nor did that freedom cease when they had been initiated into the new religion.   Their fidelity to the Christian faith was all through their subsequent life solicited by the danger in which as Christians they stood.   Only a continuous freedom of choice on their part could maintain it.   And not only did every temporal interest turn against it, but in the case at least of the more intellectual converts the activity of thought implied in their voluntary acceptance of a new belief served as a material on which the seductions of false teachers might afterwards act, unless it was controlled by an ever-living faith, and penetrated by an active charity.   The more these Christian communities multiplied, the more it was to be expected that some of them would yield to the assaults of false teachers.   It is in just such a state of things that a great dogmatic treatise was written against Gnosticism by one who stood at only a single remove from the Apostle John, being the disciple of his disciple Polycarp.   Irenæus, by birth a native of lesser Asia, enjoyed when young the instructions and intimate friendship of the bishop of Smyrna.   In his old age he delighted to remember how Polycarp had described his intercourse with John, and with those who had seen the Lord : how he repeated their discourse, and what he had heard from them respecting the teaching and the miracles of that Word of life whom they had seen with their

---

[1] Tillemont, *Hist. des Emp.* iii. 281, deduces it from a passage of Origen on St. Matt. tom. iii. p. 857 c.

own eyes. "These things," says Irenæus, "through the mercy of God I then diligently listened to, writing them down not on paper, but on my heart, and by His grace I ruminate upon them perpetually."[1] Later in life he left Smyrna, and settled in Lyons, of which Church he was a presbyter when the terrible persecution of 177 broke out there. Elected thereupon to succeed a martyr as bishop, he crowned an episcopate of twenty-five years with a similar martyrdom. He wrote, as he says, during the episcopate of Eleutherius, who was the twelfth bishop of Rome from Peter, and sat from 177 to 192. After describing at length the Gnostic errors concerning the divine nature, he sets forth in contrast the unity of the truth as declared by the Church in the following words:

"The Church, though she be spread abroad through the whole world unto the ends of the earth, has received from the Apostles and their disciples faith in one God;" and he proceeds to recite her creed, in substance the same as that now held: then he adds, dwelling with emphasis on the very point which I have been noting, the sprinkling about, that is, of distinct communities so widely dispersed, which yet are one in their belief:

"This proclamation and this faith the Church having received, though she be disseminated through the whole world, carefully guards, as the inhabitant of one house, and equally believes these things as having one soul and the same heart, and in exact agreement these things she proclaims and teaches and hands down, as having one mouth. For, though the languages through the world be dissimilar, the power of the tradition is one and the same. Nor have the

---

[1] *Frag. Epist. ad Florin.* tom. i. p. 340.

churches founded in Germany otherwise believed or
otherwise handed down, nor those in Spain, nor in
Gaul, nor in the East, nor in Egypt, nor those in the
middle of the world.   But as the sun, God's creature,
in all the world is one and the same, so too the proclamation of the truth shines everywhere, and lights
all men that are willing to come to the knowledge of
the truth.   Nor will he among the Church's rulers
who is most powerful in word say other than this, for
no one is above his teacher ; [1] nor will he that is weak
in word diminish the tradition, for the Faith being
one and the same, neither he that can say much on it
has gathered too much, nor he that can say little is
deficient."

Against the Gnostic claim to possess a private
tradition, in virtue of which each of them "depraving
the rule of the truth was not ashamed to preach himself," he sets forth the one original tradition which the
Apostles,[2] only "when they had first been invested
with the power of the Holy Ghost coming down on
them, and endued with perfect knowledge," delivered
to the churches founded by them.   "And this tradition of the Apostles, manifested in the whole world,
may be seen in every church by all who have the will
to see what is true, and we can give the chain of
those who by the Apostles were appointed bishops in
the churches, and their successors down to our time,
who have neither taught nor known any such delirious
dream as these imagine.   For, had the Apostles known
any reserved mysteries, which they taught to the perfect separately and secretly from the rest, assuredly

[1] He seems to refer to Matt. x. 24 : οὐκ ἔστι μαθητὴς ὑπὲρ τὸν διδάσ-
καλον.
[2] St. Irenæus, lib. iii. c. 2 ; lib. iii. c. 1.

they would have delivered them to those especially to whom they entrusted the churches themselves. For very perfect and irreprehensible in all respects did they wish those to be whom they left for their own successors,[1] delivering over to them their own office of teaching, by correct conduct on whose part great advantage would accrue, as from their fall the utmost calamity. But since it would be too long here to enumerate the succession of all the churches, we take the church the greatest, the most ancient, and known to all, founded and established at Rome by the two most glorious Apostles Peter and Paul. Pointing out the tradition which it received from the Apostles, and the faith which it has announced to men, reaching down to us by the succession of its bishops, we confound all those who form societies other than they ought, in any way, whether for the sake of self-fancied doctrines, or through blindness and an evil mind. For, with this church, on account of its superior principate, it is necessary that every church agree. . . .

" The blessed Apostles, then, having founded and built up the Church, committed to Linus the administration of its episcopate. . . . Anacletus succeeds him, from whom in the third place from the Apostles Clemens inherits the episcopate. . . . He is succeeded by Evaristus ; Evaristus by Alexander, who is followed by Xystus, sixth from the Apostles. Then Telesphorus, who was gloriously martyred ; next Hyginus ; then Pius ; after whom Anicetus. Soter followed Anicetus ; and now, in the twelfth degree from the Apostles, Eleutherius holds the place of bishop. By this order

---

[1] "Quos et successores relinquebant, suum ipsorum locum magisterii tradentes."

and succession the tradition from the Apostles in the
Church and the teaching of the truth have come down
to us.   And this proof is most complete that it is one
and the same life-giving Faith which has been preserved in the Church from the Apostles up to this
time, and handed down in truth. . . . With such
proofs, then, before us, we ought not still to search
among others for the truth, which it is easy to take
from the Church, since the Apostles most fully committed unto this, as unto a rich storehouse, all the
truth, so that every one, whoever will, may draw
from it the draught of life.   For this is the gate
of life : all the rest are thieves and robbers.   They
must therefore be avoided ; but whatever is of the
Church we must love with the utmost diligence, and
lay hold of the tradition of the truth.   For how ?   If
on any small matter question arose, ought we not
to recur to the most ancient churches in which the
Apostles lived, and take from them on the matter in
hand what is certain and plain.   And suppose the
Apostles had not even left us writings, ought we not
to follow that order of tradition which they delivered
to those to whom they entrusted the churches ?   To this
order many barbarous nations of believers in Christ
assent, having salvation written upon their hearts by
the Holy Spirit without paper and ink, and diligently
guarding the old tradition." [1]

This capital point of the ever-living teaching office
he further dwells on :

"The Faith received in the Church we guard in
it, which being always from the Spirit of God, like an
admirable deposit in a good vessel, is young itself, and
makes young the vessel in which it is.   For this office

[1] St. Irenæus, lib. iii. c. 3, 4.

on the part of God [1] is entrusted to the Church, as the breath of life was given to the body, in order that all the members receiving may be quickened, and in this is placed the communication of Christ, that is, the Holy Spirit, the earnest of incorruption, the confirmation of our faith, and the ladder by which we ascend to God. For, says he, in the Church God has placed Apostles, Prophets, Teachers, and all the remaining operation of the Spirit; of whom all those are not partakers who do not run to the Church, but deprive themselves of life by an evil opinion and a still worse conduct. For where the Church is, there also is the Spirit of God: and where the Spirit of God is, there is the Church and all grace: but the Spirit is Truth. Wherefore they who are not partakers of Him are neither nourished unto life from the breasts of the mother, nor receive that most pure fountain which proceeds from the Body of Christ, but dig out for themselves broken cisterns from earthly ditches, and from the filth drink foul water, avoiding the Faith of the Church lest they be brought back, and rejecting the Spirit that they may not be taught. So estranged from the truth they deservedly wallow in every error, tossed about by it, having different opinions on the same subjects at different times, and never holding one firm mind, choosing rather to be sophists of words than disciples of the truth; for they are not founded upon the one rock, but on the sand, which has in it a multitude of pebbles." [2]

And he elsewhere contrasts the certainty within, and the uncertainty without, this teaching power:

"The said heretics, then, being blind to the truth, cannot help walking out of the track into one path

---

[1] "Hoc enim Ecclesiæ creditum est Dei munus."   [2] Lib. iii. c. 24.

after another, and hence it is that the vestiges of
their doctrine are scattered about without any rule
or sequence.   Whereas the road of those who are of
the Church goes round the whole world, because it
possesses a firm tradition from the Apostles, and gives
us to see that all have one and the same faith, where
all enjoin one and the same God the Father, believe
one disposition of the Son of God's Incarnation, know
the same gift of the Spirit, meditate on the same
precepts, guard the same regimen of ecclesiastical
rule, await the same advent of the Lord, and support
the same salvation of the whole man, body and soul
alike.   Now the Church's preaching is true and firm,
in whom one and the same way of salvation is shown
through the whole world.   For to her is entrusted the
light of God ; and hence the wisdom of God, by which
He saves all men, ' is sung at her entrance, acts with
confidence in her streets, is proclaimed on her walls,
and speaks ever in the gates of the city.'   For everywhere the Church proclaims the truth : she is the
seven-branched candlestick bearing Christ's light." [1]

It has been necessary to give at considerable length
the very words of St. Irenæus, because they are stronger
and more perspicuous than any summary of them can
be, and because they exhibit a complete answer not to
this particular heresy only, but to all heresy for ever.
Such an answer, coming from one who stood at the
second generation from St. John, is of the highest
value.   Thus he meets the Gnostic error that
divine truth is acquired by the individual through
some process of his own mind, which in this particular
case is termed gnosis, but may bear many other names.
He meets it by appealing to an external standard, the

[1] Lib. v. c. 20.

Rule of Faith in the Church from the beginning, which by its unity points to its origin and lineage from the Apostles and Christ. And this serves to bring out the central idea which rules his whole mind, that " where the Church is, there also is the Spirit of God ; and where the Spirit of God is, there is the Church and all grace : but the Spirit is Truth." The deposit of which he spoke is not a dead mass, or lump of ore, requiring only safe custody, but a living Spirit dwelling in the Church, the source within her of unity, truth, and grace, using her teaching office, which is set up in her episcopate, for the drawing out and propagation of the deposit from the double fountain of Tradition and Scripture, for these her teachers as such have a divine gift of truth.[1] It is thus that he expands without altering the doctrine of his teacher Polycarp's fellow-disciple, " Where Jesus Christ is, there is the Catholic Church." [2] And from it he proceeds to what follows necessarily on such a conception, that this Church must have a visible point of unity. As then he appeals to the churches founded by Apostles as the principal centres of living tradition, so before yet one of these churches had fallen into possession of heretics,[3] before yet there was any disagreement between them, he singles out one for its superior principate, on account of which it was necessary for every church to agree with it, which he grounds on its descent from St. Peter and St. Paul, giving every link in the chain of succession during the hundred and ten years which had elapsed between their martyr-

---

[1] "Qui cum episcopatus successione charisma veritatis certum secundum placitum Patris acceperunt," iv. 26, 2 ; and 5, "Ubi igitur charismata Domini posita sunt, ibi discere oportet veritatem, apud quos est ea quæ est ab apostolis ecclesiæ successio."

[2] St. Ignatius, quoted above, p. 169.   [3] Schwane, p. 661.

dom and his own episcopate. He sees an especial
prerogative lodged in that church as the means of
securing the whole Church's organic unity ; and this
prerogative is, that it is among churches what St. Peter
and St. Paul were among Apostles ; [1] as the first general
western council expressed it, "in it the Apostles sit
daily, and their blood without intermission bears witness to the glory of God." [2]

Thus the conception expressed by Irenæus, with the
greatest emphasis and continual repetition, in order to
refute heresy, is that all truth and grace are stored up
in the one body of the Church ; to which his doctrine
of the Roman Primacy is as the keystone to the arch.
For everything in his view depends on the unity, the
intrinsic harmony, of the truth which he is describing
as lodged in the episcopate : the means therefore of
securing that unity are part of its conception. Accordingly, to see in its due force his statement that every
church must agree with the Roman Church, it must
not be severed from the context and taken by itself,
but viewed in connection with the argument as part
of which it stands. If the Church is to speak one
truth with one mouth, which is his main idea, she
must have an organic provision for such a result, which
he places in the necessary agreement of all churches
with one : and this is his second idea, subsidiary to
the first, and completing it.

Irenæus by birth and education represents in all
this the witness of the Asiatic churches ; as bishop of
Lyons, the churches of Gaul.

[1] Hagemann, p. 622.
[2] Letter of the Synod of Arles to Pope Sylvester : " Quoniam re-
cedere a partibus istis minime potuisti, in quibus et Apostoli quotidie
sedent, et cruor ipsorum sine intermissione Dei gloriam testatur."
Mansi, *Concilia*, ii, 469.

A few years after Irenæus, Tertullian in a professed treatise against heresy lays down exactly the same principles. With him, too, the main idea is the possession of all truth and grace by the one Body which Christ formed and the Apostles established. This he thus exhibits :

" We must not appeal to the Scriptures, nor try the issue on points on which the victory is either none, or doubtful, or too little doubtful. For though the debate on the Scriptures should not so turn out as to place each party on an equal footing, the order of things requires that that question should be first proposed which is the only one now to be discussed, To whom does the Faith itself belong ? Whose are the Scriptures ? From whom and through whom, when and to whom, was that discipline by which men become Christians delivered ? For wherever the truth of that which is the Christian discipline at once and faith be shown to be, there will be the truth of the Scriptures, of their exposition, and of all Christian traditions. Our Lord Jesus Christ (may He suffer me so to speak for the present), whoever He is, of whatever God the Son, of whatever substance God and Man, of whatever reward the promiser, Himself declared so long as He was on earth, whether to the people openly, or to the disciples apart, what He was, what He had been, what will of the Father He administered, what duty of man He laid down. Of whom He had attached to His own side twelve in chief, the destined teachers of the nations. One of these having fallen off from Him, He bade the other eleven, on His departure to the Father after the Resurrection, go and teach the nations, who were to be baptized into the Father, into the Son, and into the

Holy Ghost. The Apostles then forthwith, the word apostle signifying their mission of being sent, assumed by lot Matthias as a twelfth into the place of Judas. When they had obtained the promised power of the Holy Ghost to speak and work miracles, they first through Judea bore witness to the Faith in Christ Jesus, and established churches. Thence proceeding into the world they promulgated the same doctrine of the same Faith to the nations, and thereupon founded churches in every city, from which the other churches thenceforth borrowed the vine-layer of the Faith and the seeds of the doctrine, and are daily borrowing them that they may become churches. And for this cause they are themselves also counted apostolical, as being the offspring of apostolical churches. The whole kind must be classed under its original. And thus these churches so many and so great are that one first from the Apostles, whence they all spring. Thus all are the first, and all apostolical, while all being the one prove unity: whilst there is between them communication of peace, and the title of brotherhood, and the token of hospitality.[1] And no other principle rules these rights than the one tradition of the same mystery."[2]

Here is the summing up of what Irenæus had said with the force, brevity, and incisiveness which characterise Tertullian. Further on he rejects any appeal on the part of heretics to Scripture:

"If the truth be in our possession, as many as walk by the rule which the Church has handed down from the Apostles, the Apostles from Christ, and Christ from God, the reasonableness of our proposition is

---

[1] Tertull. *de Præsc.* 19, 20.
[2] The word here stands evidently for the whole body of Christian truth, rites, and discipline, the communication of which was a *sacramentum.*

manifest, which lays down that heretics are not to be allowed to enter an appeal to Scriptures, since without Scriptures we prove them to have no concern with Scriptures. For if they are heretics, they cannot be Christians, inasmuch as they do not hold from Christ what they follow by their own choice, and in consequence admit the name of heretics.[1] Therefore not being Christians, they have no right to Christian writings. To whom we may well say, Who are you? when did you come? and whence? What are you, who are not mine, doing in my property? By what right dost thou, Marcion, cut down my wood? By what licence dost thou, Valentinus, turn the course of my waters? By what power remove my landmarks? This is my possession: how are you sowing it and feeding on it at your pleasure? It is mine, I repeat: I had it of old; I had it first: I have the unquestioned title-deeds from the first proprietors. I am the heir of the Apostles. According to their will, according to their trust, according to the oath I took from them, I hold it. You, assuredly, they have ever disinherited and renounced, as aliens, as enemies. But why are heretics aliens and enemies to Apostles, save from difference of doctrine, which each at his own pleasure has either brought forward or received against Apostles?"[2]

Thus Tertullian adds the witness of the African church to that of the Asiatic and Gallic churches in Irenæus.

We have noted the great church of Alexandria as a most complete instance of the growth whereby from the mother See the hierarchy took possession of a

---

[1] That is, he opposes the word *choosers* to the word *Christians;* the one signifying those who believe what they *choose*, the other those who believe what Christ taught.

[2] *De Præscrip.* 37.

land. But the principle of such growth was the ecclesiastical rule, and its strength the energy with which that rule was preserved. This rule was two-fold: the rule of discipline, or outward regimen, what we now call a constitution; and the rule of Faith. What the church of Alexandria was in discipline has been seen above: and now just at this time we have, in the first great teacher of this church who has come down to us, the most decisive exhibition of this rule as a defence against this same Gnostic heresy. "As Circe bewitched men by her enchantments into beasts, so," says Clement, "whosoever has kicked against the tradition of the Church, and started aside into the opinions of human heresies, has ceased to be a man of God, and faithful to the Lord." . . . "There are three states of the soul, ignorance, opinion, know-ledge. Those who are in ignorance are the Gentiles; those in knowledge, the true Church; those in opinion, the adherents of heresies." . . . "We have learnt that bodily pleasure is one thing, which we give to the Gentiles; strife a second, which we adjudge to heresies; joy a third, which is the property of the Church." Again, he speaks of those who "not using the divine words well, but perversely, neither enter themselves into the kingdom of heaven, nor suffer those whom they have deceived to attain the truth. They have not indeed the key to the entrance, but rather a false key, whereby they do not enter as we do through the Lord's tradition, drawing back the veil, but cutting out a side way, and secretly digging through the Church's wall, they transgress the truth, and initiate into rites of error the soul of the irreligious. For that they have made their human associations later than the Catholic Church,

cular errors Origen may have fallen, he did not
swerve from their doctrine as to the mode of meeting error itself. "Since," says he, "there are many
who think that they hold the tenets of Christ, while
some of them hold different tenets from those who
went before them, let the ecclesiastical preaching as
handed down by the order of succession from the
Apostles, and maintained even to the present time
in the churches, be preserved : that alone is to be
believed as truth which in nothing is discordant
from the ecclesiastical and apostolical tradition." [1]
And the ground for such a principle he has given
elsewhere :

"The divine words assert that the whole Church
of God is the Body of Christ, animated by the Son
of God, while the limbs of this Body as a whole are
particular believers. As the soul quickens and moves
the body, whose nature it is not to have the movement
of life from itself, so the Word moving to what is
fitting, and working in, the whole body, the Church,
moves likewise each member of the Church, who does
nothing without the Word." [2]

The four great writers, then, of this period, Irenæus, Tertullian, Clement, and Origen, none of them
indeed from Rome, but representing the churches of
Asia, Gaul, Africa, and Egypt, exactly concur in the
principle by which they refuted heresy, the propagation, that is, of the rule of Faith in its purity and
integrity, by those who possessed the succession of
the Apostles and their office of teaching, in which
lay a divine gift of the truth.

But to those who proceeded from this basis it

---

[1] *De Principiis*, pref. p. 47. See also on Matt. tom. iii. 864, a
passage equally decisive.   [2] *Cont. Cels.* vi. 48, tom. i. 670.

was a further labour to set forth the true knowledge against the false. And we may trace the following results of heresy, quite unintended by itself, in its operation on the Church.

1. In the first place, St. Augustine continually remarks that the more accurate enucleation of true doctrine usually proceeded from the attacks of heresy; and this happened so continually that it seems to him a special instance of that law of Divine Providence which educes good from evil. "If the truth," says he, "had not lying adversaries, it would be examined with less carefulness," and so "a question started by an opponent becomes to the disciple an occasion of learning."[1] And he observes that "we have found by experience that every heresy has brought into the Church its own questions, against which the divine Scripture was defended with greater care than if no such necessity had existed."[2] Thus the doctrine of the Trinity owed its perfect treatment to the Arian assault on it; the doctrine of penance to that of Novatian; the doctrine of baptism to those who wished to introduce the practice of rebaptizing; even the unity of Christ was brought out with greater clearness by the attempt to rend it, and the doctrine of one Catholic Church diffused through the whole world cleared from its objectors by showing that the mixture of evil men in it does not prejudice the good.[3] And he illustrates his meaning by a very picturesque image: "When heretics calumniate, the young of the flock are disturbed; in their disturbance they inquire; so the young lamb butts its mother's udder till it gets

[1] *De Civ. Dei*, xvi. 2.   [2] *De dono persev.* 53.
[3] Enarr. in Ps. 54, tom. iv. 513.

sufficient nutriment for its thirst." [1]   For the doctors of the Church being called upon for an answer supply the truth which before was latent.   And there is no more signal instance of the great writer's remark than himself ; for the attacks of the most various heresies led him during forty years of unwearied mental activity into almost every question of theology.

The Gnostic heresy, then, presents us with the first instance of a law which will run all through the Church's history.   Peter, the first Apostle, meets and refutes Simon Magus, the first propagator of false-hood, who receives divine sacraments and then claims against the giver to be "the great power of God." This fact is likewise the symbol of a long line of action, wherein it is part of the divine plan to make the perpetual restlessness of error subserve the com-plete exhibition of truth.   The Gnostics denied the divine monarchy ; at once mutilated and misinter-preted Scripture ; claimed to themselves a secret tradition of truth.   We owe to them in consequence the treatises of Irenæus, Tertullian, and Clement, and a written exhibition of the Church's divine order, suc-cession, and unity, as well as a specific mention of the tie which held that unity together ; and the mention of this tie at so early a period might otherwise have been wanting to us.   But these three writers do but represent to us partially an universal result.   The danger which from Gnostic influence beset all the chief centres of ecclesiastical teaching marks the tran-sition from the first state of simple faith to that of human learning, inquiry, and thought, turned upon the objects of Christian belief.   The Gnostics had a merit which they little imagined for themselves.

[1] Serm. 51, tom. v. 288.

They formed the first doctors of post-apostolic times. Irenæus, Tertullian, and Clement are a great advance upon the more simple and external exhibition of Christianity which we find in the apologists. In them the Church is preparing to encounter the deepest questions moved against her by Greek philosophy. They are her first champions in that contest with Hellenic culture which was a real combat of mind, not a mere massacre of unresisting victims, and which lasted for five hundred years.

2. Secondly, when the Gnostic attack began, the canon of the New Testament was still unfixed. Nothing can be more certain than that the Apostles did not set forth any official collection of their writings, and that no such collection existed shortly after their death. This fact most plainly shows that the Christian religion at their departure did not rest for its maintenance upon writings. Not only had our Lord written no word Himself, but He left no command to His Apostles to write. His command was to propagate His Gospel and to found His kingdom by oral teaching; and His promise was that the Holy Ghost should accompany, follow upon, and continue with, this their action. What we find is, that they did this, and that the writings which besides they left, being from the first kept and venerated by the several churches to which they were addressed, gradually became known through the whole body of the Church. With the lapse of time they would become more and more valuable. Moreover, when the Gnostics set themselves to interpolate and corrupt them, and to fabricate false writings, the need of a genuine collection became more and more urgent. We learn from the three writers above mentioned, towards the end of

the second century, that this collection existed, and that it was based on certain principles. Firstly, only those writings were admitted which tradition traced back to an Apostle or a witness of Our Lord's life,[1] among whom Paul was specially counted. Secondly, only such writings as were attested by some church of apostolical foundation. Thirdly, only such writings as contained a doctrine which did not differ from the rule of faith orally handed down in the churches of apostolic origin, or in the one Catholic Church, excluding all such as were at variance with the doctrine hitherto received. Thus in the settlement of the canon authority as well as tradition intervened; an authority which felt itself in secure possession of the same Holy Spirit who had inspired the Apostles, and of the same doctrine which they had taught.[2]

With the reception of a book into the canon of Scripture was joined a belief in its inspiration, which rested on what was a part of oral tradition, that is, that the Apostles as well in their oral as in their written teaching had enjoyed the infallible guidance of the Holy Spirit. It is evident that such a tradition reposes, in the last instance, upon the authority of the Church.[3]

If by means of the Gnostic attacks the canon of the New Testament, as we now possess it, was not absolutely completed, it had at least advanced a very great way towards that completion, which we have finally attested as of long standing in a Council held at Carthage in 397.[4]

3. Another result of the Gnostic attack was the setting forth the tradition of the Faith, seated and

---

[1] St. Mark's Gospel would be referred to St. Peter, and St. Luke's writings to St. Paul.

[2] See Schwane, pp. 779, 780.   [3] Schwane, pp. 783, 784.

[4] " Quia a patribus ista accepimus in ecclesia legenda," n. 47.

maintained in the apostolic churches, as the rule for interpreting Scripture. The Gnostics in two ways impeached this rule, by claiming a private tradition of their own, and by interpreting such Scripture as they chose to acknowledge after their own pleasure. Irenæus, Tertullian, and Clement found an adequate answer to both errors by showing that the Faith which the Apostles had set forth in their writings could not contradict the Faith which they had established in the Church. These were two sources of the same doctrine; but it is by the permanent connection and interpenetration of the two that the truth is maintained. That which holds both together, utters and propagates the truth they jointly contain, is the teaching office, the mouth of the Church. Hence the force of the appeal in Irenæus to the succession of the Episcopate, and to the divine gift of truth which the Apostles had handed down therein with their teaching office. Hence Tertullian's exclusion of heretics from the right to possess Scriptures which belong only to the Church. Hence Clement's description of the only true Gnostic, as " one who has grown old in the study of the Scriptures, while he preserves the apostolic and ecclesiastical standard of doctrine." [1] For neither in founding churches, nor in teaching orally, nor in writing, did the Apostles exhaust or resign the authority committed to them. [2] The authority itself, which was the source of all this their action, after all that they had founded, taught, or written, continued complete and entire in them, and was transmitted on to their successors, for the maintenance of the work assigned to it. It is this

---

[1] *Stromata*, vii. c. 16, p. 896.
[2] See Kleutgen, *Theologie der Vorzeit*, iii. 957; Schwane, vol. i. 3.

case and in the other the result is that which it least
desires and intends; heresy, disbelieving and disobeying,
is made to perfect the faith and build up the hierarchy.

Now to sum up our sketch of the internal history of
the Christian Faith in the seventy-four years which
elapse from the accession of Marcus Aurelius to the
death of Alexander Severus. At the first-named date
we find that it had spread beyond the confines of the
Roman Empire, and taken incipient possession of all
the great centres of human intercourse by founding
its hierarchy in them. At the second date it has subdued the powerful and widespread family of heresies
which threatened to distort and corrupt its doctrines.
This was achieved by the vigour of its teaching office,
combining in one expression the yet fresh apostolic
tradition stored up in its churches, and the doctrine of
its sacred Scriptures. At the same time it has well-
nigh determined the number and genuineness of
these, severing them off from all other writings. The
episcopate in which its teaching office resides appears
not as a number of bishops, each independent and
severed, and merely governing his diocese upon a
similar rule, but with a bond recognised among them,
the superior principate of the Roman See. That is,
as the teaching office itself is in them all the voice of
living teachers, so its highest expression is the voice
of the living Peter in his see. And this bond as
discerned and recognised by the Asiatic disciple of
St. Polycarp, the bishop of the chief city of Gaul, is
so strong that he uses for it rather the term denoting
physical necessity than moral fitness : [1] as if he would

[1] Observed by Hagemann, p. 618, referring to the words of St.
Irenæus, "ad hanc enim Ecclesiam propter potiorem principalitatem
necesse est omnem convenire Ecclesiam," &c. It must be remembered

say: As Christ has made the Church, it must agree from one end to the other in doctrine and communion with the doctrine and communion of the Church in which Peter, to whom He has committed His sheep, speaks and rules. And so powerful is the derivation of this authority that he who sits in the place of Mark, whom Peter sent, punishes by degradation a bishop who disregards his sentence in the case of a great writer, the brightest genius of the Church in that day. And when we look at the spiritual state of the world at the beginning of the third century, we find that Christianity, having formed and made its place in human society, is penetrating through it more and more in every direction. It is then that we discern the first beginnings of that great spiritual creation, in which Reason has been applied to Faith under the guidance of authority, which the Christian Church, alone being in possession of these three constituents, could alone produce, and has carried on from that day to this. Alexandria was at this time the seat of a Jewish religious philosophy; it had just become the seat likewise of a heathen religious philosophy; there was within its church a great catechetical school, in which the Faith as taught by the apostolical and ecclesiastical tradition according to the Scriptures was communicated. It was to be expected that its teachers, such men as Pantænus, Clement, and Origen, would be led on from the more elementary work of imparting the rudiments of the Faith to the scientific consideration of its deeper mysteries; and even the

---

that the proper word for the power which held together the whole Roman Empire was Principatus, the very word used by St. Augustine to express the *original* authority of the Roman See: "Romanæ Ecclesiæ, in qua *semper* apostolicæ cathedræ viguit *principatus*." *Ep.* 43.

sight of what was going on around them among Jews and Greeks would invite them to attempt the construction of a Christian religious philosophy.

Moreover, Gnosticism, of which Alexandria was the chief focus, had raised the question of the unity and nature of the Godhead, and professed a false gnosis as the perfection of religion. By this also thoughtful minds were led to consider the true relation of knowledge to faith, and hence to attempt the first rudiments of a Theology, the Science of Faith.

To refute heathenism both as a Philosophy and as a Religion, and to set forth Christianity as the absolute truth, was the very function of such men as Clement and Origen; and the former in his work entitled "The Pedagogue" exhibits the conduct of life according to the principles and doctrines of Christianity; while his *Stromata*, or Tapestries, exhibit the building up of science on the foundation of faith.[1] We can hardly realise now the difficulties which beset his great pupil Origen, when, carrying on the master's thought, he endeavoured to found a theology. The fact that he was among the first to venture on such a deep, is the best excuse that can be made for those speculative errors into which he fell.

III. And now we turn to the conduct of the empire towards this religion which has grown up in its bosom.

At once with the accession of Marcus Aurelius a temper of greater severity to Christians is shown. The sort of toleration expressed in the rescript of Pius to the province of Asia is withdrawn. No new law about them is enacted, for none is needed, but

[1] See Kuhn, *Einleitung in die katholische Dogmatik*, i. 345, 346.

the old law is let loose.   The almost sublime clemency
of Marcus towards his revolted general Cassius, his
reign of nineteen years unstained with senatorial
blood, and the campaigns prolonged from year to
year of one who loved his philosophic studies above
all things, and yet at the call of imperial duty gave
up night and day to the rudest toils of a weary
conflict with barbarous tribes on the frontier, have
won for him immortal honour: his regard for his
subjects in general has sometimes given him in Christian estimation the place of predilection among all
princes ancient and modern.[1]   It is well, then, to
consider his bearing towards Christians.   Now among
his teachers was that Junius Rusticus, grandson of
the man who perished for the sake of liberty in
Domitian's time, and in his day no doubt a perfect
specimen of the Roman gentleman and noble, a
blending of all that was best in Cicero, Lælius, and
Cato, whom Marcus made Prefect of Rome, and to
whom when bearing that office he addressed a rescript
containing the words, "To Junius Rusticus, Prefect of
the city, our friend."   And what this friend of Marcus
thought on the most important subjects we may judge
from the sentiments of another friend and fellow-
teacher of the emperor, Maximus of Tyre, who has
left written, " How God rules a mighty and stable
kingdom having for its limits not river or lake or
shore or ocean, but the heaven above and the earth
beneath, in which He, impassive as law, bestows on
those who obey Him the security of which He is the
fountain : and the gods his children need not images
any more than good men statues.   Our vocal speech

---

[1] Guizot ranks Marcus Aurelius with St. Louis, as the only rulers
who preferred conscience to gain in all their conduct.

requires no particular characters, yet human weakness has invented the alphabetical signs whereby to give expression to its remembrance, so the nature of the gods needs not images, but man, removed from them as far as heaven from earth, has devised these signs, by which to give them names. There may be those strong enough to do without these helps, but they are rare, and as schoolmasters guide their scholars to write by first pencilling letters for them, so legislators have invented these images as signs of the divine honour, and helps to human memory. But God is the father and framer of all things, older than heaven, superior to time and all fleeting nature, legislator ineffable, unexpressed by voice, unseen by eye; and we who cannot grasp His essence rest upon words and names, and forms of gold, ivory, and silver, in our longing to conceive Him, giving to His nature what is fair among ourselves. But fix Him only in the mind; I care not whether the Greek is kindled into re-membrance of Him by the art of Phidias, or the Egyptian by the worship of animals, that fire is his symbol to these, and water to those; only let them understand, let them love, let them remember Him alone." [1]

I doubt not that Junius Rusticus was familiar with such thoughts as these, and as a matter of philosophic reflection assented to them. And now let us study the scene which was enacted in his presence and by his command.[2]

"At a time when the defenders of idolatry had proposed edicts in every city and region to compel Christians to sacrifice, Justin and his companions

[1] Maximus Tyrius, diss. 17, 12; Reiske, and diss. ii. 2, 10.
[2] *Acta Martyrum sincera*, Ruinart, pp 58-60.

were seized and brought before the Prefect of Rome, Rusticus. When they stood before his tribunal, the Prefect Rusticus said : ' Well, be obedient to the gods and the emperor's edicts.' Justin answered : ' No man can ever be blamed or condemned who obeys the precepts of our Saviour Jesus Christ.' Then the Prefect Rusticus asked : ' In what sect's learning or discipline are you versed ? ' Justin replied : ' I endeavoured to learn every sort of sect, and tried every kind of instruction; but at last I adhered to the Christian discipline, though that is not acceptable to those who are led by the error of a false opinion.' Rusticus said : ' Wretch, is that the sect in which you take delight ? ' ' Assuredly,' said Justin ; ' since together with a right belief I follow the example of Christians.' ' What belief is that, I pray ? ' said the Prefect. Justin replied : ' The right belief which we as Christians join with piety is this, to hold that there is one God, the Maker and Creator of all things which are seen and which are not seen by the body's eyes, and to confess one Lord Jesus Christ the Son of God, foretold of old by the prophets, who will also come to judge the human race, and who is the herald of salvation and the teacher of those who learn of Him well. I indeed as a man am feeble, and far too little to say anything great of His infinite Godhead : this I confess to be the office of prophets, who many ages ago by inspiration foretold the advent upon earth of the same whom I have called the Son of God.'

" The Prefect inquired where the Christians met. Justin answered : ' Each where he will and can. Do you suppose that we are accustomed all to meet in the same place ? By no means, since the God of the Christians is not circumscribed by place, but being invisible fills heaven and earth, and is everywhere adored, and His glory praised by the faithful.' The Prefect said : ' Come, tell me where you meet and assemble your disciples.' Justin answered : ' For myself I have hitherto lodged near the house of a certain Martin, by the Timiotine bath. It is the second time I have come to Rome, and I know no other place than the one mentioned. And if any one chose to come to me, I communicated to him the doctrine of truth.' ' You are, then, a Christian ?' said Rusticus. ' Assuredly,' said Justin, ' I am.'

" Then the Prefect asked Charito : ' Are you too a Christian ? ' Charito replied : ' By God's help I am a Christian.' The Prefect asked the woman Charitana whether she too followed the Faith of Christ. She replied : ' I also by the gift of God am a Christian.' Then Rusticus said to Evelpistus : ' And who are you ?' He replied : ' I am Cæsar's slave, but a Christian to whom Christ has given liberty, and by His favour and grace made partaker of the same hope with those whom you see.' The Prefect then asked Hierax whether he too was a Christian ; and he replied : ' Certainly I am a Christian, since I worship and adore the same God.' The Prefect inquired : ' Was it Justin who made you Christians ? ' ' I,' said Hierax, ' both was and will be a Christian.' Pæon likewise stood before him and said : ' I too am a Christian.' ' Who taught you ?' said the Prefect. He replied : ' I received this good confession from my parents.' Then Evelpistus said : ' I also was accustomed to hear with great delight Justin's discourses, but it was from my parents that I learnt to be a Christian.' Then the Prefect : ' And where are your parents ? ' ' In Cappadocia,' said Evelpistus. The Prefect likewise asked Hierax where his parents were,

and Hierax replied: 'Our true Father is Christ, and
our mother the Faith, by which we believe on Him.
But my earthly parents are dead. It was, however,
from Iconium in Phrygia that I was brought hither.'
The Prefect asked Liberianus whether he too was a
Christian and without piety towards the gods. He
said: 'I also am a Christian, for I worship and adore
the only true God.'

"Then the Prefect turned to Justin and said: 'You
fellow, who are said to be eloquent, and think you
hold the true discipline; if you are beaten from head
to foot, is it your persuasion that you will go up to
heaven?' Justin answered: 'I hope if I suffer what
you say, that I shall have what those have who have
kept the commands of Christ. For I know that to all
who live thus the divine grace is preserved until the
whole world have its consummation.' The Prefect
Rusticus replied: 'It is, then, your opinion that you
will go up to heaven to receive some reward?' 'I
do not opine,' said Justin, 'but I know, and am
so certain of this that I am incapable of doubt.'
Rusticus said: 'Let us come at length to what is
before us and urgent. Agree together and with one
mind sacrifice to the gods.' Justin replied: 'No
one of right mind deserts piety to fall into error
and impiety.' The Prefect Rusticus said: 'Unless
you be willing to obey our commands, you will suffer
torments without mercy.' Justin answered: 'What
we most desire is to suffer torments for our Lord
Jesus Christ and to be saved: for this will procure
for us salvation and confidence before that terrible
tribunal of the same our Lord and Saviour, at which
by divine command the whole world shall attend.'
The same likewise said all the other martyrs, adding:

' What thou wilt do, do quickly ; for we are Christians and sacrifice not to idols.'

"The Prefect hearing this pronounced the following sentence : ' Let those who have refused to sacrifice to the gods, and to obey the emperor's edict, be beaten with rods, and led away to capital punishment, as the laws enjoin.' And so the holy martyrs praising God were led to the accustomed place, and after being beaten were struck with the axe, and consummated their martyrdom in the confession of the Saviour.   After which certain of the faithful took away their bodies, and laid them in a suitable place, by the help of the grace of our Lord Jesus Christ, to whom be glory for ever and ever."

As the pillars of Trajan and Antonine faithfully record the deeds of those whose names they bear, and stand before posterity as a visible history, so, I conceive, the judgment of Ignatius by Trajan, and that of Justin by Rusticus, under the eye as it were of Marcus Aurelius and in his name, embody to us perfectly the mind and conduct of those great emperors towards Christians.   The marble of Phidias could present no more perfect sculpture, the pencil of Apelles no more breathing picture, than the simple transcription of the judicial record given above.   In the mind of Marcus the jealousy of the old Roman for his country's worship joined with the philosopher's dislike of Christian principles to move him from that more equable temper which dictated the later moderation of his immediate predecessor.   It scarcely needed the spirit which ruled at Rome to kindle passionate outbreaks against Christians in the various cities of the empire.   We have just seen the impassive majesty of Roman law declaring at the chief seat of power that to be a Christian is a capital crime.   If we go at the same time to

Smyrna, there the voices of a furious populace are demanding that an aged man venerable through the whole region for his innocent life and his virtues, be cast to the lions, because he is " the teacher of impiety, the father of the Christians, the destroyer of our gods, who has instructed many not to sacrifice to them or adore them." No grander scene among all the deeds of men is preserved to us, as described by his own church at the time, than the martyrdom of Polycarp, as after eighty-six years of Christian service he stood bound at the stake before the raging multitude in the theatre, and uttered his last prayer : " I thank thee, O God of angels and powers, and all the generation of the just who live before Thee, that Thou hast thought me worthy of this day and hour to receive a portion in the number of Thy martyrs, in the chalice of Thy Christ." Ten years later, in the great city of Lyons a similar spectacle was offered on a far larger scale. The Bishop Pothinus, more than ninety years old, is carried before the tribunal, " the magistrates of the city following him, and all the multitude pursuing him with cries as if he were Christ." But the triumph of the bishop is accompanied by that of many among his flock, of whom while all were admirable, yet the slave Blandina, poor and contemptible in appearance, surpassed the rest. " She was exposed to the beasts raised as it were upon a cross, and so praying most contentedly to God, she inspired the utmost ardour in her fellow-combatants. They saw with their bodily eyes in this their sister's person Him who had been crucified for them in order to persuade believers in Him that whoever suffers for the glory of Christ shall obtain companionship with the living God." [1] Since the wild

[1] Ruinart, p. 67.

beasts refused to touch her, Blandina and the survivors
among her fellow-sufferers were remanded to prison, in
order that the pleasure of the emperor might be taken,
one of them being a Roman citizen.   For this persecution had arisen without any command of his, and
the punishments were inflicted in virtue of the ordinary law.   After an interval, as it would seem, of two
months, a rescript was received from Marcus Aurelius
which ordered that those who confessed should be punished ignominiously, those who denied, be dismissed.
"And so at the time of our great fair, when a vast
multitude from the various provinces flock thither, the
governor ordered the most blessed martyrs to be brought
before his tribunal, exhibiting them to the people as in
theatric pomp ; and after a last interrogation those who
were Roman citizens were beheaded, and the rest given
to the wild beasts." [1]   But Blandina, after being every
day brought to behold the sufferings of her companions,
"the last of all, like a noble mother who had kindled
her children to the combat, and sent them forward as
conquerors to the king,—was eager to follow them,
rejoicing and exulting over her departure, as if invited
to a nuptial banquet, not cast before wild beasts.   At
length, after scourging and tearing and burning, she
was put in a net and exposed to the bull.   Tossed
again and again by him, yet feeling now nothing which
was done to her, both from the intensity of hope with
which she grasped the rewards of faith, and from her
intimate intercourse in prayer with Christ, in the end
she had her throat cut, as a victim, while the heathen
themselves confessed that never had they seen a woman
who had borne so much and so long." [2]

[1] Ruinart, p. 68.
[2] *Ib.* p. 69.

These three scenes of martyrdom at Rome, at Smyrna, and at Lyons, will give a notion of the grounds upon which Eusebius asserts that in the reign of Marcus Aurelius innumerable martyrs suffered[1] throughout the world through popular persecutions. Respecting the following reign of Commodus he says, on the contrary, that the Church enjoyed peace, for while the law which considered Christianity an illicit religion had not been revoked, it was made capital to inform against any one as Christian; and yet if the information took place, and the crime was proved, the punishment of death ensued, as in the case of the senator Apollonius recorded by him.[2] This state of things would seem to have lasted about seventeen years, until the year 197, when Severus, some time after his accession, became unfavourable to Christians. And it brings us to Tertullian, whose writings are full of testimonies to the sufferings endured by Christians for their Faith. For some time these sufferings would seem to fall under the same sort of intermittent popular persecution, which we have seen prevailing in the time of Marcus: but in the year 202 Severus published an edict forbidding any to become Jews or Christians. And forthwith a persecution broke out so severe and terrible, that many thought the time of Antichrist was come. It was no longer the mere action of an original law against all unauthorised religions, but an assault led on by the emperor himself, who turned directly the imperial power against Christianity as a whole. It raged especially at Alexandria, where the master of the catechetical school writes : " We have before our eyes every day abundant

---

[1] *Hist.* v. i. μυριάδας μαρτύρων διαπρέψαι στοχασμῷ λαβεῖν ἔνεστιν.
[2] *Ib.* v. 21.

The summary of the seventy-four years is this. From 161 to 180 there are nineteen years of irregular but severe persecution, followed by seventeen, from 180 to 197, wherein the denouncing of Christians is forbidden, though if brought to trial, they are punishable with death. Five years succeed, from 197 to 202, in which the favour of Severus seems lost, and the state of intermittent persecution takes effect. Then breaks out a general persecution, set on foot by the emperor himself, and we may judge if he who slaughtered his senate spared Christians. This lasts for nine years until his death in 211, whereon a time of peace returns, which is most complete during the reign of Alexander, but continues more or less from 211 to the end of his reign in 235.

On a review of the whole period it is evident that the Church has passed from its state of concealment into almost full light. The fiery trial which it met at the beginning of the third century from the hand of Severus is the best proof that can be given how greatly it had increased, how it could no longer be ignored or despised. Its organisation which was hidden from Trajan was at least partially revealed to Severus, and he saw and attempted to meet the danger which the earlier emperor would have tried to stamp out, had he divined it. But it is evident also that in proportion as the Christian Faith had grown, the heathen empire had been shaken in its foundations. Its period of just government was over; its imperial power was to fall henceforth into the hands of adventurers, with whom it would be more and more the symbol of force alone, and not of law: henceforth they would seldom even in blood be Roman, and more

seldom still in principles. Marcus was well-nigh the
last zealot for the Jupiter of the Capitol: within a
generation after him Heliogabalus will think of a
fusion of all religions in his god the sun, and Alexander Severus of a religious syncretism wherein Or-
pheus, Abraham, and Christ testify together to the
divine unity.[1] Nor is this a fancy of the prince alone.
All the thinking minds of his time have become
ashamed of Olympus and its gods. The cross has
wounded them to death. A new philosophy—the last
fortress into which retreating heathenism throws itself
—while it breaks up Roman life, prepares the way
for the Christian Faith which it strenuously combats.
The Emperor Severus, fixing the eye of a statesman
and a soldier on that Faith, contemplates its grasp
upon society, and decrees from the height of the throne
a general assault upon it; while his wife encourages a
writer[2] to draw an ideal heathen portrait as a counterpart to the character of Christ, tacitly subtracting from
the gospels an imitation which is to supply the place
of the reality. The time was not far distant when
Origen would already discern and prophesy the complete triumph of the religion thus assailed. If
Celsus had objected, that were all to do as Christians
did, the emperor would be deserted, and his power fall
into the hands of the most savage and lawless barbarians, his reply would be: "If all did as I do, men
would honour the emperor as a divine command, and
the barbarians drawing nigh to the word of God would
become most law-loving and most civilised. Their
worship would be dissolved, and that of the Christians

---

[1] Champagny, *les Antonins*, iii. 326, 338.
[2] Philostratus in his *Life of Apollonius of Tyana*, written at the
request of the Empress Julia Domna. See Kellner, *Hellenismus und
Christenthum*, c. v. s. 4, 81–4.

alone prevail, as one day it will alone prevail, by means of that word gathering to itself more and more souls." [1]

But before such a goal be reached, many a martyr's crown has yet to be won, and more than barbarian lawlessness and cruelty have to be overcome.

[1] Orig. c. *Cels.* viii. 68, tom. i. p. 793.

LECTURE XII

THE THIRD AGE OF THE MARTYR CHURCH

"Rex pacificus magnificatus est, cujus vultum desiderat universa terra."

I. The third century is that during which the Christian Church was making its way into every relation of life, and taking possession of human society. During this period it advances into full light, and becomes a manifest power. In the second century Celsus had attacked it as disclosed only to the yearning hearts of slaves, and fostered by the devotion of the weaker sex. At the distance of three generations Origen answered him, but the religion which he defended already stood avowed alike before the inquiring gaze of philosophers, the corrupt crowds of cities, and the jealous fear of rulers. Even in Rome, the sceptred head of idolatry, whose nobles the great political traditions of their city, and whose populace their sensual life, having its root in a false worship, made the most difficult to convert, the hated faith is known to have had public churches by the time of Alexander Severus, two hundred years after its first rise.[1] And much more everywhere else it had planted its foot openly on the soil of the empire. It is time, then, to view the Church as an institution offering the

---

[1] Churches in private houses, under cover of that great liberty which invested with a sort of sacred independence the Roman household, it had from the beginning: the church of St. Pudentiana in the house of the senator Pudens still guards the altar on which St. Peter offered.

twenty-five different hands. And indeed it seemed after the capture of the Emperor Valerian by the Persians, as if that great confederacy, which had just celebrated the thousandth anniversary of the imperial city's foundation, was about to break up and be resolved into its component parts. At one moment two great princesses, Victoria and Zenobia, worthy even by the avowal of Romans to wear the Roman diadem, were on the point of establishing the one an empire of the Gauls in the West, the other an empire of the East, embracing just those countries which Antony had ruled with Cleopatra at his side. A succession of great generals, all from the province of Illyricum, at last saves the empire and reasserts its unity. But the forty-nine years following the murder of Alexander Severus are filled by the struggles of twenty sovereigns and nineteen pretenders to sovereignty, scarcely any of whom reign so much as five years. Many of them are rulers of great ability and remarkable energy. Claudius, Aurelian, Probus, and Carus, and perhaps Decius, required only happier circumstances to be emperors whose fame would have matched that of Trajan or Hadrian : but their short tenure of power, occupied with the vast effort to restore unity and beat back the barbarian, prevented their doing more than preserve the imperial power and the empire itself. This whole time, then, in civil society was one of fluctuation, anxiety, disaster, alarms from beyond the frontiers and anarchy within them. The Roman peace seemed departing, and the majesty of the empire irreparably violated. Men could not tell what the morrow would bring forth. The fairest cities of the Roman world, Alexandria and Antioch, narrowly escaped perishing through internal discord or hostile surprise. Greece and Asia Minor, after reposing for centuries under the safeguard of the Roman name, found themselves swept through and desolated by barbarian hordes. Italy itself was in imminent danger of the same lot. Towards the end of this period, the senate by the election of Tacitus seems to make what may be termed its final effort to assert itself as the depository of legitimate power, the representative of civil society: and this time of confusion issues in a rejection of any such claim, and the establishment of unlimited despotism in the empire as reconstituted by Diocletian. To these straits, then, the first great and haughty enemy of the Christian Church was reduced, so that the power which a century before could look down with proud indifference on the sufferings of Christians now seemed to tremble for its own existence. And in such a condition of human society the great advance of the Church was carried on.

2. But beyond the empire to the north, advancing upon it like the multitudinous waves of the ocean on an exposed coast, lay the ever-battling legions of the northern tribes in their three great divisions of the Teutonic, Slavic, and Finnish races. If Roman society suffered throes of distress, its condition was peace compared with the instability which may be said to have been the very life of these tribes. Once at least in every century they gather themselves up for a concentrated effort against the empire whose rich civilisation lies stretched out before them as a continual prey. After the failure of Arminius to construct a German kingdom, and of Marobod to construct a Suevian, in the time of Augustus, Decebalus, in the time of Trajan, makes another effort in behalf of his

Dacians. But here the great Roman general forces barbarism to retreat, and plants a fresh citadel in its very stronghold by establishing a province north of the Danube. Then there is comparative tranquillity for sixty years. It seems as if these two generations were offered by Divine Providence to the empire yet in its unbroken strength as a time for its pacific conversion. If the empire had so willed, the eruption of the northern nations might for ever have been kept back by the unity which religious conviction would have bestowed on civilisation. It would have imparted fresh and living force to society not yet exhausted by despotic power. But with Marcus Aurelius the empire turns definitively away. A new religious revolution under Odin in Scandinavia had wakened up with redoubled force the destroying energy of barbarism. The Goths had migrated from Sweden to the Black Sea; all the tribes in the interval had been displaced and dashed upon each other by this removal. The war of the Marcomans occupied during eighteen years, from 162 to 180, the whole forces of the empire; Rome was obliged even to arm its slaves, and Italy feared an invasion more terrible than that of the Cimbri, which it cost Marcus Aurelius his life to avert.

Again, during the captivity of Valerian, another grand assault of the northern tribes takes place. The Franks attack western, the Alamans eastern Gaul; they pass the Alps and advance to Ravenna, while Alamans and Sarmatians throw themselves upon Pannonia, and the Goths seize upon Thrace and Greece. The emperors Claudius, Aurelian, and Probus are the saviours of Rome from this new flood. Of the last of these it is recorded that he dealt successively with

Franks, Burgundians, Alamans, Vandals, the Bastarnæ, and the whole barbarian brood: and seventy cities raised from their ruins, and fortifications repaired upon a line of fifteen hundred miles, were the fruits of his victories." [1]

So much for the north: while on the east the Persian empire, hereditary foe of the Roman name, had found a new and more vigorous master in the race of the Sassanidæ, who took the religion of Zoroaster to reanimate the national spirit. Ardeschir claimed once more the whole realm which Cyrus and Darius had ruled. Henceforth the Romans had a neighbour more than ever threatening their eastern frontier, and never to be wholly subdued, until the empire of Mohammed arose to detach a great part of their dominion, and to move with redoubled force upon what remained.

To the south of the Roman provinces in Africa were tribes at least as savage as those of the north. Thus the whole empire was enringed with enemies: on the east an opposing civilisation and religion; on the north and south barbarian tribes in perpetual confusion and conflict with each other. Such was the great realm of disorder which surged and heaved to the north and south of the empire; and such the second great enemy which in future times was to occupy the Christian Church, and at present offered the strongest contrast to that moral polity of peace and good-will, of loyal submission, patient endurance, and heroic fortitude, which was spreading daily in the empire.

3. But there was yet another enemy within the empire itself which from the beginning tracked the

[1] Am. Thierry, *Tableau de l'Empire Romain*, p. 412.

footsteps of the Church, grew with its increase, and everywhere attempted to dissolve its organisation and weaken its influence. The whole second century is occupied with the rise and tangled growth of the Gnostic sects. But these were not alone. From the very time of the Apostles we find the evidence of a number of sects, rising and falling, preying on and devouring each other, none without some portion of Christian truth, on which it feeds, blended with Jewish, Greek, Oriental, Egyptian, Libyan notions, prejudices, and errors; domiciled in various parts of the empire in accordance with the national or local character which they represent. They reproduce with a Christian colour the sects and the sect-life of the Greek schools of philosophy. As the wheat has its proper weed, which springs up in the midst of it and counterfeits it, so error, everywhere gathering round some portion of truth, forms itself into an antagonistic life. The force and truth of the Christian Church were shown not in the absence of these rivals, but in its triumph over their variety, in its remaining one whilst they diverged endlessly from that unchanging original type, in its continuous and uniform growth whilst they rose and fell, domineered in certain times and places, and then disappeared. In this its course the Church had to master very great difficulties, which were inherent in the manner of its rise. It had to remain one society in spite of the isolation and self-government of its local portions. It possessed in each place but a feeble minority of members compared with the mass of unbelievers. Against its assimilating power was ranged the force of national feelings which underlay the Roman authority throughout the whole empire. It had to deal entirely by

moral means with the full liberty of error to which
its adherents were exposed. Lastly, it had to do all
this amid the continual strain of threatened or actual
persecution, a state which at its best was one of in-
security, and which any local trouble, the ill-will of
a mob, the greed or ambition or fear of provincial
rulers, not to speak of the imperial state-policy, might
turn into the pressure of severe suffering.

In the face of such difficulties, if the Christian
Church continued one in its doctrine, organisation,
and manner of life, such unity was assuredly the proof
of a divine power residing in it.

I shall now proceed to show by the testimony of
eye-witnesses that such unity was its distinguishing
characteristic.

Now there was not a race or a religion in all this
Roman Empire, endless as the races and religions com-
prehended in it were, out of which individuals were
not drawn into the bosom of the one great Christian
society ; and yet within this there was a perfect union
of all hearts and minds in the conviction that the
multitude so collected was one people apart from all
other peoples. And this conviction is itself the great
marvel. How was it wrought ? For it was an utterly
new thing upon the earth. The union of race, language, and locality, with which sameness of religion
was usually interwoven, had been hitherto the bond
of such nations as had as yet existed. The great city
itself had sprung up and flourished by the strict union
of these four things. After its career of foreign conquest had substituted for the government of a city
the great Roman confederation, it had indeed, like
the preceding world-empires, in fact disregarded all
these, being supported by a force independent of them

all. But that force was material power. The great statue was of iron. It was a novelty unheard of as yet among the Gentiles and unimagined by poet or philosopher, to create a polity which, disregarding sameness of race, of language, and of locality, should exist and maintain itself throughout the whole earth solely by the force of faith and charity.

Such was the idea of Christians about themselves from the beginning. The idea preceded the fact. The prophets foretold it; the Apostles proclaimed it:[1] let us observe the fulfilment of the prophecy and the proclamation. We will take our stand in the middle of the third century, when seven full generations have passed since the day of Pentecost. In this time a people has been formed. Already a hundred and fifty years before, an eye-witness among themselves had observed the nature of this people. "Christians are not distinguished from other men either by country, or by language, or by customs: for they have no cities peculiar to themselves, nor any language different from others, nor singularity in their mode of life. . . . They dwell both in Greek and in barbarous cities, as the lot of each may be, following local customs as to raiment and food, and the rest of their life, but exhibiting withal a polity of their own, marvellous and truly incredible. They dwell in their own country, but it is as sojourners; they share in everything as citizens, yet suffer everything as strangers. Every foreign land is to them a country, and every country a foreign land. . . . In a word, what the soul is in the body, that Christians are in the world. The soul is diffused through all the limbs of the body,

---

[1] Zach. ii. 11, Is. ii. 2, Mich. iv. 1, compared with Titus ii. 14 and 1 Pet. ii. 9.

and Christians through all the cities of the world. . . .
The soul is shut within the body, of which it is the
bond, and Christians are like a garrison in the world,
which they hold together." [1]

Here a writer, calling himself a disciple of Apostles,
describes to us, at the beginning of the second century,
what the apostolic age of seventy years had wrought.
He puts his finger just upon the marvel which we are
contemplating.   Fifty years later, at the moment the
empire was culminating under the serene rule of
Antoninus, a convert from heathenism, a philosopher
who had spent his life in examining all the sects and
races of the empire, and who afterwards became a
martyr, said of Christians that being "quarried out of
the side of Christ, they were the true Israelitic race,"
"altogether being called the body, for both people and
church, being many in number, are called by one name
as one thing."   They are in fact "as one man before
the Maker of all things, through the name of His
first-born Son," the High-priest gathering up first in
the prophetical vision and then in the real fact "the
true high-priestly race" [2] in His own Person.   Thus
Justin pointed out this conception of the Christian
people to the Jew of his time as both foretold in
prophecy and exhibited in fact.   The longer that such
a people as this endured, the greater would be the
marvel.

A hundred years after this, Origen uses the same
language and points to the same marvel.   He had in
the year 249, at the entreaty of a friend and pupil,
set himself in the maturity of life, and of a renown

---

[1] *Ep. ad Diognetum*, 5, 6.
[2] St. Justin Martyr, *Tryphon*, sec. 135, 42, 116; where he refers
to and explains the vision of the high-priest Jesus in the prophet
Zacharias iii. 1.

which filled the Church as no man's before had filled
it, to answer the attack of a heathen philosopher,
Celsus, upon Christianity.   He was writing just at
the end of the longest period of peace which is found
during those three centuries.   From the death of the
Emperor Septimius Severus in 211 to that of the
Emperor Philip in this year 249, there had been,
with the exception of a short attack from Maximin,
to which his death put a stop, no general persecution
of Christians.   Thus thirty-eight years had passed of
such tranquillity as it was ever in those times the lot
of Christians to obtain.   The mother of one Emperor
had been Origen's disciple, and the emperor actually
reigning was a Christian, however unworthy of such a
profession.   Now in this work Origen speaks of the
superiority of the Christian churches in each several
place, as, for instance, at Athens, Corinth, Alexandria,
to the heathen assemblies, and of the Christian rulers
to the heathen.   He puts it as a mark of divine power
that God sending His Son, "a God come in human
soul and body,"[1] should have established everywhere
churches offering the contrast of their polity to the
assemblies of the superstitious, the impure, and the
unjust.   He considers that Christians do a greater
benefit to their country than all other men by teaching them piety to the one God, and "gathering up
into a certain divine and heavenly city those who
have lived well in the smallest cities."[2]   "We," he
says, "knowing that there is in each city another
fabric of a country, founded by the word of God, call
those who are powerful in word and of a virtuous life
to the government of churches.   We do not accept the

[1] $\dot{\omega}$ς υἱὸν Θεοῦ, Θεὸν ἐληλυθότα ἐν ἀνθρωπίνῃ ψυχῇ καὶ σώματι.   Cont.
Cels. iii. 29.   [2] Ibid. viii. 74.

covetous to such a place, but force it against their will
upon those who in their moderation would decline
taking on them this general care of the Church of
God." [1]   And the compulsion thus exercised is that
" of the great King, whom we are persuaded to be the
Son of God, God the Word."   But this other form
of country which he saw in each city is "the whole
Church of God, which the divine Scriptures assert to
be the Body of Christ, animated by the Son of God,
while the limbs of this Body are particular believers.
As the soul quickens and moves the body, whose
nature it is not to have the movement of life from
itself, so the Word moving to what is fitting, and
energising in the whole Body, the Church, moves likewise each member of it, who does nothing without
the Word." [2]   And he completes this view in another
beautiful passage wherein he describes Christ as the
high-priest Aaron, who has received upon His single
body the whole chrism, from whom it flows down
upon His beard, the symbol of the complete man, and
on to the utmost skirt of His raiment.   Every one
who partakes of Him, partakes likewise of His chrism,
because Christ is the Head of the Church, and the
Church and Christ one Body. [3]   We have here in
Origen's thought one and the same divine power, proceeding forth from the Incarnation, which forms first
the Body of the Lord, and then gathers into this
Body every individual as a copy of the Christ.   The
heathen scoffer had objected : " Why send forth one
spirit into one corner of the earth ?   It was needed
to breathe that spirit into many bodies, and to send
them forth into all the world."   " Nay," replied Origen,

---

[1] *Cont. Cels.* viii. 75.   [2] *Ibid.* vi. 48, p. 670.
[3] *Cont. Cels.* vi. 79, p. 692.

"the whole Church of God—animated by the Son of God as the soul quickens and moves the body—was enough. It needed not that there should be many bodies and many souls, like that of Jesus, in the way you suppose, for the one Word as the sun of righteousness rising from Judea was sufficient to send forth rays that should reach every soul that would receive Him." He has done far more than you suggest: every member of that one Body has received according to his measure a due portion of anointment. After the model of the Christ, they too are Christs; "so that beginning in the body He should dawn in power and in spirit upon the universe of souls which would no longer be destitute of God."

In Origen's mind, then, the greatness of the King lies specifically in this, that out of confusion He draws unity, out of those who were no people He forms a people, out of nations and tribes at enmity He moulds an indivisible kingdom, and from His own Body a Body which shall embrace a universe of souls, instinct with one life, and that His own. This was Origen's view of the work and triumph of Christ, as he saw it before him, at the eve of the great Decian persecution in 249.

Origen was writing this at a moment of great interest. It was the last year which preceded those two generations, in the course of which five great persecutions should be directed by the emperors against the Church. He was then a man of sixty-four. The son of a martyr, he had when a youth of eighteen beheld his father imprisoned for the faith, and had encouraged him to suffer the loss of all his goods, and death itself, without regarding that large family which must be left in penury, of whom Origen was the eldest.

He was burning himself to share his father's sufferings. In the persecution of which this was the opening Eusebius tells us that seven of his disciples were martyrs : and, lastly, he was to undergo such cruelties himself in the persecution of Decius, then on the eve of breaking out, that he is believed to have died of their results. Now it is in this work that he speaks of the remarkable providence of God in preserving Christians, who by their religion were bound not to defend themselves, against the attacks of their enemies. God, he says, had fought for them, and from time to time had stopped those who had risen up with the purpose of destroying them. Few and easily numbered were those who hitherto had suffered death for the Christian Faith, samples chosen by God as champions to encourage the rest, while He prevented their whole nation from being rooted out : for it was His purpose that this nation should be firmly rooted and consolidated, and the whole world be filled with its saving doctrine and discipline.[1] Thus it was by His will alone that He scattered every plot directed against them, so that neither emperors, nor local governors, nor the people should be able to indulge their wrath beyond a certain point. Origen, when he thus wrote, could look back on a period of thirty-eight years, during which, with the exception of the severe but

---

[1] Κωλύοντος τοῦ Θεοῦ τὸ πᾶν ἐκπολεμηθῆναι αὐτῶν ἔθνος. συστῆναι γὰρ αὐτὸ ἐβούλετο καὶ πληρωθῆναι πᾶσαν τὴν γῆν τῆς σωτηρίου ταύτης καὶ εὐσεβεστάτης διδασκαλίας. *Cont. Cels.* iii. 8. It must be remembered that Celsus in the passage to which this is an answer had asserted that the Christians had arisen out of the Jews through a sedition ; which makes the train of thought pertinent. For Origen is contrasting the losses which occur through exterminating wars, such as a sedition, or civil war, excites, with the losses to the Christian body through martyrdom. The comparison therefore lies between the whole number of Christians viewed *en masse* and the martyrs. Lasaulx remarks that this was written before the Decian persecution.

passing storm raised by the Emperor Maximin, peace had reigned. He had himself employed those years in unwearied labours of teaching, writing, and converting. He had directed and advised an emperor's mother, and seen a Christian emperor, and he had witnessed a wonderful increase of the Christian people. Indeed, of this increase his words above cited convey a faithful picture. He knew not the fearful trials which were to be encountered before that triumph of the truth he already anticipated should be attained: or that God was about to accept from the grey-haired man the sacrifice which the impetuous youth had affronted without success. For scarcely has he written this book when he has to fly for his life before the edict of Decius, who will attempt to destroy the Christian religion, and to whose anger Pope St. Fabian falls a victim. Amid great peril after long delay the next Pope Cornelius is chosen. And now for the first time a new danger from within assaults the Church. Novatian, a Roman presbyter of great repute, attempts after the due election and consecration of Cornelius to usurp his place, and to divide the one flock of Christ. Under circumstances so wholly altered from those in which Origen above was writing, we come to our next witness, the man in all the Western Church the most renowned, as Origen was in the Eastern.

For it was on the occasion of the first antipope, an effort, that is, within the See of Peter itself to arm the episcopal power at its very source against itself, to set an altar up against the legitimate altar, and to divide the sacraments of the Church from the Bride whose dowry they are, that St. Cyprian wrote his treatise on the Unity of the Church. " It was for the purpose of reminding his brethren that unity is the

first element of the Christian state, and that those who
break off from the principle of unity, which is lodged
in the Episcopate, even though they be confessors and
martyrs, have no portion in the hopes of the gospel." [1]
This definite purpose, so unlike that state of leisure
and tranquillity in which Origen answered by thought
and learning a speculative attack, will account for the
very remarkable precision and force of St. Cyprian's
language.

"The enemy," he says, "detected and downfallen
by the advent of Christ, now that light is come to the
nations—seeing his idols left—has made heresies and
schisms, wherewith to subvert faith, to corrupt truth,
and to rend unity." But this will all be in vain if
men will look to the Head, and keep to the doctrine
of the Master. For the truth may be quickly stated. [2]
"The Lord saith unto Peter : ' I say unto thee that thou
art Peter, and upon this rock I will build My Church,
and the gates of hell shall not prevail against it.
And I will give unto thee the keys of the kingdom of
heaven, and whatsoever thou shalt bind on earth shall
be bound also in heaven, and whatsoever thou shalt
loose on earth shall be loosed in heaven.' To him
again, after His Resurrection, He says: 'Feed My sheep.'
Upon him, being one, He builds His Church ; and
though He gives to all the Apostles an equal power,
and says : ' As my Father sent Me, even so send I you ;
receive ye the Holy Ghost : whosesoever sins ye remit,
they shall be remitted to him, and whosesoever sins ye
retain, they shall be retained ;'——yet in order to manifest
unity, He has by His own authority so placed the source

[1] Preface to the Oxford edition of St. Cyprian's treatise on the Unity
of the Church.
[2] *De Unitate*, iii. &c.

of the same unity as to begin from one. Certainly the other Apostles also were what Peter was, endued with an equal fellowship both of honour and power. Still but a beginning is made from unity, that the Church may be set before us as one. This one Church in the Canticle of Canticles doth the Holy Spirit design and name in the Person of our Lord : ' My dove, my spotless one is but one ; she is the only one of her mother, elect of her that bare her.'

"He who holds not this unity of the Church, does he think that he holds the faith ? He who strives against and resists the Church, is he assured that he is in the Church ? For the blessed Apostle Paul teaches this same thing, and manifests the sacrament of unity thus speaking : ' There is one Body and one Spirit, even as ye are called in one Hope of your calling ; one Lord, one Faith, one Baptism, one God.' This unity firmly should we hold and maintain, especially we bishops, presiding in the Church, in order that we may approve the Episcopate itself to be one and undivided. Let no one deceive the brotherhood by falsehood ; no one corrupt the truth of our faith by a faithless treachery. The Episcopate is one, of which a part is held by each without division of the whole. The Church is likewise one, though she be spread abroad, and multiplies with the increase of her progeny. So the sun has rays many, yet one light, and the tree boughs many, yet its strength is one, seated in the deep-lodged root. Again, when many streams flow down from one source, though a multiplicity of waters seems to be diffused from the bountifulness of the overflowing abundance, unity is preserved in the source itself. Part a ray of the sun from its orb, and its unity forbids this division of light ; break a branch from the tree, once broken it can bud no more ; cut the stream from its fountain, the remnant will be dried up. Thus the Church, flooded with the light of the Lord, puts forth her rays through the whole world, with yet one light, which is spread upon all places, while its unity of body in not infringed. She stretches forth her branches over the universal earth, in the riches of plenty, and pours abroad her bountiful and onward streams ; yet is there one head, one source, one mother, abundant in the results of her fruitfulness.

" It is of her womb that we are born ; our nourishing is from her milk, our quickening from her breath. The Spouse of Christ cannot become adulterate ; she is undefiled and chaste ; owning but one home, and guarding with virtuous modesty the sanctity of one chamber. She it is who keeps us for God, and appoints unto the kingdom the sons she has borne. Whosoever parts company with the Church and joins himself to an adulteress, is estranged from the promises of the Church. He who leaves the Church of Christ, attains not to Christ's rewards. He is an alien, an outcast, an enemy. He can no longer have God for a Father who has not the Church for a mother. If any man was able to escape who remained without the ark of Noah, then will that man escape who is out of doors beyond the Church. The Lord warns us and says : ' He who is not with Me is against Me, and he who gathereth not with Me, scattereth.' He who breaks the peace and concord of Christ, sets himself against Christ. He who gathers elsewhere but in the Church, scatters the Church of Christ. The Lord says : ' I and the Father are one ; ' and again of the Father, the Son, and the Holy Ghost it is written : ' And these three are one.' And does any one think that oneness, thus pro-

Certainly if any idea has ever been put forth clearly and definitely, it would seem to be the idea of organic unity here delineated by Cyprian, as necessary not merely to the well-being but to the essence of the Church. Nor does one see what words he could have found more expressly to reject the notion that the individual bishop in his diocese was the unit on the aggregation of which the Church was built, and to assert in contradiction that the Church was built on the Primacy of Peter as its generative, formative, controlling, and unifying power. According to him the whole order and government of the Church are bound up in the Lord's words to Peter : while as to the Church herself three ideas are in his mind so compacted together, so running into and pervading each other, that they cannot be severed ; and these ideas are Unity, Grace, and Truth. The symbols of the Sun, the Tree, and the Fountain, the Lord's Coat, the one Flock tethered in one Fold under one Shepherd, the one House as opposed to sundry self-chosen domiciles, the Mother embracing her whole progeny in her womb, illustrate and enforce each other. All contain the three ideas, and Grace and Truth are, as it were, the warp and woof in the substance of the one web. For Unity, Truth, and Grace, viewed as attributes of the Church, are blended together in the light and warmth of the sun, in the sap vivifying every branch of the tree, and giving it fruitfulness from the root, in the fountain of water, under which image our Lord has so often summed up His whole gift to man. Again, they are imaged in the flock which the Shepherd has chosen, and for which He cares, in the house where the master dwells and collects his family, in the one robe encompassing and containing the virtue of the Wearer, in the prolific womb giving birth to the whole sacred race. The force of all these images lies in their unicity : plurality would not modify, but destroy them. Yet even these symbols are surpassed by that argument from the divine Unity which he sets forth as the type and cause of the Church's unity. From created likenesses——the fairest and choicest which the world presents——he passes to the uncreated nature, and from the divine immutability, wherewith these three, the Father, the Son, and the Holy Ghost, the divine Exemplar of Unity, Truth, and Grace, are one, deduces the Unity of the Church their dwelling-place.

Cyprian, then, cannot sever the Church of his heart, the Church for which he lived and died, from Unity, or from Truth, or from Grace : and this Church is to him founded on the Primacy of Peter, and developed from his person. The one Episcopate, whose golden chain he looks upon as surrounding the earth in its embrace, "of which a part is held by each without division of the whole," wherein therefore joint possession is dependent on unity, would have no existence without the bond of the Primacy, from which it was developed and which keeps it one. Take away this, and the office of each bishop is crystallised into a separate mass, having no coherence or impact with its like : bishops so conceived would hold indeed a similar office, but being detached from each other would not hold joint possession of one Episcopate. Separate crystals do not make one body ; nor a heap of pebbles a rock. But it was a Rock on which Christ built and builds His Church, that Rock being His own Person, from which He communicated this virtue, wherein the cohesion and impact of the whole Episcopate lies, to the See of him whom He constituted His Vicar.

Finally, Cyprian contrasts pointedly the people of Christ *which cannot be rent* with the twelve tribes of Israel, which were torn asunder. It is as if he would beforehand repudiate that parallel between the Synagogue and the Church, in the question of unity, which has before now been resorted to as a refuge by minds in distress, who failed to see the tokens of the Bride of Christ in the community to which they belonged.

In Origen and in Cyprian we put ourselves back into the middle of the third century. In the words of the latter we see portrayed to the life that idea which had filled the hearts of Christians through seven generations of labours and sorrows from the day of Pentecost down to his time. But whence arose this perfect union of all hearts and minds in the early Christians, who were penetrated with the conviction that the Church was the home of truth and grace? We may answer this question thus: No catechumen was received into the fold without a clear and distinct belief in that article of the earliest creed, and part of the baptismal profession, " the Holy Catholic Church." A new word was made to express a new idea, the glorious and unique work of that ever-blessed Trinity whom the creed recited: the Home and House in which the Triune God, whom the Christian glorified, by indwelling made the fountain of that grace and that truth which God had become Man in order to communicate. The catechumen's baptism into the one Body was the foundation of all the hope in which his life consisted ;[1] the integrity, duration, sanctity of that Body being component parts of the hope. And with regard at least to all Gentile converts this precise and definite catechetical instruction was reinforced by the

---

[1] τῇ γὰρ ἐλπίδι ἐσώθημεν.

new sense which at their conversion was impressed on them of the heathenism out of which they were then taken. In how many of them was the remembrance of their past life connected with the guilt of deeds and habits which their new Christian conscience taught them to regard as fearful sins. Nay, the notion of sin itself—as a transgression of the eternal law and an offence against the personal Majesty of God—was a Christian acquisition to the corrupted heathen. Thus the passage into the one Body and the divine Kingdom was contemporaneous in their case with a total change of the moral life. It is Cyprian, again, who has given us a vivid account of this change, which took place at a time of mature manhood in his own life, and which will serve as a graphic sketch of what had happened to the great mass of adult converts besides himself.

Let us suppose a man forty-five years of age speaking: "For me, while I yet lay in darkness and bewildering night, and was tossed to and fro on the billows of this troublesome world, ignorant of my true life, an outcast from light and truth, I used to think that second birth, which divine mercy promised for my salvation, a hard saying according to the life I then led: as if a man could be so quickened to a new life in the laver of healing water as to put off his natural self, and keep his former tabernacle, yet be changed in heart and soul. How is it possible, said I, for so great a conversion to be accomplished, so that both the obstinate defilement of our natural substance, and old and ingrained habits, should suddenly and rapidly be put off; evils whose roots are deeply seated within? When does he learn frugality, to whom fine feasts and rich banquets have become a habit? Or he who

in gay sumptuous robes glisters with gold and purple,
when does he reduce himself to ordinary and simple
raiment?   Another whose bent is to public distinctions and honours cannot bear to become a private
and unnoticed man ; while one who is thronged by
a phalanx of dependents, and retinued by the overflowing attendance of an obsequious host, thinks it
punishment to be alone.   The temptation still un-
relaxed, need is it that, as before, wine should entice,
pride inflate, anger inflame, covetousness disquiet,
cruelty stimulate, ambition delight, and lust lead
headlong.

"Such were my frequent musings ; for whereas I
was encumbered with the many sins of my past life,
which it seemed impossible to be rid of, so I had
used myself to give way to my clinging infirmities,
and, from despair of better things, to humour the
evils of my heart, as slaves born in my house and my
proper offspring.   But after that life-giving water
succoured me, washing away the stain of former years,
and pouring into my cleansed and hallowed breast the
light which comes from heaven, after that I drank in
the heavenly Spirit, and was created into a new man
by a second birth, then marvellously what before was
doubtful became plain to me, what was hidden was
revealed, what was dark began to shine, what was
difficult now had a way and means, what had seemed
impossible now could be achieved, what was in me of
the guilty flesh now confessed that it was earthy,
what was quickened in me by the Holy Ghost now
had a growth according to God.   Thou knowest well,
thou canst recollect as well as I, what was then taken
from me, and what was given by that death of sin,
that quickening power of holiness.   Thou knowest, I

name it not.   Over my own praises it were un-
welcome to boast, though reason for gratitude never
for boasting, which is not ascribed to man's virtue
but is confessed to be God's bounty.   To sin no
more has come of faith, as heretofore to sin had
come of human error.   From God, I say, from God is
all we can be; from Him we live, from Him we grow,
and by that strength which is from Him accepted and
ingathered we learn beforehand, even in this present
state, the foretokens of what is yet to be.   Let only
fear be a guard upon innocency, that that Lord who
by the influence of His heavenly mercy has graciously
shone into our hearts, may be detained by righteous
obedience in the hostelry of a mind that pleases Him;
that the security imparted to us may not beget sloth-
fulness, nor the former enemy steal upon us anew." [1]

Add to this that Christians were marked out as one
Body by the Jewish and heathen persecution which
tracked them everywhere.   But the sects were not
persecuted.   The various schools of the Gnostics all
agreed in this, that it was not necessary or desirable
to suffer martyrdom for the faith.   Their view was,
that they could believe with their minds whatever
they pleased, though an enemy might force them by
threats of suffering to utter with the mouth what
they abhorred; and with this convenient distinction
they escaped imprisonment, poverty, bereavement, and
death.   But the Christian was bound—when the
fitting circumstances came—to repeat the confession
of his Lord before Pilate.   Joined therefore to his
baptismal belief, and to the utter change of life involved in his conversion, was the bond of common
suffering which held together Christians as one Body

[1] Ep. 1, Oxford translation.

throughout the world. Hence the words of an old martyr bishop: "The Church, for that love which she bears to God, in every place and at every time sends forward a multitude of martyrs to the Father, whereas all the rest not only have no such thing among themselves to show, but deem not even such a witness necessary." [1]

Moreover, as a fourth cause, the historic origin of their name and belief led them up to that day of Pentecost when the descent of the Spirit of God constituted the formation of that body in belonging to which was all their hope and trust. Their faith was identified in its existence, their charity engendered in its communion. As the birth and the life and the passion of Christ were that subject-matter on which their whole faith grew, so the creation of their existence as a people was a definite act in which the Redeemer showed Himself the Father of His Race, creating them as His children and generating them by His Spirit. The loving thought of Christians in every age ran along this line to its source. Nature herself presents us with an image of what this idea of the Church was to them. As the great river whose water is the symbol of blessing and the bearer of fertility leaps down a giant birth from its parent lake, ever blazing under the splendour of a tropical sun, yet ever fed by sources springing from snow-crowned mountains, and changes in its course the desert into earth's fruitfulest region, so the river of God, welling forth on the day of Pentecost from the central abyss of the divine love, bore down to all the nations the one water of salvation, and wheresoever it spread, the desert retreated,

[1] St. Irenæus, lib. iv. 33 g.

and the earth brought forth corn and wine in abundance.   And the idea of this divine stream was from
the beginning as deep as it was clear in every Christian heart.   It is one of a very few doctrines, such as
the unity of the Godhead, whereof indeed it is the
image and the result, of which there is not only an
implicit belief but a definite consciousness from the
first.   For the thought of the kingdom is inseparable
from that of the king: and he could be no Divine
Sovereign whose realm was not one and indivisible :
and that this realm should break in pieces and consume all other kingdoms,[1] but itself stand for ever,
was the trust on which the whole Christian life of
endurance and hope was built.

The Christian society through its whole structure
was marked with the seal of that great act on which
it grew, the assumption of human nature by a divine
Person.   Its whole government, its whole worship,
and the whole moral and spiritual being of its people
radiate from that Person as King, as Priest, and as
Prophet.   Take first the character of the individual
Christian.   It is in all its gradations, in that marvellous range of the same being which stretches from the
highest saint matured in acting and suffering to the
most imperfect penitent received into the bosom of the
one mother, a copy, more or less resembling, of our
Lord Himself.   He, the divine Image, is the original
from which every Christian lineament is traced, and
every one of His race repeats Him in some degree.
Every virtue is such as a transcript of some portion of
His character; and the whole life of the individual
resolves itself into an imitation of Him.   Thus He is

---

[1] Dan. ii. 44.   Compare Apoc. i. 9. ὁ ἀδελφὸς ὑμῶν καὶ συγκοινωνὸς ἐν
τῇ θλίψει καὶ ἐν τῇ βασιλείᾳ καὶ ὑπομονῇ Ἰησοῦ Χριστοῦ.

the Prophet not only declaring the whole divine will to men, but leading them in it by His own example. The divine Painter is but representing in every one of His children a copy in some sort of that life, which He set forth in full in the thirty-three years: a thought which we have seen Origen expressing in the chrism which descended from the head of Aaron to the utmost skirt of his raiment.

But likewise in His Priesthood a parallel derivation ensues. First He multiplies Himself in His Apostles: they again in the Bishops whom they create; while each of these communicates himself in his priests. A triple transfusion suffices to form the whole hierarchical order. Nothing can be conceived more simple, yet nothing more efficient supposing that He is what He proclaimed Himself to be. The victim which He appoints to be offered by this priesthood is Himself, and His Body so offered is the food, the life, and the bond of the whole spiritual Body thus created. That Person with which He took the manhood is the centre of all this worship, of which the manhood so taken is the instrument. Thus it is that His second office of Priest, bound up so entirely with Himself, is yet communicated through His divine manhood to the whole Body which He forms. And this order remains through all ages, as intimately connected with His Person now, as eighteen centuries ago, and as it will be when all the centuries to come are evolved.

One office remains; His office of King. And here, again, the jurisdiction which He created for His kingdom springs from His Person, and that not only in its origin but in its perpetual derivation. He was Himself[1]

[1] Κατανοήσατε τὸν ἀπόστολον καὶ ἀρχιερέα τῆς ὁμολογίας ἡμῶν Χριστὸν Ἰησοῦν. Heb. iii. 1.

the Apostle : as such He first multiplied Himself in
the Twelve, whom from Himself He named Apostles.
His public life on earth is an image of the whole mission or government which He would set up after His
Ascension.   He lives with the Twelve : He teaches
them : He is their Instructor, Father, and Friend.
When His Apostles afterwards created Bishops, this
form of our Lord's life on earth was exactly reproduced
in the earliest dioceses.   Thus St. Mark went forth
from the side of Peter, and the mode of his living
and the family which he drew around him at Alexandria was after this pattern.   He, the Bishop, is
the image of Christ, and his twelve presbyters of the
Apostles.   This model is continually set forth by St.
Ignatius as a divine command and institution, he
being himself the occupant of the great Mother See of
the East, the third See of Peter, and that wherein he
first sat.[1]   Thus the canonical life was formed by the
exactest imitation of our Lord's public life, and its
reproduction throughout the various dioceses formed
the Church.   Such was the life which St. Augustine
afterwards practised and reduced to rule ; and those
who planted the Christian Faith throughout the north,
Apostles to new and barbarous races, had this model
before them.   The diocese was first a family, in which
the Bishop as a father presided over his priests, and
sent them forth to their work.   The Eucharist which
he consecrated was from the beginning dispensed from
his church to all his flock.   The diocese, then, in its

---

[1] Thus St. Gregory the Great wrote to Eulogius, Patriarch of Alex-
andria, that the three original patriarchal Sees were all Sees of Peter :
"Cum multi sint Apostoli, pro ipso tamen principatu sola Apostolorum
Principis Sedes in auctoritate convaluit, quæ in tribus locis unius est."
Epist. lib. vii. 40.   The patriarchal authority is a derivation from the
Primacy, which is the well-head.

earliest form was an image of our Lord's intercourse with the Twelve, wherein the Bishop represents Him, and the Priesthood His Apostles.

But the whole Church in its Episcopate or mass of dioceses no less represented His public life. For as He was the Head, the Living Teacher and Guide of His Apostles, and as He came to establish one Kingdom, and one only,[1] wherein the Twelve represented the whole Episcopate, and contained in themselves its powers, so the Primacy which He visibly exercised among them, He delegated, when He left them, to one of their number. Peter, when he received that commission to feed His sheep, took the place on earth of the great Shepherd, and in him the flock remains one.

Thus the double power which expresses the divinely-established government of the Church, the Primacy and the Episcopate, is as close a transcript of the Lord's life on earth with His Apostles as the diocese taken by itself. In His intercourse with His Apostles He is the germ of the Bishop with his priests ; in His Vicariate bestowed upon Peter He repeats or rather continues His visible Headship on earth.

But spiritual jurisdiction is the expression of Christ's sovereignty on earth, and in the order just described it is linked with His Person as strictly as the worship exercised by means of His Priesthood, and the spiritual character which every one of His children bears. Surely no kingdom has ever been so contained in its king, no family in its father, no worship in its object, as the Christian kingdom, family, and worship, which together is the Church. Is it, then, any wonder that all Christian hearts from the first were filled with the blessing of belonging to such

[1] Κηρύσσων τὸ εὐαγγέλιον τῆς βασιλείας. Matt. iv. 23.

a creation as this, in which to them their Redeemer lived and reigned, penetrated them with His own life, and gathered them in His kingdom ?   Are not the words of St. Cyprian just what we should expect those to utter who overflowed with this conviction ?   At the same time that Cyprian was so writing, Dionysius, the Archbishop of Alexandria, addressed Novatian the antipope in these words : " It was better to suffer any extremity in order not to divide the Church of God.   And martyrdom endured to prevent schism were not less glorious than that endured to refuse idolatry, but in my opinion more so.   For in the one case a man suffers martyrdom for his own single soul, but in the other for the whole Church." [1]

But let us trace the chronological sequence in history of that great institution, the real as well as logical coherence of which has just been set forth.   The Church was a fact long before its theory became the subject of reflection.   It came forth from the mind of the Divine Architect and established itself among men through His power ; and it is only when this was done that the creative thought according to which it grew could be delineated.

The fact, then, exactly agrees with the theory, and history here interprets dogma.

It is during the great forty days that our Lord founded the Primacy, when He made St. John and the rest of the Apostles sheep of Peter's fold.   The period of thirty-eight years ·which follows is the carrying into effect His design in the first stage.   The Church grows around Peter.   First in Jerusalem he forms a mass of disciples ; then for a certain number of years at Antioch.   In the second year of Claudius,

[1] St. Dionys. Alex. Ep. 2.   Gallandi, iii. 512.

the thirteenth after the Ascension, he lays the foundations of the Roman Church. In the sixtieth year of
our era he sends forth St. Mark to found the Christian
society in Alexandria. Thus he takes possession of
the three great cities of the empire, of east, west, and
south. In the meantime the labours of St. Paul and
the other Apostles, in conjunction with those of Peter
and in subordination to them, plant the Christian root
in a great number of cities. As St. Paul toils all
round the northern circuit of the empire, through
Asia Minor, Macedonia, Illyricum, to Spain, his work
has a manifest reference to the work of Peter in the
metropolis of the east, of the south, and of the west.
In the latter he joins his elder brother, and the two
Princes of the Apostles offer up their lives together on
the same day in that city which was to be the perpetual citadel of the Christian Faith, the immovable
Rock of a divine Capitol. Thus was it Peter, "from
whom the very Episcopate, and all the authority of
this title sprung,"[1] and what Pope Boniface wrote in
422 is a simple fact of history : that "the formation
of the universal Church at its birth took its beginning
from the honour of blessed Peter, in whose person its
regimen and sum consists. For from his fountain the
stream of ecclesiastical discipline flowed forth into
all churches, as the culture of religion progressively
advanced."[2] Thus the whole initial movement was
from above downwards, and St. Cyprian was not only
enunciating dogma but speaking history when he
wrote that the Lord built the Church upon Peter. In
one generation the structure rose above the ground,

---

[1] Answer of Pope Innocent I. to the Council of Carthage in 416,
among the letters of St. Augustine.
[2] Constant. *Epist. Rom. Pontif.* p. 1037.

and during all that time St. Peter's hand directed the work.

Just at the end of this time, on the point of being thrown into prison, whence he only emerged to martyrdom, Paul was at Rome with Peter, and he describes in imperishable words the work which had been already accomplished. Again it is not only dogma but history, not only what was always to be, but what already was, which he set forth as it were with his dying voice : the one Body, and the one Spirit, the one Lord, one Faith, and one Baptism, as there is one God. That Body in which Apostles, Prophets, Evangelists, Pastors and Teachers were fixed, that the visible structure might grow up to its final stature, in whose accordant unity was the perpetual safeguard against error. When Paul so wrote,[1] the Body was formed, and its headship was incontestably with Peter. He had no need to remind them of the man with whom he was labouring, of whose work the whole Church from Rome to Antioch and Alexandria was the fruit. But he places the maintenance of truth, and the perpetual fountain of grace, in the unity of the Church, which was before those to whom he wrote an accomplished fact.

Two generations pass and the aged St. Ignatius, on his way to martyrdom, attests the same fact. " Where Jesus Christ is," he says, " there is the Catholic Church." The King is in His Kingdom ; the Master in His House ; the Lord in His Temple. The bishops throughout the world inseparably linked together are His mind : and the presidency of charity, which is the inner life of all this spiritual empire, is at Rome. St. Ignatius and the author of the letter to Diognetus

[1] Ephes. iv., written during St. Paul's imprisonment at Rome.

write just after the expiration of the apostolic period; and they both regard Christians as one mass throughout the world, living under a divine form of spiritual government. No one who studies their words can doubt that the one Body and the One Spirit were as visible to their eyes and as dear to their heart as to St. Paul.

We pass two generations further and St. Irenæus repeats the same testimony. The interval has been filled by incessant attacks of heresies, and the Bishop of Lyons dwells upon the fact that the Church speaks with one voice through all the regions of the earth as being one House of God, and that the seat of this its unity is in the great See founded by the Princes of the Apostles at Rome. He reproduces at great length the statements of St. Paul that the safeguard of truth lies in the one apostolic ministry, for which he runs up to the fountain-head in Rome. It is in the living voice and the teaching office of the Church that he sees a perpetual preservative against whatever error may arise. Thus it has been up to his time, and thus it will ever be.

Another period of seventy years runs on, and we come to the just-cited testimony of Cyprian, who therefore said nothing new, nor anything exaggerated; but when the truth was assailed in its very citadel, he spoke out and described wherein its strength lay. He gathers up and gives expression to the two hundred and twenty years between the day of Pentecost and his own time. Here are the creative words of our Apostle and High-priest explained and attested and exhibited as having passed into fact by four witnesses, first St. Paul, then Ignatius, thirdly St. Irenæus, fourthly St. Cyprian. Between all the five there is no shadow of divergence, between the Master who designed the building and the servants who described its erection; between the Prophet who foretold and the historians who recorded. The one said, " Upon this rock I will build My Church; " the others pointed out that the work was accomplished.

The original and fundamental conception of all this work is expressed by St. Matthew and St. Mark when they speak of our Lord at His first going forth as " proclaiming the gospel of the kingdom." His three years' ministry is the germ and type of the perpetual mission which He founded. It was to be from first to last a work of personal ministry, beginning from above, not spreading from below; its power and virtue descending from Him through those whom He chose, the people being the work of the Prince, their government a delegation from Him, as their moral condition lay in following Him, and their life and support in feeding on Him. And He declared that the original conception should be carried out to the end, and that " the gospel of the kingdom " should be proclaimed through the whole world as a witness to all nations, until the consummation should come.[1]

The chief events of the third century brought out more and more the unity of the Church and the Primacy of St. Peter's See as the power within the Church by which that unity is produced and maintained.

With this century the great persecutions begin. That of Septimius Severus arose in the year 202. Now a persecution which assaulted the mass of Chris-

---

[1] This text is continually used by St. Augustine against the Donatists, as containing an express divine prophecy that the one Catholic Church should continue to the end of the world. The Gospel *of* the Kingdom, and the Gospel *without* the Kingdom, are ideas far as the poles apart.

tians was the occasion of fall and apostasy to some, of martyrdom to others. Hence the question became urgent how those should be treated by the Christian society who through fear of suffering had failed to maintain the confession of their faith. It was necessary to lay down more distinctly rules as to what crimes should be admitted to penance, and what that penance should be. The practice here involved doctrine ; it raised immediately the question of the power which the society itself had to grant pardon, and to receive the guilty back into its bosom. And here the authority of the chief Bishop was at once called out. We find as a matter of fact Pope Zephyrinus in the first years of this century determining the rules of penance, and a small party of rigid disciplinarians, among whom Tertullian was conspicuous, who considered his rules as too indulgent. It is in the vehement pamphlet with which Tertullian assails the Pope that we have one of the earliest expressions of the great authority claimed by him. " I hear," he exclaims, " that an edict has been set forth, and a peremptory one. The Pontifex Maximus, in sooth, that is, the Bishop of Bishops, issues his edict : ' I pardon to those who have discharged their penance the sins both of adultery and of fornication.' " [1] Twenty years later Pope Callistus carried the indulgence yet further, receiving to penance those who had committed murder or idolatry. [2] Once more, after a period of thirty years, the breaking out of the Decian persecution raised afresh the question of admitting great sinners to penance, and the actual discipline of the

---

[1] *De Pudicitia*, § 1. See Hagemann, p. 54.
[2] He is so represented by Hippolytus, *Philosophumen*, lib. ix. p. 209. See Hagemann, p. 59.

Roman Church, as established under Zephyrinus and Callistus, is set forth in a letter to Cyprian by Novatian, then one of the most esteemed presbyters of that church. By the discipline which these facts attest it is determined that the Church has lodged in her the power of pardoning any sin whatsoever according to the rules of the penance which she imposes. And it is the Roman Church which herein takes the guidance. She maintained the ancient faith, severity, and discipline, yet tempered with that consideration which the full possession of the truth alone bestows.[1] Thus she received back without hesitation those who returned from heresy or schism, as well as those who had fallen in the conflict with persecution.

For another question of great importance which her guidance determined was that concerning the rebaptization of heretics; and in this she went against the judgment of Cyprian with his council, of Firmilian, and of other bishops. It had been the custom that those who had received baptism among heretics, provided it was with the proper rite, should, when they sought admission into the Church, be received only by an imposition of hands, not by the iteration of baptism. And though Cyprian and a great majority of African bishops, through their horror of schism and heresy, wished to modify this rule, and to insist that baptism given outside the Church was invalid, Pope Stephen resisted, and maintained the ancient rule, with the

---

[1] "Nec hoc nobis nunc nuper consilium cogitatum est, nec hæc apud nos adversus improbos modo supervenerunt repentina subsidia: sed antiqua hæc apud nos severitas, antiqua fides, disciplina legitur antiqua; quoniam nec tantas de nobis laudes Apostolus protulisset dicendo: Quia fides vestra prædicatur in toto mundo, nisi jam exinde vigor iste radices fidei de temporibus illis mutuatus fuisset: quarum laudum et gloriæ degenerem fuisse maximum crimen est." *Epist. Cleri Rom. ad Cyprian.* 31.

decision that nothing save what had been handed down should be done.

It is evident that the question of penance and that of rebaptization touched the whole Christian society, and here accordingly we find the superior Principate of the Roman Church exert itself. In fact, the right decision as to both these questions involved the right conception of the Church herself, her constitution, power, and prerogatives. The rigorism [1] with which some had endeavoured to exclude certain sinners from the faculty of receiving penance, and the view which led them to confine the validity itself of baptism to its reception within the one Church, led when fully developed in the following century to the obstinate schism and heresy of the Donatists. These dangerous tendencies were resisted, when they first appeared, by the Roman See, and we owe to such resistance the application by Tertullian to the Pope of the title of "Pontifex Maximus" and "Bishop of Bishops," about the year 202, as the expression of the power which he then claimed and exercised.

Another question likewise touching the whole Christian society, which the Roman Pontiff had already decided against the practice of the influential and ancient churches of Asia Minor, was the time of holding Easter. Pope Victor insisted that the practice of the Roman Church must be followed, which kept the day of the Crucifixion invariably on the Friday, and that of the Resurrection on the Sunday, and not the Jewish practice of the Asiatics, which took the 14th and the 16th days of the month Nisan, on whatever days of the week they might fall, for that purpose. And here in the peremptory tone of Pope Victor, and

[1] Hagemann, p. 77.

in the threat of excommunication which he issued, the consciousness was shown that the right to determine lay with him, while subsequent times justified his judgment and followed it.   Nor was it of little importance that the greatest festival of the Church should be celebrated by all her children both on the same day and in the same spirit.

We have then now traced up to the end of the third century the inner growth and constituent principles of that great institution, which out of every language, tribe, and religion in the empire or beyond it had formed and welded together one people, the bearer of that Truth and that Grace which the Son of God in assuming manhood had conveyed to the world.   It remains rapidly to review the relations of the empire with this people during seventy-eight years, from the death of Alexander Severus in 235 to the edict of toleration in 313.

II. The seizure of the empire by Maximin was accompanied by a violent attack upon Christians, whom Alexander was held to have favoured.   It is on this occasion that we learn from Origen [1] that churches were burnt, and thus their existence as public buildings is attested.   The clergy were especially threatened, and amongst them Ambrosius, the friend of Origen, and Origen himself.   But Maximin, after reigning three years with extraordinary cruelty, was slain by his own soldiers.   And then during eleven years a period of comparative tranquillity for Christians ensued.

It is with the accession of Decius that the severest trials of the Church begin.   In the sixty-four years, which elapse from this to the edict of toleration the force of the empire is five times directed by its

[1] In Matt. tom. iii. 857 c.

rulers against the Christian name.   The cause of this
is disclosed to us by St. Cyprian, mentioning incidentally the very words of that emperor whose name is
associated with the bitterest hatred to Christians.   He
praises Pope Cornelius,[1] who succeeded Pope Fabian
in "the place of Peter and the rank of the sacerdotal
chair."   He "sat fearless in that chair at Rome at
the moment when the tyrant who hated God's priests
uttered every horrible threat, and with much more
patience and endurance heard the rise of a rival
prince than the appointment of God's priest at Rome."
But why should Decius regard with such dislike the
nomination of a Roman Bishop?   Why, but that the
emperors had now come clearly to discern the organisation of the Church as a visible kingdom of Christ,
at the head of which the Roman Bishop stood.   That
kingdom, whose whole moral and religious doctrine,
together with the life founded upon it, they felt to be
in contradiction with the heathen life and the maxims
of polity on which from time immemorial the empire
had been based, that kingdom Decius saw to be
summed up and represented in him who held, to use
the words of Cyprian, "Peter's place."   With that
religious association which Decius saw extending round
him on every side, and gradually drawing into its
bosom the best of the two sexes, there was no way of
dealing but either to yield to those new maxims which
it set forth, or to destroy it.   In proportion as the
emperors were zealous for the worship of the Roman

---

[1] "Cum Fabiani locus, id est, cum locus Petri et gradus cathedræ
sacerdotalis vacaret." *Epist.* lii. p. 68.   "Sedisse intrepidum Romæ
in sacerdotali cathedra eo tempore cum tyrannus infestus sacerdotibus
Dei fanda atque infanda comminaretur, cum multo patientius et tolera-
bilius audiret levari adversus se æmulum principem quam constitui
Romæ Dei sacerdotem." *Ibid.* p. 69.

grand attack of the empire on the Church is thus
described by Cyprian in the interval which followed
the persecution of Decius and preceded that of Gallus;
and the words of one who not only taught but died
for his teaching carry with them no common force.
" As long repose had corrupted the discipline which
had come down to us from God, the divine judgment
awakened our faith from a declining, and if I may so
speak an almost slumbering state; and whereas we
deserved yet more for our sins, the most merciful
Lord has so moderated all, that what has passed has
seemed rather a trial of what we were than an actual
infliction.   Every one was applying himself to the
increase of wealth, and forgetting both what was the
conduct of believers under the Apostles, and what
ought to be their conduct in every age, they with
insatiable eagerness for gain devoted themselves to
the multiplying of possessions.   The priests were
wanting in religious devotedness; the ministers in
entireness of faith; there was no mercy in works, no
discipline in manners.   Men wore their beards dis-
figured, and women stained their complexion with a
dye.   The eyes were changed from what God made
them, and a lying colour was passed upon the hair.
The hearts of the simple were misled by treacherous
artifices, and brethren became entangled in seductive
snares; ties of marriage were formed with unbelievers;
members of Christ abandoned to the heathen.   Not
only rash swearing was heard, but even false; persons
in high place were swollen with contemptuousness;
poisoned reproaches fell from their mouths; and men
were sundered by unabating quarrels.   Numerous
bishops, who ought to be an encouragement and
example to others, despising their sacred calling,

engaged themselves in secular vocations, relinquished their chair, deserted their people, strayed among foreign provinces, hunted the markets for mercantile profits, tried to amass large sums of money while they had brethren starving within the Church, took possession of estates by fraudulent proceedings, and multiplied their gains by accumulated usuries." [1]

Such was the end of the long peace which succeeded the persecution of Septimius Severus, and yet it was followed at once by that ten years' conflict which, if stained with apostasies at first, soon became rife in martyrdoms. And as the former relaxation seems to prove that the third century among Christians was no ideal time in which moral corruptions and abuses did not largely exist, so the improvement which trial and suffering at once produced, calling forth some of the greatest triumphs the Faith has ever known, seems to indicate that the divine power of the Church lies not in forming a community free from imperfections, or even secured from scandals, but in building up a portion of her children to sanctity. At all times the wheat and the chaff lie together on her threshing-floor, and the flail of suffering winnows them. But those who seek for a time when all professing believers were saints, will find it neither when the Apostles taught nor afterwards.

The Emperor Valerian, after being during four years more kindly disposed to Christians than any preceding emperor, and after filling his palace with them, was instigated by an Egyptian magician into becoming a most bitter persecutor.[2] This was ended in less than three years through his capture by the Persian monarch, when his son Gallienus restored the

---

[1] *De Lapsis*, iv. pp. 182, 183, Oxford translation.
[2] Euseb. *Hist.* l. vii. c. 10.

sacred places to the Christians, and ordered the bishops
not to be disturbed.[1]   The empire during the following
eight years seemed through the supineness of Gallienus
to be on the point of dissolution; it is the time when
nineteen commanders in various provinces assume the
purple, and successively perish.   At last Gallienus is
put out of the way by a council of officers, and the
empire is restored by Claudius and by Aurelian.   The
latter, after being for some years fair to Christians,
ends by persecuting them.   But he too is speedily
removed by death.   It is remarkable that all these
persecutions, by Maximin, by Decius, by Gallus, by
Valerian, and by Aurelian, are of short duration:
none of them continue more than three years.   After
Aurelian's death in 275 a whole generation ensues
in which Christians by the ordinary operation of the
empire's laws, according to which their religion was
illicit, were liable to suffer much in individual cases.
Thus it is in a time not reckoned persecuting, shortly
after Maximianus had been made his colleague in the
empire by Diocletian, that one of the most merciless
acts of tyrannical cruelty took place, which gave an
occasion for several thousand men at once to offer
up their lives.   Unresisting victims, yet brave soldiers
with arms in their hands, they endured two decima-
tions, and when remonstrance had proved in vain,
piled their arms, and let themselves be massacred to
the last man rather than violate their conscience.
The place where they suffered took the name of their
heroic captain, Maurice.   The churches of that Alpine
valley to this day bear witness to that most illustrious
act of Christian sacrifice by placing his figure over
their altars.   A monastery has for thirteen hundred

[1] Euseb. *Hist.* l. vii c. 13.

and fifty years guarded the sepulchre of that martyred legion, it being itself amongst the most ancient houses of prayer.

It cannot be doubted that in the last twenty-five years of the third century the number of Christians was being largely increased, and moreover they were daily gaining the higher ranks of society.   Diocletian had reigned for eighteen years, and seemed effectually to have stopped that incessant succession of soldiers gaining the throne by assassination and yielding it in turn to their assassins, which for fifty years threatened to destroy the state.   At such a moment it was that Diocletian, belying all the past conduct of his life, let loose against the Christian Church the last, the fiercest, and the longest of the heathen persecutions.

It was in truth scarcely less than the rending in pieces the whole social framework when a proclamation of the Emperors Diocletian and Maximian, in the year 303, declared that the Christian Faith should cease to exist.   How entirely that faith had now penetrated all ranks was shown in Diocletian's own household, wherein his most trusted[1] chamberlains, beloved as his children, were cruelly tortured because they refused to worship the heathen gods, while his wife Prisca and his daughter Valeria purchased immunity for the present by compliance.   We have the emperor described by an eye-witness of those times as himself sitting in judgment,[2] and putting men to the

[1] See the martyrdom of the favourite chamberlain Peter, who, says Eusebius (*Hist.* viii. 6), was violently scourged, and then slowly roasted alive.

[2] "Diocletianus . . . excarnificare omnes suos protenus cœpit.   Sedebat ipse atque innocentes igne torrebat. . . .   Omnis sexus et ætatis homines ad exustionem rapti; nec singuli, quoniam tanta erat multitudo, sed gregatim circumdato igni amburebantur," &c. Lactant. 14, 15.

torture of fire. The same power was delegated to the governors throughout the provinces. "It was," says Eusebius, "the nineteenth year of Diocletian's reign, in the month of March, when the festival of the Lord's Passion was drawing near, that imperial edicts were everywhere published, ordering the churches to be levelled, the Scriptures to be burnt, those of rank to be deprived of it, the common people, if they remained faithful, to be reduced to slavery. This was the first edict against us; another soon came enjoining that all those who ruled the churches should first be imprisoned, and then by every means compelled to sacrifice."[1] Lactantius adds that every action at law was to proceed against Christians, while they should not be allowed to claim the law for any wrong inflicted, or spoliation suffered, or dishonour done to their wives.[2] Many in consequence of these edicts suffered willingly terrible torments: many others at first gave way. What these torments were Eusebius describes: some were beaten; some torn with hooks.[3] "It is impossible to say how many and how great martyrs of Christ might be seen in every city and country." A man of the highest rank in Nicomedia, from an impulse of zeal when the edict first appeared, tore it down. He was seized, and not merely tortured but slowly roasted alive,[4] which he bore with unflinching patience, preserving joyousness and tranquillity to his last breath. The emperors polluted the provinces subject to them, by the slaughter of

---

[1] Eusebius, *Hist.* viii. 2.
[2] Lactantius, *de Morte Persecutorum*, 13.
[3] Euseb. viii. 4.
[4] "Statim productus non modo extortus sed etiam legitime coctus cum admirabili patientia, postremo exustus est." Lact. *de Morte Pers.* 13; Euseb. viii. 5.

men and women who worshipped God, as if it had
been in a civil war, with the exception of Constantius,[1]
who ruled the Gauls and Britain, and preserved his
soul pure from this stain.   But it was so much worse
than a war in which the conquered have only to
suffer servitude or at most death, whereas in this case
what was committed against those who refused to do
wrong passes all description.   They used against
them every imaginable torture, and thought it little
to slay those whom they hated, unless by cruelty
having first exposed their bodies to mockery.   If they
could persuade, by terror, any to violate the faith to
which they were bound, and to agree to the fatal
sacrifice, these they praised and with their honours
destroyed, but on the others they exhausted the whole
ingenuity of their butchery, calling them desperate as
disregarding their own body.[2]   For two years the
whole Roman world ruled by Diocletian, Maximian,
and Galerius was exposed to this misery : when on
the retirement of Diocletian and Maximian in 305
Galerius became the chief emperor, the persecution
continued in all its intensity, save in the territory
subject to Constantius.   " It is impossible to describe
the individual scenes which took place throughout the
world.   The several governors having received their
commission carried it out according to their own
ferocity.   Some through excess of fear did more than
their orders ; some were inspired by personal enmity ;
some by natural cruelty ; some sought to advance
themselves ; some were precipitate in the work of
destruction, as one in Phrygia,"[3] where, says Eusebius,

---

[1] Euseb. *de Vita Constant.* l. i. 13.
[2] Lactant. *Divin. Institut.* l. v. 9; Gallandi, tom. iv, 313, 314.
[3] Lactant. *Divin. Institut.* l. v. 11.

the soldiers surrounded a Christian town and burnt it with all its inhabitants, " men, women, and children, calling upon the name of Christ, the God of all." [1] " And in devising various kinds of tortures they aim at gaining a victory. They are well aware that it is a struggle between champions. I myself saw in Bithynia a governor beside himself in joy, as if he had subdued some barbarous nation, because one who for two years had with great virtue resisted was seen to fail. They inflict therefore exquisite pains, only avoiding to put the tortured to death, as if it were only death that made them blessed, and not likewise those torments which in proportion to their severity produce a greater glory by the virtue they exhibit." [2]

Eusebius declares that such cruelties were perpetrated not for a short time, but during several years; that ten, twenty, thirty, sixty, and as many as a hundred men, women, and children would be slain in a day by various tortures. " When I was in Egypt myself I saw a crowd in one day, some beheaded, some burnt; with my own eyes I beheld the marvellous ardour, the truly divine virtue and alacrity of those who believed in Christ. Scarcely was sentence passed against the first, when a fresh number hastened before the tribunal, professing themselves Christians : with joy, gaiety, and smiles they received the award of death, singing hymns and returning thanks to their last breath." [3]

Among those distinguished for their learning in all Grecian studies, and for the universal honour in which they had been held, Eusebius mentions especially a bishop of Thmuis named Phileas. While he lay in

---

[1] Euseb. *Hist.* viii. 11.   [2] Lactantius, as above.
[3] *Hist.* viii. 9.

prison under sentence of death, which was afterwards executed by beheading, he wrote a letter to his people, detailing the scenes in which he bore a part. This letter the historian has happily preserved for us. "Inasmuch," he says, "as the Holy Scriptures presented us with so many fair ensamples, and lessons, the blessed martyrs who are with me felt no hesitation. They fixed their mind's eye steadily upon the God of all, formed the conception of death suffered for piety's sake, and clung firmly to that to which they were called. For they knew that our Lord Jesus Christ had become man for our sakes in order to cut up all sin by the root, and to supply us with food on that journey by which we enter into eternal life. For He thought it not robbery to be equal with God, but emptied Himself by taking the form of a slave, and being found in fashion as a man humbled Himself to death, and that death the cross. Hence it was that the martyrs, bearing Christ within them, in their zeal for the greater gifts endured every suffering and all the various inventions of torture not once, but some of them a second time, and all the threats of their guards, which did not stop with words in their zeal to overcome them, without their resolution being broken, because perfect charity casts out fear. What words can I find to enumerate their virtue and their endurance in each particular trial? Since they were left exposed to any one's outrage, some being struck with clubs, others with rods, others with scourges, some with lashes, some with ropes. The sight of the tortures presented every variety, but great suffering throughout. These with hands bound behind them were distended on the wood, and had every limb stretched by machinery; and thus their tormentors by command attacked the whole body,

tearing them not on the sides alone as murderers are
treated, but on the stomach, the knees, and the cheeks.
Others were hung by one hand from the portico, and
this tension of the sinews and limbs caused a more
terrible pain than any.   Others were bound to pillars
face to face, the feet not reaching the ground, but the
weight of the body tightening the bonds, and this they
suffered not during the time of examination only, or
while the governor was engaged with them, but almost
the whole day.   For when he went to others, he left
his officers watching over these, to see if the extremity
of torture should cause any to give way : and he
charged them to be bound without mercy, but when
at their last gasp to be let down and dragged along
the ground.   For he said that no account at all was
to be taken of us, but we were to be both reputed
and treated as non-existent.   This last was a second
torture which they superadded to their blows.   There
were those also who after their tortures were put in
the stocks with their feet distended to the fourth hole,
where they must needs lie down, not being able to
hold themselves up through their wounds gaping over
the whole body.   Others flung on the pavement lay
there through the repeated violence of their racking,
the many signs of suffering over their body presenting
a more fearful spectacle to those who looked on than
the racking itself.   Thus treated, some died under the
torture, putting their adversary to shame by their
endurance ; some shut up in prison half-dead, after a
few days expired through the extremity of their pains ;
the rest having treatment applied became still more
resolute through the time spent in prison.   And so
when the choice was presented to them either to touch
the abominable sacrifice, and depart unmolested, gain-

ing by this course an execrable deliverance, or, not sacrificing, to receive sentence of death, without any doubt they joyfully went to death. For they knew what the sacred writings enjoin : ' He that sacrifices to other gods shall be rooted out,' and 'Thou shalt have no other gods but Me.' " [1]

This may suffice as a specimen of what was done during a course of years throughout the dominion of Galerius, Maximin, and Maxentius. It is in this persecution especially that the virgin martyrs suffered the extremity of the heathen malignity in the threatened loss of that purity which they valued more than life. And here a fellow-Christian at Alexandria, disguising himself as a soldier, was to St. Theodora the guardian which her angel himself became to St. Agnes at Rome. In this persecution also St. Vincent repeats in Spain the trial and the triumph of St. Laurence at Rome. The authentic account of his martyrdom shows the utmost point to which the most ingenious and the most ferocious cruelty could reach on the one side, and the most enduring patience on the other. But the numberless details concerning the sufferings of this time preserved to us show that it was indeed a conflict prolonged during eight years, in which the Roman State put forth the utmost strength which unlimited power guided by unhesitating cruelty could exert to destroy the Christian Church and name.

At the end of this time the conflict was terminated by the Emperor Galerius, the chief mover of the whole persecution, being struck by a mortal disease, in which, reduced to impotence by his sufferings, he withdrew his edicts against the Christian Faith. One after another the persecuting emperors are taken away

[1] Euseb. *Hist.* viii. 10.

by death.   Constantine, inheriting his father's justice towards Christians and preserving them in his own territory from these outrages, gradually appears as their champion.   It is when advancing to Rome against Maxentius that he sees in the Cross the token of victory over all enemies : enrolling it on his banner he rules with Licinius the Roman world, and by a decree issued at Milan in 3 1 3 assures to all Christians the free exercise of their religion.

In the year 64 Nero had declared, by initiating a persecution against Christians, that their religion was illicit, and fell under the ban of the old Roman laws which forbade the exercise of any worship not approved by the senate.   From that time down to the edict of Constantine no Christian could stand before a Roman tribunal plainly avowing his faith in one God and one Christ without incurring the liability of capital punishment.   In this period of two hundred and forty-eight years it is true that there were intervals of comparative peace when the emperors did not themselves call into action the laws against Christians.   During the whole second century there would seem to be no emperor who set himself to destroy the Christian name and people as a whole.   In the time of Commodus it was even forbidden to accuse a Christian of his religion ; yet even then, if the accusation was made and proved, it was a capital offence, followed, and that too in the case of a senator after defence before the senate, by the infliction of the penalty.   Alexander Severus is the first of whom it is said that " he suffered the Christians to be " ; Philip also favoured them ; so again Valerian at first ; Gallienus gave back their churches ; Diocletian trusted them and filled his palace with them : but no one of these emperors ventured to declare the

Christian religion to be according to the laws of Rome a "licit" religion, and no one therefore enabled Christians to avow it without danger of suffering. The most favourable suspended the action of the laws either by positive edict, or by letting it be understood that they did not wish Christians to be disturbed. A change either of the ruler, or of the ruler's inclination, as was seen in the cases of Valerian, Aurelian, and Diocletian, induced at once that full state of penality under which Christianity was as much forbidden as homicide or treason, and in virtue of which Roman magistrates could as little refuse to judge the crime of being a Christian as those other crimes. Thus it is that we find martyrdoms assigned to times at which there is not known to have been any general persecution. In unnumbered cases Christians won their crown through private enmity or local tumults, when any one of the thousand motives which awaken ill-will was sufficient to cause an appeal to that great and unchanged enemy, the Law of Rome, which proscribed them. To Constantine belongs the glory of having removed this enemy. He made the profession of Christianity no longer a crime. He accomplished that which Justin and Tertullian and every Christian apologist had asked for in vain, that every Christian in the Roman Empire might profess and practise the Christian Faith without suffering punishment for it.

LECTURE XIII

THE CHRISTIAN CHURCH AND THE GREEK PHILOSOPHY

PART I

"*Socrates.* It is, then, necessary to wait until we learn how we ought to be disposed towards gods and men.

"*Alcibiades.* But when, Socrates, will that time arrive? and who shall teach us it? For it seems to me that I should with the greatest pleasure see that man.

"*Socrates.* It is he who cares for thee." [1]   *Second Alcib.* § 22.

IN the three preceding lectures we have witnessed a great spectacle, a spectacle in all history unique and without a rival, the encounter, that is, with the forces of the great world-empire of a voluntary society which bears in its bosom and propagates a body of truth, and this encounter carried on without respite during ten generations of men. The elements of this conflict are, on the one side, power, throned in civilisation, and defended by that sword before which nothing hitherto had stood. On the other, appears a belief testified by suffering and patience, the possession of a society which is itself dropped as a seed into the earth's bosom and silently fills its expanse. Attention must now be called to another aspect of the same encounter. Rome, as we have said, pre-eminently wielded power; not the power of her legions only, immense as that was, but the

---

[1] Σωκ. Ἀναγκαῖον οὖν ἐστὶ περιμένειν ἕως ἄν τις μάθῃ ὡς δεῖ πρὸς θεοὺς καὶ πρὸς ἀνθρώπους διακεῖσθαι.

Ἀλκ. Πότε οὖν παρέσται ὁ χρόνος οὗτος, ὦ Σώκρατες; καὶ τίς ὁ παιδεύσων; ἥδιστα γὰρ ἄν μοι δοκῶ ἰδεῖν τοῦτον τὸν ἄνθρωπον τίς ἐστιν.

Σωκ. Οὗτός ἐστιν ᾧ μέλει περὶ σοῦ.

power of her laws, and the power of that many-sided and as it seemed triumphant all-embracing civilisation, of which she was the golden head. The mind, how-ever, the thought of the world which she ruled, belonged to the great Hellenic race. It therefore remains to consider the contest waged by this mind against the truth for which the Christian Church suffered. The sword hews away limbs ; the fire destroys bodies ; and the martyrs offered freely their limbs and their bodies to sword and flame. But the martyrs were inspired with a mind ; they carried Christ in them. The mind opposed to theirs was the mind animating that ancient civilisation ; the mind which had erected such shrines as Diana of Ephesus and the Parthenon at Athens ; the mind which dictated the laws of Solon and Lycurgus ; the mind which taught in the Acade-mus, the Lyceum, the Portico, and the Garden ; the mind which built Alexandria for the world's emporium and university, and raised Antioch to be the gorgeous throne of eastern magnificence. We have to consider how this heathen mind encountered the Christian ; in short, how, " after that in the wisdom of God the world by wisdom knew not God, it pleased Him through the folly of Christian preaching to save those that believed." [1] Let us trace the encounter of heathen wisdom——that is, Philosophy——with Christian wisdom, that is, the truth of a God incarnate and crucified, with all its consequences, as upborne by the Christian Church and planted among men.

Now the system of polytheistic worship which was then in possession of the Græco-Roman world had been subjected for many ages to all the analytic power of human reason as exercised by the most gifted of

[1] 1 Cor. i. 21.

races which have hitherto embodied their genius in a corresponding civilisation. The philosophy of Greece is in fact such an analysis, and the rise of this philosophy is carried back by the ablest inquirers to the time of Thales and Pythagoras in the sixth century before Christ. In the beautiful climate of Ionia and Southern Italy there arose at this time men who attempted by the efforts of their own reason to form a physical and a moral theory of the world which surrounded them. Philosophy is not merely thought, but methodical thinking, thinking consciously directed upon the knowledge of things in their connection with each other. Nor is it content merely with the collecting of observations and the knowledge so derived, but proceeds to gather the individual instances into a whole, to draw to a centre what was scattered, and to form a view of the world resting upon clear conceptions and at unity with itself.[1] This was the nature of that work which Thales and Pythagoras began. Let us give a glance at the race which bore them, and of which they were representative men.

This race had dwelt for some ages in Greece, and from thence occupied by emigration the shores of Asia Minor, Sicily, and Southern Italy, with a part of Africa. Pythagoras, the father of Italian philosophy, had migrated from Samos to Crotona, having visited Egypt, examined and gathered from all the stores of its knowledge. A century later Herodotus, the father

---

[1] Zeller, *die Philosophie der Griechen*, 2te Aufl. vol. i. pp. 6 and 35, "Philosophy," says Grote, *Plato*, vol. i. v. "is, or aims at becoming, reasoned truth: an aggregate of matters believed or disbelieved after conscious process of examination gone through by the mind and capable of being explained to others:" who quotes Cicero's "Philosophia ex rationum collatione consistit."

of Greek history, migrated likewise from his country
Halicarnassus, and after spending many years in
extensive travels through Egypt and Western Asia
settled at Thurii. In the succeeding century Plato
travelled in like manner with similar purposes. He
was familiar with Sicily as with his own Attica, not to
speak of Egypt or Phœnicia. These three great men,
Pythagoras, Herodotus, and Plato, are specimens herein
of the cultured Greek, the gentleman, as we should
call him. Thus though Greece proper was a very
small country, the whole region from middle Italy,
including Sicily, and the rich coast-land of Northern
Africa from Carthage to Egypt, with again Phœnicia
and Syria, and the continent to the depth of perhaps
a hundred miles round the three sides of Asia Minor
watered by the sea, were in a larger sense the Greek's
country, a field of Grecian thought, and enterprise,
and observation, a sphere in which his mind was
enlarged, and his judgment of men and things
matured.[1] Generally speaking these regions were
singularly favoured as to richness of soil and convenience of situation. Herodotus himself has marked
the climate of Ionia as the most beautiful and best-
tempered of the earth ; and with a far wider knowledge of its regions we should not venture to dispute
the justness of his remark. Some modern writers are
wont to dwell on the effect which climate exercises
upon man's mind. However this may be, it is certain
that the race whose energies were diffused over this
region was most highly gifted with natural endowments. When out of the world which Christianity

[1] Thus Herodotus says of Solon, τῆς θεωρίης ἐκδημήσας εἵνεκεν, i. 30 ;
and presently, ξεῖνε Ἀθηναῖε, παρ᾽ ἡμέας γὰρ περὶ σέο λόγος ἀπῖκται
πολλὸς, καὶ σοφίης εἵνεκεν τῆς σῆς καὶ πλάνης, ὡς φιλοσοφέων γῆν πολλὴν
θεωρίης εἵνεκεν ἐπελήλυθας.

has mainly formed, and from the bosom of nations which have grown through the struggle of a thousand years, and with perpetual competition among each other, into a rich civilisation, we look back on that ancient and simpler world, we find in Hellenism the most perfect expression of the natural man, as a plastic, artistic, poetical, philosophical, and generally intellectual race, wherein matter was most completely permeated by mind. The language which they used even yet presents a very perfect image of such a race, as not being formed from the corruption of other idioms, but a mother tongue, the most brilliant of the Aryan sisters. In its union of strength with beauty, of pleasing sound with accurate sense, in its power to convey the most subtle distinctions of philosophic thought, or the most radiant images of sensuous loveliness, the gravest enunciations of law, or the tenderest dreams of romance, it was well calculated to be the organ of a people wherein bodily form and immaterial intellect alike culminated. Our own language is full of nerve and vigour. With its northern force and habit of incorporating the material stores of other languages it is well suited to the descendants of sea-kings, who have provinces all over the world. But without inflections our English tongue is deprived of cases and genders, and is defective in marking time, whereas the Greek in all these is most rich and flexible : the one resembles the torso of a Hercules without its limbs, the other an Apollo as he touches the earth in his perfect symmetry. Then compare its sound with that of the old Hellenic tongue, and we seem to hear the poet's " stridor ferri tractæque catenæ," beside the voice of a lute ; while as to texture, it is like the train of a railway matched with the golden network, fine as the

spider's web, indissoluble as adamant, which the poet
feigns to have been wrought by Vulcan: the English
imprisons thought in a rude and cumbrous iron, while
the Greek exhibits it in a rich and ductile gold.   As
was the language, so was the people: fond of society
and intercourse, skilful, crafty, commercial, enterpris-
ing, with a most human and genial intellect, with a
keen and critical judgment, and a vivid imagination.
When such a race turned itself to a scientific consideration of the world, it might well produce what we
are now to pass in review, the Greek philosophy.

And here it is well to lay down first the standing-
point of the Greek mind.   The Hellenic religion was
a natural religion, inasmuch as according to it man
had no need to raise himself above the surrounding
world and his own nature in order to connect himself
with the Deity.   As he was originally constituted, he
felt himself related to it: no inward change in his
mode of thought, no struggle with his natural impulses and inclinations, was required of him for this
purpose.   All that to him was humanly natural seemed
to him to have its justification in regard to the Deity
likewise; and so the most godlike man was he who
worked out most completely his powers as man, and
the essence of religious duty consisted in that man
should do for the honour of the Deity what is in
accordance with his own nature.[1]

But this natural religion of the Greeks differed
from that of others in that neither outward nature as
such, nor the sensuous being of man as such, but
human nature in its beauty, as illumined by mind, is
its point of excellence.   The Greek did not, like the
Eastern, lose his independence before the powers of

[1] Zeller, i. 39, quoted.

nature, nor revel like the northern savage in boundless liberty, but in the full consciousness of his freedom saw its highest fulfilment in obedience to the general order as the law of his own nature. And as the purely Grecian deities are the ideals of human activity, he thus stands to them in a calm and free relation, such as no other nation of antiquity felt, because they are the mirror of his own being, but his being exalted, so that he is drawn to them without purchasing this at the cost of the pain and toil of an inward struggle.[1]

How the features of his own land served to image out to his fancy the Greek's religious attitude a poet has told us in exquisite verses, worthy of the beauty which they describe; the apotheosis of nature.

"Where are the Islands of the Blest?
    They stud the Ægean sea;
And where the deep Elysian rest?
    It haunts the vale where Peneus strong
    Pours his incessant stream along,
    While craggy ridge and mountain bare
    Cut keenly through the liquid air,
    And in their own pure tints arrayed,
    Scorn earth's green robes which change and fade,
    And stand in beauty undecayed,
        Guards of the bold and free."[2]

It seems to me essential to bear in mind throughout our whole inquiry this standing-point of the Greek mind, because through all the succession of schools and the fluctuations of doctrines, it remains, so to say, the groundwork on which they are embroidered. It is the very texture of Hellenic thought upon which first Pythagoras, then Plato, Aristotle, Epicurus, Zeno, Cleanthes, Panætius, and even Plotinus and Por-

[1] Zeller, i. p. 38.
[2] Newman, *Verses on Various Occasions;* Heathen Greece, p. 158.

phyrius spin their web. They vary the decoration, but the substance remains unaltered. This standing-point rules the conception of virtue, and therefore of the whole moral world. It reaches also to the final end of man, and determines it.

Moreover as the intellectual power of man seems to have culminated in the Hellenic race, so it would seem that a state of things existed among that people which left the human reason practically more to its own unaided resources than we find to have been the case elsewhere. No doubt the Greek mind had lived and brooded for ages upon the remains of original revelation, nor can any learning now completely unravel the interwoven threads of tradition and reason so as to distinguish their separate work. However, it is certain that in the sixth century before Christ the Greeks were without a hierarchy, and without a definite theology: not indeed without individual priesthoods, traditionary rites, and an existing worship, as well as certain mysteries which professed to communicate a higher and more recondite doctrine than that exposed to the vulgar gaze. But in the absence of any hierarchy holding this priesthood together, and teaching anything like a specific doctrine about divine and human things, a very large range indeed was given to the mind, acting upon this shadowy religious belief, and reacted upon by it, to form their philosophy. The Greeks did not, any more than antiquity in general, use the acts of religious service for instruction by religious discourse.[1]

---

[1] Zeller, i. p. 43. "Aber es liegt überhaupt nicht in der Weise des Alterthums, die gottesdienstlichen Handlungen zur Belehrung durch Religionsvorträge zu benützen. Ein Julian mochte in Nachahmung christlicher Sitte dazu den Versuch machen, aus der klassischen Zeit selbst ist uns kein Beispiel hievon überliefert."

In other words, there was no such thing as preaching among them. A domain therefore was open to the philosopher on which he might stand without directly impeaching the ancestral worship, while he examined its grounds, and perhaps sapped its foundations. He was therein taking up a position which their priests, the civil functionaries of religious rites scarcely any longer retaining a spiritual meaning or a moral cogency, had not occupied.

The Homeric and Hesiodic poems exhibit a multitude of gods and goddesses, beings with a personal character and will, who were supposed to divide the government of the world between them, with a more or less recognised sovereignty of one chief. In the midst, then, of a people practising this traditional worship, arose men who set themselves by the light of reason to think steadily and continuously how that world in which they were living had become what it was. Such a movement of mind indicated in itself dissatisfaction with the existing religion, wherein the gods were considered the causes of things, and their wills the rulers of them, though in the background even here loomed the idea of fate, the representative, as it were, of brute matter, from which the Greek mind could never disengage itself. Yet we do not find that these philosophers set themselves openly to attack the existing religion; rather leaving it in possession, and themselves usually complying with its forms, they pursued their own train of thought, as it were by its side, not choosing to look whither it would lead them.

Such very much appears the position of inquirers in the first period of Greek philosophy, which is generally made to extend from its rise under Thales to the time of the Sophists and Socrates. Their thoughts were mainly occupied with the appearances of the physical world: they speculated how it could have arisen. Thus Thales, we are told, imagined its first principle to be water; Anaximander, boundless matter; Anaximenes, air; the Pythagoreans said, all is number; the Eleatic school, all is the one unchangeable being.[1] On the contrary Heracleitus conceived the one Being as ever in motion, involved in perpetual change: in accordance with which he nowhere finds true knowledge, and thinks the mass of men have no understanding for eternal truth.[2] Empedocles of Agrigentum sets forth the four elements, earth, water, air, and fire, as the material principles or roots of things, attaching to these two ideal principles as moving forces, Love as the unitive, and Hatred as the severing.[3] Anaxagoras, over and above mechanical causes, to which he limited himself in the explanation of everything in particular, recognises a divine spirit, which as the finest of all things is simple, unmixed, passionless reason, which came upon chaos, forming and ordering the world out of it.[4] Democritus of Abdera takes for his principles the Full and the Empty, identifying these with Being and Non-being, or Something and Nothing. His Full consists of indivisible atoms.[5]

The remarkable thing about all these systems, if we may so call them, is, that while the existing popular religion teemed over, so to say, with the idea of a number of personal agents directing human things, these philosophers nearly all concurred in the attempt

---

[1] Zeller, i. p. 141. [2] *Ibid.* i. pp. 449–452.
[3] Ueberweg, *Grundriss der Geschichte der Philosophie*, drit. Aufl. i. p. 65. [4] *Ibid.* i. 68. [5] *Ibid.* i. 72.

to find some one agent, and that material, from which
all should spring. As yet even the radical distinction
of matter and spirit was not clear to their minds: [1]
the soul of the individual man was to them merely
a particle of the vital power which disclosed itself
through the universe, the purest portion, but a portion
still, of primal matter. In their conception of the
constituent cause, while they advanced towards unity
they receded from personality. Even the world-
forming Intelligence of Anaxagoras, who first distinctly declares that spirit is not mixed with matter,
works only as a power of nature, and is portrayed
to us in a semi-sensuous form, as a finer matter. [2]

After Greek philosophy had run out during about
a hundred and fifty years in this sort of vague and
imaginative speculation upon the physical world, it
underwent a great change, which marks the transition
to its second period. These successive opinions of
philosophers led a class of men who arose at Athens
about the middle age of Socrates to the conclusion,
that it would be more profitable to turn the course
of human thought from such cosmological reveries
to the question of the perception itself of truth by
man. He who accomplished this was Socrates, who
turned his reflection by preference upon man himself
as the subject who thinks and wills. [3]   And herein

[1] Döllinger, *Heidenthum und Judenthum*, p. 272, and Zeller, i. p. 139,
who states this of the Eleatics, Heracleitus, Democritus, and even the
Pythagoreans, who, though they put Number instead of Matter, yet
conceived incorporeal principles as material, and so considered from the
same point of view the soul and the body, the ethical and the physical,
in man.

[2] Zeller, *ibid.*

[3] Ueberweg, i. 75. "Die Sophistik bildet den Uebergang von der
kosmologischen zu der auf das denkende und wollende Subject gerich-
teten Philosophie," p. 76. "Sokrates . . . theilt mit den Sophisten
die allgemeine Tendenz der Reflexion auf das Subject, tritt aber zu

his character had an influence over Greek philosophy
which is strikingly marked through the whole of its
second period. This period embraces the Sophists,
Socrates himself, Plato and Aristotle, and the Stoics
and Epicureans; finally those Sceptic and Eclectic
schools which rose naturally from the criticism
detecting what is untenable in preceding systems.
During the six hundred years which elapse from the
teaching career of Socrates to the death of Marcus
Antoninus we may say that one great line of inquiry
occupied among philosophers the human mind; it
was man himself, as the subject of logical thought
and moral will.[1] The chief endeavour was to form
a science of ethics, and a science of reasoning, to
which physical and mathematical studies, though at
times warmly pursued and never wholly neglected, were
yet subordinate.[2]

Who is this man of singular ugliness, with a face
like a Silenus, with a body enduring hunger and
impervious to heat and cold, who for thirty years
frequents from morning to night the agora, the
streets, the porticoes of Athens; who can drain the
wine-cup through the night, and with reason unimpaired discuss philosophy through the following day;
never alone, ready to converse with all in whom he
discerned the germ of inquiry? He neither courts

ihnen dadurch in Gegensatz, das seine Reflexion sich nicht bloss auf die
elementaren Functionen des Subjects, die Wahrnehmung und Meinung
und das sinnliche und egoistische Begehren, sondern auch auf die höch-
sten gestigen, zur Objectivität in wesentlicher Beziehung stehenden
Functionen, nämlich auf das Wissen und die Tugend richtet."

[1] Ueberweg, i. 76.

[2] Thus Zeller throughout his great work perpetually deplores that
through this long period, and with increasing force after Aristotle's time,
pure science, *die reine Wissenschaft*, was not studied for its own sake,
but was subordinate to a moral purpose, the question, that is, of man's
greatest good, and his happiness.

the high nor despises the low. Beside him may
be found the reckless beauty of Alcibiades and the
staid gravity of Nicias, the admiring gaze of Plato
even in youth majestic, and the sober homage of
plainer Xenophon. Who is this, the man most social
of men where the whole population is a club, the
club of Athenian citizenship; whose tongue arrests
the most volatile and inconstant of peoples; whose
reason attracts and by turns draws out or silences
the most opposite of characters; whose whole life is
publicity; of spirit at once homely and subtle, simple
and critical, parent both of philosophic certitude and
philosophic scepticism? This is Socrates, the son of
Sophroniscus, to whom Greek philosophy will look
back as on one that had given its bent and directed
its course during a thousand years, until the last of
its defenders [1] will fight a hopeless battle with triumphant Christianity, as the gods of Greece vanish, never
more to return, and the lurid star of a false prophet
teaching a false monotheism appears above the horizon,
and takes the place, which they have left vacant, to be
chief foe of the Christian name.

The special principle of Socrates is thus described
to us by an historian of Greek philosophy.[2] "It is
not merely an already existing mode of thought
which was further developed by Socrates, but an
essentially new principle and proceeding which were
introduced into philosophy. Whilst all preceding
philosophy had been directed immediately on the
object, so that the question of the essence and
grounds of natural appearances is in it the radical
question, on which all others depend, Socrates was

[1] Simplicius, in the sixth century.
[2] Zeller, i. p. 117.

the first to give utterance to the conviction that
nothing can be known respecting anything which
meets our thought, before its general essence, its
conception, be determined. It follows from this that
the trial of our own representations by the standard
of the conception is philosophical self-cognition, the
beginning and the condition of all true knowing.
Whilst those who preceded him had arrived through
the consideration of things only to distinguishing between the representation of things and the knowing
of them, he, reversing this, makes all cognition of
things dependent on the right view of the nature
of knowledge."

Another [1] says : "It is stated in Aristotle's *Meta-
physics* [2] that Socrates introduced the method of
Induction and Definition, which proceeds from the
individual to the determination of the conception.
Aristotle marks [3] the domain of ethics as that on
which Socrates applied this method. According to
him the fundamental view of Socrates was the indivisible unity of theoretical prudence and practical
ability on ethical ground. Socrates conceived all
the virtues to be prudences, inasmuch as they are
sciences.[4] These statements are fully borne out by
the portraits of Xenophon and Plato : Aristotle has
only given point to their expression. Thus Xenophon
says,[5] 'He was ever conversing about human things,
inquiring what was piety and what impiety; what
honour and what turpitude; what just and what
unjust; what sober-mindedness and what madness;
what courage and what cowardice; what policy and

---

[1] Ueberweg, i. p. 88.   [2] xiii. 4.   [3] *Metaph.* i. 6.
[4] Σωκράτης φρονήσεις ᾤετο εἶναι πάσας τὰς ἀρετάς· . . . λόγους τὰς
ἀρετὰς ᾤετο εἶναι· ἐπιστήμας γὰρ εἶναι πάσας. *Ethic. Nic.* vi. 13.
[5] Xen. *Mem.* i. 1. 16.

what politician; what the government of men and
who capable of it; and suchlike things; and those
who knew these he esteemed men of honour and
goodness, those who knew them not to be justly
called of servile mind.' 'Never did he cease inquiring with those who frequented him about what
everything was.'[1] 'And he did not distinguish between wisdom and temperance, but he asserted that
justice and every other virtue was wisdom.'[2] With
this view hang together the convictions that virtue
can be taught, that all virtue in truth is only one,
and that no one is willingly wicked, but only through
ignorance.[3] The good is identical with the beautiful
and the expedient. Right dealing, grounded upon
prudence and practice, is better than good fortune.
Self-knowledge, the fulfilment of the Delphic Apollo's
injunction, 'Know thyself,' is the condition of practical ability. External goods do not advance. To
need nothing is godlike; to need the least possible
comes nearest to the divine perfection.[4] Cicero's
well-known expression is substantially correct,[5] that
Socrates called down philosophy from heaven to
earth, introduced it into cities and houses, and required it to study life, morals, goods and evils, which
constituted a progress from the natural philosophy
pursued by his predecessors to ethics whose province is man. But Socrates possessed no complete
system of ethical doctrines, only the mainspring of
inquiry; and so it was natural that he could only
reach definite ethical statements in conversation with
others. Thus his art was Mental Midwifery,[6] as

---

[1] Xen. *Mem.* iv. 6. 1.   [2] *Ibid.* iii. 4. 9.
[3] *Ibid.* iii. 9, iv. 6; *Sympos.* ii. 12. Plat. *Apol.* 25 e; *Protag.*
p. 329 b.   [4] *Memor.* i. 6. 10.
[5] *Tusc.* v. 4.   [6] ἡ μαιευτική, Plat. *Theæt.* p. 149.

Plato designates it. His confessed non-knowledge, resting on the firm consciousness of the essence of true knowledge, stood higher than the imagined knowledge of those who conversed with him. And to it was attached the Socratic Irony ; that apparent recognition paid to the superior wisdom and prudence of another until this is dissolved into its nothingness by the dialectic examination which measures what is maintained as a generalisation by the fixed point of the particular case. Thus it was that Socrates exercised the charge of examining men,[1] which he was convinced had been imposed upon him by the Delphic god in the oracle elicited by Chærepho, that he was the wisest of men.

The opinion, practice, and teaching of Socrates concerning the gods and the Godhead are set forth most graphically by his disciple Xenophon in two chapters of his *Memorabilia*. Scarcely could a Christian moralist exhibit more lucidly the argument from design in proof of a Divine Providence which has formed and which rules the world ; more than this, which has produced the seasons of the year, the plants, the animals, for the good of man. In the eyes of Socrates the human body itself is a never-failing proof of the divine love of man. He details the wisdom with which it is put together, and forces the opponent, who is introduced as not sacrificing, nor praying to the gods, nor believing in divination, to confess : " When I consider this, assuredly these things seem the device of some wise world-maker, the lover of living things." [2] Another he compels by a long enumeration of divine benefits to man to come to

---

[1] ἐξέτασις, Plat. *Apol.* p. 20.
[2] Xen. *Mem.* i. 4. 7.   σοφοῦ τινὸς δημιουργοῦ καὶ φιλοζώου.

a similar conclusion.[1] "Certainly, Socrates, the gods seem to have a great care for men." "Besides," he replies, "when we cannot foresee in the future what is good for us, they help us by revealing through divination what is to come, and instructing us as to the best course." "Nay, Socrates," rejoins the other, "they seem to treat you even more kindly than other men; for without being asked by you, they signify before to you what you should do and what leave undone." "That I say true," answers Socrates, "even you, O Euthydemus, will acknowledge, if you do not wait until you see the forms of the gods, but are contented, when you behold their works, to worship and honour them. And consider that the gods themselves point this out to you: for not only do the rest of them, when they give us good things, not exhibit themselves to our senses in so doing, but he [2] who co-ordinates and holds together the whole universe, in whom are all beautiful and good things, and who provides them for the perpetual use of men free from waste, disease, and old age, so that they help us unfailingly, quicker than thought, is discerned in the greatness of his operations. And while he administers these to us he is himself invisible. And take thought that the sun, who seems to be manifest to all, allows not men to examine him closely, but should any one attempt to look at him shamelessly,

---

[1] Xen. *Mem.* iv. 3.

[2] ὁ τὸν ὅλον κόσμον συντάττων τὲ καὶ συνέχων, ἐν ᾧ πάντα τὰ καλὰ καὶ ἀγαθά ἐστι, καὶ ἀεὶ μὲν χρωμένοις ἀτριβῆ τε καὶ ὑγιᾶ καὶ ἀγήρατον παρέχων, θᾶττον δὲ νοήματος ἀναμαρτήτως ὑπηρετοῦντα, οὗτος τὰ μέγιστα μὲν πράττων ὁρᾶται, τάδε δὲ οἰκονομῶν ἀόρατος ἡμῖν ἐστι. Compare the famous passage of St. Paul, Rom. i. 19, 20. διότι τὸ γνωστὸν τοῦ Θεοῦ φανερόν ἐστιν ἐν αὐτοῖς· ὁ γὰρ Θεὸς αὐτοῖς ἐφανέρωσε· τὰ γὰρ ἀόρατα αὐτοῦ ἀπὸ κτίσεως κόσμου τοῖς ποιήμασι νοούμενα καθορᾶται, ἥτε ἀΐδιος αὐτοῦ δύναμις καὶ θειότης εἰς τὸ εἶναι αὐτοὺς ἀναπολογήτους. Socrates draws precisely the conclusion which St. Paul asserts that the premises warrant.

takes away his sight.   And the ministers of the gods too you will find evading our senses; the lightning shoots from on high, and is master wherever it alights, but is seen neither in its approach, nor in its stroke, nor in its departure.   The winds themselves are invisible, but their works are manifest, and we feel them as they come.   Nay, and man's soul too, or if there be anything else in man participating the divine, manifestly rules in us as a king, but is not seen. Bearing in thought these things we must not despise the invisible, but learning their power by their results, honour that which is divine." [1]   "Indeed, Socrates," says Euthydemus, "for my part I am quite resolved not the least to neglect what is divine; but my trouble is, that it seems to me that no single man can ever be duly thankful for the kindnesses of the gods."   "Do not let this trouble you, Euthydemus, for you see the god at Delphi, when any one asks him how to be grateful to the gods, answers, 'By your country's law.' Now it is surely law everywhere to please the gods by sacrifices, as best you can.   How then can any one honour the gods better or more piously than by doing what themselves bid?   Only we must not be behind our power: for any one who is so behind surely is manifest therein as not honouring the gods.   Our duty is to honour them to the utmost of our power, and then to take heart and hope from them the greatest goods.   For a man cannot show a sound mind in hoping from others greater goods than from those who have the power to give the greatest aid; nor from those in any other way than by pleasing them. And how can one better please them than by the most unfailing obedience to them?"   Now, by saying such

[1] τὸ δαιμόνιον.

things, and himself doing them, he was ever bringing those who were in intercourse with him to piety and a sound mind.

The last words of this man to his judges were: " And now it is time that we depart, I to death, and you to life; but which of us are going unto the better thing is not clear to any one save to God."[1]   And when the hemlock was reaching his heart,[2] he uncovered his head, and said with his last utterance, " O Crito, we owe a cock to Æsculapius : pay it, and do not neglect it."

I have cited at length these passages because I think that they exhibit clearly the opinions and convictions of Socrates on the most important of all subjects.   We behold here a man of a very religious mind, holding with the utmost tenacity the idea of a Providence, the Benefactor of men and their Judge, since it discriminates between them by reward and punishment.   Nor is it an impersonal Providence, an abstract Reason, but " a wise world-maker," who loves man and does him good, and whose operations in this very purpose of doing him good indicate unity of design and perfection of execution.   And yet in his conception of the Godhead itself he halts between unity and plurality, and beside a statement such as we might read in a Pauline epistle of the one God who orders in harmony the universe and holds it together, we find him passing to the recognition and worship of many gods.   Beside words to his judges most sublime and most pathetic, concerning the issue of life and of death, we find him with his last breath directing his friend to discharge the sacrifice of a cock which he had promised to Æsculapius.   He does not attempt

---

[1] Plato, *Apol.*, at the end.   [2] *Phædo*, p. 118.

to solve either the rational or the moral antagonism between many gods and one ; but practically he throws himself into the worship of his country, referring to the law of each place as that which should determine for every man the question how the gods are to be honoured.   And in this I believe that he is typical of the whole race of philosophers at whose head he stands.   Like him they spoke of one God, and they offered the cock to Æsculapius.   If we seek the highest expressions concerning the divine unity, wisdom, and power which are to be found in their writings, they approach St. Paul : if we consider other expressions, and above all, their practice, it is in the main that other word of Socrates, " Worship according to the law of your country."   In the doctrine attributed to him both by Xenophon and Aristotle, that he identified virtue and prudence, and believed that no man is willingly wicked, but only out of ignorance, we have a proof which can scarcely be exceeded in force how entirely the standing-point of Socrates was that above attributed to the Greek mind in general, that of a religion according to nature.   It ignores in the most emphatic, because in the most unconscious way, the inclination to evil in man.   The relation between God and man is simply that of greater and less. There is a physical affinity and a numerical proportion between that mighty nature which is ruled through all its length and breadth by a pervading reason, and the portion of it contained in man's body and soul.[1]

[1] The view here taken would be powerfully confirmed by citing at length the interview of Socrates with the hetæra Theodote, as given by Xen. *Mem.* iii. 11.   The unconscious absence from the mind of Socrates of any notion of turpitude in the occupation of Theodote is very striking indeed.   One is reminded that Socrates took lessons in

It is curious to imagine what would have been the effect of the life and the death of Socrates had he lived and died just as he did with one sole exception, that Plato and Xenophon had not been his disciples. Socrates wrote nothing : oral discourse was his sole instrument of teaching. When its last memories had faded away, we might have known as little of him as we really know of Pythagoras. He would still indeed have been the greatest of heathen names because he died for his moral convictions. This might have been all, and it would have been very much. This, however, was not to be. In Xenophon's *Memorabilia* we have an accurate life-portrait of the man, while in the great genius of Plato we have the application of what may be termed Socratic principles to the formation of an ethical, logical, and physical system. The Megaric [1] school of Euclides, and Phædo's school of Elis, took indeed one side of his doctrine, the dialectic, for their special subject of inquiry ; the Cynic school of Antisthenes and the Cyrenian school of Aristippus another side, the ethical : but it was Plato who embraced in one comprehensive scheme the whole grasp of his master's thought, as well as the collective approved elements of former systems.

The principle of Socrates concerning the union of knowledge and virtue invited his followers to work out a system of dialectics and ethics.[2] And further

rhetoric of that Aspasia, herself the hetæra of Pericles, who is recorded to have educated a school of Theodotes. Thus Plutarch, *Pericles*, 24, says of her, παιδίσκας ἑταιρούσας τρέφουσα. In the Menex imus, p. 235, Socrates claims her as being his διδάσκαλος οὖσα οὐ πάνυ φαύλη περὶ ῥητορικῆς, quoted by Wallon, *de l'Esclavage*, vol. i. p. 190.

[1] Ueberweg, i. 92, 93.

[2] *Ibid.* i. 91.

the dialectic process of induction and definition, which Aristotle tells us that Socrates introduced, was made by Plato the foundation of his philosophy.[1] Its central point is the doctrine of Ideas. Now the Platonic Idea is the object of the conception. As a single object becomes known by its representation, so the Idea becomes known by its conception. It is not the essence as such which dwells in many similar individual objects, but that essence as represented perfectly in its kind, unalterably, in unity, independence, and self-existence. The Idea points to the general, but is represented by Plato as an original image of the individual projected as it were outside of time and space. Conceive individuals having a similar being, or belonging to the same class, delivered from the limits of time and space, of materiality and individual imperfections, and so reduced to that unity which is the groundwork of their existence, and such unity is the Platonic Idea. The highest Idea is the Idea of the good,[2] which is as it were the sun in the realm of Ideas, viewed as the first cause of being and of knowledge. Plato seems to identify it with the highest Godhead. Thus the method to attain the knowledge of Ideas is dialectics, which comprehend the double path of rising to the general and returning from the general to the particular.

As to the generation [3] of the doctrine of Ideas, Aristotle states it as the common product of the doctrine of Heracleitus that everything which meets the senses is subject to change and flux, and of the Socratic view of the conception. From Socrates Plato learnt that when once this is rightly formed, it

[1] Ueberweg, i. 117.   [2] Ibid. i. 118.
[3] Ibid. i. 120, from Aristotle, Metaph. i. 6 and 9, and xiii. 4.

can be held fast unchangeably. He would not then apply it to anything that meets the senses, but inferred that there must be other beings which are the objects of the knowledge acquired by the conception, and these objects he named Ideas. The filiation,[1] then, between Socrates and Plato is this: Socrates was the first to require that all knowledge and all moral dealing should proceed from the knowing of the conception, and endeavoured to execute this by his inductive process, while with Plato the same conviction formed the starting-point of a philosophical system. Thus, what with Socrates was simply a rule of scientific procedure was carried out by Plato to an objective intuition, and when Socrates said, "Only the knowing of the conception is true knowledge," Plato added, "Only the being of the conception is true being."

Thus in Plato we have a man of great original mind attempting with this instrument of induction and definition to form a scheme of the universe, which divides under his hand into a triple aspect of ethics, physics, and dialectics.[2] No doubt his main intention was to offer to the cultured and reflective few,—that inner circle to which his teaching and his writings were directed,—a philosophy which should serve them as a religion,[3] which should fill up the gaps and remove the anomalies of the existing worship, purifying and restoring it, while it preserved amity with it notwith-

---

[1] Zeller, i. 119.

[2] Ueberweg, i. 120, remarks: "Die Eintheilung der Philosophie in Ethik, Physik und Dialektik (die Cicero *Acad. pos.* i. 5, 19, Plato zugeschreibt), hat nach Sextus Empir (*adv. Math.* vii. 16) zuerst Plato's Schüler Xenocrates förmlich aufgestellt: Plato aber sei, sagt Sextus mit Recht. δυνάμει ihr Urheber, ἀρχηγός."

[3] See Zeller, vol. ii. part 2, p. 599. Döllinger, p. 299, sec. 122; p. 279, sec. 87.

standing.   Such being his intention, the manner in
which he treats the doctrine of the Divine Being is
the more remarkable.   Instead of basing his philosophy upon it, and showing its relation as a part of
his system of physics, ethics, and dialectics, he speaks
of it frequently indeed, but always incidentally.[1]   It is
not so with other doctrines which he has at heart.
Three of his finest dialogues are dedicated to setting
forth as many aspects of his doctrine as to the soul's
immortality ; the Phædrus treats of its pre-existence ;
the Banquet of the influence of immortality on the
relations of the present life ; the Phædo of death as
the means of a happy futurity.[2]   But no one collects
together and lucidly exhibits his view of the divine
nature.   This has to be picked out of his writings, a
bit here, and another there, and put together by the
student.   No doubt he felt, as he has said,[3] "with
regard to the Maker and the Father of this universe
it is hard to find Him out, and when you have found
Him impossible to describe Him to all men."   He was
intimately convinced that the great mass of mankind
was quite unsuited to receive the conception of the
Divine Being which he had formed.   But I believe
there to have been another reason of greater force
with him for his not having presented as a whole his
conclusions on this central doctrine of all.   It was
not merely that the fate of his master Socrates was
ever before him,[4] but the singular position which he

---

[1] Zeller, ii. part 1, p. 598. "Ueber diese beiden Gegenstände (die
Religion und die Kunst) hat sich Plato ziemlich häufig, aber immer
nur gelegenheitlich geäussert."

[2] Döllinger, p. 290, sec. 110.   [3] *Timæus*, 28.

[4] Thus Grote, *Plato*, i. 230, speaks of " the early caution produced
by the fate of Socrates," and believes "such apprehension to have
operated as one motive deterring him from publishing any philosophical
exposition under his own name, any Πλάτωνος σύγγραμμα," p. 231.

held with regard to the established worship. He wished to correct, not to destroy it; he wished to reduce it to monotheism, and yet to preserve polytheism. The two are bound together in his mind. If then his writings be carefully analysed, and every reference to the Supreme Being put together into a sort of mosaic,[1] we should find the following picture. The everlasting essence of things, with which Philosophy deals, is the highest object. Ideas are those everlasting gods after the pattern of which the world and all things in it are formed, and the Godhead, taken absolutely, is not distinct from the highest Idea. Plato sets forth the causality of Ideas and the sway of reason in the world together with the impossibility to explain what is generated save by an Ingenerate, motion save by a soul, and the ordered disposition of the world, working out a purpose, save by reason; and in all which he declares respecting the Godhead, the Idea of Good, of the highest metaphysical and ethical perfection, is his guiding-point. As this highest Idea stands at the head of all Ideas as the cause of all being and knowledge, so the one everlasting invisible God, the Former and Father of all things, stands at the head of all the gods, alike difficult to find and to describe. Just as the above Idea is distinguished by the conception of the Good, so Plato selects goodness as God's most essential attribute. It is on this ground that he maintains the Godhead to be absolutely good and upright, and its operation to be merely good and upright; against the old notion which imputed envy to it, and derived evil from it.

---

[1] This has been done by Zeller, vol. ii. part 1, pp. 599–602, from whom I take it. He supports his analysis with a great number of references to various works of Plato.

transgression unpunished and no virtue unrewarded; its goodness, which makes the best provision for all. He rejects, as notions taken from man, not merely the Godhead's having a body, but likewise all those tales which impute passions, quarrels, crimes of every kind to the gods. He declares them to be exalted above pleasure and displeasure, to be untouched by any evil; and is full of moral indignation at the thought that they allow themselves to be won over, or rather corrupted, by prayers and offerings. Moreover he shows that everything is ordered and ruled by Divine Providence, which extends over the least as well as the greatest, and as regards men is especially convinced that they are a carefully-tended possession of the Godhead, and that all things must issue in good to those who through virtue gain its goodwill. If the unequal and unjust distribution of men's lot is objected, his reply is, that virtue carries its reward and wickedness its punishment immediately in itself; further, that both are sure of a complete retribution in the after-world, while already in this life as a rule in the end the upright goes not without recognition and thanks, nor the transgressor without universal hate and detestation. As to the general fact that there is evil in the world, it seemed to him so inevitable that it was not requisite expressly to defend the Godhead on that score. All these statements carry us back at last to one and the same point. It is by applying the Idea of the Good that Plato produces so exalted a doctrine of God. In the like spirit he will consider only the moral intention in acts of worship. He alone can please the Godhead who is like it, and he alone is like it who is pious, wise, and just. The gods cannot receive the gifts of the wicked; the virtuous alone have a right to invoke them. God is goodness; and he who bears not the image of that goodness in himself stands in no communion with Him.

The doctrine here set forth is the highest ever reached by purely heathen Greek speculation; but we must remember that it is not thus collected into a head by Plato himself, still less is it put into such a relation to his physical, his logical, and his moral system as such a doctrine ought to bear. A man who had reached so lofty a conviction of the divine unity and moral perfection as this must, if he would make it effectual, give to it in his system the place which it really holds in the world. If there be indeed a Maker and Father of the universe by whom all things consist, all that Plato taught should have been subordinated to this its first principle, and the sum of his teaching to men should have been to set him forth. So far is this from the position which Plato really took, that in his ideal Republic no other religion but the traditional Greek religion was to subsist; he changes nothing in the very forms of the polytheistic worship; he refers the decision on many points to the Delphic Apollo.[1] And when in his last book on the Laws [2] he sets forth the notion of a second-best state, one which can be realised under actual circumstances, wherein he gives a mass of practical directions for the needs of the lower classes, religion in its purely polytheistic dress is the soul of his teaching, the groundwork of his structure. Men are to worship first of all the Olympian gods, and the gods who are the patrons of the city; then the gods of the earth; then demons and heroes; and all

[1] Döllinger, p. 297, sec. 119, quoted.
[2] So likewise Zeller remarks, vol. ii. part 1, p. 604: "Die Gesetze, welchen die philosophischen Regenten fehlen, behandeln die Volks-religion durchweg als die sittliche Grundlage des Staatswesens."

these in the traditional way by offerings, prayers, and vows. All good in public life is their gift; every thing is to be consecrated to them; to violate their shrines is the greatest of crimes. In fact, after all, but few of mankind are capable of understanding or receiving the philosophic God. However imperfect [1] the popular belief in the gods may be, and however unsatisfactory to him the allegorical interpretations of it then so much in vogue, yet is it in Plato's conviction indispensable to all those who have not had a scientific education. Men must first be taught with lies, and then with the truth : the popular fables and the worship grounded on them is therefore for all the *first*, and for most the *only* form of religion. [2] The philosopher, it is true, sees deeper and despises them in his heart. Thus the monotheist in speculation is a polytheist in practice : as Socrates, the model and exemplar of Greek philosophy, with his dying breath, so Plato, its most inspired teacher with all the voice of his authority, sacrificed the cock to Æsculapius.

But moreover, this supreme God, who has to be disinterred from the recesses of the Platonic teaching, and conciliated with the worship practically paid to a host of subordinate gods, is in Plato's conception neither absolutely personal nor free. He is not the Creator, only the Former of the world. In Plato's theory there is co-eternal with him a first matter, without form or quality, which exists independently of him. This moreover is inhabited and swayed to and fro in disorderly heavings by a sort of soul, the

---

[1] Zeller, p. 605.

[2] Here Zeller remarks : "Diese Voraussetzung liegt der ganzen Behandlung dieser Gegenstände bei Plato zu Grunde. . . . Dass die philosophische Erkenntniss immer auf eine kleine Minderheit beschränkt sein müsse ist Plato's entschiedene Ueberzeugung."

what they are only by participation of something higher, it is no wonder that in describing that one Reason, the Idea of the Good, the highest and most general of all, which forms and governs the world, his language oscillates between the personal and the impersonal. But if his philosophical reasons tend one way, it must be allowed that the heart and affections of the man, and the whole moral sense of the teacher, decide another.

The ethical system of Plato appears to be a strict deduction from his physical. As man in his view is a compound of matter, vivified by a portion of the world-soul, which the divine reason takes and unites with a portion of itself, so his virtues correspond to this threefold composition.[1] For man has an immortal portion in his soul, the reason, the godlike, in him; but the divine reason, in joining a portion of the world-soul with matter, invests it with two mortal parts, one the courageous, or manly, the other, sensuous desire, or the female element, having their seat in the body's activity. To these answer respectively the virtues of prudence, of courage, and of temperance, while justice comes in afterwards as a right ordering of the three, or as prudence applied to practice. The seat of all irregular desires, of all evil, in fact, is to Plato in this union of the soul with matter. As this matter is primordial, evil in its origin does not indeed spring from God, but it is beyond his power. It springs from that state of things which existed before the action of God on chaos.[2] It must stand over against

der Persönlichkeit fehlt, und die Vernunft nicht selten als allgemeine Weltvernunft in einer zwischen Persönlichem und Unpersönlichem unsicher schwankenden Weise gedacht wird." *Zeller*, p. 454.

[1] Döllinger, p. 286, sec. 103. Zeller, vol. ii. part 1, p. 538.

[2] *Theætetus*, p. 176. Σωκ. 'Αλλ' οὔτ' ἀπόλεσθαι τὰ κακὰ δυνατόν, ὦ Θεόδωρε· ὑπενάντιον γάρ τι τῷ ἀγαθῷ ἀεὶ εἶναι ἀνάγκη· οὔτ' ἐν θεοῖς αὐτὰ ἱδρῦσθαι, τὴν δὲ θνητὴν φύσιν καὶ τόνδε τὸν τόπον περιπολεῖ ἐξ ἀνάγκης.

the good, and of necessity encompasses this mortal nature and the place of its habitation.   To man it lies not in the perverted use of free-will, but in his original composition, wherein his body is its seat.   But in this triple composition of man Plato does not seem to have clearly apprehended a human personality at all : he has not even attempted to explain [1] in what the unity of the soul consists besides these its three portions, two of which, being tied to the body, drop off at death.

It is in the practice of Plato as a teacher that we can most fitly consider the conception which the Greek philosophers in general had concerning the whole method of studying and imparting philosophy.   It was about the fortieth year of his life, and twelve years after the death of his master Socrates, that Plato, having already travelled widely, settled at Athens.[2] Here he purchased a fixed residence at the Academia, which became from that time a philosophical school for study, conversation, oral lectures, and friendly meetings.   Here he drew around him an inner circle of scholars to whom he addressed his unwritten doc-trines,[3] especially his doctrine of Ideas, the key to his whole system, according as they were able, after pre-paration, to receive them : and here besides he gave lectures which might be attended not only by that inner circle of choice disciples but by studious persons in general.   This residence of Plato served for three hundred years, from 387 before Christ until the siege of Athens by Sylla in 87, as the centre of Plato's philosophy viewed as a teaching power.   Now in this

---

[1] See Zeller, vol. ii. part 1, pp. 541–544, who points out a string of difficulties on the subject of personality, free-will, as maintained by Plato, and his doctrine that no one is willingly wicked.

[2] See Grote's *Plato*, i. pp. 133, 134.   [3] Ueberweg, i. p. 116.

Plato had before him the great example of Pythagoras, in the first age of Greek philosophy. Concerning the doctrines of that philosopher we know little with certainty,[1] but all are agreed as to his manner of teaching them. His attempt was to establish a community which should carry in its bosom, propagate, and perpetuate a doctrine in morals, politics, religion, and philosophy. His whole procedure was by oral teaching, for he left not a word written. It was in fact a religious order of life which he first practised in his own person, and then endeavoured to communicate to others. Into this order trial for every one preceded reception.[2] His scholars were for a long period required to practise silent obedience and unconditional submission to the authority of the doctrine delivered to them. Severe daily examination was imposed upon all. The publishing of his doctrine, especially his speculation as to the nature of God, was strictly forbidden. The upright life, the learning which then could only be attained by personal inquiry, the persuasiveness of Pythagoras, were together so effective that he succeeded in establishing such a community both in Crotona and in other cities of Southern Italy. It was persecuted and suffered continual disasters, but still this Pythagorean community, bearing on its founder's doctrines and manner of life, existed for several generations after his death, during which many of the most distinguished Greeks belonged to it. Such was the poet Æschylus, whose mind was formed on Pythagorean principles. In Plato's time the

---

[1] So Zeller sets forth at length, i. p. 206; and Ueberweg, i. p. 47.

[2] Ueberweg, i. p. 50. Plato calls it ὁδόν τινα βίου, for which Pythagoras αὐτός τε διαφερόντως ἠγαπήθη, καὶ οἱ ὕστερον ἔτι καὶ νῦν Πυθαγόρειον τρόπον ἐπονομάζοντες τοῦ βίου διαφανεῖς πη δοκοῦσιν εἶναι. *Polit.* x. p. 600.

affection assert of them that which is just the contrary
to their real office. For they will breed forgetfulness
in the minds of those who learn them, who will slight
the faculty of memory, inasmuch as relying on what
is written externally in the types of others they do not
exercise remembrance by an inward act of their own.
The spell you have found is good, not for fixing in the
mind, but for reminding. And as to wisdom, you
offer to those who learn them not its reality but its
appearance. For they will indeed hear much, but as
this will be without teaching, they will seem to have
many minds but generally no judgment, and be hard
to comprehend, having become wiseacres instead of wise
men.' 'O Socrates,' says Phædrus, 'you are one who can
easily tell stories from Egypt or any other country.'
'My dear Phædrus, it was in the temple of Dodonean
Jupiter that they made the first oracular words to proceed from an oak. The men of that day, not being
wise as you young men, were satisfied in their simplicity
to listen to an oak or a rock, if they only spoke the
truth. Perhaps it makes a difference to you who the
speaker is, and from what country ; for you do not
look merely whether it is true or not.' 'Your rebuke,'
says Phædrus, 'is just, and what the Theban says about
letters seems to me to be right.' 'Well then,' says
Socrates, 'the man who thinks to leave an art in writing, and he also who receives it as being, when written,
something clear and certain, must be very simple, and
be really ignorant of Ammon's oracle, when he thinks
that written words are something more than a reminder
to one who knows the subject of the matters about
which they are written.' 'Exactly so, Socrates.' 'For
surely, Phædrus, writing shares this troublesome characteristic with painting. The productions of painting

stand there as if they were alive, but if you ask them a question, preserve a solemn silence. Just so it is with writing. You may think that they speak with some meaning, but if you ask what that meaning is, there they stand with just the same word in their mouth. When once a thing is written, it is tossed over and over by all who take it in, whether it concerns them or not, and is unable to speak or to be silent with the proper persons. And if it is maltreated or slandered, it wants its father always to help it, for it can neither defend nor help itself.' 'What you say now is also very true indeed.' 'But,' says Socrates, 'can we not find another word, this one's lawful brother, and see the process by which it arises, and how much better and abler than the former it is?' 'What word is this, and how does it arise?' 'The word which is written on the disciple's soul together with true knowledge, which is able to defend itself, and knows how to speak and to be silent with the proper persons.' 'You mean the living and animated word of one who has knowledge, whereof the written word may justly be called the shadow?'[1] 'I mean that indeed. Tell me now; an intelligent gardener, who had seeds that he cared for, and wished to bear fruit, would he hurry with them in summer to the gardens of Adonis, plant them, and rejoice to see them springing up with a fair show in a week? Or would he do this for amusement, and in festival-time, if he did it at all? Would he not rather use his gardener's art, sow them at the fitting time, and be too glad if, seven months afterwards, he saw them coming to perfection?' 'Certainly, Socrates, that would be the differ-

---

[1] τὸν τοῦ εἰδότος λόγον λέγεις ζῶντα καὶ ἔμψυχον, οὗ ὁ γεγραμμένος εἴδωλον ἄν τι λέγοιτο δικαίως.

ence between his sport and his earnest.' ' Shall we, then, say that he who possesses the science of justice, honour, and goodness, has less intelligence than the gardener for his own seeds? Surely not. He will not, then, hurry to write them with a pen in ink with words, which cannot on the one hand help themselves with speech, and on the other hand are incapable to teach the truth sufficiently.' ' I should think he would not.' ' He will not; but as for these written flower-borders, he will sow and write them, when he does write them, for amusement, storing up reminders for himself, should he come to a forgetful old age, and for every one who pursues the same footsteps, and he will take pleasure in seeing them springing up tenderly. So when other men fall to other amuse-ments, lubricating themselves at the banquet, or other such things, he will take his amusement here.' ' In this, Socrates, you would substitute a very seemly amusement for a bad one, when the man who can play with words sports upon the subject of justice and suchlike.' ' So it is, my dear Phædrus, but it is, I take it, earnest in a far higher sense, when one, using the art of dialectics, takes hold of a fitting soul, and plants and sows with true knowledge words able to help both themselves and their planter. They are words bearing seed, whence growing up in a succession of minds they will from age to age produce an immortal line,[1] and will make their possessor happy as far as man can be.' "

In these words, put in his master's mouth, Plato, if I mistake not, has given us the whole purpose of his life, and the manner in which he hoped to accomplish it. It was in the Academia that he sought to establish

---

[1] ἔχοντες σπέρμα, ὅθεν ἄλλοι ἐν ἄλλοις ἤθεοι φυόμενοι τοῦτ᾽ ἀεὶ ἀθάνατον παρέχειν ἱκανοί.

that immortal line of living words, who should speak
as the possessors of real knowledge upon justice, truth,
and goodness.   He is describing a living culture by
living teachers, of whom he aspired to be himself the
first.   And the written dialogues which he has left are
in his intention, and so far as they enter at all upon
the higher points of his doctrine,[1] reminders of what
he had set forth to chosen auditors by word of
mouth, the word which was able, as he says, to explain
and defend itself, and to answer a question put to it.

This, then, was the relation existing in the mind
of the prince of Greek philosophers between the
written and the spoken word as instruments in imparting true knowledge or science.   The written word
he regarded as subsidiary, as presupposing instruction
by question and answer, and still more the moral
discipline of a life earnestly given up to the study of
the subjects in question.   Without this a writing by
itself was like a figure in a picture, which makes an
impression on the beholder, but when asked if it is the
true impression, keeps, as he says, a solemn face, and
makes no reply.   It is the same to all, the earnest
and the indifferent, and cannot treat them according
to their merits.   He laughs at the notion of such a
writing being by itself any more than sport.   And let
us remember that he who said this has enshrined his
own philosophy in the most finished specimens of
dramatic dialogues which the Greek mind produced.
These are the statements of the man who wrote Greek
in his countrymen's opinion as Jupiter would have
spoken it.   There are, then, in Plato's mind three
constituents of teaching : first, the choice of fitting

---

[1] See his averseness to write on such doctrines at all set forth in his
7th epistle.

subjects for it, and what is therein implied, the imposition of a moral discipline upon them regulating their life to the end in view; secondly, the master's oral instruction conveying gradually and with authority to minds so prepared the doctrine to be received; and thirdly, the committing such doctrine to writing, which shall serve to *remind* the disciple of what he has been taught. And this was what he carried into effect.[1] He fixed himself at the Academia, over which he presided for forty years. He was succeeded therein by his nephew Speusippus, who held his chair for eight years. Xenocrates followed in the same post during twenty-five years; and the line was continued afterwards by Polemon, Crantor, Crates, Arcesilaus, and others in uninterrupted series. Plato thus established the method of Greek philosophy, and his example herein was followed by Aristotle, Zeno, and Epicurus.

His great disciple Aristotle came to him at the age of seventeen, and studied under him during twenty years. At a later age, when, after completing the education of Alexander, he fixed himself in middle life at Athens, he set up there a second philosophical school at the Lyceum on its eastern side, and on the model of that of Plato. Attached to this museum were a portico, a hall with seats, one seat especially for the lecturing professor, a garden, and a walk, together with a residence, all permanently appropriated to the teacher and the process of instruction.[2] When

---

[1] Grote observes, *Plato*, i. 216: "Plato was not merely a composer of dialogues. He was lecturer and chief of a school besides. The presidency of that school, commencing about 386 B.C., and continued by him with great celebrity for the last half (nearly forty years) of his life, *was his most important function.* Among his contemporaries he must have exerted greater influence through his school than through his writings."

[2] Grote, *Plato*, i. p. 138.

Aristotle died in the year 322 B.C., his friend Theo-
phrastrus presided over his school during five and
thirty years, and the line continued on. We learn
that there were periodical meetings, convivial and
conversational, among the members both of the
Academic and Peripatetic schools, and laws for their
regulation established by Xenocrates and Aristotle.
It was in the shady walks of his garden that this
great philosopher taught by word of mouth the choicer
circle of his disciples : for the more general hearers he
gave lectures sitting.[1] His instructions were divided
into two classes, those he gave on rhetoric, the art of
discussion, knowledge of civil matters, and such-like,
which were exoteric, and those touching the finer
and more subtle points of philosophy, which were
termed acroatic, as addressed to the ears.[2] Again,
his dialogues he called "public" or "issued" discourses, things made over to the general public, in
distinction from what was not so disclosed, but reserved for the philosopher's own meditation, to be
subsequently communicated either by oral lecture or
by writing to the private circle of scholars who gave
themselves up entirely to his philosophy. These
Aristotle called "philosophical" or "teaching" discourses, proceeding, that is, from the principles proper
to each branch of learning, and not from the opinions
of the lecturer. These latter were termed "tentative,"
as belonging to the exoteric. Simplicius, one of the
latest writers on Greek philosophy, defines exoteric as
"the common, and what concludes by arguments
which are matter of opinion ; " and Philoponus, as
discourses "not of strict proof, and not directed to

[1] Ueberweg, i. p. 140, from Diogenes.
[2] Aulus Gellius, *N.A.* xx. 5, quoted by Ueberweg.

lawfully-begotten hearers," that is, trained and prepared, "but to the public, and springing from pro-
babilities."[1]   Thus in Aristotle, the largest in grasp
of mind, the most observant of facts, the most accurate
in definition among Greek writers, the philosopher in
fact and "master of those who know,"[2] for all future
ages, we find the same three constituents of teaching
as in Plato, and in the same order of importance:
first, hearers selected for their natural aptitude, and
then submitted to a moral discipline and a common
life; secondly, the instruction of such hearers by
word of mouth, question and answer, discussion and
cross-examination; and lastly, the committing of doctrines to writing.   With him too his written philosophical discourses were *reminders* of his oral teaching,
which they presupposed and required as a key to their
full meaning, and especially for the comprehension of
their harmony as a system.

The order of teaching which I have thus sketched
as being followed in practice by the two most eminent
Greek philosophers belonged to them all.   They had
no other conception respecting the method of communicating a doctrine efficiently to men.   They none
of them considered philosophy merely or chiefly as a
literature : none of them attributed to a book the
power of teaching it.   Their conception was, a master
and his scholars, and the living together, the moral

---

[1] Ἐν κοινῷ γιγνόμενοι λόγοι . . . ἐκδεδομένοι λόγοι· οἱ κατὰ φιλοσοφίαν
λόγοι, or διδασκαλικοὶ λόγοι, οἱ ἐκ τῶν οἰκείων ἀρχῶν ἑκάστου μαθήματος
καὶ οὐκ ἐκ τῶν τοῦ ἀποκρινομένου δοξῶν συλλογιζόμενοι, which last are
λόγοι πειραστικοί.   Simplicius calls τὰ ἐξωτερικὰ, τὰ κοινὰ καὶ δι' ἐνδόξων
περαινόμενα ; Philoponus, λόγοι μὴ ἀποδεικτικοί, μηδὲ πρὸς τοὺς γνησίους
τῶν ἀκροατῶν εἰρημένοι, ἀλλὰ πρὸς τοὺς πολλοὺς, ἐκ πιθανῶν ὡρμημένοι.
Quoted by Ueberweg, i. p. 146.

[2] Vidi il maestro di color che sanno
Seder tra filosofica famiglia.   Dante, *Inf.* iv. 131.

subordination and discipline which this involved. This
school of education or training in knowledge [1] was
their primary thought: the committing of their doctrine to writing was both subsequent and secondary.
Their writings were intended, as Plato says, to be
recollections [2] of their teaching, and failed to convey
the real knowledge to those who had not the stamp
of this teaching impressed on their minds.

As Plato made a local habitation for himself and
his doctrine in the Academia, and Aristotle in the
Lyceum, so Zeno, the founder of the third great
philosophic school, took up his abode in the Portico
at Athens, a court surrounded with pillars, and
adorned with the paintings of Polygnotus. Here he
began to teach about 308 B.C., and here he continued
teaching as some say for fifty-eight years. It is said
that the character of Socrates, as drawn by Xenophon
and by Plato in his *Apology*, filled him with aston-
ishment and admiration. [3] The Stoics afterwards
drew their doctrine of the wise man, which they
endeavoured to image out and realise, from that
living example of it, [4] an instance of the connection
of doctrine with person which is full of interest and
suggestion. Zeno was succeeded in his office of
teaching by Cleanthes, and Cleanthes by Chrysippus
and a long line of teachers, who for several hundred
years continued, with variations, the same general
doctrine of ethics.

Just in the same way and at the same time Zeno's
great rival Epicurus fixed the seat of his school in
the Garden at Athens, which thenceforth became for
thirty-six years the central point of the teacher's

---

[1] διδασκαλία.   [2] ὑπόμνησις.
[3] Ueberweg, i. p. 188, from Diogenes and Themistius.
[4] *Ibid.* from Noack, *Psyche*, v. i. sec. 13.

activity. About him gathered a circle of friends whom similarity of principles and the enjoyment of cultivated intercourse bound together with unusual intimacy. It speaks for the special character of his philosophy that from the beginning women and even hetæræ formed a part of this society. But he succeeded during this long period of teaching in impressing upon his school so strong a character that it is recognised without essential change during hundreds of years.[1]

We should do injustice to the character and the work of Plato, Aristotle, Zeno, and Epicurus, the founders of the four great schools of Greek philosophy, if we did not take into account what was in their day no doubt of greater influence than their writings, that is, their function as teachers, their oral teaching itself, and those fundamental principles of philosophic education which lay at the bottom of it. Plato has left us very little of doctrine put out in his own name. He is not a speaker in his dialogues. He puts what he would say in the mouth of others, especially of Socrates. He tells us that he has purposely done this in order that men might not say, "Here is Plato's philosophy:"[2] and the reason of this was that he

---

[1] Zeller, vol. iii. part 1, p. 343.

[2] Ep. vii. p. 341. οὔκουν ἐμόν γε περὶ αὐτῶν ἐστι σύγγραμμα, οὐδὲ μή ποτε γένηται· ῥητὸν γὰρ οὐδαμῶς ἐστὶν ὡς ἄλλα μαθήματα, ἀλλ' ἐκ πολλῆς συνουσίας γιγνομένης περὶ τὸ πρᾶγμα αὐτὸ καὶ τοῦ συζῆν ἐξαίφνης, οἶον ἀπὸ πυρὸς πηδήσαντος ἐξαφθὲν φῶς, ἐν τῇ ψυχῇ γενόμενον αὐτὸ ἑαυτὸ ἤδη τρέφει· and much more to the same effect ; after which he says, ὧν ἕνεκα νοῦν ἔχων οὐδεὶς τολμήσει ποτὲ εἰς αὐτὸ τιθέναι τὰ νενοημένα, καὶ ταῦτα εἰς ἀμετακίνητον, ὃ δὴ πάσχει τὰ γεγραμμένα τύποις. So again in his second letter, p. 314. πολλάκις δὲ λεγόμενα καὶ ἀεὶ ἀκουόμενα καὶ πολλὰ ἔτη μόγις, ὥσπερ χρυσὸς, ἐκκαθαίρεται μετὰ πολλῆς πραγματείας. . . . μεγίστη δὲ φυλακὴ τὸ μὴ γράφειν ἀλλ' ἐκμανθάνειν· οὐ γὰρ ἔστι τὰ γραφέντα μὴ οὐκ ἐκπεσεῖν. Grote seems to me fully justified in counting these epistles as genuine, against the attacks of some modern German sceptics.

utterly distrusted his own or any man's power to
disclose to others such a system in a set form of
words. It is, then, the more remarkable that he has
said in his own person what were his most settled
convictions as to intercourse by word of mouth, and
continuous written discourse, viewed as instruments
for attaining and communicating truth. He expresses
his absolute disbelief that men can reach true conceptions by their being set forth in the immutable form
of writing. It is a far other and more difficult work
which has to be accomplished. In a word, not even
aptness for learning and memory will give the power
to see the truth as to virtue and vice to one who is
not kin to the subject. Nor, again, will this kinship
be efficient without such aptitude and memory. When
both are joined, then out of living together, after
much time,[1] by the continual friction of name, definition, acts of sight and perception, by thought and
meditation, the hearing and answering the objections
of others, the process of mutual cross-examination discharged without envy or jealousy, and with sincere
love of the truth, a sudden flash of fire kindles in the
mind, and nourishes itself, disclosing the knowledge
required. Thus it is that prudence and intelligence
on each subject shining out in this beam of light, go
forward as far as man may reach. The view here
propounded, if reflected upon, will convey to us what
the living work first of Pythagoras, and then of Plato,
Aristotle, Zeno, Epicurus, and their successors, was.
Both the conception indeed and the realisation seem

---

[1] Μετὰ τριβῆς πάσης καὶ χρόνου πολλοῦ, ὅπερ ἐν ἀρχαῖς εἶπον· μόγις δὲ
τριβόμενα πρὸς ἄλληλα αὐτῶν ἕκαστα, ὀνόματα, καὶ λόγοι ὄψεις τε καὶ
αἰσθήσεις, ἐν εὐμενέσιν ἐλέγχοις ἐλεγχόμενα καὶ ἄνευ φθόνων ἐρωτήσεσι καὶ
ἀποκρίσεσι χρωμένων, ἐξέλαμψε φρόνησις περὶ ἕκαστον καὶ νοῦς, συντείνων
ὅτι μάλιστ᾽ εἰς δύναμιν ἀνθρωπίνην. Ep. vii. p. 344.

to have been most complete in Pythagoras. The philosophic living together was its basis. Instruction was oral. Learning was effected by the collision of mind with mind, by objection and answer. It was the Socratic principle inherited from these schools that nothing passed muster for knowledge which did not stand the test of cross-examination.[1] An unchangeable text was utterly unsuited, according to Plato, to debate the question under treatment in such fashion, while on the other hand the mind of the reader was passive in receiving the impression which it conveyed. On neither side therefore did the conditions of knowledge exist, but this was reached under the circumstances of personal intercourse above mentioned, and might be recalled in the written form to the minds of those who had thus first attained it.

Down to the end of Greek philosophy the same conception as to the method of teaching prevailed. Ammonius Sakkas, the founder of Neoplatonism, delivered his doctrine only by word of mouth, which his chief disciples, Erennius, Origines, and Plotinus, engaged not to make public.[2] It was when one of them, Erennius, had broken this promise, that another, Plotinus, after delivering lectures at Rome, wrote down his philosophy; but his scheme was to carry it out by collecting his disciples together in one city, and thus realising Plato's republic.

---

[1] Grote, *Plato*, i. 229. "When we see by what standard Plato tests the efficacy of any expository process, we shall see yet more clearly how he came to consider written exposition unavailing. The standard which he applies is, that the learner shall be rendered able both to apply to others and himself to endure a Socratic Elenchus or cross-examination as to the logical difficulties involved in all the steps and helps to learning." Without this "Plato will not allow that he has attained true knowledge" ($\epsilon\pi\iota\sigma\tau\eta\mu\eta$). Compare the system pursued in the mediæval schools and universities.

[2] Ueberweg, i. pp. 242, 243.

LECTURE XIV

THE CHRISTIAN CHURCH AND THE GREEK PHILOSOPHY

PART II

THE mind of the next great teacher who arose in Greece after Plato presented an almost complete contrast to that of the master under whom he had so long studied. Aristotle's power consisted in a parallel development of two forces which do not often co-exist.[1] He joined together a rare degree of consistent philosophic thinking with an equally rare degree of accurate observation. This double faculty is shown in what he effected. He made the sciences of logic, ethics, and psychology: he built up those of natural history and politics with the wealth of knowledge which his experience had accumulated.[2] Thus his analytic and synthetic genius embraced the whole range of human knowledge then existing. As Plato threw his vivid fancy and imagination and his religious temper into everything which concerned the human spirit, so Aristotle fixed his gaze upon nature, which with him in all its manifestations was the ultimate fact. As Plato rose from the single being to his conception of the true, the good, the beautiful, of which the Idea to him was everything, so Aristotle, steadfastly discarding his master's doctrine of Ideas, took his stand on the single being, examining it with the closest observation

---

[1] Zeller, vol. ii. part 2, p. 632.   [2] Döllinger, pp. 304, 305.

and the subtlest thought, and the knowledge thus conveyed to him is everything. Plato's conception of God
is that of the great world-former, orderer, and ruler.
Aristotle's conception of God is that of a pure intelligence, without power, an eternal, ever-active, endless,
incorporeal substance, who never steps out of that
everlasting rest into action: who is the world's first
cause, but is unconscious of it, His action upon the
world being likened to the influence of the beloved
object upon the lover. Plato's dualism is summed up
in the expression, God and Matter; Aristotle's dualism,
in God and the World. Plato represents the action
of the Deity as the working-up of the original matter
into the millions of forms which the world exhibits:
but these millions of forms are taken by Aristotle as
if they had existed for ever; the World, as it is, and
the Deity, are co-eternal.

Aristotle's doctrine of the human soul is that it
exists only as that which animates the body, without
which its being cannot be known.[1] It is the principle forming, moving, and developing the body;
the substance only appearing in the body formed
and penetrated by it, and working continuously in
it, as the life which determines and prevails over its
matter. Thus the body is of itself nothing; what
it is, it is only through the soul, whose being and
nature it expresses. The body is the medium, in
which the purpose, that is, the soul, realises itself.
Thus the soul cannot be thought of without the body,
nor the body without the soul: both come into their
actual state together. In the soul Aristotle distin-
guishes three parts, the vegetative, the sensitive,
and the thinking. This last, the peculiar property

[1] Döllinger, pp. 309, 310, sects. 137, 138.

of man, is further divisible into the passive and
the active, of which the former is linked to the soul
as the soul is to the body, as form is to matter,
multiplies itself with individuals, and is extinguished
with them. But the reason, or pure intelligence,
has nothing in common with matter, comes from
without into man, and exists in him as a self-con-
sisting indestructible being, without multiplying or
dividing itself. Accordingly this intellect or reason
suffers the soul to sink back with the body into the
nothing from which both have been together produced.
It alone continues to subsist as what is ever the same
and unchangeable, since it is nothing but the divine
intelligence in an individual existence, enlightening the
darkness of the human subject in the passive part of
the understanding, and so must be considered as the
first mover in man of his discursive thinking and
knowing, as well as of his willing.[1] As that which
is properly human in the soul, that which has had a
beginning, must also pass away, even the understanding, and only the divine reason is immortal, and as
memory belongs to the sensitive soul, and individual
thinking only takes place by means of the passive
intellect, all consciousness must cease with death.
And again, clearly as Aristotle maintains that man is
the mover and master of his own actions, and has it
in his power to be good or evil, and thence repudiates
the assumption of Socrates and Plato that no one is
willingly evil, yet he cannot find a place for real
freedom of the will between the motion which arises
from sensitive desire, and that which proceeds from
the divine intelligence dwelling in the soul. Necessity arises on both sides, from the things which deter-

[1] Döllinger, p. 310, sec. 139.

mine the passive understanding, and from the divine intelligence.[1]   Thus his physical theory, as in the case of Plato noted above,[2] prevents a clear conception of the human personality.   His notion of man in this point corresponds to his notion of God : he does not concern himself with questions respecting the goodness, justice, and freedom of God, inasmuch as his God is not really personal :[3] so with regard to man we find in him no elucidation as to the question of moral freedom, nor of the origin and nature of wickedness in man.   Wickedness is with Aristotle the impotence to hold the mean between too much and too little : it presents itself therefore only in this world of contingency and change, and has no relation to God, since the first or absolute good has nothing opposed to it. He has not the sense of moral perversion with regard to evil.   Therefore the end of all moral activity with him is happiness, which consists in the well-being arising from an energy according to nature ; as virtue is the observing a proper mean between two extremes. And the highest happiness is contemplative thought, the function of the divine in man, the turning away from everything external to the inner world of the conceptions.

The religious character, which belongs conspicuously to Plato's philosophy, fails, it will be seen, in that of Aristotle.   Whereas Plato strove to purify the popular belief, and urged as the highest point of virtue to become like to God by the conjunction of justice and sanctity with prudence,[4] Aristotle divides morality from

---

[1] Döllinger, p. 311, sec. 140.   [2] See p. 338, above.
[3] Döllinger, pp. 307 and 311.
[4] Διὸ καὶ πειρᾶσθαι χρὴ ἐνθένδε ἐκεῖσε φεύγειν ὅτι τάχιστα· φυγὴ δὲ ὁμοίωσις Θεῷ κατὰ τὸ δυνατόν· ὁμοίωσις δὲ δίκαιον καὶ ὅσιον μετὰ φρονήσεως γενέσθαι.   κ. τ. λ.   Theætet. p. 176.

religion as his God is separated off from the world.[1]
His scientific inquiries have not that immediate relation to the personal life and the destiny of man in
which the religiousness of Platonism most consists.
His whole view of the world goes to explain things as
far as possible from their natural causes.[2]   Thus he
admits in the whole direction of the world the ruling
of a divine power, and of a reason which reaches its
purpose.   He believes in particular that the gods care
for men, take an interest in him who lives in accordance
with reason, and that happiness is their gift.   He con-
tradicts the notion that the godhead is envious, and so
could withhold from man knowledge, the best of its
gifts.   But this divine providence coincides for him
entirely with the working of natural causes.   In his
view the godhead stands in solitary self-contemplation
outside the world, the object of admiration and reverence to man.   The knowledge of it is the highest
task for his intellect.   It is the good to which in
common with everything that is finite he is struggling; whose perfection calls forth his love.   Yet
little as he can expect a return of love from it, so
little does he find in it any co-operation distinct from
the natural connection of things, and his reason is the
only point of immediate contact with it.

Religion [3] itself Aristotle treats as an unconditional
moral necessity.   The man who doubts whether the
gods should be honoured is a subject fit not for instruction but for punishment, just as the man who
asks whether he should love his parents.   As the
natural system of the world cannot be imagined without God, so neither can man in it be imagined without

[1] Zeller, vol. ii. part 2, p. 623.   [2] *Ibid*. ii. 2, p. 625.
[3] *Ibid*. p. 629.

religion.   Still he can give us no other ground save political expediency for resting religion upon fables so apparent as the stories of the popular belief.   He sometimes himself uses these fables, as he does other popular opinions, to illustrate some general proposition, as, for instance, Homer's verses on the golden chain show the immobility of the first mover.   Similarly in other cases he likes to pursue his scientific assumptions to their least apparent beginnings, and to take account of sayings and proverbs.   But if we except the few general principles of religious belief, he ascribes to these fables no deeper meaning, and as little does he seem to care about purifying their character.   For his state he pre-supposes the existing religion, as in his personal conduct he did not withdraw from its usages, and expressed his attachment to friends and relations in the forms consecrated by it.   No trace is found in him of Plato's desire to reform religion by means of philosophy.   As to his politics he allows in the existing worship even what in itself he disapproves, as for instance, unseemly words, inscriptions, and statues. Thus the relation of the Aristotelic philosophy to the actual religion is generally a very loose one.   It does not disdain indeed to use the points of connection which the other presents, but has no need of it whatever for itself.   Nor does it seek on its own side to purify and transform religion, the imperfection of which it rather seems to take as something unavoidable.   The two are indifferent to each other ; philosophy pursues its way without troubling itself about religion, without fearing any interruption from it.

In the seventy-seven years which elapsed from the death of Socrates, 399 B.C., to that of Aristotle, 322 B.C., Greek life had suffered a great change.   That dear-loved independence which every state had cultivated, and which concentrated every energy of the mind in civil life had vanished. During the forty years of Plato's work as a teacher it was becoming less and less; Chæronea gave it the death-blow; while Aristotle is the son of a time at which scientific study had already begun to take the place of active political life.[1] But the conquest effected by his great pupil Alexander completed this change. He opened the East to the Greek mind, bringing it into close contact with Asiatic thought, beliefs, and customs. Under his successors Alexandria, Antioch, and Seleucia, Tarsus, Pergamus, and Rhodes became great centres of Greek culture: but Greek self-government was gone. Athens with the rest of the Greek cities had lost its political independence, but it remained the metropolis of Greek philosophy. From the last decade of the fourth century before Christ four great schools, the Platonic, Peripatetic, Stoic, and Epicurean, all seated here, as embodied in the dwelling-place and oral teaching of their masters, stand over against each other. The point most interesting to our present subject is this, that all these schools take up a common ground, one which we consider to belong properly to religion, that is the question wherein the happiness of man consists, and how to attain it.[2] Thus the political circumstances of the land gave the tone to its philosophy. What the time required was something which would compensate men for the lost position of a free citizen and a self-governed fatherland. The cultivated classes looked to philosophy for consolation and support. The answers to this question which the various systems gave were very different from each other, but an answer they all

[1] Zeller, vol. iii. part 1, p. 7.　　　[2] *Ibid.* p. 14.

attempted. What they have in common is, the draw-ing-back of man upon himself, his inner mind, his consciousness, as a being who thinks and wills.[1] On the other hand the mental view was widened from the boundaries of a narrow state to that which touches man in general. The field of morality opened out beyond the range of this or that city, territory, or monarchy. Thus two hundred full years were occu-pied with the struggles of the Stoic and Epicurean schools, and the sceptical opposition to them of the middle and later Academy. At the very beginning of this time the man who sat first in Aristotle's chair after him, and therefore the head of the most specula-tive school, Theophrastus, had shocked the students of philosophy by declaring that fortune, not wisdom, was the ruler of the world. It was precisely against the despondence resulting on the mind from this conviction that the Stoics struggled with their doc-trine of apathy, Epicurus with his self-contentment, the Sceptics with their tranquillity of indifference.[2] These all sought to cure those whom the fables of the popular religion were insufficient to satisfy, those who felt the evils and trials of life and knew not whither to turn in their need. But the Stoic and the Epicu-rean cures stood in the strongest contrast to each other.

Zeno[3] of Cittium in Cyprus, after listening for twenty years to the teaching of various Socratic masters in Athens, founded a school himself, and wished it to be a school of virtuous men rather than of speculative philosophers. It was a system of complete materialism rigorously carried out. He

[1] Zeller, vol. iii. part 1, p. 18.   [2] *Ibid.* p. 12; Döllinger, p. 318.
[3] Döllinger, pp. 319–321.

admitted only corporeal causes, and two principles—
matter, and a force eternally indwelling in it and
shaping it.   These two principles, matter and force,
were in fact to the Stoic mind only one eternal being
viewed in a twofold aspect.   Matter for its subsistence
needs a principle of unity to form and hold it together:
and this, the active element, is inconceivable without
matter as the subject in which it dwells, works, and
moves.   Thus the positive element is matter viewed
as being as yet without qualities, while the active
element which runs through and quickens everything
is God in matter.   In real truth God and matter are
one thing, or, in other words, the Stoic doctrine is a
pantheism which views matter as instinct with life.[1]
God is the unity of that force which embraces and in-
terpenetrates the universe, assuming all forms, and as
such is a subtle fluid, fire, ether, or breath.   In it
are contained all forms of existence belonging to the
world-body which it animates, and from this world-body
develop themselves in order.   It lives and moves in
all, and is the common source of all effect and all desire.   God, then, is the world-soul, and the world itself
no aggregate of independent elements, but a being,
organised, living, filled and animated by a single soul,
that is to say, by one original fire manifesting itself in
various degrees of tension and heat.   If in Aristotle's
theory the world is a total of single beings, which are
only bound together unto a higher aim by a community of effort, in the Stoic system on the contrary
these beings all viewed together are members of a
surpassingly perfect organisation, and as such, so bound
in one, that nothing can happen to the individual
being, which does not by sympathy extend its opera-

[1] The doctrine of Hylozoismus.

tion to all others.   Thus on His physical side, God is
the world-fire, the vital all-interpenetrating heat, the
sole cause of all life and motion, and the necessity
which rules the world.   On His moral side, inasmuch
as the first general cause can only be a soul full of
reason and wisdom, He is the world-reason, a blessed
being, the originator of the moral law, ever occupied
with the government of the world, being in fact Himself the world.   Thus everything is subject to the law
of absolute necessity; everything eternally determined
through an endless series of preceding causes, since
nothing happens without a cause, and that again is
the working of a cause before it.   What, then, is
called, or seems to be, chance, is merely the working
of a cause unknown to us.   The will of man is accordingly mere spontaneity.   He wills, but what he wills
is inevitable: he determines himself, yet always in
consequence of preceding causes.   And since here
every cause is something subject to the conditions of
matter, something purely inside the world, it becomes
unalterable destiny.   Inasmuch, however, as the series
of causes leads back to the first, and this first cause
has an intellectual as well as a physical side, that
which is called fate or destiny may also be termed
Providence, a divine arrangement, under the aspect
of inevitable necessity.

With such a doctrine it is evident that all morality
was reduced to a matter of physics: and yet no sect
of Greek philosophers struggled so hard to solve the
great problem of moral freedom as the Stoics.[1]   But
the iron grasp of their leading tenet was ever too much
for them.   Man's soul is of the same substance as the
world-soul, that is, breath or fire, of which it is a

[1] Döllinger, pp. 322-324.

portion. In man it manifests itself as the force from which knowledge and action proceed, as at once intelligence, will, and consciousness. It is, then, closely allied with the Divine Being, but at the same time corporeal, a being which stands in perpetual action and reaction with the human body. It is that heat-matter bound to the blood, which communicates life and motion : it is perishable, though it lasts beyond the body, perhaps to the general conflagration. It has therefore, in the most favourable view, the duration of a world-period, with the out-run of which it must return to the universal ether or godhead : its individual existence and consciousness end.

As to the popular religion,[1] the Stoics admitted that it was filled with pretended deities, false doctrines, and rank superstition ; that its wilderness of fables about the gods was simply contemptible : but that it was well to retain the names of gods consecrated in public opinion, who were merely descriptions of particular incorporations of the one world-god.

The Stoics did not represent the component elements of human nature as struggling with each other, like Plato.[2] With them nature and reason is one thing. Their virtue,[3] or highest good, is life in accordance with nature, that is, the concurrence of human conduct with the all-ruling law of nature, or of man's will with God's will. Thus it was that the Stoic sought to reach his doctrine of philosophical impassibility : and to this system the majority of earnest and thinking minds in the two centuries before Christ inclined.[4]

---

[1] Döllinger, p. 324.   [2] *Ibid.* p. 326.
[3] ὁμολογουμένως τῇ φύσει ζῆν. Ueberweg, i. p. 198.
[4] Döllinger, p. 340.

At the very same time as Zeno, Epicurus set up at Athens a school destined through all its existence to wage a battle with Stoicism, yet aiming by different means at the same end, the freedom of the individual man from anxiety and disturbance.[1] If Zeno's world was an intelligent animal, that of Epicurus was a machine formed and kept in action by chance. He assumed the atomic theory of Democritus, that all bodies—and there are nothing else but corporeal things—have arisen originally from atoms moving themselves in empty space. They are eternal and indestructible, without quality, but not without quantity, and endlessly various in figure. As these from mere weight and impulse would fall like an everlasting rain in empty space without meeting each other, Epicurus devised a third motion, a slight declension from the perpendicular, in virtue of which their agglomeration is produced. Thus it is a work of pure chance that out of these, the countless worlds which frame the universe began to be. Any order or higher guidance of the universe, as directed to a purpose, is not to be thought of, any more than necessary laws, according to which the appearances of nature reproduce themselves. For a law would ultimately lead to a lawgiver, and this might re-awaken fear, and disturb the wise man's repose. He utterly denied the intervention either of one god or of many gods in the forming or the maintenance of the world. The main purpose indeed of his philosophy was to overthrow that religious view which saw in the argument from design a sure proof of a Divine Providence.[2] Nothing, he thought, was more perverted than the opinion that nature was directed for the good of man,

[1] Döllinger, p. 330.   [2] Zeller, vol. iii. part 1, p. 370.

or generally for any object at all; that we have tongues
in order to speak, or ears in order to hear, for in fact
just the reverse is true.   We speak because we have
tongues, and hear because we have ears.   The powers
of nature have worked purely under the law of necessity.   Among their manifold productions some were
necessarily composed in accordance with an end.
Hence resulted for man in particular many means
and powers.   Such result must not be viewed as in-
tentional, rather as a purely casual consequence of
naturally necessary operations.   Gods, such as the
people believed, he utterly repudiated.   Not he who
denied such gods, but he who assumed their existence,
was godless.   He allowed, indeed, that there existed
an immense multitude of gods, beings of human form,
endued with subtle, ethereal, transparent indestructible
bodies, who occupied the intermundial spaces, free
from care, regardless of human things, enjoying
their own blissful repose.[1]   His gods are in fact a
company of Epicurean philosophers, possessing everything which they can desire, eternal life, no care, and
perpetual opportunity of agreeable entertainment.

The soul of man is a body made out of the finest
round and fiery atoms; a body which, like heated
air, most rapidly penetrates the whole material frame.
The finest portion of the soul, the feeling and thinking spirit, which as a fourth element is added to the
fiery, aerial, and vaporous portions, dwells in the
breast.   In these elements all the soul's passions and
impulses are rooted.   When death destroys the
body, the sheltering and protecting home of the
soul's atoms, these evaporate at once.   It was clear
that in such a system the soul could not outlive the

[1] Zeller, vol. iii. part 1, p. 398.

body, but Epicurus laid a special stress on this, since thereby only could men be delivered from the greatest impediment to repose and undisturbed enjoyment of life, the torturing fear of the world below, and of punishments after death. It was the crown of his system, to which ethics, physics, and such logic as he admitted were entirely subordinate, to emancipate men from four fears—the fear of death, the fear of natural things, the fear of the gods, the fear of a Divine Providence, which was the same thing as fate.[1] Nevertheless, the followers of Epicurus had no scruple, after the manner of their master, who had spoken of the worship of the gods like a priest, to visit temples and take part in religious ceremonies. These, it is true, were useless, since they had nothing to fear and nothing to hope from the gods, but it was an act of reason, and could do no harm, to honour beings naturally so high and excellent.[2]

Of this school we learn that it gradually became the most numerous of all. Its social force really lay in setting forth as a model the undisturbed security of individual life. It agreed at the bottom with Stoicism that man's wisdom and highest end was to live in accordance with nature. Zeno, it is true, called this living in accordance with nature, virtue, man's highest and only good; Epicurus called it pleasure; but Zeno's virtue consisted essentially in the absence of passions, the pleasure of Epicurus in the mind's undisturbedness.[3] The Epicureans were more attached to their master's memory than any other school. They were renowned for their

[1] Döllinger, pp. 331–333.   Zeller, vol. iii. part 1, p. 392.
[2] Döllinger, p. 335.
[3] Zeller, vol. iii. part 1, p. 427.   ἀπαθία and ἀταραξία.

friendship with each other. Epicurus's Garden at
Athens meant the highest refinement of Athenian
life, the enjoyment of everything that was pleasant
in the society of like-minded men.[1]   It was this side
of his philosophy which made it popular.

While the schools of Zeno and Epicurus seated at
Athens were powerfully influencing Grecian thought,
the former especially drawing to it the stronger and
more thinking minds, resistance arose to them both
in the chair of Plato. First Arcesilaus and then
Carneades, who had succeeded to this office, set up
in the middle Academy the school of Scepticism.
While Stoics and Epicureans alike sought peace of
mind through knowledge of the world and its laws,
they on the contrary maintained that this same
peace of mind could only be attained by renouncing
all such knowledge.[2]   They held that no truth and
no certainty were given to man by the representations
of his senses, by his feelings, and by his consciousness of these, which do not enable him to know the
real being of anything.[3]   Those who held this view
would not say downright that what they contradicted
was untrue : they were of opinion that it might be
true, only there was no certitude of this, and therefore it must be left undetermined. The uncertainty
was as great on the one side as on the other.
Sextus Empiricus defined the state of skepsis to be
" skilfulness in so setting forth appearances and re-
flections against each other, as to be brought through
the equilibrium of opposing facts and grounds in their
favour first to a suspension of judgment, and then to
imperturbable tranquillity."

[1] Zeller, i. p. 107.   [2] Ibid. p. 435.
[3] Döllinger, p. 336, who quotes Sextus, Hypot. i. 8.

Carneades, whose life occupied the greater part of the second century before Christ, and who is extolled by Cicero as the keenest and most copious of disputants, was the man in whom this school of thought reached its highest point. He had appeared at Rome among a deputation of philosophers in the year 155, when his eloquence and earnestness made a great impression on his Roman hearers. This scepticism of the younger Academy however ran in accordance with the direction which the collective philosophy of the Greeks naturally took. It was carried out with an acuteness and a scientific ability which makes us recognise in it an important member of philosophical development.[1]   Carneades subjected the Stoic doctrine as to God in particular to a criticism the range of which went far beyond the dogmas of this school, and in fact tended to represent every conviction as to the existence of the Godhead, and every religious belief, as something impossible and untenable.[2]   This, however, as Cicero repeatedly assures us, was not done for the purpose of destroying belief in the gods, but only to point out the weakness and groundlessness of Stoic doctrines.   It is chiefly in his assaults on the assertions and assumptions of his adversaries that Carneades is victorious.   When he attempts anything positive on his own side, it amounts to this, that a rational man will take probability for his guide, when he cannot be assured of truth : and his chief merit appears to have been in more accurately determining the degrees of probability.[3]

The contests of these schools bring us down to the

[1] Zeller, vol. iii. part 1, p. 477.
[2] Döllinger, p. 338.
[3] For a full account of the line of thought followed by Carneades, see Zeller, vol. iii. part 1, pp. 454–477.

middle of the second century before Christ, when Greece fell under the dominion of Rome. From this time forth not only were Greek philosophers of eminence drawn to live themselves at Rome, and so to meet her statesmen and nobles in habits of intercourse, but the higher classes of the great capital commonly completed their education by visiting and studying at Athens, Rhodes, and other centres of Grecian thought. Thus by the fusion of Greece with the empire, while her political importance dwindled away, her influence upon the mind of her subjugators was immensely increased. But the Roman on his side obtained a sort of victory. As a rule he was anything but an original thinker. He was an essentially practical man : he had a steady instinct which led him to distrust first causes and general principles. The Greek schools were to him of value only as they might fit into his daily life, not as coherent systems of thought. The spirit therefore in which he regarded their differences was to select from them what best suited his tastes and feelings. If he had no power to originate, he could choose. But such likewise had been the result among the Greeks themselves of two centuries of conflict, in which the rival systems of Stoicism, Epicureanism, and Scepticism had stood over against each other. They sprung from the same soil ; they might even be termed three branches of one stem,[1] inasmuch as their common root was the desire to find for the individual man something which would give him tranquillity of mind, happiness in fact, independent of his civil circumstances. In this they all took up a practical rather than a theoretical ground, the ground indeed which is now assigned to religion. Utterly

[1] Zeller, vol. iii. part 1, p. 436.

opposed, then, as they were in their means, they sought the same end, and it was not in nature that the collision of their various arguments should not at length kindle the spirit of eclecticism. Thus the temper of the Roman statesman and noble, and the course of Greek philosophy itself, combined to produce this spirit, which from the beginning of the first century before Christ pervaded the thinkers of the Græco-Roman world.[1] But eclecticism betokens a weakening of the philosophic mind, that weariness which is unable to take a firm grasp of truth, an absence of the keen aim and high desire involved in that grasp. It is a confession that no one system possesses the truth. In this state of things nothing remains for the individual except to choose for himself out of different systems those morsels of truth which approve themselves most to his taste or tact, or, as he would term it, his truth-seeking sincerity.

It is not too much to say that the whole spirit of later antiquity, so far as it interested itself in the discovery of truth, from the time that Greek philosophy was diffused over the Roman world, leant more or less to eclecticism. Its most able, most distinguished, and most interesting representative is Cicero.[2] He lived at a time when rival criticism had searched out and exposed every weak point in the different systems of thought. To found new systems there was no further creative force; his eclectic position was the necessary result. His genius supplied him with no means to overcome it. His philosophical writings are

[1] Zeller, vol. iii. part I, pp. 482, 492.
[2] Ueberweg, i. p. 218; and Zeller, iii. part I, p. 593, calls him "neben seinem Lehrer Antiochus den eigentlichsten Vertreter des philosophischen Eklekticsimus in dem letzten Jahrhundert vor dem Anfang unserer Zeitrechnung."

scarcely more than transcripts from various Grecian
sources, wherein he uses his skill as a rhetorician and
his unfailing wealth of words to set forth with lawyer-
like balancing the arguments of different schools.   We
can yet detect the originals, from which in the short
intervals of enforced absence from political life before
and after the death of Cæsar he transfused with such
rapidity into a Latin shape the products of Greek discussion.[1]   Thus his treatise on the Republic and on
Laws are in form imitations of Plato's writings with
the same title, while for their contents Cicero applies
Platonic, Aristotelian, and Stoic doctrines to his own
political experiences, making also much use of Polybius.   His *Paradoxa* explain Stoic propositions.   The
groundwork of his *Consolatio* is Crantor's writing upon
Grief.   The *Lost Hortensius* is drawn from an exhortation of Aristotle to Themison, a prince of a city of
Cyprus, or from a similar work of the academician
Philo of Larissa.   His books *De Finibus* are taken
from   works   of   Phædrus,   Chrysippus,   Carneades,
Antiochus, as well as from the studies which Cicero
himself in his youth made while attending lectures.
His *Academica* is traced to the writings and partly also
to the lectures of the best-known Academicians; his
Tusculan Disputations to the influence of Plato and
Crantor, the Stoics and Peripatetics.   The first book
on the *Nature of the Gods* is taken from the writing
of an Epicurean, which has been discovered in the
rolls of Herculaneum, and was first supposed to be a
treatise of Phædrus, but is now known to be a work of
Philodemus.   His critique on the Epicurean standing-
point is drawn from the Stoic Posidonius; the second
book from Cleanthes and Chrysippus; the third from

[1] Ueberweg, i. pp. 221, 222.

Carneades and Clitomachus.   Of his books on *Divina-tion,* the first is taken from Chrysippus, Posidonius, Diogenes, and Antipater; the second from Carneades, and the Stoic Panætius.   His treatise on *Fate* from the writings of Chrysippus, Posidonius, Cleanthes, and Carneades: his *Elder Cato* from Plato, Xenophon, Hippocrates, and Aristo of Chius: his *Lælius* mainly from a writing of Theophrastus on Friendship.   His main authority for the first two books on *Offices* is Panætius; and for the third Posidonius; while besides Plato and Aristotle he has made use of Diogenes of Babylon, Antipater of Tyre, and Hecato.

Now in this selection from rival and antagonistic schools—this oscillation between the positive and sceptical tone of thought, this sitting as a judge rather than obeying as a disciple — Cicero very exactly represented the tone and attitude of the cultivated classes in his own time and in the century following his death.   Originality of mind in philo-sophic studies was gone; nor was any system as a whole believed in.   The sceptic and eclectic turns of mind are but the reverse sides of the same mental coinage : he who selects from all is convinced by none. Neither his doubts nor his choices satisfied Cicero, or any one of those who followed him in that most important century, the eighth of the Roman city, fifty years of which preceded and fifty followed the coming of Christ.   In its philosophical productions no preceding century had been so poor as this.   It had only to show the school of the Sextii, which arose at Rome about the beginning of our era, and took a sort of middle standing between Pythagorean, Cynic, and Stoic principles.[1]   This school was of small im-

[1] Ueberweg, i. 219, 223.

portance, and soon became extinct.   With this exception, from Cicero to Seneca no names of distinction
appear.   There is a gap in philosophical thought.   A
period so influential on the destinies of man in its
events, so celebrated for its polite literature, on which
the world has since been feeding, is barren in the
highest realm of inquiry.   For this reason there is a
particular justice in taking Cicero as an exponent of
heathen thought and spirit, the living specimen of
the kind, inasmuch as he is the last philosophic writer
before Christian thought appears in the world, and
chose for himself the function of summing up what he
thought of value in the ages before him.

We omit therefore nothing in our review if we
place ourselves at the end of this century, in the
reign of Claudius, and cast a glance backward over
that prodigious labour of human reason through which
we have hastily travelled, and which had then lasted
six hundred years.   The problem was, given the universe, what will man's reason in the most gifted, cultivated, inquiring, dialectic race of the ancient world do
with it ?   And more particularly, to what results will
reason come as to the power which has formed, or
is ruling it ?   How will it view the purpose of man's
existence, his nature, and the end to which he is ever
advancing ?   How the duties by which he is bound to
this creating, or at least maintaining and ruling power ?
How those offices which he owes to his fellow, the individual to the individual, the civil community to the community ?   It was to these points especially that the
greatest character in the whole movement—the single
heathen who knew how to die for his convictions—turned
the thoughts of those who followed him.   Again, at the
very starting-point of Greek philosophy a man of most

virtuous conduct, gifted likewise with great powers of attraction, had sought to realise in a society the philosophic life. And we have seen this conception of the mode of propagating truth to lie at the bottom of Greek teaching, and to have been pursued by Plato, by Aristotle, by Zeno, by Epicurus, to have been the original and even the only form of teaching which they recognised. What was the result in this respect also? In the four hundred and forty years following the death of Socrates had reason produced a consistent doctrine, and a society of which that doctrine should be the law and bond? Had the immortal race of that living word, which Plato contemplated, fashioned a fitting body for its soul to tenant? Time there had been enough, and even a superfluity of genius: but there were also two great outward events which might be expected to favour and advance such a result.

The first of these was the subjection of the whole East to the influence of the Greek mind by the conquest of Alexander, the effect of which continued in the kingdoms carried on by his successors. Originally the civil position of the Greek, as the free citizen of a free state, had been all in all to him. His country was his single measure. But during the lifetime of Plato and Aristotle this position had been more and more altering. The philosophy of Zeno and Epicurus was set up by men who had lost it altogether, who were thrown back on themselves, on the intrinsic nature of man, for support. Their inmost thought was how to produce tranquillity of mind and, so far as might be, happiness, for man, in something independent of his civil position. The loss of self-government had opened to them perforce a field far wider than the narrow confines of a provincial citizenship. Henceforth the schools of Plato, Aristotle, Zeno, and Epicurus issued their mental legislation not for the inhabitant of Attica, but for all that fusion of races which occupied the eastern coasts of the Mediterranean, was ruled by Greek potentates, and spoke the Hellenic tongue. Thus the ground taken up by philosophy was at once religious and cosmopolitan ; the former because it attempted to deal with the nature of man as man, and to give him inward contentment ; the latter because the mind, which used as its organ the Greek language, swayed large and independent empires, embracing various races of men. Then, if ever, it might have been expected that heathenism would make a great spring,[1] would cast aside what was local and accidental in the various customs, races, and beliefs brought under the fusing influence of one spirit, and idealise out of them a religion bearing the stamp and showing the force of that human reason of which Greece was the great representative. But the three centuries which witnessed the birth, the vigorous growth, and the incessant contests of the schools of Zeno and Epicurus, together with the scepticism which from Plato's chair passed judgment on them both, produced no such result. Rather they terminated in that balancing of opposite systems, and the selection of fragments from each, which we have seen in Cicero.

The second great event which we have to note is that when the Greek mind had thus been for three hundred years in possession of society throughout the East, the Roman Empire came to bind in unity of government not only all those races which the suc-

[1] Döllinger, p. 313.

cessors of Alexander had ruled, but the wide regions
of the West as well, and their yet uncivilised inhabitants.   Here, again, the Greek mind was not dethroned,
but married, as it were, to Roman power.   Philosophy
made a sort of triumphal entry into Rome in spite of
Cato and all the conservative force of the old Roman
spirit.   And if fusion had been the thought, the desire,
and the attempt of the Ptolemies and the Seleucidæ,
even more certainly was it the only spirit by which
Augustus and Tiberius could hope to rule in peace the
world made subject to them.   And not less than the
extinction of Greek autonomy did the loss of self-
government accompanying the institution of the empire
force the Roman also back upon himself.   When
Cicero could no longer sway the senate, he studied
philosophic systems at Tusculum : and certainly his
book of Offices has been more valued by all posterity
than his speeches against Catiline or his defence of
Milo.   A long train of writers from the Fathers downwards have seen in the civil unity of the Roman Empire
a providential preparation for a great religion.   But
the field on which that empire arose had already, so far
as concerns the thinking classes, long been occupied by
the Greek philosophy.   The two forces come into
operation now together.   Seventy years had elapsed
since the battle of Actium.   Augustus and Tiberius
had completely established one ruling authority, and
for two whole generations the vision of an empire,
seemingly conterminous with civilisation itself, had
been set before the eyes of men.   At this stage we
may fairly ask what philosophy had done towards
producing a corresponding unity of doctrine, and a
society sustaining and propagating it.

If, then, we take our stand at the moment when

Claudius began to reign, and count a century backwards, it is impossible to mention a time when philosophy was more impotent for good, and when the higher classes of the Roman Empire were more thoroughly irreligious and unbelieving. To understand the reason of this we must take into account first the negative and then the positive action of philosophy up to that time. As to the former, there can be no doubt that the effect of philosophy in all its schools and through all its shades of thought had been hostile to a simple belief in polytheism and its mythology. Human reason had been turned with pitiless severity on its mass of fables, its discreditable stories, its manifold contradictions. As early as the sixth century before Christ it had used the key of allegory in order to infuse into these some better meaning, and this was carried out into full detail by Metrodorus, a follower of Anaxagoras. Thus if Homer, the mirror in which the Greek saw his religion reflected, described Jupiter as suspending Juno between heaven and earth, Heracleitus was indignant with the atheists who did not see that it meant how the world and the elements were formed.[1] By this process indecent personal agencies melted away into physical effects, or were even sublimated into moral lessons. Men were told that only soft Phæacians could see in the loves of Mars and Venus a consecration of adultery : to the man of sense it meant that valour and beauty were worthy of each other. Through all the following centuries this tone of mind continued. As to the Stoical philosophers in particular, this physical allegorising was the perpetual instrument by which they reconciled their stern system of material Pantheism with all the stage scenery

[1] Döllinger, p. 254.

of the poet's Olympus. Epicurus, on the contrary, recognised the existence of gods in countless numbers, but they were beings who lived in the enjoyment of his philosophy, far removed from the cares of providence and the thought of human things. On the other hand, Plato's attempt to purify, while he recognised, polytheism, and to sweep away all its fables as purveyors of evil thoughts and desires, met with little success, though his conception of the Godhead as the Idea of goodness, remained the highest ever reached in that long process of thought. Through all this period the best and purest minds found in him a support against that bewilderment of the reason which the vulgar religion inflicted on them. But few and far between were those who followed Plato in this his highest conception, while the literature of that last century, in the midst of which Christ appeared, remains an abiding proof that the critical, scoffing, negative spirit of philosophy had spread itself over all the cultured classes. We seek in vain in Julius Cæsar and Cicero, in Lucretius, Catullus, Virgil, Manilius, Horace, Ovid, in Polybius, Dionysius, Diodorus, or Strabo, for any real belief in the immortal gods whose names appear in their writings. The poets use them for stage-effect, the statesmen as part of the machinery of government, the historians as names interwoven with the events which they recount. Yet the life of all these men was filled with the frequentation of rites and ceremonies, as a matter of law and custom, having reference to a multitude of gods, concerning whom they had a contemptuous disbelief, though none of them were without many a dark superstition.

Such was the negative influence of philosophy; but

what inward support had it given to minds whose
ancestral belief, still entertained by the mass of men
all around, was thus eaten out ?   What substitute had
it provided for this discredited polytheism with its
ridiculed mythology ?

1. First, did the Greek philosophy teach the unity
of the Godhead ?   If by this question be meant, did
philosophy ever go forth into the midst of the temples
and smoking sacrifices with which every city teemed,
and proclaim, These gods whom you worship are no
gods : there is one Maker and Ruler of the universe,
and the homage due to Him alone is usurped by a multitude of pretended deities ?——then there is no doubt
about the answer, that this, is what neither Socrates,
nor Plato, nor Aristotle, nor Zeno, nor any other
philosopher thought of doing.   The philosophic god
was never set in the forefront of the battle after
this fashion.   He dwelt in the most secret shrine of
Plato's mind, hard to be discovered, and to be confessed, if at all, in secret.   If with Aristotle he was
a pure spirit, yet he abode apart from the world,
working on it indeed, as the magnet on the iron, but
unconscious of it, not ruling it with free-will.[1]   And,
save so far as this is an exception, the Greek mind
from beginning to end never succeeded in absolutely
separating God from matter.   And as time went on,
this original defect showed itself more and more,
until in the Stoic system, which prevailed over all the
rest as to the conception of a world-ruling power, what
was called God was simply a force pervading all
matter.[2]   The Stoics could, indeed, as in the hymn of

---

[1] Döllinger, p. 307.   "Er wirkt also zwar auf die Welt, aber ohne
sie zu kennen, wie der Magnet auf das Eisen, und seine Action auf
die Welt ist keine freiwollende."

[2] Döllinger, pp. 340, 572.

Cleanthes, invest this god of theirs with many beautiful, grand, and attractive attributes. His was almighty
power;[1] he was the author of nature; he ruled all
things with law; and the world willingly obeyed his
will. And this common law passed through all things,
so that evil mixed with good resulted in a general
order. Thus they could address him as Father and as
King, guiding all things with justice; and this being
they termed Jupiter. But this is only a poetic[2] exhibition of their genuine thought and meaning that
"all which was real was corporeal; matter and force
are the two chief principles; matter in itself is motion-
less and formless, though capable of assuming every
motion and every form. Force is the active, moving,
and forming principle; it is indivisibly joined with
matter: the operating force in the whole of the world
is the Godhead."[3] " By the names World-soul, World-
reason, Nature, Universal Law, Providence, Fate, the
same thing is indicated, the one Primal Force determining everything with absolute regularity, interpenetrat-
ing the whole world." "And even the opposition
between the material and the spiritual description of
the Godhead disappears upon closer examination, for
on Stoic principles the Godhead can only then be considered as real when considered as body.[4] It was to

---

[1] Ζεῦ, φύσεως ἄρχηγε, νόμου μέτα πάντα κυβερνῶν·—
Σοὶ δὴ πᾶς ὅδε κόσμος ἑλισσόμενος περὶ γαῖαν
Πείθεται ᾗ μὲν ἄγης,καὶ ἑκὼν ὑπὸ σεῖο κρατεῖται—
Ἀλλὰ σὺ καὶ τὰ περισσὰ, ἐπίστασαι ἄρτια θεῖναι,
Καὶ κοσμεῖς τὰ ἄκοσμα, καὶ οὐ φίλα σοὶ φίλα ἐστίν.
῝Ωδε γὰρ εἰς ἓν ἅπαντα συνήρμοκας ἐσθλὰ κακοῖσιν,
῝Ωσθ᾽ ἕνα γίγνεσθαι πάντων λόγον ἀὲν ἐόντα.

[2] Cleanthes preferred expressly the poetic form; see the note in
Zeller, vol. iii. part 1, p. 289; for poetry and music are better suited
to reach the truth of divine contemplation than the bare philosophical
expression. [3] Ueberweg, i. p. 195.

[4] Zeller, vol. iii. pp. 130, 131; see the many authorities he produces,
pp. 126–131.

such a unity that Greek philosophy advanced, receding more and more from that imperfect conception of personality with which it had started.   Further, the idea of creation is wanting to Greek philosophy from its beginning to its end.   The power it contemplates is evermore confronted with matter, which it can permeate, fashion, move through a natural alchemy of endless changes.   Over against this power it is not free to create or not to create, not even free to prevent the evil which lies therein as a sort of blind necessity. As there was always Force, so was there always Matter. To the conception of a free Creator of spirit and of matter the Greek mind never rose : nor accordingly to that of a free Ruler of the universe : and this is only to say in other words, that the conception of personality—that is, of self-consciousness and moral freedom, as applied to a Being of infinite power, wisdom, and goodness—was imperfect and confused.   Plato in his highest flight had seemed to recognise one God, whom to enjoy is the happiness of man ; but Plato and all who followed him had endured, had countenanced, had taken part in the polytheistic worship.   And again, neither he, nor Aristotle, nor Zeno showed any inclination to suffer for their doctrines.   This philosophic god, gradually evolved by the reasoning mind, produced the very smallest effect upon the unphilosophic world. Cicero has preserved for us the Stoic argument from final causes, and acknowledged its force in very remarkable words.[1]   It generated no martyrs.   Was it merely from

[1] He says of the opposite theory of Epicurus, the construction of the world from the chance falling-together of atoms : "Hoc qui existimat fieri potuisse, non intelligo, cur non idem putet, si innumerabiles unius et viginti formæ literarum, vel aureæ vel quales libet, aliquo conjiciantur, posse ex his in terram excussis annales Ennii, ut deinceps legi possint, effici : quod nescio an ne in uno quidem versu possit tantum valere fortuna."   *De Nat. Deor.* ii. 37.

want of earnestness that the philosophers tolerated and practised the polytheism all around them, and avoided all suffering for their opinions by compliance with a worship which they disbelieved? Or was it that their standing-ground, in all more or less pantheistic, was identical with that which they impugned?[1] Were the gods of Olympus powers of nature personified, while their god was simply one power inhabiting nature? Or was it that they never reached the one personal creating God, and were consequently unable to maintain His absolute distinction from the world together with His relation to it as Creator and Ruler? That which they cherished as a private philosophical good, which they cared so little to exhibit to the world, was in fact incapable of conquering the world, for the human heart cannot live upon an impersonal god, and will not suffer for a conception of the reason. But it was in this conception that philosophic thought had terminated. And here we find the chief cause of its powerlessness to improve and purify the mythology which it attacked, and much more to affect the lives and conduct of those who professed its tenets. For the old mythology had at least a strong consciousness of personality in its gods. In Homer himself the original tradition, of which his religion was a corruption, still spoke of the father of gods and men as the ruler and judge of the world. In the heathen mind generally such a conception still existed. Nor is it too much to say

---

[1] So Zeller remarks, iii. 1, p. 296 : " A Pantheism, such as the Stoic, could take up into itself the most boundless polytheism, a double liberty only being allowed, that of passing on to derived beings the name of deity, from the Being to whom alone originally and in the strict sense it belonged, and that of personifying as God the impersonal, which is an appearance of divine power."

that the common people among the Greeks and
Romans were nearer to the truth of one personal
God than the philosopher; and the philosopher himself when he listened at any moment of danger and
anxiety to the promptings "of the soul naturally
Christian" within him, than when he indulged in his
esoteric problems.

2. But the conception of personality in God rules
the conception of personality in man. As throughout the
Greek philosophy the former was weak and imperfect,
until in the Stoic system it vanished, so the latter.
The physical theory of the Greek overmastered and ex-
cluded the conception of free-will in his mind, first as to
God and then as to man. As he had no better solution
for the existence of evil throughout the world than to
place its seat in matter which was co-existent with the
divine reason, and as reason so conceived was powerless
to subdue matter, so in the smaller world of man. In
him a portion of the divine reason was united with
matter. If Plato, Aristotle, and the Stoics arranged
somewhat differently the mode of this composition, yet to
all of them alike from the one side and the other the
notion of physical necessity came in. The material
constituent tended to evil, the reasoning constituent to
good: in the man who was made up of the two there
was a perpetual jar. There was no room left in their
theory for the conception of the soul as a self-
originating cause of action. No sect struggled so
hard and so persistently to maintain a doctrine of
free-will as the Stoic: but it went down before that
central tenet of their system, physical necessity, the
inexorable sequence of cause and effect, that "common
law" of theirs, by which the world was ruled. The
conception of an all-wise, all-good, and all-powerful

personal Creator, in whose nature the eternal law is based, not being clear to their minds, so neither was the conception of sin, as the infringement of that law. The law of physical necessity took the place of the eternal moral law. The physical constituents of a man were responsible for his actions. The evil which he did was physical rather than moral: and he was not responsible for what he could not prevent. The questions of free-will, of evil viewed as sin, and of responsibility, are inextricably bound up with the doctrine of the human personality; and on all these the philosophic mind was dark and confused.

If the Greek's physical theory stood in the way of his conceiving clearly the human personality in this life, much more did it impede his conception of that personality as continuing after death. For as the union of a portion of the divine reason with matter constituted man, and as death put an end to that union, the compound being ceased to exist, the portion of the divine reason reverted to its source, but the sensitive soul, as well as the body, was dissolved and came to nothing. There was in his mind no " individual substance of a rational nature" to form the basis of identity, and maintain the conception of personality. In the absence of this, he who had felt, thought, and acted, was no more. He could not therefore receive retribution for his deeds, since there was no personal agent on whom the retribution was to fall.

3. A god who was not personal and did not make man,—man in whom free-will, the mark of personality, was not recognised, so long as he lived, and in whom after death no personal agent continued to exist,— these correspond to each other, and these were the last result of Græco-Roman philosophic thought up

to the time of Claudius.   But what sort of duty did
man, being such, owe to such a god?   Cicero's book
on Offices had been written upwards of eighty years,
but nothing that followed it during that time equalled
it in reputation or ability.   It was the best product
that his Roman thought could draw from all the preceding Grecian schools : and it was accepted for centuries as the standard of heathen morality.   Let us,
then, first note that in this book [1] there is nothing
like a recognition of God as the Creator and Common
Father; no call upon the human soul to love him as
such, and for his own perfections; no thought that
the duty of man consists in becoming like to him, nor
his reward in attaining that likeness.   The absence of
such a thought gives its character to the whole book,
and measures its level.   The second point to be noted
is, that the happiness of man consists not in being
like God, and consequently, in union with Him, but in
virtue, which is living according to nature.   In his
reasonable nature every one possesses a sufficient standard of moral action under every circumstance which
may arise.   Thirdly, throughout the whole of his
treatise Cicero makes no use of the doctrine of man's
immortality.   His happiness, then, is left to consist in
virtue—life according to reason, which again is life
according to nature—without respect to any future
state of existence.   Now, if Cicero stood alone in
these three points, his book would only represent his
own authority, but he is in fact the mouthpiece herein
of that whole preceding heathen philosophy which he
criticised, and from which he selected.   Even Plato

[1] See Hasler, *Verhältniss der heidnischen und christlichen Ethik*,
p. 28; and Zukrigl's commentary on the same, *Tübingen theol. Quar-
talschrift*, 1867, pp. 475–482.

himself, by far the highest and best of Greek philosophers in this respect, though he had in single expressions indicated that the happiness of man was to
be made like to God, constructed no system of ethics
in dependence on that conception.   If it be true, it
is of all-constraining influence, and is to the whole
moral system what the law of gravity is to the
material universe.   Plato's ethical system was a strict
deduction from his physical theory of the three parts
in man, to each of which he assigned its virtue.   Far
less did Aristotle connect morality with God.   The
Stoics, indeed, who occupy by far the largest space in
Greek philosophy, seem to be an exception.   It is
said that "their whole view of the world springs from
the thought of the Divine Being who generates all
finite beings from himself.   He includes them all in
himself, penetrates them with his power, rules them
with his unchangeable law, and thus merely manifests
himself in them all."   Hence their system "is funda-
mentally religious, and scarcely an important statement
in it which is not in connection with their doctrine of
God."   Thus with them "all moral duties rest on a
religious ground, all virtuous actions are a fulfilment
of the divine will and law." [1]   This God, indeed, is but
a name for the sternest and most absolute system of
material necessity : a God without a moral nature,
without freedom, without personality.   Under that
name, in fact, force and matter making up one thing
are substituted for a living God, who, in virtue of the
laws of nature, is swept out of His own universe.
So, again, Cicero's statement that man's happiness
consists in virtue, or life according to nature, is the
general doctrine of philosophy, which the Stoics in

[1] Zeller, iii. 1, pp. 288, 289.

particular had elaborated. If there be any one expression which would sum up in a point the whole
heathen conception of what man should do, it would
be "Life according to nature." So, again, the exclusion of any thought of immortality, and a consequent
retribution, in its bearing on morality, was common to
all the schools of Grecian thought, if we except the
faltering accents and yearning heart of Plato, and most
of all was truly Stoic. The imperfection and unclear-
ness of their view as to the divine personality, and
as to the human, in the reasonable being, the image
and reflection of the divine, accords but too truly, while
it accounts for, this detachment of man from God in
the field of moral duty.

4. What, then, remained to man, after such deduc-
tions? There remained the earthly city, the human
commonwealth. And when, passing beyond the bounds
of any particular nation, and man's civil position
therein, philosophy grasped the moral life as the relation between man as man,[1] and conceived human
society itself as one universal kingdom of gods and
men, it made a real progress and reached its highest
point. But this was the proper merit of the Stoics.[2]
Plutarch attributes to Zeno, their founder, this precise idea, that we ought not to live in cities and
towns, each divided by peculiar notions of justice,
but esteem all men as tribesmen and citizens, who
should make up one flock feeding in a common pas-
ture under a common law. The grandest passages of

[1] Zeller, iii. 1, 12.

[2] Καὶ μὴν ἡ πολὺ θαυμαζομένη πολιτεία τοῦ τὴν Στωϊκῶν αἵρεσιν κατα-
βαλλομένου Ζήνωνος εἰς ἓν τοῦτο συντείνει κεφάλαιον, ἵνα μὴ κατὰ πόλεις
μηδὲ κατὰ δήμους οἰκῶμεν, ἰδίοις ἕκαστοι διωρισμένοι δικαίοις ἀλλὰ πάντας
ἀνθρώπους ἡγώμεθα δημότας καὶ πολίτας, εἷς δὲ βίος ᾖ, καὶ κόσμος, ὥσπερ
ἀγέλης συννόμου νόμῳ κοινῷ τρεφομένης. Plutarch, Alex. M. Virt. i. 6,
p. 329, quoted by Zeller, iii. 1, p. 281.

Cicero are those in which he clothes in his Roman diction this Stoic idea, as for instance : [1] "They judge the world to be ruled by the power and will of the gods, and to be a sort of city and polity common to gods and men, and that every one of us is part of this world." The bond of this community is the common possession of reason,[2] "in which consists the primal society of man with God. But they who have reason in common, have also right reason in common. And as this is law, we are as men to be considered as associated with the gods by law also. Now they who have community of law, have likewise community of rights. This latter makes them also to belong to the same polity. But if such pay obedience to the same commands and authorities, then are they even much more obedient to this supernal allotment, this divine mind and all-powerful God. So that this universal world is to be considered one commonwealth of gods and men." "Law is the supreme reason, implanted in nature, which commands all things that are to be done, and prohibits their contraries." "The radical idea of right I derive from nature, under whose guidance we have to draw out the whole of this subject-matter." Thus the great Roman lawyer and statesman, robing philosophy in his toga, propounded admirably to his countrymen, filled with the greed of universal conquest, the result of Stoic thought. This was that human society in general rested on the similarity of reason in the individual, that we have no ground for restricting this common possession to one people, or to consider ourselves more nearly related to one than another. All men, apart from what they have done for themselves, stand equally near to each other, since

---

[1] *De Finibus*, iii. sec. 19.   [2] *De Legibus*, i. 7, 6.

all equally partake of reason. All are members of one body, since the same nature has formed them out of one stuff, for the same destination.[1]

Greek philosophy has undoubtedly the merit of bringing out into clear conception this purely human and natural society. It thus expressed in language the work of Alexander, and still more the work of the Roman Empire, as it was to be ; and more than this, it herein supplied a point of future contact with Christian morality. The advance from the narrowness of the Greek mind in its proud rejection of all non-Hellenic nations, and no less from the revolting selfishness of Roman conquest, is remarkable. And it is an advance of philosophic thought. As the older thinkers considered the political life of the city to be an immediate demand of human nature, so the Stoics considered the unitedness of man as a whole together, the dilatation of the particular political community to the whole race, in the same light. Its ground was the common possession of reason. The common law ruling this human commonwealth was to live according to the dictation of reason, that is, according to nature, in which therefore virtue consists,[2] being one and the same in God and in man, and in them alone.[3] Such virtue branches into four parts, the prudence which discerns and practises the truth : the justice which assigns his own to each ; the courage which prevails over all difficulties ; the self-restraint and order which preserves temperance in all things. These being bound up together cover the whole moral

[1] Zeller, iii. 1, p. 278, from Seneca and Marcus Aurelius, who here, however, only enlarge on Cicero's idea, or rather Zeno's.

[2] "Jam vero virtus eadem in homine ac Deo est, neque ullo alio ingenio præterea. Est autem virtus nihil aliud quam in se perfecta, et ad summum perducta natura." *De Legibus*, i. 8.   [3] *De Officiis*, i. 5.

domain, and embrace all those relations within which human society moves, and, as having their root in the moral nature of man, are a duty to every one.

This human commonwealth enfolds in idea the whole earth. It is the society of man with man. But it closes with this life. It has no respect to anything beyond. It was the Stoics who most completely worked out this system of moral philosophy; who urged the duty of man's obedience to nature, of his voluntary subjection to that one universal law and power which held all things from the highest to the lowest in its grasp; and who likewise most absolutely cut him off from any personal existence in a future state. The virtue in which they placed his happiness was to be complete in itself; it was the work of man without any assistance on the part of God.[1] It made man equal to God. It found its reward in itself. If it was objected that the highest virtue in this life sometimes met with the greatest disasters, sorrows, pains, and bereavements, the system had no reply to this mystery. It did not attempt to assert a recompense beyond the grave.

As little did it attempt to account for or to correct the conflict between man's reason and his animal nature. That perpetual approval of the better and choice of the worse part stood before the Stoic as before us all. He admitted that the vast majority of men were bad, and his wise man was an ideal never reached. But he had no answer whatever to the question, why, if vice is so evil in the eye of our reason, it so clings to our nature; why, if so contrary to the good of the mass, it dwells within every individual.[2]

---

[1] Cic. de Nat. Deor. iii. 36. "Virtutem nemo unquam acceptam deo retulit. Nimirum recte. Propter virtutem enim jure laudamur, et in virtute recte gloriamur : quod non contingeret, si id donum a deo, non a nobis, haberemus."   [2] Champagny, Les Césars, iii. 333.

The human city or community of men is the highest point which this moral philosophy contemplates. Each particular commonwealth should be herein the image of the one universal commonwealth which their thought had constructed. But what, then, is the relation of the individual man to the whole of which he is a part? This nature, which is the standard to the whole ideal commonwealth, is, as we have seen so often, in fact a law of the strictest necessity. If virtuous, man follows it willingly; if vicious, he must follow it against his will. There was no real freedom for the individual in the system as philosophy. What was disguised under the name of law, reason, and God, was a relentless necessity before which every one was to bow. But transfer this philosophy to any political community, and consider in what position it placed the individual with regard to the civil government. Human society is considered as supreme: but his own state represents to him that society, and as all things end with this life, no part of man remains withdrawn from that despotism which requires the sacrifice of the part for the good of the whole. Man's conscience had no refuge in the thought of a future life; no reserve which the abuse of human power could not touch. And so we find that in matter of fact there was no issue out of such a difficulty except in the doctrine of self-destruction. They termed it in truth *The Issue*,[1] when disease, or disaster, or pain, or the abuse of human power, rendered it impossible any longer to lead a life in accordance with nature. In this case

---

[1] "'Εξαγωγὴ ist bei den Stoïkern der stehende Ausdruck für den Selbstmord." Zeller, vol. iii. part i, p. 284 n. 2, who quotes Diog. vii. 130. Ἐλλόγως τέ φασιν ἐξάξειν ἑαυτὸν ἀπὸ τοῦ βίου τὸν σοφὸν καὶ ὑπὲρ πατρίδος καὶ ὑπὲρ φίλων, κἂν ἐν σκληροτέρᾳ γένηται ἀλγηδόνι, ἢ πηρώσεσιν, ἢ νόσοις ἀνιάτοις.

all the Stoic authorities justified it, praised it, and termed it the Door which Divine Providence had benignantly left ever open.

While therefore it must be acknowledged that the Stoical conception of the whole earth as one city [1] was a true result of Greek thought, and at the same time the highest point it reached, and a positive result of great value, yet it must also be said that it was one rather big with rich promises for the future than of any great present advantage. It required indeed to be completed by another conception of which its framers had lost their hold, the doctrine, that is, of a future retribution, redressing the inequality, the injustice, the undeserved suffering so often falling upon virtue in the present life. When that conception came to complete and exalt the Stoic idea, the need of self-destruction as an issue of the wise man, as soon as he could not live according to nature, ceased, for man himself ceased to be a part of a physical whole governed by necessity. The human city relaxed its right over the individual in presence of a divine city, which embraced indeed man in his present life, but taught him to look for its complete realisation in another.

Up to the time of Claudius the last word of heathen philosophy was expressed by the human commonwealth and individual man therein, ruled by prudence, justice, fortitude, and temperance, but both commonwealth and individual terminating with this life.

We have seen that from the time the Greek race was absorbed in the Roman Empire the systems of philosophy were broken up by the eclectic spirit, which, engendered within already by the ferment of

---

[1] "Qui omnem orbem terrarum unam urbem esse ducunt." Cicero, *Paradoxon* 2.

opinions, was strengthened and developed by the
accession of the practical Roman mind. Variety of
belief is indeed marked as "the essential feature of
Greek philosophy" from its outset, and "the antagonist force of suspensive scepticism" as including some
of its most powerful intellects from Xenophanes five
hundred years before to Sextus Empiricus two hundred years after the Christian era.   One of its historians stamps it as "a collection of dissenters, small
sects each with its own following, each springing
from a special individual as authority, each knowing
itself to be only one among many."[1] It is therefore no
wonder that if Plato's grand conception of an immortal
line of the living word thus came to nought, philosophy proved itself much more incapable of founding a society impregnated with its principles than it
had even been of constructing a coherent doctrine
which should obtain general reception.   And to
judge of the actual impotence of philosophy in the
century ending with the principate of Claudius, we
must rest a moment on this second fact. Philosophers calling themselves Platonic, Peripatetic, Sceptic, Stoic, Epicurean, or these in various mixtures,
were to be found at the various seats of learning,
Athens, Rhodes, Alexandria, for instance, or at Rome
as the seat of empire, or travelling like wandering stars over her vast territory, but these scattered, nebular, and disjoined luminaries shone with
a varying as well as a feeble light, which rather
confused than satisfied human reason. They were
utterly powerless to transfer their doctrine into
any number of human hearts living in accordance
therein.   The only exception to this statement

[1] Grote, *Plato*, vol. i. p. 87.

seems to prove its real truth. By far the most united of the sects was that of the Epicureans, who held with great tenacity to their founder's views and mode of life, which may be summed up in denial of God and Providence, and enjoyment to the utmost of this world's goods; the fair side of it being a general benevolence, courtesy, friendship, in short, a genial appreciation of what we understand by the word civilisation. These antagonists of Stoic principles and of the highest morality which heathen thought had constructed were the most numerous of existing sects, and we are told that hundreds of years after their founder's death they presented the appearance of a well-ordered republic, ruled without uproar or dissension by one spirit, in which they formed a favourable contrast to the Stoics. With the exception of a single fugitive, Metrodorus, never had an Epicurean detached himself from his school.[1] Philosophy must have the credit of having created this single form of social life according to its tenets in a sect whose doctrines were a reproach among the heathens themselves. The failure of Pythagoras, of Plato, of Aristotle, of Zeno, was the success of Epicurus. The age of Augustus and Tiberius was ready to expire in sensuality and unbelief, and even in exhaustion of the philosophic mind, for no period is so barren of scientific names, which carry any weight, as the fifty years pre-ceding Claudius.[2] We have seen above that all these philosophers aimed at forming a society which should carry out their principles; that this was their original

[1] Döllinger, p. 315, from Numenius, quoted by Eusebius. Ueber-weg, i. 205, says of them, that up to the rise of Neoplatonism they were the most numerous of all.

[2] See Döllinger, pp. 341 and 572–584; so Champagny, Les Césars, iii. 294.

and their only idea of teaching; that with a view to
make it permanent they created a chair of teaching,
a living authority who was to continue on their
doctrine. But the chair of Plato alone presented [1]
five Academies with dissentient doctrines; and a
Platonic or Stoic city no one had seen. Thus viewing their united action upon the polytheistic idolatry,
we may say that while they could discredit its fables
in reflecting minds, while they could even raise an
altar in their thoughts "to the unknown God," they
left society in possession of the temples and observant
of a worship which they pronounced to be immoral,
monstrous, and ridiculous. They had destroyed in
many the ancestral belief; they had awakened perhaps in some a sense of one great Power ruling the
universe; but having taken up the religious ground
and professed to satisfy man's desire for happiness,
they had been utterly powerless to construct a religion. They failed entirely in the union of three
things,[2] a dogma and a morality founded on that
dogma, both of which should be exhibited, brought
before the eyes and worked into the hearts of men
by a corresponding worship. To unite these three

[1] Ueberweg gives them thus: to the first Academy belong Plato's
successor Speusippus, who taught 347–339 B.C.; Xenocrates, 339–314;
Polemo, 314–270; Crates, a short time. The second Academy was
founded by Arcesilaus, who lived 315–241, taking more and more a
sceptical direction, which was carried out to the utmost by Carneades,
214–129, in the third: in the fourth, Philo of Larissa, about 80 B.C.,
returned to the dogmatic direction; and Antiochus of Ascalon,
Cicero's friend, founded the fifth, in which he fused Platonic, Aristotelian, and Stoic doctrines together. St. Augustine, De Civ. Dei,
viii. 3, puts his finger on the variations of the Socratici.

[2] Lier ensemble les dogmes, une morale, et un culte, c'est-à-dire
donner à la société une foi, une règle, et des pratiques, c'était l'œuvre
que le genre humain appelait de ses vœux, et sur laquelle pourtant
tous les efforts humains semblaient échouer." A. Thierry, Tableau
de l'Empire Romain, p. 328.

things was needed an authority of which above all they were destitute. Their dogma was without the principle of faith; their morality without binding power; but the worship which should blend the two they had not at all. And so they presented no semblance of the society which should carry these three things in its bosom. They could not in the least satisfy the doubts or the yearnings which they had raised.

The period beginning with the rise of Greek philosophy and ending with the principate of Claudius will ever remain of the highest interest and importance. It exhibits what human reason, putting forth its highest powers in the race in which it culminated, but at the same time more thoroughly separated from belief, tradition, and authority than anywhere else, did actually achieve. It is in this respect that the heathen philosophers, together with the poets and historians who precede the publication of the Christian religion in the Roman world, possess a value far beyond any intrinsic merit of their own. It is a study of pathology the results of which are far as yet from being gathered in. It is only by carefully examining what the philosophers taught in theology and morals—for they aspired to be and were both the theologians and the moralists of those ages—that we can at all form an adequate judgment of the real work which the Christian Church has wrought in the world. It is only by using the historians and poets as a mirror of that general society to whose cultured classes the philosophers spoke, that we can estimate what the great mass of mankind then was, and what effect the philosophers produced on them. The difference between their world and their society

and ours is the measure of Christian work. The
hundred years preceding Claudius, which include in
them almost all the greatest names of Roman literature, are the most important of all in this point of
view, both as containing the result of scientific thought
in the five preceding centuries, and as giving the
depth of the moral and intellectual descent. We
learn from this whole long period the fulness of the
truth conveyed in those words of the angelic doctor
at the beginning of his great work: " Even for
those things which can be investigated concerning
God by the force of human reason, it was necessary for man to be instructed by a divine revelation,
because few only, and they after long inquiries, and
with the admixture of many errors, would convey to
man the truth concerning God as searched out by
reason.[1]

What the philosophers from the time of Thales had
taken as their special work was to measure and estimate
the visible world. And for the last four centuries of
this period especially they made the nature and the
needs, the supreme good and the happiness, of man
their chief concern, in subordination to which they
continued their physical inquiries. And surely the
judgment which an inspired writer formed of their
travail must recur to the mind with great force at the
end of the preceding review : " If they knew so much
as to be able to estimate the visible world, why did
they not more easily discover its Lord ? "[2]   Why from
the goods which they beheld had they not power to
know the sole possessor of being, nor when they gave
attention to his works, recognised their artificer ?

[1] St. Thomas, *Summa*, p. I. 9. I. a. I.
[2] *Sap.* xiii. 9.

Why did they esteem fire or breath, rapid air or circling stars, or the force of water, or the lights of heaven, rulers of the universe? For if the visible beauty of these delighted them so that they conceived them to be gods, how did they not draw the conclusion that the Lord of these was so much better than they? For it was the Author of beauty who created them. If they were struck dumb with the sense of their power and operation, why did they not conceive how much more powerful He who made them was? For from the greatness and the beauty of creatures the parent of them is by the force of reason discerned.[1]

From their capital error in this—which the same writer declares to be inexcusable[2]—proceeded their other errors concerning man, his nature, his supreme good, and his final end. It is here sufficient to note that down to the age of Claudius there is no appearance that either of these great errors would be corrected. Still less was there any sign that the rise of a great religion would cause the multitudinous altars of heathenism to disappear before the altar of the Unknown God, and that it would construct a City of God. Divergent systems of philosophy had eaten out in thinking minds belief in the babel of false gods, without implanting belief in a personal Creator, the author and the end of man.

---

[1] Reading with St. Chrys. and St. Gregory ἐκ μεγέθους καὶ καλλονῆς κτισμάτων ἀναλόγως, cognoscibiliter, *i.e.* by a conclusion of reason.

[2] Μάταιοι μὲν γὰρ πάντες ἄνθρωποι φύσει, οἷς παρῆν Θεοῦ ἀγνωσία· . . . πάλιν δὲ οὐδ' αὐτοὶ συγγνωστοί. *Sap.* xiii. 1, 8.

INDEX

END OF VOL. II.

BURNS AND OATES, LIMITED, LONDON

BURNS & OATES'
SELECTED LIST
M·CM·XVI
ARRANGED ALPHABETICALLY
CHIEFLY UNDER *the* AUTHORS' NAMES

NOS·NE·CESSES
THOMA·TVERI

28 ORCHARD STREET
LONDON
W

Telegrams
Burns Oates London

Telephones
5911 & 2706 Mayfair

THE YEAR'S WORK

WE have published one new book or new edition for every week of 1915. No one lacking experience of the labours of a publisher can, we think, realize what that simple statement means. Nor do we follow the common course of allowing our printers and our binders to throw together our books for us. To the least detail everything is considered and designed ; and so we have been able to set a standard of comeliness and artistic honesty. The year's work does not only represent a record in number : much more important, it is a record in quality. Among the authors are Mgr R. H. Benson (two books), Cardinal Mercier, G. K. Chesterton, C. M. Antony, Father Martindale, Sir Bertram Windle, Father Rickaby (two), Father Thurston (two), Miss Monica Gardner, Father McNabb, Miss E. M. Wilmot-Buxton, the author of " Aunt Sarah and the War." Not less important than the books of these are the new "Ordo Administrandi Sacramenta," "Ritus Servandus," "Excerpta," "Epistles and Gospels—the Pulpit edition"; or the new edition of Bishop Challoner's "Meditations," and Mother M. Loyola's " Little Children's Prayer Book."

Of undertakings in the immediate future, the most significant is the series of English and Latin texts called "The Liturgy for Layfolk." For this the Publishers have secured the services of Bishop Butt, Abbot Cabrol, Dr Adrian Fortescue, Father Thurston, and the Benedictine Nuns of Stanbrook Abbey.

A large new showroom has been added to our Orchard Street premises for the better service of our clients. Purchasers of church decorations and furnishings are realizing in constantly growing numbers that our goods have nowhere else any equal for beauty, quality and value; and now they will be able to examine in comfort a multitude of varieties of whatever it is they need. We are confident that this extension is to be the scene of a big development in the movement for supplying to churches beautiful and craftsmanlike goods.

A SELECTION *from* BURNS & OATES' CATALOGUES OF PUBLICATIONS

N.B.—NEW BOOKS are marked with an asterisk.

ACTON, LORD.

Lord Acton and His Circle. Edited by Cardinal Gasquet. Large 8vo. With an Engraved Portrait of Lord Acton. 15s. net (postage 6d.).

À KEMPIS, THOMAS.

Of the Imitation of Christ. *Popular Edition*, 6d. net and 1s. (postage 2d.). *Pocket Editions*, 1s. 6d. to 10s. *Presentation Edition*, 3s. 6d. to 15s. *The Seraphic Edition.* Being an entirely new translation from the Latin by Father Thaddeus, O.F.M. Very finely printed in red and black. Cloth, 6s. net; leather, 7s. 6d. net (postage 5d.).

LATIN EDITIONS from 2s. net. FRENCH, SPANISH and ITALIAN EDITIONS also in stock.

Lesser Imitation of Christ, The. By Thomas à Kempis. 2s. 6d.

St Lydwine of Schiedam. By Thomas à Kempis. Translated by Dom Vincent Scully, C.R.L. 3s. net (postage 4d.).

ALLEN, CARDINAL.

Father Edmund Campion and His Companions. A briefe historie of the glorious martyrdom of twelve reverend priests. With contemporary verses by the Venerable Henry Walpole, and the earliest engraving of the martyrdom. Edited by the Rev. J. H. Pollen, S.J. Demy 8vo. 4s. net (postage 5d.).

Souls Departed. Cheaper Edition, with Portrait. 3s. 6d.

ALLIES, T. W. (K.C.S.G.)

*A Journal in France and Letters from Italy (1845–1849). By T. W. Allies. Cr. 8vo. 6s.

A Life's Decision. Cr. 8vo. 5s.

The Formation of Christendom Library. New Editions. Cr. 8vo.
The Christian Faith and the Individual. 5s.
The Christian Faith and Society. 5s.
The Christian Faith and Philosophy. 5s.
As seen in Church and State. 5s.
The Throne of the Fisherman. 5s.
The Holy See and the Wandering of the Nations. Demy 8vo. 10s. 6d.
Peter's Rock in Mohammed's Flood. Demy 8vo. 10s. 6d.

ALLIES, MARY.

Thomas William Allies, 1813-1903. With Portraits and other Illustrations. 3s. 6d. net (postage 5d.).

ALLIES, MARY—*continued*.

Pius the Seventh, 1800-1823. Cr. 8vo, cloth, gilt. 5s.

Leaves from St Augustine. 6s. net (postage 5d.).

Leaves from St John Chrysostom. 6s.

History of the Church in England, from the Accession of Henry VIII to the Death of Queen Elizabeth. 3s. 6d.

How to Help the Dead. A translation of the De cur gerenda pro mortuis of St. Augustine. Cloth, gilt, with frontispiece in photogravure. 1s. net (postage, 2d).

ANDERDON, BLANCHE (Whyte Avis).

The Catholic Girl in the World. *First Series*. 2s. 6d. net (postage 4d.).

The Catholic Girl in the World. *Second Series*. 2s. 6d. net (postage 4d.).

ANTONY, C. M.

*St. Catherine of Siena : Her Life and Times. One volume demy 8vo. With many illustrations. 6s. net. (postage 6d.).

This vivid sketch on broad outlines is designed to present the life of the great mystic and politician in such a way that no one aspect of her career obscures another. The wonderful romance of that career has never been so movingly presented as in this notable work.—*Prospectus, etc., on application.*

*AUNT SARAH AND THE WAR. A Tale of Transforma-tions. Wrappers, 1s. net. (postage 2d.). Fortieth Thousand

Its depth of feeling should make every reader proud and grateful.—*Pall Mall Gazette.*

BAKER, VEN. FATHER AUGUSTINE (O.S.B.)

Holy Wisdom (*Sancta Sophia*). Directions for the Prayer of Contemplation, etc. Edited by Abbot Sweeney, D.D. Cloth 3s. 6d. With leather back, 5s.

BAKER, B. ANSTICE.

A Modern Pilgrim's Progress. With important contributions by way of Preface and Introduction by Mgr R. H. Benson and Father Sebastian Bowden of the Oratory. New popular edition, 1s. net. Postage 4d.

BARRY, CANON WILLIAM.

*The Knights of the Red Cross. A Sermon preached at a Requiem for fallen Catholic soldiers. Demy 8vo. Well printed and wrappered. With frontispiece. 3d. net (postage 1d.).

4

CATALOGUES OF PUBLICATIONS

BEARNE, FATHER (S.J.)

The Curé's Brother: A Laumant Story. 1s. 6d.

Nick Roby: A Story of his Childhood. 1s. 6d. and 2s.

Charlie Chittywick: or, Ridingdale in the 'Sixties. 3s. 6d.

Ridingdale Boys. Illustrated, 5s. net. Boards, 2 vols, 4s. net (postage 5d.).

A Ridingdale Year. Illustrated. Cloth, gilt, 5s. net (postage 5d.).

Ridingdale Stories. Illustrated. 3s. 6d. net (postage 5d.).

Sanctity's Romance. 2 vols, 2s. net each (postage 5d.).

The Golden Stair: A Chronicle of Havenhurst. 3s. 6d.

Portraits. Stories for Old and Young. Wrapper, 6d. net, 1s. 6d. net (postage 3d.).

The Organist of Laumont. 2s. net (postage 3d.).

Jack South and some other Jacks. 3s. 6d.

Roddy the Dreamer. 5s. net (postage 5d.).

Romance of the Silver Shoon. 3s. net (postage 5d.).

BENSON, MGR R. H.

*Poems. In one volume, with a portrait in photogravure. Attractively bound in cloth, with seventeenth-century design in gold. 2s. 6d. net (postage 2d.). **Third Impression.**

Very beautiful, tender, and of deep devotional impulse.—*Daily Chronicle.*
He must be reckoned of the line of Herbert and Vaughan, and Donne and Crashaw. —*Sunday Times.*

*Memorials of R. H. Benson. By Blanche Warre-Cornish, Shane Leslie, and others of his friends. With a portrait-miniature exquisitely reproduced in colours, and nine mounted plates of great interest. Uniform with the " Poems." 2s. 6d. net (postage 3d.). **Second Impression.**

Loneliness. Mgr Benson's last novel. 6s.

Oddsfish ! A Tale of the times of Charles II. 6s.

Come Rack ! Come Rope ! 6s. *Cheap edition,* 1s. net. (postage 3d.).

An Average Man. A Story of Conversions. 6s.

Initiation. 6s.

The Religion of the Plain Man. 2s. 6d. net (postage 4d.).

An Alphabet of Saints. Rhymed by Mgr Robert Hugh Benson, Reginald Balfour, C. Ritchie. Illustrated by L. D. Symington. Fancy binding, 2s. 6d. net. Paper, 1s. net (postage 3d.).

The King's Achievement. A Tale of the Suppression of the Monasteries by Henry VIII. 6s.

By what Authority? A Tale of the Times of Queen Elizabeth. 6s.

The Light Invisible. The Life-Stories of an Old Priest. 3s. 6d.

5

BIBLES, NEW TESTAMENTS, etc.

> *N.B.—New Illustrated List giving full particulars of Bindings, etc., sent post free on application.*

Holy Bible. POCKET EDITION (size 5¼ by 3¼ inches). Cloth, 2s. 6d. Leather bindings, from 4s. 6d. to 7s. 6d. each. OCTAVO EDITION (size 9 by 6 inches). Cloth, 5s. And in a great variety of leather bindings, from 8s. to 35s. net.

New Testament, The. POCKET EDITION. Limp cloth, 6d. net (postage 2d.). Grained roan, red edges, 1s. Roan, gilt edges, 1s. 6d.

India Paper Edition: Paste grain, round corners, 3s. 6d. net. Best calf or morocco, 5s. 6d. each net. Russia limp, 10s. 6d. net.

LARGE TYPE EDITION. With Annotations, References, Historical and Chronological Index, and a Family Register, Cr. 8vo (size 7½ by 5 inches). 500 pp. Cloth, boards, gilt lettered, 2s.; and in handsome leather bindings at 4s. 6d. and 8s. 6d.

The "Prize" New Testament. An impression especially prepared for Presentation purposes. Finely printed in large type on Oxford India Paper. Buckram, gilt, 3s. 6d. net. Roan, gilt, red under gold edges, 5s. 6d. net. Finest morocco, gilt, red under gold edges, 7s. 6d. net (postage 4d.).

In this impression the purpose has not been to compress the text into the smallest conceivable space but, on the contrary, to provide a library volume printed in large clear type and with generous margins.

Novum Testamentum. From 2s., unbound, to 4s., bound.

Book of Psalms, The. 32mo, cloth, 1s. 6d. Calf, red edges, 5s.

Liber Psalmorum. Unbound 1s. net. Bound from 2s. 6d.

BOWDEN, REV. H. S. (of the Oratory).

*Crumbs of Comfort. Edited from "The Dialogue of Comfort of B. Thomas More," by H. S. Bowden, of the Oratory. With a Preface. Cloth, 1s. 6d. net (postage 2d.).

The Religion of Shakespeare. Chiefly from the Writings of Mr Richard Simpson. Cr. 8vo. 7s. 6d.

Dante's Divina Commedia: Its Scope and Value. From the German of Franz Hettinger, D.D. 8vo. 10s. 6d.

Natural Religion. Being Vol. I of Dr Hettinger's "Evidences of Christianity." With Introduction on "Certainty." 7s. 6d.

Revealed Religion. The Second Volume of Dr Hettinger's "Evidences." With Introduction on the "Assent of Faith." 5s.

BOWDEN, REV. H. S. (of the Oratory)—*continued.*

Miniature Lives of the Saints, for every Day in the Year. 2 Vols. 18mo, cloth, gilt, 767 pp., 4s. Also in Monthly packets of Single Leaves for distribution, 4d. per Packet. Or the Complete Set of Packets for the Year, 3s. 6d.

Mementoes of the English Martyrs. For every day of the year. 1s. net (postage 2d.).

Miniature Life of Mary. Cloth, 6d. Cloth extra, with steel plate frontispiece, 1s.

Guide to the London Oratory. Illustrated, 1s. Or with fewer illustrations, 6d.

BRIDGETT, FATHER (C.SS.R.)

A History of the Holy Eucharist in Great Britain. Edited with Notes by Father H. Thurston, S.J. Folio. Illustrated. One Guinea net (postage 10d.).

Life and Writings of Blessed Thomas More. 6s.

Life of the Blessed John Fisher. New Edition. 6s.

Our Lady's Dowry. Illustrated. 5s.

Ritual of the New Testament. 5s.

Wisdom and Wit of Sir Thomas More. Edited, with Introduction, by Rev. T. E. Bridgett, C.SS.R. 6s.

BUCKLER, REV. REGINALD (O.P.)

A Spiritual Retreat. 3s. 6d. net (postage 5d.).

Spiritual Instruction on Religious Life. 3s. 6d. net (postage 5d.).

Spiritual Perfection through Charity. 5s.

*BURIAL SERVICE, THE. The complete Latin and English of the Order of Burying Adults and Infants ; together with the Mass for the Dead in full, with the various propers. Well printed in large type. This is the only edition in conformity with the 1915 Ordo Administrandi Sacramenta. Stout wrappers, 3d. net. ; cloth, gilt, 6d. net (postage 1d.).

BUTE, THE MARQUESS OF (FROM THE BREVIARY OF).

A Form of Prayers following the Church Office. For the use of Catholics unable to hear Mass upon Sundays and Holidays. Cloth, 1s. net (postage 2d.) ; leather, 2s. 6d. net (postage 3d.).

Lenten Readings. From the Writings of the Fathers and Doctors of the Church as found in the Roman Breviary. Done into English by John Patrick, Marquess of Bute, and arranged by Father John Mary, O.S.F.C. 2s. 6d.

Mary Immaculate. From the same sources. Cloth, 1s. net (postage 2d.) Leather, 2s. 6d. net (postage 3d.).

BUTLER, REV. ALBAN.

> **People's Edition of the Lives of the Saints.** Twelve Pocket Volumes, each Volume containing the Saints of the Month, and an Additional Volume containing a Complete General Index. Neat cloth binding, gilt lettered, 1s. 6d. each. Or the complete set of 13 volumes, in handsome cloth case, to match, £1.

BUTLER, LIEUT.-GENERAL SIR WILLIAM (G.C.B.)

> **The Wild North Land.** The Story of a Winter's Journey with Dogs across Northern North America. Illustrated. 5s.
>
> **The Great Lone Land.** An Account of the Red River Expeditions 1869-1870. With 15 Illustrations and a Map. 5s.
>
> **Red Cloud.** A Tale of the Great Prairie. 3s. 6d.
>> A new edition, with Portrait and Memoir of the Author, and new illustrations.

BUTT, BISHOP.

> *The Marriage Rite: the English and Latin Texts of the Order of Marriage, the Nuptial Mass, and the new Blessing without the Mass. With an Instruction on the significance of the Sacrament by Bishop Butt. Printed throughout in red and black, and wrappered in parchment, gilt, 6d. net (postage 1d.).

CABROL, ABBOT FERNAND (O.S.B.)

> *The Layfolk's Ritual, with notes by (see page 31).
>
> *The Day Hours of the Church, with Introduction by (see p. 31).

CAMM, DOM BEDE (O.S.B.)

> **Tyburn Conferences:** Oxford, Douay, Tyburn. Conferences on the Martyrs of the English Seminaries. 2s. 6d. net (postage 3d.).
>
> **The Voyage of the " Pax."** An Allegory. Cloth, gilt, Illustrated. 2s. 6d. net (postage 4d.).
>
> **In the Brave Days of Old.** Historical Sketches of the Elizabethan Persecution. New Edition. Cr. 8vo. 2s. 6d.
>
> **Lives of the Blessed English Martyrs.** Edited by Dom Bede Camm, O.S.B. Vol. 1.—"The Martyrs under Henry VIII." Cr. 8vo. 7s. 6d. net (postage 5d.). Vol. II—"The Martyrs under Queen Elizabeth." 7s. 6d. net (postage 6d.).

CAPES, F. M.

> **St Catherine de Ricci.** Her Life, her Letters, her Community. With a Treatise on the Mystical Life by Fr Bertrand Wilberforce, O.P. With Portrait and other Illustrations. 8vo. 7s. 6d. net (postage 6d.).

CARMICHAEL, MONTGOMERY.

The Solitaries of the Sambuca. Cloth, gilt, with 3 illustrations. 5s. net (postage 5d.).

The striking story of an English gentleman of wealth and culture who decides to go into complete solitude, like the Fathers of the desert. It is deeply suggestive in ts handling of that most fascinating subject, the solitary life.

In Tuscany. New Edition, with numerous Illustrations. Large Cr. 8vo. 6s. net (postage 5d.).

John William Walshe. The Story of a Hidden Life. 5s. net (postage 5d.).

The Lady Poverty. A Thirteenth-Century Allegory. Translated by Montgomery Carmichael. 3s. 6d. net (postage 2d.).

CATECHISMS.

Catechism of Christian Doctrine. With Prayers, Hymns, and other Aids to Devotion, and four Holy Pictures printed on special paper. 100 pp. Stiff wrapper, 1d. Per 100, 5s. net (postage 10d.).

Catechism for Infants and Standard I. ½d.

Children's Companion to Bible History and Explanatory Catechism. Wrapper, 96 pp. 2d.

Explanatory Catechism of Christian Doctrine. With an Appendix. 32mo, wrapper, 96 pp. 2d.

Little Catechism: or, Short Abridgment of the Catechism of Christian Doctrine. Wrapper, ½d. Per 100, 3s. (postage 3d.).

Little Catechism Explained. By Rev. Bernard Kelly. 2d.

Meanings of the Words of the Catechism, to which are added the Miracles of the Gospels. 32mo, wrapper. 2d.

Bible History for School and Home Use. Wrapper. 2d.

CATHOLIC BELIEF: or, A Short and Simple Exposition of Catholic Doctrine. By Very Rev. Joseph Faà di Bruno, D.D. Wrapper, 6d. net (postage 2½d.); cloth, boards, 10d. (postage 2½d.). Better paper edition, cloth, 2s.

***CATHOLIC DIRECTORY,** The Official Ecclesiastical Register, and Almanac (Annual). Over 1000 pages. Prices: Directory, 1s. 6d. net; Directory and Ordo, 2s. net (postage on either, Inland 6d., Foreign 10d.).

***CATHOLIC WHO'S WHO** (Annual). Over 4,000 brief Biographies of Catholics of importance, together with their Addresses; also an important Year-Book section and an Approved List of Catholic Convents, Colleges and Schools. Cloth, gilt, 3s. 6d. net (postage 5d.).

CECILIA, MADAME (of St Andrew's Convent, Streatham).

From the Sepulchre to the Throne. 426 pages. Bound in

CECILIA, MADAME (of St Andrew's Convent)—*continued.*

    art canvas, gilt, with six plates in lithographic offset. 5s. net (postage 5d.).

The Training of Girls in their Teens. 1s. net (postage 2d.).

Girls' Clubs and Mothers' Meetings. 1s. 6d. net (postage 2d.).

Home Truths for Mary's Children. 3s. 6d.

More Home Truths for Mary's Children. 3s. 6d.

CHALLONER, BISHOP.

    *Meditations for every Day in the Year. An entirely new edition of pocket size. About 960 pages, printed on toned Oxford India paper in the original " Fell " type; with many full-page engravings. Cloth, 3s. 6d. net; French morocco, in case, 5s. net ; finest Turkey morocco, gilt edges, gold roll, in case, 10s. 6d. net (postage 3d.).

    This remarkably attractive edition of Bishop Challoner's masterpiece measures 6 by 3¾ by ¾ inches, and weighs 8½ ozs., against the 7½ by 5 by 1 inches, with a weight of 19 ozs., of the edition it supersedes, and withal **the type is much larger and clearer,** and is one of the beautiful seventeenth-century "Fell" series of the Oxford University Press.

" By far the most valuable and useful body of practical divinity in our language," wrote Bishop Milner of this work.

    *The Garden of the Soul. A faithful re-issue of Bishop Challoner's original edition. Printed throughout in red and black in a large type. Cloth, 1s. 6d. net, and in fine leather bindings at from 2s. 6d. net to 30s. net (postage 3d.).

Modern prayer-books called " The Garden of the Soul " have but little in common with Bishop Challoner's beautiful original, which is here made available for the first time in over one hundred years. It is designed to be a brief guide to the spiritual life, containing not prayers only, but information, instruction, meditation, and much practical advice.

The format of this red-and-black edition is very fine indeed, and the type is larger than that of any other " Garden of the Soul."

    *Penny Meditations Series. Messrs. Burns & Oates have just issued a very attractive series of reprints of Bishop Challoner's meditations in penny booklets, well printed on good paper, strongly wrappered, and of a convenient shape for carriage in the pocket. The price of 1d. each is net, and postage is extra ; but orders of one hundred and over have a preferential price. The following are the titles : Advent, Christmas Week, Passion Week, Holy Week, Mary Immaculate, Our Saviour in Glory, The Holy Ghost, Corpus Christi, Holy Communion, The Eucharistic Sacrifice, Confession, The Lord's Prayer.

CHALLONER, BISHOP—*continued.*

*Exhortations from the old Ordo Administrandi Sacramenta. Uniform with the 1915 Ordo (which does not contain them). Exhortations before and after Baptism, Conversion, Marriage, Communion of the Sick, Extreme Unction, etc. Japon vellum, wrappers, 6d. net (postage 1d.).

CHASLE, ABBÉ LOUIS.

Sister Mary of the Divine Heart (Droste zu Vischering), Religious of the Good Shepherd, 1863-1899. Illustrated. 6s.

CHESTERTON, G. K.

*Poems. Buckram, gilt, with portrait in photogravure. 5s. net (postage 4d.).

It is genius.—*Daily News.* An almost miraculous skill.—*Everyman.* A level of unwonted beauty and fine expression.—*Manchester Guardian.*

CHILDREN'S HOUR (THE): An anthology for children, of poems by Father Tabb, Francis Thompson, Katharine Tynan, etc.; together with a Talk (with Tales and Texts) by Father Vincent McNabb, O.P., and illustrations on nearly every page by L. D. Symington. Printed in red and black. Japon vellum and gold, 1s. net (postage 2d.).

CHURCH AND KINDNESS TO ANIMALS, THE.

Illustrated. 2s. 6d.

CLARE, FATHER, (S.J.)

A Voice that is Still: the Sayings of Fr Clare. 48mo. Leather, gilt edges, 2s.

CONVERSION AND A VOCATION, A. Sister Mary of the Sacred Heart. (Sophia Ryder.) 2s. 6d.

COOPER, ERIC T.

Soliloquies of a Subaltern Somewhere in France. Wrappers. 1s. net (postage 1d.).

A book or verses, written for the most part in the very trenches.

CUTHBERT, FATHER (O.S.F.C.)

A Tuscan Penitent. Being the life and legend of St Margaret of Cortona. With Illustrations. 4s. 6d. net (postage 5d.).

DAHLMANN, FATHER.

Outline Conferences for Children of Mary. With a Preface by Madame Cecilia (of Streatham). 2s. 6d.

DALGAIRNS, FATHER BERNARD, of the Oratory.

The Holy Communion : Its Philosophy and Practice. A new, well printed and well bound edition. In two volumes. Crown 8vo. Price 7s. net (postage 6d.).

Devotion to the Heart of Jesus. A new, well printed and well-bound edition. 3s. net (postage 5d.).

DE MONTFORT, BLESSED GRIGNON.
    Treatise on the True Devotion to the Blessed Virgin Mary. Father Faber's Translation. 12th revised edition. 2s.

DE SEGUR, MGR.
    Familiar Instructions and Evening Lectures on all the Truths of Religion. 2 vols. 3s. each.

DIGNAM, FATHER (S.J.)   *See also under Miss Taylor.*
    A Daily Thought from the Writings of Father Dignam, S.J. 48mo, bound in maroon leather, gilt edges. 2s.

EGGER, REV. JOSEPH (S.J.)
    The Devout Guide for Catholics in Service. Wrapper, 6d. net. Cloth, 1s. net. (postage 1d.)
    Meditations on the Sacred Heart. 2s. 6d.
    Consolations of the Sick-Room. Wrapper, 3d. net (postage 1d.).

EMMERICH, SISTER ANNE CATHERINE.
    Dolorous Passion of Our Lord Jesus Christ. With a Preface, and a Life of Anne Catherine Emmerich. 20th Edition. 3s. 6d.

*EPISTLES AND GOSPELS : the Pulpit Edition. Demy 8vo, printed in large Fell type. Cloth, 3s. 6d. net (postage 5d.). Also in roan at 7s. 6d. net, and morocco at 10s. 6d. net.

This is the only edition of the Epistles and Gospels (in the Douay version authorised for public use) fitly designed for the single purpose of pulpit use. Its type is nearly twice as big as that of any other edition, and turning overleaf in the middle of an epistle or gospel has been largely avoided.

*EXCERPTA e libro cui titulus Ordo Administrandi Sacramenta in usum cleri extra loca sancta ministrantis. Published by command of H.E. Cardinal Bourne. Printed in red and black, and of a convenient vest-pocket size. Cloth, 1s. 6d. net ; French morocco, 2s. net ; finest Turkey morocco, 4s. 6d. net (postage 1d.).

FABER, FATHER.
Centenary Re-issue of the Works of Father Faber. In 12 uniform volumes. Cr. 8vo, on good paper, strongly and handsomely bound in cloth, gilt. 2s. 6d. net each (postage 5d.). The volumes are sold singly.

    All for Jesus, or, The Easy Ways of Divine Love.

A book written for " peopl. living in the world and trying to be good there."

    Bethlehem.

Father Faber used to say that he had written the rest of his works to please others, but this (his masterpiece on the Incarnation) to please himself.

    Growth in Holiness, or, The Progress of the Spiritual Life.

Father Faber's *magnum opus* on conduct.

    Hymns. Complete Edition.

CATALOGUES OF PUBLICATIONS

FABER, FATHER—*continued.*

Notes on Doctrinal and Spiritual Subjects. Two vols.

The purpose of this collection was to create a storehouse of suggestions, thoughts and frameworks for sermons during retreats and parochial sermons.

Spiritual Conferences.

Delivered during Advents, Lents, and months of Mary at the London Oratory.

The Blessed Sacrament, or The Works and Ways of God.
The Creator and the Creature, or, The Wonders of Divine Love.
The Foot of the Cross, or, The Sorrows of Mary.
The Precious Blood, or, The Price of our Salvation.
The Life and Letters of Frederick William Faber, D.D., By Rev. John E. Bowden, of the Oratory.

Tales of the Angels. Containing (1) "The Last Children," "Philip, or the Pains of Children," (2) "The Weeping Angel" and (3) "The Child to Whom Nobody was Kind." Profusely illustrated by L. D. Symington. Cloth, extra gilt, 3s. 6d. Or the three parts can be had separately in wrappers, with all the illustrations, price 1s. net each (postage 2d.).
Devotion to the Holy Ghost. Wrapper, 3d. net. Cloth, 6d. net (postage 1d.).
Father Faber's May Book. 18mo, cloth, gilt edges. 2s.
Ethel's Book: or, Tales of the Angels. Cloth, gilt, 2s. 6d.
The Easiness of Salvation. 1s.
The Spirit of Father Faber : Selections from his writings. With an Introduction by Wilfrid Meynell, and a portrait in photogravure. Cloth, 1s. 6d. net ; limp leather, 3s. net (postage 2d.).

FIDELIS, MOTHER MARY.

Growth in the Knowledge of Our Lord. Meditations for every Day of the Year. Adapted from the Original of the Abbé de Brandt. In Three Volumes. 21s. net (postage 6d.).
In Holiest Troth: The Story of St Encratida, one of the Martyrs of Saragossa, A.D. 304. 2s. 6d.

FULLERTON, LADY GEORGIANA.

Ellen Middleton. New and Cheap Edition. 2s. 6d.
Faithful and True. Cloth, 1s.
Grantley Manor. A Novel. Cloth, gilt extra. 3s. 6d.
Laurentia. A Tale of the Jesuit Missions in Japan. 2s. 6d.
Life of Mère Marie de la Providence, 2s. net (postage 4d.).
Life of St Frances of Rome. 2s.
Seven Stories. 2s. 6d.
The Strawcutter's Daughter, and The Portrait in My Uncle's Dining-Room. 2s. 6d.

13

FUNK, DR. F. X.

The History of the Church. Translated by Dr. Perceballi, and edited, with additional notes, by Father W. H. Kent, O.S.C. Handsomely printed and bound, two large volumes, with Tables and Appendices. 15s. net the set (postage 6d.).

GALLERY, DAVID (S.J.)

The Life of Mother Mary of Jesus, Foundress of the Society of Marie Réparatrice. Translated from the French of Father P. Suau, S.J. With three portraits. Cloth, gilt, 6s. net (postage 5d.).

GALLWEY (S.J.), FATHER.

The Watches of the Sacred Passion. Two vols. 8s. net (postage 7d.).

GARDNER, MONICA M.

*Poland : A Study in National Idealism. By the author of " Adam Mickiewicz." Cr. 8vo. 3s. 6d. net (postage 4d.).

The purpose of this important volume is to interpret the soul of Poland to English readers. It is illustrated with copious translations, many of them hitherto inaccessible, from Polish literature; but its purpose is less literary criticism than the study of the national mysticism and idealism.

GASQUET, CARDINAL (O.S.B.)

Lord Acton and his Circle. Edited, with Notes, by Cardinal Gasquet. With portrait. 15s. net (postage 6d.).
Leaves from my Diary, 1894-1896. 2s. 6d. net (postage 2d.).
The Order of the Visitation. Illustrated. 2s.

GAVIN, M. (S.J.)

Memoirs of Father Peter Gallwey, S.J. Cloth, gilt, with Frontispiece. 3s. 6d. net (postage 5d.).
The Sacrifice of the Mass. 2s.

GAY, MGR CHARLES.

The Religious Life and the Vows. 5s.

GIBERGUES, MGR DE.

Faith. Translated from the French of the Bishop of Valence. Cloth, gilt, with Frontispiece. 2s. 6d. net (postage 3d.).
Holy Communion. A Book of Counsel, Exhortation and Instruction. Cloth, gilt, with Frontispiece. 2s. 6d. net (postage 4d.).

GIBSON, REV. HENRY.

Catechism made Easy: being a Familiar Explanation of th Catechism of Christian Doctrine. 5s.

CATALOGUES OF PUBLICATIONS

GRANVILLE POPULAR LIBRARY of Entertaining, Instructive, and Amusing Books. All handsomely bound in cloth, extra, and suitable for Prizes. Over two hundred volumes, from 1s. to 3s. 6d. A complete list sent post free on application.

One Hundred Books selected from this Library, to the value of £8—viz. 42 books at 1s., 24 at 1s. 6d., 16 at 2s., 8 at 2s. 6d., and 10 at 3s. each—will be sent, carriage paid, to any part of the United Kingdom on receipt of £5 5s. net cash.

GRANVILLE SERIES of Reading Books, History Readers, Poetry Books, etc. *List on application.*

HALL, H. E.
The Shadow of Peter. With a Preface by Cardinal Gasquet. Cloth, 2s. net (postage 3d.). Second Impression.

HEDLEY, BISHOP.
A Bishop and his Flock. Cr. 8vo, cloth gilt, gilt top. 6s.
Light of Life, The. Set forth in Sermons. 6s.
The Christian Inheritance. 6s.
Our Divine Saviour. 6s.
A Retreat. For the Use of the Clergy, Religious, and Others. In handsome binding, with leather back. 6s.

*HOLY WEEK BOOK. A new (1915) and complete edition, embodying all the Reforms of the Offices. All the Latin as well as all the English. Most convenient and simplest arrangement. Fewer cross-references in the Psalms than in any other edition. Finely printed from large type, on thin but opaque paper. Cloth, 1s. net; limp leather, gilt or red edges, 2s. 6d. net (postage 2d.).

HOLY WEEK BOOK, according to the Dominican Rite. 1s. 6d. net (postage 3d.).

HYMN BOOKS.
The Hymn Book. The only Collection authorized by the Catholic Hierarchy, in the order prescribed by the Bishops' Committee. Wrappers, 2d. net; limp cloth, 4d., cloth boards, 8d., limp lambskin, 1s.

INNES-BROWNE, MRS.
Honour without Renown. A Story. 3s. 6d.

JESSOPP, AUGUSTUS.
One Generation of a Norfolk House. The Story of the Life and Death of Father Walpole, martyred in 1595. Cloth, 7s. 6d. net (postage 5d.).

KEENAN, REV. STEPHEN.
  Controversial Catechism. 2s.

KENNEDY, M. M.
  *Thirty-one Days with Our Lady.** With seven illustrations
    by Ciceley Butt. Cloth, 2s. 6d. net (postage 4d.).
  The story of Our Lady's life told in simple language for little children. Each
  chapter is designed to make a sufficient reading for one day of Our Lady's month.
  The Holy Child seen by His Saints. The Legends retold to
    children. With full page illustrations by L. D. Syming-
    ton. Cloth, 2s. net (postage 4d.).

LANDRIOT, ARCHBISHOP.
  The Valiant Woman. A Series of Discourses intended for the
    use of Women living in the World. *A new edition, attrac-
    tively printed.* Cloth, 2s. net. (postage 3d.).

LASSERRE, HENRI.
  Our Lady of Lourdes. The History of the Miraculous Sanctu-
    ary of our Lady of Lourdes. 3s. 6d.

LECHNER, DOM PETER.
  Life and Times of St Benedict, Patriarch of the Monks of
    the West. Illustrated. 5s.

LE MASSON, DOM INNOCENT.
  Spiritual Reading for Every Day in the Year. Translated by
    Rev. K. D. Best, of the Oratory. Popular Edition. Cloth.
    1s. net (postage 3d.). Large type edition. Cloth, 2s. net
    (postage 5d.).

LITTLE BREVIARY OF THE SACRED HEART OF JESUS.
    From the Life and Works of the Blessed Margaret Mary.
    1s. 6d.

LOUGHLIN, JOHN.
  The Server's Manual. 1s. net (postage 2d.).

LOYOLA, MOTHER MARY (of the Bar Convent, York). Edited
    by Rev. H. Thurston, S.J.
  *The Little Children's Prayer Book.** Entirely new (1915)
    edition. With many fine illustrations, including a
    series of the Mass, by Dom Bernard (of Caldey Abbey)
    and L. D. Symington. Stiff boards, 6d. net. Cloth, 1s.
    net. Cloth, extra gilt, 1s. 6d. net. Leather, 2s. 6d. net,
    and in a special white presentation binding for First
    Communion, 3s. 6d. net (postage 1d. and 2d.).

LOYOLA, MOTHER MARY—*continued*.

Heavenwards. A chapter for every week in the year. Cloth, 3s. 6d. net (postage 5d.).

Home for Good : Talks to girls for the difficult time of their leaving school. With Frontispiece. 3s. 6d. net (postage 5d.).

Jesus of Nazareth. The Story of His Life. Written for Children. With 24 full-page illustrations. 5s. net (postage 5d.).

Welcome. Holy Communion before and after. Small cr. 8vo, cloth, 3s. 6d. net. Prayer-book size edition, handsomely bound in leather, 5s. net (postage 4d.).

First Communion. A Book of Preparation for First Communion. With numerous illustrations. 3s. 6d.

The Children's Charter: Being "Talks to Parents and Teachers on preparing Children for their First Communion." Cloth, 2s. net (postage 2d.).

The Child of God : or, What comes of our Baptism. With five full-page illustrations. Boards, 2s. 6d. Cloth, gilt, 3s. 6d.

The Soldier of Christ : or Talks before Confirmation. Illustrated. Cr. 8vo, cloth, 5s.

Confession and Communion. Intended for the use of Religious and those who communicate frequently. 1s. 6d.

MADONNA OF THE POETS, THE.

An Anthology of only the best Poems written about the Blessed Virgin. With illustrations after favourite Old Masters. Cloth, 1s. 6d. net (postage 3d.).

McNABB, FATHER VINCENT J. (O.P.)

*The Wayside : A Priest's Gleanings. 3s. 6d. net (postage 4d.). An attractive book of essays, sketches, etc.

Our Reasonable Service. A new volume of Essays. 3s. 6d.

The Decrees of the Vatican Council. 8vo. 2s.

Where Believers May Doubt. 3s. 6d.

MANNING, CARDINAL.

Confidence in God. 32mo. 1s.

Life of the Blessed Curé d'Ars. Wrapper, 1s. net. Cloth, 2s. 6d. net (postage 3d.).

Miscellanies. First and Second Series in one vol. 7s. 6d.

Pastime Papers. 2s. 6d. net and 1s. net (postage 3d.).

Sermons on Ecclesiastical Subjects. 6s.

Sin and its Consequences. 4s.

The Eternal Priesthood. 3s. 6d.

The Four Great Evils of the Day. 2s. 6d.

The Fourfold Sovereignty of God. 2s. 6d.

MANNING, CARDINAL—*continued.*

The Glories of the Sacred Heart. 4s.

The Grounds of Faith. 1s. 6d.

The Holy Ghost the Sanctifier. 32mo. 2s.

The Independence of the Holy See. 2s. 6d.

The Internal Mission of the Holy Ghost. 5s.

The Love of Jesus to Penitents. 32mo. 1s.

The Temporal Mission of the Holy Ghost. 5s.

The True Story of the Vatican Council. 2s. 6d.

The Workings of the Holy Spirit in the Church of England.
1s. 6d.

Why I became a Catholic (Religio Viatoris). 1s.

MARTINDALE, FATHER C. C. (S.J.)

*The Goddess of Ghosts. Cr. 8vo, finely printed. 3s. 6d.
net (postage 4d.).

These stories are alight and alive with the brightness of the author's own heart
and mind. The title-story is a perfect and poignant piece of writing.—*Pall Mall
Gazette.*

Father Martindale's genius . . . not promises but fulfilment ; not blossom, but
fruit.—*The Month.*

MATHESON, ANNIE. Collected by.

Sayings from the Saints. Leather, 3s. 6d. net (postage 4d.).

MEISTERMANN, FATHER BARNABAS (O.F.M.)

New Guide to the Holy Land. With 25 coloured maps and 110
plans of towns and monuments. Translated from the
French Edition by the order and sanction of the Most Rev.
Father Custodian of the Holy Land. With a Preface by
the Bishop of Salford. 7s. 6d. net (postage 5d.).

MERCIER, CARDINAL.

*Pastoral Letter : "Patriotism and Endurance" (Christmas,
1914). The official translation, of which over one hundred
thousand copies have been sold. Pamphlet edition, 2d.
net. Japon vellum, boards, 1s. net (postage 1d.). An
edition in French, 2d. net.

Modernism. Translated by M. Lindsay. 2s. net (postage 3d.).

MEYNELL, ALICE.

Collected Poems. With a portrait in photogravure Buckram,
gilt, 5s. net (postage 5d.).

Collected Essays. With a frontispiece in photogravure.
Uniform with the author's "Collected Poems." Buckram,
5s. net (postage 5d.).

The Shepherdess and other Poems. In *"The Hound of
Heaven" Series.* Japon wrapper, with a portrait, 1s. net.
Limp leather, 3s. net (postage 1d.).

MEYNELL, ALICE—*continued.*

The Madonna: A Pictorial Record of the Life and Death of the Mother of our Lord Jesus Christ, by the Painters and Sculptors of Christendom, reproduced from more than 500 of their Works. Translated from the Italian of Adolfo Venturi, with an introduction by Alice Meynell. Medium 4to. 15s. net (postage 9d.).

MEYNELL, EVERARD.

*The Life of Francis Thompson. New (1916) edition, uniform with Thompson's " Works." Buckram, gilt, 6s. net (postage 5d.).

MEYNELL, WILFRID.

Cardinal Newman. New and Revised Edition. With 15 Illustrations. 2s. 6d.

Cardinal Bourne. A Record of the Sayings and Doings of Francis, Fourth Archbishop of Westminster. Compiled by Wilfrid Meynell. With many hitherto unpublished portraits. Wrappers, 1s. net. Cloth gilt, 2s. 6d. net (postage 3d.).

MONNIN, L'ABBÉ.

The Spirit of the Curé of Ars. Translated from the French. With 17 additional Exhortations. New Edition. 2s.

MULHOLLAND, FLORENCE M.

Princess Melody and other Stories. Illustrated by L. D. Symington. Sm. 4to. Cloth, extra gilt, 2s. 6d. net (postage 5d.).

MULHOLLAND, ROSA (LADY GILBERT).

The Story of Ellen. With Illustrations. 5s.
The Squire's Grand-daughters. A Novel. 5s.
The Wicked Woods. A Novel. 5s.
The Wild Birds of Killeevy. A Novel. 3s. 6d.

NEWMAN, CARDINAL.

The Spirit of Cardinal Newman : Selections from his writings. With a Preface by Father C. C. Martindale, S.J., and a portrat in photogravure. Cloth, 1s. 6d. net. Leather, 3s. net (postage 2d.).

Loss and Gain: A Story of Oxford Life and a Conversion. Wrapper, 6d. net. Limp cloth, 1s. net (postage 3d.). Illustrated Edition, on superfine paper, cloth, gilt edges, 3s. 6d.

Callista: A Sketch of the Third Century. Crown 8vo, wrapper, 6d. net. Limp cloth, 1s. net (postage 3d.). Illustrated Edition, printed on superfine paper. Cloth, extra gilt, gilt edges, 3s. 6d.

NIEUWBARN, REV. FATHER (O.P.)
   The Holy Sacrifice. A mystical and liturgical explanation
   of its meaning. With illustrations, 2s.

NOYES, ALFRED.
   The Carol of the Fir Tree. Printed in red and black, with
   frontispiece in photogravure. Japon vellum, 1s. net.
   Velvet calf, 3s. net (postage 1d.).

O'BRIEN, MRS WILLIAM.
   Rosette: A Tale of Paris and Dublin. 3s. 6d. net (postage
   5d.).

*ORDO ADMINISTRANDI SACRAMENTA. The new edition
   published by order of the Hierarchy of England and
   Wales. Finely printed in red and black. Buckram, 5s.
   net. Calf boards, 8s. 6d. net. Finest morocco, 10s. 6d.
   net (postage 5d.).

   This edition has been edited by a committee appointed by the Hierarchy; and the
   publishers, for their part, have spared neither pains nor cost to make it the most
   beautiful liturgical publication of a generation. It is printed from a large "face"
   of the original type imported by Bishop Fell in the seventeenth century for the
   Oxford University Press. The press-work, in red and black, has been done with
   the greatest care; and the paper is that beautiful and durable japon vellum which
   has been so much appreciated in the new Ritus Servandus.

**PRACTICAL MEDITATIONS FOR EVERY DAY IN THE
   YEAR,** of the Life of Our Lord Jesus Christ. By a Father
   of the Society of Jesus. In Two Volumes. 9s.

PRAYER-BOOKS, etc.

   ¶ *The new Illustrated List giving full particulars of Bindings, etc., sent post free on request.*

   ¶ *Owing to the great increase in the costs of production,
   all our prayer books are now strictly net.*

   ¶ *The Ordo Administrandi, Excerpta, Pulpit Epistles and
   Gospels, and the Ritus Servandus are catalogued separately
   under their titles. See pages* 20, 12, 12, *and* 25 *respectively.*

   Catholic Piety. A Popular Manual of Catholic Devotion, containing all the ordinary Prayers and Services of the Church,
   with Epistles and Gospels. 48mo EDITION (size 3⅝ by 2¼
   inches). Leather bindings, from 1s. to 5s. DEMY 32mo
   EDITION (size 4 by 2¼ inches). From 1s. 6d. to 4s. 6d. ROYAL
   32mo EDITION (size 5 by 3¼ inches), without Epistles and
   Gospels. Cloth, 6d. net (postage 2d.) Or complete, in six
   different styles, at 1s., 1s. 6d., 2s., 2s. 6d., and 4s. 6d.

   Catholic's Vade Mecum: or, Select Prayers for Daily Use, The.
   (Size 5½ by 3½ inches.) Leather, 3s. 6d. Calf, red edges,
   5s. 6d. German-calf or morocco, limp, 6s. each. German
   calf, padded, 7s., Russia, padded; morocco circuit or with

PRAYER-BOOKS, etc.—*continued*.

    clasp, 8s. 6d. each and in handsome leather bindings, beautifully finished, at 10s. 6d. to 21s. With 6 Photographs, mounted, calf or morocco, 12s., and Russia leather, 15s.

*Day Hours of the Church. The complete text of the Horæ Diurnæ in Latin and English. Printed throughout in red and black on toned Oxford India paper, about 1,000 pages. From 6s. net upwards (postage 5d.). See announcement on p. 31.

This book has been edited, and many of its translations have been made, by the Benedictine Nuns of Stanbrook Abbey. It is in all respects in accord with the latest changes in the Divine Office. There is an explanatory preface by the Editors, which makes easy the proper use of the book for public and private devotion, and an historical introduction by Abbot Fernand Cabrol, O.S.B.

Devotions for Holy Communion. From the Missal, Breviary, Writings of the Fathers, the Hymns of the Church, etc. With the Ordinary of the Mass. Finely printed, 250 pages. Cloth, 3s. 6d. net; leather, 5s. net (postage 4d.). The preface by Alban Goodier, S.J. Second edition.

Devotional Library for Catholic Households. Containing New Testament, Book of Psalms, Imitation of Christ, Devout Life, Spiritual Combat. All neatly bound in cloth, red edges, with cloth case to match. 5s. net (postage 5d.).

Flowers of Devotion: A collection of Favourite Devotions. New (1912) Edition, printed on India paper, containing the Ordinary of the Mass in Large type. Roan, 1s. net. French morocco, 1s. 6d. Polished paste grain, 2s. 6d. German calf, limp, 4s. Polished morocco, limp, 4s. Russian leather, calf-lined, 5s. Polished morocco, silk lined, with pockets for Visiting Cards, etc., 6s.

*Garden of the Soul (The). The only reprint (1916) of Bishop Challoner's original masterpiece. See under author's name, page 10.

Garden of the Soul (The) and **Key of Heaven (The).** New and finely printed uniform editions, containing the Epistles and Gospels, and the Latin and English of the Ordinary of the Mass as well as the devotions proper to each book. ¶ Their small compass, 3 by 4½ inches, and extreme slimness, make them the ideal travelling and pocket Prayer Books. **Ordinary Paper editions,** with red border and collotype frontispiece. Cloth, 6d. net, and in various fine bindings up to 7s. 6d. **India Paper editions,** with red border and collotype frontispiece. Paste grain, 2s. 6d. Calf Boards, 4s. Pol. Persian, 6s. 6d. Calf limp and Morocco limp, 5s. Russia limp, 7s. 6d. Russia padded, silk ends, 10s. 6d.

PRAYER-BOOKS, etc.—*continued.*

Garden of the Soul, The.   Containing all the Popular Devotions, with the Mass, Vespers, Benediction, and Epistles
and Gospels for Sundays and Festivals.

48mo EDITION (size 3⅝ by 2¼ inches).   In strong cloth
binding, 6d., and in handsome leather bindings, with red
line borders, from 1s. to 6s. ; or in Two Volumes, in leather
cases, in various styles, from 3s. net to 10s. 6d. net.

DEMY 32mo EDITION (size 4 by 2¾ inches).   In leather
bindings, from 1s. 6d. to 4s. 6d.

IMPERIAL 32mo EDITION (size 5⅝ by 3½ inches).   Without
Epistles and Gospels, cloth, 6d. net (postage 2d.) ; or
complete in 18 different styles, from 1s. to 10s. 6d.

18mo EDITION, with larger type.   Cloth, 1s., without
Epistles and Gospels; or complete, from 1s. 4d. to 5s. 6d.

Golden Manual, The.   The choicest collection of Prayers,
Public and Private, with Epistles and Gospels (size 5¾ by
3¾ inches), 900 pages.   Paste grain, limp, or French
morocco, stiff, 6s. each.   Rutland roan, 7s.   English calf,
8s. 6d.   German calf, or morocco limp, 8s. 6d. each.
Morocco boards, 8s. 6d.   Also in handsome leather bindings, in a variety of styles, from 10s. 6d. to 30s. net.

Horae Diurnae. Roman. From 4s. 6d. net. **Monastic. 5s. net.**

Key of Heaven, The.   Containing all the Popular Devotions,
Prayers, and Services of the Church, Epistles and Gospels.

48mo EDITION (size 3⅝ by 2¼ inches).   Cloth, 6d. net.
In handsome leather bindings, with red borders, from 1s.
to 6s.

DEMY 32mo EDITION (size 4 by 2¼ inches).   In six different
styles of leather bindings, from 1s. 6d. to 4s. 6d.

ROYAL 32mo EDITION (size 5 by 3¼ inches), without
Epistles and Gospels.   Cloth, 6d. net (postage 2d.)   Or
complete, in various styles, from 1s. to 4s. 6d.

*Little Children's Prayer Book.   *The perfect Prayer Book for
children of all ages.*   By Mother Mary Loyola.   From 6d.
net to 4s. 6d. net.   *See under author's name on p. 16.*

*Manual of Prayers for Congregational Use.   Compiled and
prescribed by the Bishops of England and Wales.   A new
(1916) edition, carefully revised to bring it down to date,
and rearranged for greater convenience.   Vest-pocket
edition (size 3 by 4½ inches).   From 6d. net upwards.   The
new Sanctuary Edition is described below.

*Manual of Prayers for Congregational Use.   Compiled and
prescribed by the Bishops of England and Wales.   A new
(1916) Sanctuary edition.   Demy 8vo (8¾ by 5½ inches),
very finely printed in a large face of the famous Fell Type

PRAYER-BOOKS, etc.—*continued*.

(the exclusive property of the Oxford University Press) on good paper, and strongly bound in canvas, gilt, 5s. net. Also in calf and morocco. Uniform with the Pulpit edition of the Epistles and Gospels (see page 12).

*The Missal. Every year since its first publication in 1911, the Publishers have been obliged to go to press with a large new impression of this most popular book. The 1916 impression has been revised from cover to cover by Dr. Adrian Fortescue, who equips it also with an historical introduction ; and it is the only Missal in entire conformity with the most recent reforms. The only Missal printed throughout in red and black, on the finest India paper. By far the smallest and neatest Missal published. Thickness, when bound, less than ¾-in. The Leather bindings are models of fine workmanship. Cloth, gilt or red edges, 5s. net. Roan, gilt edges, 6s. net. Rutland, red under gold edges, 7s. 6d. net. Calf boards, red edges, 8s. 6d. net. Finest Morocco, limp, handsomely tooled, red under gold edges, 10s. 6d. net. And up to 30s. net. (Postage 4d.) *Copies sent on approval.*

Missals, Latin only. From 4s. 6d. net to 16s. Altar Missals. From 16s. to 5 guineas, with English or other Supplements.

*Office of Our Lady. A new (1915) edition (the Latin text only) of the reformed Office, most attractively printed. French morocco, 1s. net (postage 1d.).

Our Lady of Perpetual Succour. A Manual of Devotion for every Day of the Month. Translated by Rev. T. Livius, C.SS.R. 32mo, cloth, 1s. net. (postage 2d.). Leather bindings at 2s. net, 2s. 6d. net and 4s. 6d. net (postage 2d.).

Our Lady of Perpetual Succour, Manual of. From the Writings of St Alphonsus Liguori. By a Redemptorist Father. 18mo, cloth, 1s. net (postage 2d.). Leather, 2s. net.

Paradise of the Christian Soul, The. A new edition of the Paradisus Animæ. This exquisite work of Devotions, which has gone through many editions in the original Latin, has always been a favourite Prayer Book among Catholics. The Life of Alban Butler, author of the "Lives of the Saints," tells us that he greatly preferred it to other devotional manuals; and Cardinal Manning did not hesitate to describe it as "beautiful almost beyond compare."

PRAYER-BOOKS, etc.—*continued.*

The present fine edition is printed in bold type and upon India paper, with a red border round each page, and in a *format* (5¾ by 3¼ in.) that is both comely and convenient. Cloth, round corners, gilt or red edges—a supple and durable binding, 5s. net. Smooth roan, limp, gilt cross, round corners, gilt or red edges, 6s. net. Rutland, limp, red under gold edges, 7s. 6d. net. English calf, boards, red edges, 8s. 6d. net. Turkey morocco, limp, round corners, red under gold edges, 10s. 6d. net.

Path to Heaven, The. A Revised Edition of the Cheapest and most complete Book of Devotions ever issued. (Size 5⅝ by 3⅞ inches.) Cloth, 2s. and 2s. 6d. Roan, 3s. Paste grain, gilt edges, 4s. French morocco, gilt, with clasp, 4s. 6d. Persian calf, red edges, 4s. 6d. Rutland roan, limp, 6s. English calf, 7s. 6d. Turkey morocco, 7s. 6d. German calf or morocco, limp, 7s. 6d. each ; also soft cushioned, 8s. 6d. each.

Pax Vobiscum. Specially adapted for Sick Persons and Invalids. Large type. Cloth, 2s. 6d. net. Leather, 4s. net (postage 2d.).

Prayers of St Gertrude and St Mechtilde. Cloth, 1s. Leather, 2s. and 4s. 6d. each. With the Exercises of St Gertrude, in one Vol., English calf, 6s. 6d.

Raccolta, The, or Collection of Indulgenced Prayers and Good Works. By Father Ambrose St John. 4s. 6d. net (postage 5d.). In calf or morocco, 8s. 6d. net.

*Ritual, The Layfolk's. Edited by the Benedictines of Farnborough Abbey, with an important series of notes to the different Offices by Abbot Fernand Cabrol, O.S.B. In this book are given all those Offices from the Ritual at which the layman has occasion to assist—the full Latin and English texts, finely printed with the rubrics in red. Cloth, 3s. net, and in leather bindings up to 10s. 6d. net. *Ready early in* 1916. *For others in the series see page* 31.

Spirit of the Sacred Heart. A large type Manual of Prayers. Cloth, 3s. 6d. Paste grain roan, gilt, 5s. 6d. Also in better bindings at 8s. 6d. net and 12s. 6d. net (postage 4d.).

Spiritual Combat, The. Pocket Edition. Cloth, 6d. net (postage 2d.) and 1s.; also leather bound at 2s. 6d., and 4s. 6d. Larger edition (foolscap 8vo), cloth, 1s.

RAWES, FATHER (D.D.)

The Bread of Life; or, St Thomas Aquinas on the Adorable Sacrament of the Altar. Third Edition. 3s. 6d.

Devotions for the Souls in Purgatory. 32mo. 1s.

St John the Evangelist; or, The Beloved Disciple. 2s. 6d.

CATALOGUES OF PUBLICATIONS

RICKABY, REV. JOSEPH (S.J.,

*The Lord my Light. Demy 8vo, cloth, gilt, 6s. net (postage 5d.). Papers on a wide variety of subjects which aim at instructing the Catholic layman on points of theology he ought to know. They must also be helpful to all inquirers who wish to understand the Catholic system better.

*The Spiritual Exercises. The text of the original Spanish, a new translation, and a commentary. Demy 8vo, 5s. net (postage 5d.).

Notes on St Paul. 5s. net (postage 5d.).

Waters that go Softly: or Thoughts for Time of Retreat. 2s. 6d.

Of God and His Creatures. An Annotated Translation, with some Abridgments, of the "Summa Contra Gentiles" of St Thomas Aquinas. Foolscap folio, 21s. net (postage 10d.).

*RITUS SERVANDUS in solemni epositione et benedictione SSmi Sacramenti. Quarto, magnificently printed in red and black on japon vellum. Buckram, gilt, 5s. net. (postage 6d.).

A new impression of the 1912 Edition, which is thereby made conformable with the latest Rituale Romanum.

RODRIGUEZ ON CHRISTIAN PERFECTION. For Persons living in the World. 2 vols. 5s. net (postage 5d.).

ROE, CANON MCDERMOTT.

*The Kingdom of God. With a Preface by Cardinal Vaughan New edition. Cloth, 1s. net (postage 2d.).

RUSSELL, REV. MATTHEW (S.J.)

He is calling me. 2s. 6d. net (postage 3d.).

A Soggarth's Last Verses. 2s. net (postage 2d.).

At Home near the Altar. 1s. net (postage 1½d.).

Close to the Altar Rails. 1s. net (postage 1½d.).

Moments before the Tabernacle. 1s. net (postage 1d.).

Jesus is Waiting. Appeals and reproaches from the Prisoner of Love. Cloth, 2s. 6d. net (postage 3d.). *Second Edition.*

ST CATHERINE OF GENOA.

Treatise on Purgatory. With Preface by Cardinal Manning. New 32mo Edition. 1s.

ST FRANCIS DE SALES, THE WORKS OF.

Introduction to the Devout Life. Cloth, red edges, 1s. 6d. Calf, red edges, 5s. Morocco, gilt edges, 5s. 6d.

ST IGNATIUS OF LOYOLA.

Spiritual Exercises, in Spanish and English (*see under* Rickaby, Rev. J., S.J., *above*).

Manresa: or, The Spiritual Exercises of St Ignatius. 3s.

Text of the Spiritual Exercises. 2s. 6d.

SALOME, MOTHER M.

Stories for You and Me. With Illustrations by L. D. Symington. 2s. 6d.

Good-Night Stories. Illustrated. 2s. 6d.

Some Little London Children. A Story. 2s. 6d.

The Feasts of Mother Church. With Hints and Helps for the Holier Keeping of them. With Illustrations. 3s. 6d.

Mary Ward, a Foundress of the Seventeenth Century. With an Introduction by the Bishop of Newport. Illustrated. 5s.

Wide Awake Stories, told in the Nursery. 2s. 6d.

SCHOOL BOOKS, Stationery, and General School Requisites. Supplied on the best terms. *Catalogue sent free on request.*

SCHOUPPE, REV. F. X. (S.J.)

Purgatory: Illustrated by the Lives and Legends of the Saints. Revised edition, with Notes by Father Kent, O.S.C. 6s.

Abridged Course of Religious Instruction, Apologetic, Dogmatic, and Moral, for the Use of Catholic Schools. 3s.

SERVERS' MANUAL of the Archconfraternity of St Stephen. Compiled by a Priest of the Archdiocese. With a Preface by the Archbishop of Westminster. 1s. net (postage 2d.).

SHEEHAN, CANON P.A. (D.D.)

The Souvenir of Canon Sheehan. With a Portrait in Photogravure, and a facsimile of MS. Cloth, 2s. net. Postage 3d.

A book of extracts from Canon Sheehan's writings for every day of the year, made by the Nuns of Doneraile.

A Spoiled Priest, and Other Stories. With nine illustrations by M. Healy. Cr. 8vo, cloth, 2s. 6d. net. A Selection of these Stories, printed on thinner paper, is issued under the title of Canon Sheehan's Short Stories. cloth. 1s. net (postage 4d.).

The Triumph of Failure. A Novel. Illustrated Edition. 2s. 6d. net (postage 5d.).

SHIPLEY, ORBY (M.A.) Edited by.

Carmina Mariana. An English Anthology in Verse in honour of, or in relation to, the Blessed Virgin Mary. First and Second Series. 7s. 6d. each.

SNEAD-COX, J. G.

The Life of Cardinal Vaughan. New, cheap, but unabridged, edition. 2 vols. Two Portraits. 10s. net (postage 7d.). *Sixth Thousand.*

Original large paper edition, 21s. net (postage 9d.).

SPIRITUAL CLASSICS OF ENGLISH DEVOTIONAL LITERATURE, THE. A New Series. Cloth, gilt top, Portrait in

SPIRITUAL CLASSICS—*continued.*

    Photogravure, 1s. 6d. net ; Leather, gilt top, Silk Marker Portrait in Photogravure, 3s. net (postage 2d. each).
    The first two volumes are :

    The Spirit of Father Faber : Extracts from his writing. Preface by Wilfrid Meynell.

    The Spirit of Cardinal Newman : Extracts from his writings. Preface by the Rev. C. C. Martindale, S.J.

STRAPPINI, W. D. (S.J.).
    Meditations Without Method. 3s. 6d. net (postage 4d.).

SUSO, H.
    Suso, The Life of Blessed Henry. By Himself. Translated from the original German by T. F. Knox, with an Introduction by Father Sebastian Bowden of the Oratory. Cloth gilt, 3s. 6d. net (postage 5d.).

SWEENEY, ABBOT (O.S.B.)
    Sermons for all Sundays and Festivals of the Year. Cheaper Edition. Cr. 8vo, bound in quarter leather. 7s. 6d.

TABB, FATHER JOHN BANISTER.
    Poems. Selected, with an appreciation, by Mrs. Meynell. 2s. 6d. net (postage 2d.).
    Later Poems. 2s. 6d. net (postage 2d.).

TAYLOR, MOTHER MAGDALEN (S.M.G.).
    Memoir of Father Dignam. 5s. net (postage 5d.).
    Father Dignam's Retreats. 6s. net (postage 5d.).
    Conferences given by Father Dignam, S.J. 6s. net (postage 5d.).
    Inner Life of Lady Georgiana Fullerton, The. With Notes of Retreat and Diary. 5s. 6d. net (postage 5d.).
    Holy Confidence. 1s. 6d. net (postage 2d.).
    Convent Stories. 3s.
    Dame Dolores. A Tale. 3s. 6d.
    Lost, and other Tales for Children. 2s.
    Stoneleighs of Stoneleigh, and Other Stories. 2s. 6d.
    Tyborne: A Tale of Queen Elizabeth's Days. 3s. 6d.

THERESE OF LISIEUX, SŒUR.
    Life, Letters, Poems, Favours, etc., of Sœur Thérèse. With 14 illustrations in photogravure. A handsome volume of 448 pages. Printed in red and black. Edited and translated by Father T. N. Taylor. Preface by Cardinal Bourne. Cloth gilt, 6s. net (postage 6d.).

THERESE OF LISIEUX, SŒUR—*continued*.

The Little Flower of Jesus. Being the Autobiography of Sister Teresa, of the Child Jesus and the Holy Face, Carmelite Nun. With three Portraits. 2s. 6d. net (postage 4d.).

The Cause of the Beatification of the Little Flower of Jesus. Containing a detailed account of many of her miracles. With a portrait. Cloth gilt, 2s. 6d. net (postage 4d.).

TERESA, SISTER MARY, O.S.B. (of Princethorpe Priory).

Conferences for Children on the Gospel of St John. With a Preface by the Abbot of Ampleforth. 2s. 6d. net (postage 3d.).

THEOLOGY, MORAL OR DOGMATIC: Gury, Pesch, Hurter, Noldin, Tanquerey, Lehmkuhl, Morino, Matharan, Genicot, Billot, Haine, Jungmann, Antonelli, etc. Any work procured to order.

THOMPSON, FRANCIS.

The Works of. Definitive edition in three volumes. Vols. I and II, The Poetry; Vol. III, The Prose. Buckram gilt, bevelled boards, with three portraits in photogravure. 6s. net each (postage 4d. each volume). *Sold singly.*

The Hound of Heaven. Wrapper, 1s. net. Velvet calf, 3s. net (postage 1d.). Printed in red and black. With a Portrait.

The Selected Poems of Francis Thompson. With a Biographical Note by Wilfrid Meynell, and a Portrait of the Poet. 5s. net (postage 4d.).

Health and Holiness. A Study of the Relations between Brother Ass, the Body, and his Rider, the Soul. Cloth, 2s. net. Semi-limp leather, 3s. 6d. net (postage 2d.).

Shelley. An Essay. With an appreciation by the Rt Hon. George Wyndham, M.P. 2s. 6d. net (postage 3d.).

The Life of St Ignatius. (Not included in "The Works.") Edited by Father J. H. Pollen, S.J., with 100 illustrations by H. W. Brewer and others. 10s. 6d. net (postage 7d.).

THURSTON, FATHER HERBERT (S.J.).

*The War and the Prophets.** An Examination of Current Predictions concerning this latter age. Cr. 8vo, 2s. 6d. net (postage 4d.).

*The Memory of Our Dead.** A succinct historical account of the origins and practice of prayer for the dead. Cr. 8vo, 2s. 6d. net (postage 4d.).

TYNAN, KATHARINE.

Men, not Angels. And other Tales told to Girls. By KATHARINE TYNAN. Cloth gilt, with many full page illustrations. A collection of Catholic short stories by the most popular living writer for girls. 3s. 6d. net. Postage 4d.

TYNAN, KATHARINE—*continued*.

The Flower of Peace. A Collection into one volume of the Religious Poetry of Katharine Tynan. Printed on Dutch handmade paper, with a frontispiece in photogravure after Giotto, real parchment, gilt, 5s. net (postage 3d.).

The Rhymed Life of St Patrick. With a Foreword by Lieut-General Sir William Butler, G.C.B., and 26 illustrations. Printed in Green and Black. Wrapper, 1s. net (postage 2d.). Cloth, 2s. 6d. net.

VATICAN EDITIONS.

Kyriale, Graduale, etc. By Desclée, Dessain, Schwann, Pustet, in Gregorian and modern notation. *The supply of these is now somewhat uncertain.*

VAUGHAN, CARDINAL.

The Young Priest. Conferences on the Apostolic Life. Edited by Mgr Canon J. S. Vaughan. Second Edition. With Portrait. 5s. net (postage 5d.).

VAUGHAN, REV. DOM JEROME (O.S.B.) Edited by.

The Spiritual Conflict and Conquest. With Preface and Notes. 5s.

Pax Animae. By St Peter of Alcantara. Wrapper, 6d. net (postage 1d.) ; cloth, 1s. net.

VAUGHAN, REV. DOM JEROME (O.S.B.) Translated by.

The Practice of Humility. A Treatise, edited by H.H. Leo XIII. Cloth gilt, 1s. 6d. Wrapper, 6d. net (postage 1d.).

VAUGHAN, MGR JOHN S. (Bishop of Sebastopolis).

Time or Eternity. And other Preachable Sermons. 5s. net (postage 5d.).

Faith and Folly. Revised Edition. 5s. net (postage 5d.).

VILLESBRUNE, JEHANNE DE LA.

*The Giant Tells. Breton folk tales and legends told to children. Attractively illustrated. Cloth, 2s. 6d.

WARD, MARY, THE LIFE OF. With Two Portraits. Introduction by Abbot Gasquet, O.S.B. 2s. net. (postage 3d.).

WHITE, C. L.

Saint Benedict Joseph Labre (Votary of Holy Poverty and Pilgrim). With Portrait and other Illustrations. 2s. 6d.

WILBERFORCE, WILFRID, AND A. R. GILBERT.

Her Faith against the World. A Novel. Crown 8vo. 3s. 6d.

WILMOT-BUXTON, E. M. (F.R.Hist.S.).

    *A Book of English Martyrs. With seven fine illustrations, including a frontispiece in colour, by M. Meredith Williams, and a Preface by Dom Bede Camm, O.S.B. Cloth, richly gilt, 3s. 6d.

      "The story is told in an attractive way, and the excellent taste shown in the production of the book leaves nothing to be desired. I hope it will be in great demand as a prize-book. It is perhaps the only form of spiritual reading that the average boy really enjoys."—*Mother Mary Loyola*.

WINDLE, SIR BERTRAM, M.D., F.R.S., LL.D., etc.

    *A Century of Scientific Thought. And other Essays. Cloth, 5s. net (postage 5d.).

WISEMAN, CARDINAL.

    Fabiola. A Tale of the Catacombs. New Cheap Edition. Wrapper, 6d. net ; limp cloth, 1s. net (postage 3d.). Illustrated Edition on superfine paper, cloth, richly gilt. 3s. 6d.

    Meditations on the Sacred Passion of Our Lord. 4s.

MAGAZINE SUBSCRIPTION DEPARTMENT

MESSRS BURNS & OATES accept Subscriptions (not less than six months) for any of the Catholic or other Journals, weekly, monthly, or quarterly. The special service of the Subscription Department enables it to despatch journals immediately on publication and with machine-like regularity.

THE DUBLIN REVIEW. 5s. 6d. net per Quarterly Issue; 21s. net a Year, post free.

THE TABLET. One Year, post free, inland, 24s.; abroad, 26s.

THE IRISH ROSARY. A Catholic Illustrated Monthly of Fiction and Affairs. Single copies 4d. (postage 3d. extra). One Year, post free, 6s. 9d.

THE MONTH.   One Year, post free, 14s.

THE CATHOLIC WORLD.   One Year, post free, 15s.

30

LITURGY FOR LAYFOLK

A NEW UNIFORM SERIES OF LATIN-ENGLISH TEXTS, FINELY PRINTED THROUGHOUT IN RED AND BLACK.

THE LAYFOLK'S RITUAL. The complete text, in Latin and English, of all those Offices of the Ritual at which layfolk have occasion to assist. With an historical introduction to each Office by Abbot Fernand Cabrol, O.S.B. Printed throughout in red and black. Prices from 3s. net. *Early in* 1916.

THE DAY HOURS OF THE CHURCH. The complete text of the Horæ Diurnæ in Latin and English. Edited by the Benedictines of Stanbrook Abbey. With an introduction by Abbot Fernand Cabrol, O.S.B. Printed on toned Oxford India paper, about 1,000 pages. From 6s. net upwards. Postage 5d. *Early in* 1916.

THE MISSAL FOR THE LAITY. The 1916 impression has been revised from cover to cover by Dr. Adrian Fortescue, who equips it also with an historical introduction ; and it is now in entire conformity with the most recent reforms. Printed on toned Oxford India paper. Prices from 5s. net to 30s. net. Postage 4d. *Early in* 1916.

THE RITE OF MARRIAGE, THE NUPTIAL MASS AND BLESSING, and the new Blessing without the Mass. With an Instruction on the significance of the Sacrament by His Lordship Bishop Butt. Wrappered in parchment. 6d. net. Postage 1d. *Early in* 1916.

THE ORDER AND CANON OF THE MASS. Wrappers, 3d. net. Postage 1d. *Early in* 1916.

THE PRIMER. Containing the reformed Little Office of Our Lady, The Office for the Dead (and the Chant), Grace Before and After Meals, The Penitential Psalms, etc. The complete text in Latin and English. With an historical introduction by Fr. Herbert Thurston, S.J. Price from 3s. 6d. net. *Early in* 1916.

BURNS & OATES, LTD.
28 ORCHARD STREET
LONDON, W.